SUPERPOWERS DEFEATED

DATE DUE

SUPERPOWERS DEFEATED

Vietnam and Afghanistan Compared

DOUGLAS A. BORER

Virginia Polytechnic and State University

FRANK CASS
LONDON • PORTLAND, OR

#3996332b   8-16-04

First Published in 1999 in Great Britain by
FRANK CASS PUBLISHERS
Crown House
47 Chase Side, Southgate,
London N14 5BP

and in the United States of America by
FRANK CASS PUBLISHERS
c/o ISBS, 5824 N.E. Hassalo Street
Portland, Oregon 97213-3644

Website: www.frankcass.com

Copyright © D. Borer 1999
Reprinted 2001

British Library Cataloguing in Publication Data

Borer, Douglas A., 1962–
 Superpowers defeated : Vietnam and Afghanistan
 compared
 1. Vietnamese Conflict, 1961–1975 2. Afghanistan – History –
 Soviet occupation, 1979–1989
 I. Title
 958.1'045

ISBN 0-7146-4851-5 (cloth)
ISBN 0-7146-4409-9 (paper)

Library of Congress Cataloging-in-Publication Data

Borer, Douglas A., 1962–
 Superpowers defeated: Vietnam and Afghanistan compared /
 Douglas A. Borer.
  p. cm.
 Includes bibliographical references (p.   ) and index.
 ISBN 0-7146-4851-5 (cloth). – ISBN 0-7146-4409-9 (paper)
 1. Vietnamese Conflict, 1961–1975 – United States. 2. Afghanistan –
 History – Soviet occupation, 1979–1989. 3. United States – Politics
 and government – 1945–1989. 4. Soviet Union – Politics and
 government – 1945–1991. I. Title.
 DS558.B67 1999
 959.704'3373–dc21   98-31628
                                                         CIP

Typeset by Vitaset, Paddock Wood, Kent
Printed and bound by Antony Rowe Ltd, Eastbourne

To Jodi and Stella

Contents

Acknowledgements

My motivations for writing this book are embedded in my earliest memories, those from the Vietnam War. As a young boy I watched Vietnam on television in the mid 1960s. I was impressed the most by the simple bar graphs denoting tons of bombs dropped and the daily comparative body counts. It was clear from these charts we were kicking some commie butt. I always knew that we would win the war in the near future. By 1970, at the age of eight, it began to dawn on me that I might have to fight in Vietnam. For some reason we just weren't winning. Some of the big kids in my neighbourhood didn't come home, some did, but they were different. I remember a big kid named Doyle Daniels showing me an ugly scar, a Purple Heart and a tiny piece of metal that he said could have killed him. I thought he was kidding, Doyle used to kid me all the time, but he didn't seem to be kidding about that little piece of steel which looked nothing like a bullet to me. It was the beginning of my confusion about Vietnam. By 1973 I understood that I would not be fighting because the president said we had won the war, even though the news men said we had lost. I was more confused. When President Nixon resigned from office in 1974, my true political awakening began. I had believed in Nixon, after all he was the president of the United States. When he resigned from office, something changed in me. Like many of my generation, Richard Nixon made a permanent impact on my life. It was not until the mid 1980s that I was mature enough to grasp the reality of the war. We had lost the war through our own devices, the war itself was wrong, President Nixon was in fact a criminal, and American politics was not as clean and good as I wanted it to be. In sum, I began to comprehend the true nature of power. Fearing it, I have been studying politics and war ever since.

This book evolved out of my master's thesis at the University of Montana (1988) and my PhD dissertation from Boston University (1993). In the course of its final creation I had a good deal of help along the way. I would like to acknowledge the generous financial assistance provided by the Institute for the Study of World Politics which provided early funding for my research. I would also like to thank a number of individuals who had a major impact on my professional development during the research leading to this book: Marty Farrell at Ripon College; Bill Chaloupka, Forrest Grieves and Lou Hayes at the University of Montana; David Mayers, Al Shockley and Mark Silverstein at Boston University; and Andy Markovits at the University of California at Santa Cruz. I would also like to thank the many family members, friends and colleagues who have assisted me, tolerated me and supported me over the years. Last but not least, I would like to reserve special thanks for my marvellous friend and editor Dr John Guardiano, who has helped to correct and mould my less than elegant prose on this and other projects.

Abbreviations and Glossary

AFV	American Friends of Vietnam
ARVN	Army of the Republic of Vietnam
CIA	(United States) Central Intelligence Agency
Comintern	Communist International (operational spearhead for the spread of worldwide revolution)
Contras	Opposition force to Sandinistas in Nicaragua
CPSU	Communist Party of the Soviet Union
DRA	Democratic Republic of Afghanistan
DRV	Democratic Republic of Vietnam
FCP	French Communist Party
Geneva Accords	Settlement (1954) by which Vietnam was partitioned at the 17th parallel and principle of free elections established
GVN	Government of Vietnam
ICP	Indochinese Communist Party
KGB	Soviet Committee of State Security (popularly regarded as secret police)
Khalq	(lit. Masses) Faction of the PDPA, headed by Taraki
MAAG	Military Assistance Advisory Group
MAC	Military Assistance Command
Mandate of Heaven	Divine authority to rule Vietnam (adopted Chinese concept)
Mujahideen	Afghan freedom-fighters opposing Soviet occupation
NATO	North Atlantic Treaty Organization
NFF	National Fatherland Front (Afghan nationalist organization)
NLF	National Fatherland Front (organized by North Vietnamese to co-ordinate activities between North and South Vietnam)
NSC	National Security Council (United States)
Parchem	(lit. Banner) Faction of the PDPA, headed by Babrak Karmal

PDPA	People's Democratic Party of Afghanistan (First Communist Party of Afghanistan)
PRC	People's Republic of China
RVN	Republic of Vietnam
SEATO	Southeast Asia Treaty Organization
SRV	Socialist Republic of Vietnam (North Vietnam)
TASS	Soviet official news-agency
UN	United Nations
USSR	Union of Soviet Socialist Republics
VC	Viet Cong (Vietnamese Communist)
Viet Minh	Vietnamese Party of Ho Chi Minh (leading party of Vietnamese nationalism)
VNA	Vietnamese National Army

Introduction

This is an old-fashioned treatise on war and politics. As such, this book is part of an enduring tradition among scholars of international politics dating to Thucydides' classic history of strife between Sparta and Athens in the Peloponnesian War of ancient Greece. In the midst of other mutable factors, war has consistently played a major role in determining the success and failure of all important international actors, past and present. One enduring truth of international politics is that no great state ever rose to regional or global primacy without victory in war, and no great state has ever fallen from pre-eminence without war's having been a contributing factor. Two major conflicts during the latter half of the twentieth century reconfirm the crucial importance of war in global power dynamics. War loss in Vietnam clearly marked the downward trajectory in the global hegemonic power of the United States, a hegemony that had been established since its rise to superpower status by the end of the Second World War. Likewise, war loss in Afghanistan was a vital contributing factor in ending the Cold War between the United States and the Soviet Union, and more important, the Afghan War was a significant factor in both the wholesale collapse of Soviet hegemony in Eastern Europe and in the destruction of the Soviet Union itself in 1991.

In the immediate context of their own times, because of the apparent power disparities of the combatants, both of these war losses came as a surprise to many of the participants and observers. No political or military analyst in the near aftermath of the Second World War would have predicted that the two newly emergent superpowers – spectacularly successful in crushing the imposing military machines of Nazi Germany and Imperial Japan – would later be humiliated by lightly armed insurgents in two countries of such seemingly trivial military strength as Vietnam and Afghanistan. In April 1975, when Vietnam was unified by military forces directed by the communist government in Hanoi, the complexities and realities of the global Cold War power struggle were forever altered. The United States had lost its first war, the perception of American military invincibility had been destroyed, America's commitment to its international partners and to its own ideals were questioned, and the domestic political system and social order of the United States were rocked by turmoil. A decade later, as the Islamist rebels in

Afghanistan successfully maintained their insurgency to oppose the Red Army forces that occupied their country, the global perception of Soviet power also began to change. By the mid 1980s a widely held view among observers was that the United States's war in Vietnam and the Soviet Union's war in Afghanistan were analogous events: commonly the war in Afghanistan was referred to as 'the Soviet Vietnam'. When Soviet troops finally withdrew in humiliation in 1989, the Afghans' successful rebellion against Moscow's domination was mirrored quickly in a new explosion of political unrest, both in Eastern Europe and among various national groups within the Soviet Union. In Afghanistan the Soviet Union had lost its first war, perceptions of the fearsome power of the Soviet war machine had been shattered, and Soviet commitments to both the international communist movement and its own governing ideology had been severely eroded. In short order the open rebellion against Soviet hegemony spread from Afghanistan to Eastern Europe and finally throughout non-Russian republics and Russia alike.

In retrospect, a number of initial similarities buttress the analogy between the two wars. Each of the superpowers had deployed its troops in the territory of a weak client state and each had failed to achieve its political goals despite the utilization of massive military force. Instead, both wars had developed into long and costly 'quagmires' in which the superpower and its client regime was pitted against a highly motivated opposition force that was supported both materially and politically by the other superpower. After approximately a decade of immense effort, both interventions proved too costly in human and material terms to be politically sustainable for the superpowers, and in the end both were thwarted in their original war goals and withdrew in disgrace. As a result, the parallelism between the US experience in Vietnam and the Soviet experience in Afghanistan has largely become accepted as a historic truism.[1]

This book is an attempt not only to provide a greater degree of substance to the apparent truth that Vietnam and Afghanistan are analogous events but also to explore the important differences between these two watershed events in post-Second World War history. Despite the initial close resemblance between the Vietnam and Afghanistan wars, if one digs further into the story, the similarities derived from the initial comparison and the apparent clarity of the analogy begin to blur. In what ways are Vietnam and Afghanistan truly similar, and how are they different? In answering these questions, and throughout my analysis I will stress two important concepts: *legitimacy* in the domestic politics of each of the parties involved (Vietnam, the United States, Afghanistan and the Soviet Union); and *credibility* in the international arena for each of the superpowers. This book is based on the idea that the 'lessons of Vietnam and Afghanistan' are found by answering two fundamental questions. First, why were the United States and the Soviet Union and their respective allies in Vietnam and Afghanistan unable to create and maintain political legitimacy? Second, why was the American political system (in both the international and domestic spheres) able to survive the stresses of war loss in the Vietnam War, whereas the Soviet Union and the 'socialist commonwealth' in Eastern Europe collapsed so soon after the end of the Afghan War?

THE CONTEMPORARY LEGACY OF DEFEAT

Twenty-five years after the withdrawal of US military forces from Indochina the Vietnam War continues to resonate in the collective consciousness of America. In the wake of the 1973 withdrawal of American combat forces, the trauma of the Vietnam war has resurfaced at sundry points in American politics. After Vietnam any consideration of US military intervention, from Iran in the late 1970s to Nicaragua and Panama in the 1980s and Iraq, Somalia and Bosnia in the 1990s, has invoked the spectre of destruction, defeat and disgrace of Vietnam. In the domestic politics of the United States, recriminations continually emerge from the shadow of Vietnam. During the 1992 election campaign, presidential candidate Bill Clinton's draft avoidance and his direct involvement in antiwar protests raised doubts in some quarters about his ability to function effectively as commander in chief of the US armed forces. Later President Clinton's decision in 1994 to normalize diplomatic relations with Vietnam once again raised hackles in some circles by highlighting the emotional issue of possible American prisoners of war remaining in Indochina. Two years later, in 1996, media scrutiny regarding the display of a 'V' citation on the uniform of the US navy's highest officer, Admiral Jeremy 'Mike' Boorda, drove him to commit suicide over his disputed combat role in Vietnam. Boorda's highly publicized death is only the latest evidence that the Vietnam War still actively lurks just under the surface of mainstream American society and even continues to claim casualties long after its apparent end.[2]

On a more general front, the Vietnam War influences American politics in more subtle ways. As the years go by, a growing number of both its foot soldiers and protesters have entered the age of political maturity and been elected to local, state and national office, and both military and civilian members of the 'Vietnam Generation' now command the highest echelons of America's elite. They have become the captains of industry and commerce, they dominate the boardwalks and boardrooms of Hollywood and Wall Street, and they determine the nation's most important decisions in the cloakrooms and war rooms of Congress and the Pentagon. Concurrently, the less fortunate alumni of the Vietnam War also constitute a significant component of the nation's lowest social echelons. They are a large sector of the physically disabled, the residents of mental wards, the homeless population, and many

''Nam' veterans suffer long-term – or permanent – alienation from family, community and country.

For this observer, Admiral Boorda's suicide may be understood as a microcosm of America's tragedy in Vietnam, a tragedy reminiscent of age-old human discord over questions of morality, idealism and power politics. In the person and persona of Boorda the ideals of the American system – fair play, hard work, and rewards based on merit – existed to perfection incarnate. He had started his career as lowly enlisted 'E-1' ensign at the age of seventeen, yet he rose to the top of his profession, becoming an officer, an admiral and finally Chief of Naval Operations – doing so through individual effort, hard work, and perseverance. However, when investigative reporters were on the verge of revealing an apparent discrepancy between the ideals that Boorda embodied and the reality of his military record, a credibility gap was in the making.[3] Thus, on a microlevel scale, the divergence between Boorda's claims to valour in war and the reality of his Vietnam wartime experience are similar to the macrolevel collective discord suffered by American society as a whole. For the first time since the Second World War, the ideals of the American dream and America's role in the world were severely undermined as the truth about the Vietnam War seeped into and corroded the collective moral conscience of the nation.

Should America have been in Vietnam? Was the war just? In the late 1960s a significant minority of American society began vociferously to question the validity and legitimacy of US government policy. As the Vietnam War dragged on in the late 1960s, the growing chasm between the rhetoric of politicians and the reality of the war as reported by the press seemed to be steadily backfilled with a growing number of corpses – consisting of both the young American soldiers who had been sent by their leaders to fight for the ideals of their beloved country, and of innocent Vietnamese civilians caught in the cross-fire of bullets, napalm and indiscriminate strategic bombing. By 1968 the perceived failure of the war effort had filtered to the highest levels of public office, and the growing public unrest over the war's lack of legitimacy drove President Lyndon Johnson to withdraw from the upcoming election – one of the great political suicides of modern American history. The conduct of the final withdrawal of American ground forces from Vietnam under President Richard Nixon served to erode further the legitimacy of the American government. In the process of fulfilling his problematical campaign pledge to end America's involvement in Vietnam by achieving 'peace with honour', Nixon mounted an exceptionally lethal disengagement that included the initiation of an illegal ground and air war into Cambodia and a massive increase in the use of strategic bombers in both North and South Vietnam. Nixon's premeditated violation of US law in the secret Cambodian war was part of a broader pattern of unconstitutional activities that later emerged more clearly in the Watergate scandal, an event that shook the

American political system to its very core. The events surrounding Nixon's eventual resignation from office make it arguably the most traumatic event in American domestic politics since the Civil War, with his dishonour and deceit having sullied the office of the presidency and psychologically imprinted on a generation of Americans a fundamental distrust of government. Even in the late 1990s the extent of Nixon's criminal activities are yet to be fully realized, with recent transcriptions of Oval Office audiotapes revealing the president ordering his subordinates to burglarize the Brookings Institution in Washington, DC. On the tapes Nixon is heard ordering his minions to seize copies of the *Pentagon Papers*, the US government's own secret history of the Vietnam conflict.[4] When later published in full, the five-volume *Pentagon Papers* revealed the dishonesty, deception, duplicity and outright lies to which the American public had been subjected by the highest political leaders, dating back through the Johnson, Kennedy, Eisenhower and Truman administrations.

In similar fashion, nearly a decade after the withdrawal of Soviet forces, the Afghan War resonated powerfully in both the Russian Republic and throughout the other successor states of the Soviet Union. The carnage among civilians and the mass exodus of refugees that occurred during the decade-long occupation of Afghanistan was hauntingly replicated in Russia's civil war in the breakaway Republic of Chechnya during the period 1994–97. Many of the leading public figures and decision-makers in Russia's civil war in Chechnya were drawn directly from the ranks of the *Afghanets* (veterans of the Afghan War). Just like American veterans who have taken opposite sides in debates over post-Vietnam US military operations, the *Afghanets* are a fragmented group, consisting of both vocal supporters and harsh opponents of President Boris Yeltsin's decision in 1994 to use force to re-establish Russian Federation sovereignty in Chechnya. The architect of Yeltsin's military response, then defence minister General Pavel Grachev, and Grachev's most well-known critic, former security chief and presidential candidate General Alexsander Lebed, were both Afghan veterans whose opposing views on Yeltsin's Chechnya policy flowed directly from their war experience in Afghanistan. Sadly, like the Vietnam War in the United States, the Afghan War also continues to claim casualties in Russia. For instance, in November 1996, in a dispute over control of a lucrative tax-exempt charity for Afghan veterans, the lives of thirteen people were lost in a bomb blast at a memorial service for the recently deceased head of the Russian Fund for Invalids of the Afghan War.[5] Likewise, Russian border-patrol troops stationed in neighbouring Tajikistan have steadily suffered casualties while interdicting both smugglers and Islamist guerrillas seeking to spread a fundamentalist revolution outside of Afghanistan's borders.

Should the Soviet Union have been in Afghanistan? Was the war just? While these questions remain salient for some post-Soviet citizens in Russia and the successor states, the emotional need to answer them is contextually and substantively different from that of Americans in their soul-searching over Vietnam. Contextually, the most important difference is the obvious fact that the Soviet Union no longer exists as a unified state. Though the war in Afghanistan is certainly part of the living history of many people in the post-Soviet order, the ruling state that was responsible for conducting the war has now passed into the annals of history. Hence Russian soul-searching over Afghanistan is often merged or submerged in a morass of ongoing debates over what Russia should be as a state, a society and an international actor in the post-Soviet era. In the fourteen other Soviet successor states, Russian expansionism, territorial annexation and attempts at coerced cultural assimilation are part of each nation's own historic relations with Moscow. As a result, many non-Russians view the Afghan War as an integral component of a long historical record of Russian imperialism, with many seeing the Afghans' experience as similar to their own imperial struggle against Russia.

POLITICAL LEGITIMACY AND INTERNATIONAL CREDIBILITY: A UNIFYING THEME

As I have noted, this book hinges on two fundamental questions regarding the superpowers' defeats in Vietnam and Afghanistan. First, why were the United States and the Soviet Union and their respective allies in South Vietnam and Afghanistan unable to create and maintain political legitimacy? Second, why was the American political system (in both the international and domestic spheres) able to survive the stresses of war loss in Vietnam, while the Soviet 'socialist commonwealth' and Soviet government collapsed so soon after the end of the Afghan War? One way to grapple with these questions is through the concept of political legitimacy: political legitimacy and its various manifestations, ramifications and meanings remain some of the most perplexing and enduring questions of political scholarship. Some would argue that legitimacy is rooted in legal authority, others argue that legality is less important than morality, culture or religion, and others argue that legitimacy can be derived from coercive power. These debates have raged throughout the ages. From Thucydides' *Melian Dialog* and Plato's *Republic* in ancient times to Marx's *Communist Manifesto* and Gingrich's *Contract with America* in modern times, political thinkers have attempted to define the correct form, function and justification of legitimate governing authority.

Within all polities controversy over legitimacy, the support for and opposition to a government or government policy, is at the core of all political discourse; however, it is not the purpose of this book to discover any single truth about legitimacy. Rather, it is my intent to seek out and explore the nature of legitimacy in each of the polities under study, proceeding from the assumption that legitimacy will most likely be found to be very different in each case. A soundly utilitarian framework for doing so was provided by the German sociologist Max Weber. Like others, Weber believed that the legitimacy of governing authority was derived from a multitude of sources and processes which, in the interest of analytical enquiry, he also thought could be classified into three ideal types: charismatic, traditional and legal (or rational–legal). While these classifications have been scrutinized over the years by a multitude of supporting and dissenting voices,[6] I find this framework to be especially useful in doing cross-cultural comparisons. Though my study is not a Weberian examination of the Vietnam and Afghanistan wars, Weber's typology of legitimacy claims will resurface occasionally in the chapters to come and will help to guide the analysis.

For the purposes of this book, on the domestic level I will focus on the legitimacy of ruling states, which will also be referred to interchangeably as 'governments' or 'regimes'. In the broadest of terms I define domestic political legitimacy as *the basis for social unity, cohesion, and stability within any given polity, with the polity comprising the ruling state apparatus and the citizenry of a given territory*. Legitimacy is a function of the state's ability to govern effectively a society in which citizens see the state's power over them as being correct and just. Thus, it is a fundamental assumption in this book that in all of its manifestations political legitimacy is derived from the beliefs, perceptions, and/or convictions of the ruled and their willingness to accept and obey the authority of those who rule them. In all societies obedience to governing authority is embedded in a shared understanding of the basic correctness of the state's right to rule, regardless of the type or form of government or regime. Hence it is clear that legitimacy can and does exist in widely different regime types, including democratic, quasi-democratic, and non-democratic governments.[7] For any polity to survive in the long term, the ruling state must have political legitimacy. States that fail to acquire legitimacy at their inception and to maintain it over time will eventually fail. States can rule without legitimacy, but not well, and not for long. In this regard I agree with Rodney Barker, who asserts that '[a] state which can only coerce its subjects is not governing them, it is at war with them'.[8]

States that are born illegitimate or that lose legitimacy over time all eventually fail, sometimes peacefully, but more commonly as a result of civil war. Two types of legitimacy crisis will be discussed in later chapters of this book: crises of state or regime creation, as in Vietnam and Afghanistan, and crises of state maintenance, as in the United States and the Soviet Union. There are thus two closely related underlying hypotheses that unify the historical narrative and the comparative analysis in this book. The first hypothesis is that the many similarities attending the wars in Vietnam and Afghanistan are best understood as being rooted in problems of domestic political legitimacy – or, perhaps more accurately, in political illegitimacy. The second hypothesis is that any understanding of these wars as very different events can be best achieved in an analysis of the impact of foreign military intervention on both the domestic political legitimacy and international credibility of the superpowers themselves.

For all governments throughout history, relations with the 'outside world' have ultimately been shaped by the necessities, urges and demands of the domestic polity. Or, as articulated more axiomatically by the late great Speaker of the US House of Representatives, Thomas 'Tip' O'Neill, one of the fundamental lessons of political leadership is that '*All politics is local*'. Although O'Neill meant it literally, the statement's logic is applicable to questions of political legitimacy on the international level as well. In this book I will review the impact of the Vietnam and Afghan wars not only on the superpowers' domestic legitimacy but also on their respective relations with other countries, primarily those in their alliance structures: the Western and Eastern blocs. In a broad sense, an international alliance – or for that matter, the international community itself – is a type of polity. However, relations between and among states are contextually and qualitatively different from relations between the rulers and the ruled in a domestic polity. Because of this difference, this book will employ the concept of *credibility* to analyse the impact of US and Soviet policies on the perceptions and reactions of countries other than Vietnam and Afghanistan. I define international credibility as *the basis for being believed by other actors within the international system*. It is thus clear that credibility and legitimacy are closely related concepts, with credibility in the international sphere being akin to legitimacy in the domestic sphere. Likewise, it will become clear in later chapters that this definition of credibility applies to the domestic sphere as well, with widely different ramifications in the United States and the Soviet Union.

In summary, our ability to understand the 'lessons' of Vietnam and Afghanistan is premised on our understanding that these wars were concurrently domestic and international in character. While political strife in Vietnam and Afghanistan originated in disputes between rival factions that claimed the exclusive right to organize and rule the domestic polity, I will show that the failures of the incumbent regimes are inextricably linked to the role played by their superpower patrons in worsening the various crises of creation that all new states or regimes encounter at birth. In other words, it is impossible to discuss the legitimacy problems of the Republic of South Vietnam that declared its independent status in 1956 as being separate from the role played by the United States. Likewise, it is impossible to discuss the legitimacy problems of communists who declared the new Democratic Republic of Afghanistan in 1978 as being separate from the role played by the Soviet Union. This interconnectedness exists in reverse as well. It is impossible to understand the impact of these wars on state legitimacy in US and Soviet domestic society without a discussion of what serves as the foundation of political unity within the polities of the superpowers. And, in similar fashion, I will attempt to explain how and why these war losses affected the domestic legitimacy and international credibility of each of the superpowers in very different ways with very different outcomes.

ORGANIZATION AND STRUCTURE OF THE BOOK

The chapters of this book are structured in roughly similar fashion, with comparisons differentiated by chronological periods. Chapter 1, which addresses ancient times through to 1940, reviews the interesting and crucially important histories of previous foreign interventions in Afghanistan and Vietnam, focusing primarily on the British in Afghanistan and the French in Vietnam. The evolution of domestic sources of political legitimacy in Vietnam and Afghanistan are also reviewed, and the chapter shows how both the British and the French attempted to shape these domestic polities to achieve the goals of their nineteenth-century imperial programmes. The ultimate failure of these imperialist efforts foreshadowed the later experiences of the United States and the Soviet Union. Chapter 2 looks at the period from 1940 to 1955 and provides an analysis of the origins of superpower military activities and intervention in Vietnam and Afghanistan as an integral part of the ideological and geopolitical struggle of the Cold War. The domestic roots of US and Soviet foreign policy are examined, with especial focus on the sources of state legitimacy in each of the superpowers' domestic polity. This chapter emphasizes the conflicting ideals of domestic state legitimacy as the core foundation for the Cold War itself. Chapters 3 and 4 then recount the superpowers' various attempts to create legitimate client states in Vietnam and Afghanistan, discussing why these attempts failed before the decision was made to commit large-scale military forces. In the case of Vietnam, Chapter 3 looks at the period 1956–65 and, in the case of Afghanistan, 1956–79. In these two central chapters I also develop the term 'detainment' – as opposed to containment – as a useful way of reconceptualizing US and Soviet foreign policies that were directed toward client states wanting in domestic legitimacy. Chapter 4 also reviews the rationale behind, and the eventual failure of, the use of military force to achieve victory by comparing the period of 1965–73 in Vietnam with 1980–89 in Afghanistan. The analysis in Chapter 4 reaches the conclusion that while military intervention did postpone victory by the superpowers' opponent, in doing so military intervention actually undermined any chance of building domestic political legitimacy and sealed the fate of the very regimes that were supposedly being aided. Chapter 5 then concludes with a multistranded analysis of the impact of the superpowers' defeats in Vietnam and Afghanistan on both the domestic polities and the international standing of the United States and the Soviet Union.

AUTHOR'S NOTE

It may be helpful, too, to make clear what this book is not, and what are some of its limitations. First, like many 'big-picture' comparisons, this book's primary limitation is a function of scope and space – a broad scope of analysis delivered in a relatively short space. It should be emphasized that this book is more concerned with the politics of war than with the details of warfare on the battlefield. I am more interested in the relationship between war and domestic politics in comparative perspective than I am in the details of weapons systems, tactics, and logistics and their impact on the outcome of these wars. However, the grand strategy of warfare, as characterized by von Clausewitz's well-known dictum 'War is the continuation of politics by other means', is an integral component of my comparative analysis. Second, as the title *Superpowers Defeated* suggests, this book is as much about the foreign and domestic politics of United States and Soviet Union as it is about the culture and politics of Vietnam and Afghanistan. Much has been written about Vietnam, Afghanistan and the foreign policies of the superpowers. This book seeks new insights and generalizations that can be generated through a comparative framework of the existing literature. Third, this book is not an attempt to revise the empirical histories of the Vietnam and Afghanistan wars on the basis of newly discovered documents that trickle forth from various archives in Washington and Moscow. What is interesting in this regard is the awareness that, while most new documents have served to deepen and enrich our understanding of the complexities of Vietnam and Afghanistan, the perceptions and interpretations of these wars have for the most part been reconfirmed by the most recent findings.[9] The basic facts about these wars are well known, and any new details that emerge over the years will surely broaden our understanding. However, I believe it is the interpretation of these facts, the arguments made by various analysts, and the ensuing debates that analysis engenders, that hold the true social value of contemporary scholarship on Vietnam and Afghanistan. I hope this book's contribution will add something to the body of knowledge that is useful to students of history, warfare and politics.

NOTES

1. For a common example see, John M. Goshko, 'Windup of "Soviet Vietnam": Afghan Power Fight Continues', *Washington Post* (17 April, 1992): A1.
2. At the time of his death, Boorda was scheduled to do an interview with two *Newsweek* correspondents who were planning to question the Admiral on his Vietnam service on a navy destroyer. The destroyer had provided fire-support to ground troops in Vietnam; however, according to the Navy, such an action did not entitle Boorda to wear a 'combat V' (for valour) citation on two of his Vietnam service medals.

Apparently, the wearing of the dubious citations synergized in his mind a clash between the idealism for which his career had become axiomatic, and the reality that his rise to the top had included honours claimed but unmerited.

3. Apparently, even an inkling that his virtue was under fire was enough to make death preferable to living with personal disgrace, and perhaps more importantly, to living with the knowledge that his minor falsehood would cause additional disgrace on his beloved yet beleaguered navy which had been rocked by various scandals in the notorious Tailhook incidents and criminal conduct at the naval academy.

4. Evan Thomas and Lucy Shackelford, 'Nixon Off the Record', *Newsweek* (3 November 1997): 52–4.

5. *Open Media Research Institute, Daily Digest*, No. 218, 11 November 1996. Hereafter, *OMRI*. See, http://www.omri.cz/Index.html.

6. For a good example see, J.G. Merquior, *Rousseau and Weber: Two Studies in the Theory of Legitimacy* (London: Routledge & Kegan Paul, 1980).

7. Ibid., pp. 4–9.

8. Rodney Barker, *Political Legitimacy and the State* (New York: Oxford University Press, 1990) p. 138. However, it should also be remembered that not all states which are legitimate survive, with some few falling victim to unusually violent and powerful natural disasters, but with most falling victim to unusually violent and powerful human competitors.

9. Two examples illustrate this point. The crimes of Richard Nixon have been well documented over the years; however the level of subterfuge, dirty dealing and shocking vulgarity of the man have been reconfirmed by the release of new secret Oval Office tapes. See Stanley Kutler, *Abuse of Power: The New Nixon Tapes* (New York: The Free Press, 1997). Translations of Russian material on Afghanistan have also reconfirmed most earlier political analysis; nonetheless, the new material certainly adds to the richness of detail. For example, see *The Bear Went Over the Mountain: Soviet Combat Tactics in Afghanistan*, trans. and ed. Lester W. Grau (Washington, DC: National Defense University Press, 1997). Grau's text is a translation of a 1991 study published by the Department of History of Military Art at the Frunze Military Academy.

AFGHANISTAN

Outline map showing main towns and cities, roads, rivers and contours

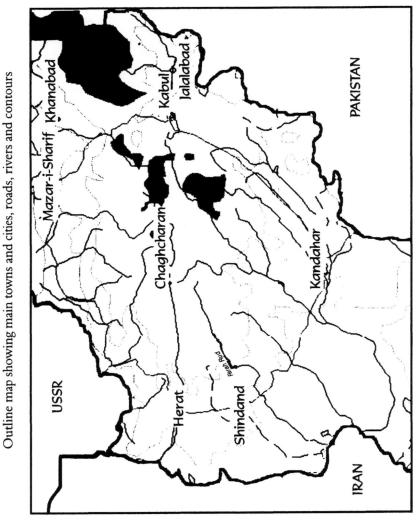

Source: Mark Galeotti, *Afghanistan: The Soviet Union's Last War* (London, Frank Cass, 1995), p. 5.

NORTH AND SOUTH VIETNAM
Showing corps tactical zones

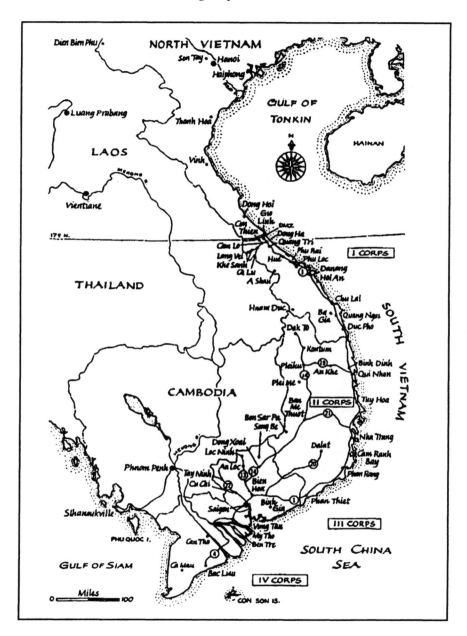

Source: Ronnie E. Ford, *TET 1968: Understanding the Surprise* (London: Frank Cass, 1995), p. xviii.

1

Afghanistan and Vietnam in World Affairs: The Historical Background

Before fighting wars with the United States and the Soviet Union, Vietnam and Afghanistan were little-known entities in twentieth-century world politics. In many respects, despite their widely divergent cultural traits, Afghanistan and Vietnam share several remarkably similar political characteristics. The historic predecessors of both states were of central importance to the political dynamics, wars and imperial fortunes of their respective regions dating back to the earliest records of written history. Both states have witnessed numerous migrations of peoples and rulers, and both have fallen victim to or have been manipulated by the political aspirations of larger and more powerful states. An understanding of the basic political events that shaped Vietnam and Afghanistan will be of crucial importance in understanding how peoples of these relatively small, weak, 'premodern' nations defeated the two greatest military powers of all time.

In this chapter the comparative histories of Afghanistan and Vietnam and their relations with the United States and the Soviet Union before the Second World War are broadly reviewed. Before the Second World War the United States had negligible relations with Vietnam, becoming involved there only as a result of the Japanese occupation of French Indochina in 1944. The Soviet Union, however, as Russia's successor, had a distinctly different historical experience in Afghanistan, with continual interaction that dates back to the pre-Soviet period of the Tsars. As will be seen in later chapters, a pervasive ignorance in the halls of power in Washington and Moscow of Vietnamese and Afghan history certainly seems to have had no positive effect on superpower policies toward these countries after the Second World War. Knowledge of local history in both countries might have shown national policy-makers in Washington and Moscow that their global approach to Cold War politics clashed with the specific realities in these two states.

THE FOUNDATIONS OF POLITICAL LEGITIMACY IN AFGHANISTAN

Afghanistan did not exist as a nation-state in the modern sense before the eighteenth century, when geopolitical consolidation into a recognizable state with defined territories occurred with the advent of British and Russian imperialism. Previously, the territory of Afghanistan, justly known as 'the highway of conquest' was periodically subjected to military invasions and cultural migrations, with a corresponding variety of political sovereigns. These events added to the multiplicity of ethnic communities and cultures in the form of various Afghan tribal groups, but rarely did the region experience political, economic, or cultural unity.[1] The list of invaders and conquerors who have influenced Afghanistan's political and social development reads like a *Who's Who* in the history of Asian aggression. The Indo-Aryans are the first people on record to have invaded the area, probably before the sixteenth century BC. They were followed by the Persians, Greeks, Kushans, Huns, Turks,[2] Mongols, again the Turks, again the Persians, and finally the British and the Russians.[3] The major ethnic groups of the twentieth century demographically reflect this history of military conquest. The region north of the Hindu Kush mountain range, often referred to as Afghan Turkestan, is populated primarily by Uzbeks, a people of Turkish origin. In the western areas of the Hindu Kush, the Hazaras peoples, who descend from Mongolian stock, are dominant. The peoples closest to a true ethnic 'Afghan' are known locally as Pathans, who are subdivided into two groups (western and eastern) based on linguistic distinctions, with the western Pathans often being referred to as Durranis. Living in between these two groups and in the southern region near Pakistan are the ethnic Ghilzais, who are said not to be 'true' Pathans but rather a mixture of ethnic groups. Around Kabul, the capital, live the Qizilbashes, descendants of Iranian garrison troops imported by a nineteenth-century Afghan ruler (Nadir Shah) to shore up his rule. These ethnic Qizilbashes, like other Iranians, are followers of Shia Islam, while most of the other ethnic groups (the most notable exception being the Hazaras) of Afghanistan are followers of Sunni Islam.[4]

Creating a unified 'national' polity out of this mosaic of peoples, traditions, languages and cultures has never truly succeeded in Afghanistan. However, the importation of Islam by the Turks in the tenth century had a major impact on all future events in Afghanistan. As a cultural force capable of partially integrating a hitherto politically divided amalgam of peoples, Islam was a cross-cultural element upon which national identity could be built, and which would later prove crucial to the defeat of the Soviet Union. Indeed, Islam was the single most important factor in the initial creation of what can be characterized as a very limited national polity in modern-day Afghanistan. Islam introduced the idea of a community that was based on law as well as on religion, and Islam's missionary universalism was able to provide under the banner of one god a unifying element that eventually assimilated the wide variety of polytheistic migratory ethnic groups into one faith. According to Vartan Gregorian, 'The Muslim conquest brought Afghanistan within a greater political entity, stimulated trade in the region, and preserved the country's geographic importance as a crossroads between India, Central Asia, and the Mediterranean world.'[5]

Concurrently with the spread of Islam, there also evolved a loosely affiliated, centralized, tribal-based political structure that was very similar to the political structures of premodern Europe. The polity of nineteenth-century Afghanistan could best be described as a feudal estate in which personal identity and political loyalty were focused primarily on extended family/clan ties. Among clans themselves loyalty was next accorded to the tribe (generally based on a common language in addition to blood relations). Next, vacillating levels of deference by clan and tribal leaders were paid to the leadership of the most militarily and economically powerful tribe, which nominally ruled as the 'national' government. At the head of each clan sat a patriarchal leader who was a son of the most noble family of the tribe. The favourite son was elected for life by the assembled elders of the tribe, whose decision was then usually acknowledged by the 'central' government (and other tribes) as a matter of course. Within each clan, social organization and social relations were strictly dictated by religious law. Despite this commonality, like their Christian counterparts in the European feudal order, conflict was rife between clans and tribes all professing the same universal faith in Islam. As in the political economy of European feudalism, feudal politics in Afghanistan revolved around personal loyalty, patronage and protection. The family/clan that headed the central government was in power because it could command more loyalty among the tribes than any other single tribe or group of allied tribes. Like other feudal orders, the Afghan central government maintained power through patronage by granting land to vassals in exchange for military service and the sharing of tax revenues. As in medieval Europe this was a very unstable order. Political society in Afghanistan alternated randomly between periods of uneasy truce and warfare, with no single tribe, clan or family ever being able to entirely defeat the others, with no central government leader ever ruling without challenges from would-be usurpers, in a political reality that can be characterized as a fluctuating balance-of-power system, until the arrival of the British and the Russians.

Political legitimacy in Afghanistan thus existed only marginally on the national level. In the sociology of Weber, traditional and charismatic authority were of much greater importance than the legal/rational legitimacy of the central government. In political terms, Afghanistan was a society of loosely affiliated and highly autonomous subnational polities, each governing itself largely free of central government control. Any single leader who attempted to concentrate and centralize governing power met fierce resistance. Certainly the power of the central government was feared by regional and local authorities, and hence central authority was often supported and given due respect by local rulers – but only if it did not try to infringe on the traditional right of tribal leaders to organize and conduct their own affairs. In short, there were two pillars of political legitimacy in Afghanistan: the religion of Islam that was shared by all, and, perhaps most important, respect for the variety of traditional cultures as characterized by the autonomy of each extended family/clan/tribal unit.

Afghanistan in world affairs until 1940

Because of its remote location, Afghanistan was of little concern to the principal powers in the Western world until the nineteenth century, when British economic interests and political rule expanded northward throughout what is today India and Pakistan. The East India Company, acting as Britain's representative in Asia, signed the Anglo-Afghan Treaty of 1809 with Shah Shuja, known as the 'King of Kabul'.[6] However, Shah Shuja's centralized influence over the territories and peoples of today's Afghanistan was tenuous at best. Entry of the British further disrupted the local balance of power, and as a result political anarchy reigned in Afghanistan during the next two decades. Warring tribal factions, dominated by the Sikhs of northern India, struggled for control in the early 1800s. Shah Shuja fled to Lahore in 1813 and remained under British protection until a local Pathan chieftain, Dost Muhammad Khan, consolidated Afghan tribal power in 1836. Dost Muhammad sought British sanction of his new position as Amir [King] and appealed for British aid against Persia, which sought to gain power in what today consists of Afghanistan's western provinces.[7]

The British, who viewed events in Afghanistan as a component of the European balance of power, rejected the request for recognition on the grounds that Dost Muhammad had previously sought aid from the Russians. The British were wary of the independent-minded and potentially pro-Moscow Afghan Amir, and acted to remove him by military force. In restoring their puppet leader Shah Shuja to the throne in Kabul, the British military aroused a countrywide revolt in support of Dost Muhammad, a struggle that became known as the First Anglo-Afghan War (1838–42).[8] During the war Shah Shuja was driven from the throne in Kabul, and the British expedition that placed him there was defeated utterly by Dost Muhammad's forces. The First Anglo-Afghan War is one of the most humiliating defeats in the chronicles of British military history. Most accounts by European historians report that of more than 4,500 fighting men and 12,000 camp followers who started the expedition into the Afghan interior, a single person (the lowly but lucky assistant surgeon Dr William Brydon) made it back to British-controlled territory alive. These accounts are only partially correct. Actually, eighty-six British officers and over 2,000 camp followers remained in Afghanistan as hostages, prisoners of war, or refugees, and were liberated at the war's end by a British punitive expedition. Nonetheless, Dr Brydon was the only European to survive independently the entire length of the original expedition, and the magnitude of the British defeat at the hands of the Afghan tribesmen remains undiminished.[9]

In response, in the autumn of 1842, a British punitive expedition entered and destroyed Kabul and laid waste to other cities upon leaving the country, with the death toll at the war's end estimated at 70,000 Afghans. The tribes of Afghanistan remained unified under Dost Muhammad's leadership, and the fiasco of the war caused the fall of Lord Melbourne's government in Britain.[10] Anglo-Russian rivalry in Asia and Europe increased, and Afghanistan was the key geographic playing field of what has since become known as 'the Great Game'. The main concern of Afghan leaders over the next half-century was to prevent their country from being swallowed up either by the Russian Bear or the British Lion.

The nineteenth century marked the zenith of Russian imperial expansion. Tsarist foreign policy at this time focused on the subjugation and annexation of vast reaches of territory to the east and south of the Urals. As the British pursued their colonial endeavours in India, the Russians slowly moved south through Central Asia toward Afghanistan. The Russians viewed the British invasion of Afghanistan (1838–42) as a direct threat to their interests, and in response they continued to conquer and occupy the independent Central Asian Khanates, or reduced them to political and economic dependency through treaties and trade. By 1870 Russian influence extended to the banks of the Amu Darya River.[11]

The British and Russian governments, as members of the Concert of Europe, were concerned that their expanding empires in Asia would precipitate a European war, and they attempted to settle their differences over Afghanistan by diplomatic means. The result was a number of treaties and agreements worthy of note. The first such accord was the Granville–Gorchakoff Agreement of 1873. This agreement established the Amu Darya River as the southern boundary of the Russian sphere of influence. Afghanistan was to be regarded as a *de facto* neutral zone between the British and Russian empires. Lord Granville and Prince Gorchakoff reached agreement without conferring with the reigning Afghan Amir Sher Ali, a factor that added to the confusion, distrust and lack of communication that eventually resulted in the Second Anglo-Afghan War (1878–80).[12]

Sher Ali viewed the expanding Russian forces with suspicion and apprehension. In 1873 he asked for a definite British commitment to aid Afghanistan in case of Russian aggression. In July an Afghan delegation met with British representatives who advised the Afghans not to worry about Russian manoeuvring because the Russians had agreed to honour the Amu Darya as the northern boundary of Afghanistan. Sher Ali distrusted the British, and Anglo-Afghan relations became strained.[13] In 1874 Benjamin Disraeli became prime minister of Britain. Disraeli changed the character of British policy toward Russia. He implemented what was known as the 'Forward Policy'.

This policy, a forerunner of the American 'containment' following the Second World War, actively sought to blunt Russian expansionism toward India with more active engagement in Afghan affairs.[14] British fears of Russian encroachment in South Asia were often fuelled by Russian newspaper articles. An article appearing in the *Moscow Gazette* (19 July 1878) reflects the Russian attitude at the time:

> The time has arrived for Russia to establish her influence over the whole of Central Asia, and this is all the more easy as the Ruler of Afghanistan is not on good terms with England – our foe in Central Asia. The concentration of our influence on the frontiers of the territory of the Empress of India would be a natural answer to the English seizure of Cyprus and all the approaches to India ... In Asia there are two political Powers confronting each other, and they must inevitably come into collision ...[15]

In the summer of 1878 the Russians sent a diplomatic mission to Kabul without receiving prior permission from Sher Ali. The British demanded an explanation and in return sent their own delegation, which was denied permission to enter Afghanistan. The British considered Sher Ali's action a national insult and decided to invade Afghanistan – and thus began the Second Anglo-Afghan War. Sher Ali died in early 1879, and his son Yaqub Khan was forced to sign the Treaty of Gandamak with the British military delegation. The major features of this treaty were the delivery of control of Afghan foreign policy to the British and the subjection of Afghanistan to external British supervision.[16] The other Afghan tribes soon revolted in protest over British intervention, and in July 1879 the British envoy, Sir Louis Cavagnari, was murdered. In the face of significant tribal military forces, and lacking re-inforcements, the British troops withdrew from Afghanistan, losing a sizeable force during the course of their retreat.[17]

To the north, the Russians continued their policy of expansion into Central Asia. In 1881 Khiva was annexed, in 1884 Merv, and in 1885 Afghan and Russian troops fought over control of an oasis a hundred miles south of Merv in what is known as the 'Panjdeh Incident'. The British, fearing that the ultimate Russian goal was to seize the strategic Afghan city of Herat, mobilized forces in India. Only a successful arbitration by Denmark pre-vented war, and in 1887 the Anglo-Russian Agreement of St Petersburg was signed.[18] The Russians agreed to make no further territorial advances southward, and Anglo-Russian conflict was again averted in 1895 when a similar agreement was signed that further defined Afghan borders.[19]

The most significant diplomatic event affecting the long-term fortunes of Afghanistan was the agreement fixing the Durand Line as the border between Afghanistan and the northern territory of British India. The problem with the Durand Line is typical of many such demarcations created during

the British colonial period. The border was drawn for reasons of administrative and strategic convenience. Subsequently, the indigenous tribal groups
that populated the region were divided by the arbitrary decision of British
surveyors. This boundary separated one-third of the Pathan tribe (Afghanistan's dominant ethnic group) from its traditional territorial homeland. In
1893 the British forced the Afghan Amir Abdur Rahman into recognizing
the Durand Line as the formal border between Afghanistan and what is today
Pakistan. It has been hotly disputed by both sides whether the final agreement
stipulates actual boundary demarcations, or merely defines the respective
spheres of influence of the British government and the Afghan Amir.
Ironically, the Durand Line was designed to bring political stability to the
frontier region, but in fact this border has proved to be strategically indefensible, and has been the major cause of friction between Pakistan and
Afghanistan into the 1990s.[20]

The latter part of the nineteenth century saw the waning of the Great
Game between Britain and Russia. Both the British and the Russians feared
a reinvigorated Germany and turned their attentions away from Afghanistan.
After its defeat in the 1904–5 Japanese War, Russia was preoccupied with
solving its internal problems. In 1905 the new Afghan Amir, Habibullah,
offered the British control over Afghan foreign relations in return for a
subsidy of 18 lakhs of rupees a year (160,000 British pounds) and access to
military supplies through India.[21]

The final major agreement of the Great Game period was the Anglo-
Russian Convention of 1907. This agreement had four important provisions.
First, Persia was divided into two zones of influence: Russian in the north
and British in the east and south, thus protecting the western frontier of
Afghanistan from Russian penetration. Second, Britain and Russia recog-
nized China's control of Tibet and agreed not to interfere in this area. Third,
Russia agreed that Afghanistan was outside the Russian sphere of influence
and agreed to confer directly with the British on matters relating to
Afghan–Russian affairs. Fourth, Britain was not to occupy or annex any part
of Afghanistan, nor interfere in any way in the internal affairs of Afghanistan.[22]
A final article stated that the Afghan Amir must agree to the Convention in
order to make it legal and binding. Habibullah, who was not consulted during
deliberations, declared the Convention illegal. The Amir, bolstered by the
Russian defeat by the Japanese in 1905, wanted the British to join him in an
attack on Russian Turkestan to recover lands lost to the Tsars in the 1880s.
The British refused and joined the Russians in ignoring Habibullah's protests,
unilaterally declaring the Convention legal and binding on the Afghans.[23]

In early 1912 Russian military activities precipitated a war scare in
Afghanistan when it was reported that attempts were being made to build a
bridge across the Amu Darya River. The Russians were reportedly frustrated
by the relatively minor benefits they obtained from the 1907 Convention and
blamed the British for convincing the Afghan Amir that any Russian overtures

were sinister. Russia also requested British aid in extracting Russians held in Afghan prisons, basing its request on the third component of the Convention. The British were reluctant to help foster any sort of Afghan–Russian rapprochement and refused to pressure the Amir on behalf of the Russian prisoners. Secret negotiations between Russia and Britain took place in which the Russians indicated a willingness to make concessions in regional matters, such as disputes over Tibet, in return for more influence in Afghanistan. These negotiations continued inconclusively until the outbreak of the First World War, at which time they were terminated.[24]

During the First World War, Afghanistan declared and maintained a strict neutrality, despite German and Turkish attempts to draw it to their side. Both attempted to use Afghanistan as an instrument to undermine Russian and British influence in the region. Afghanistan signed a treaty of friendship with Germany in January 1916. This treaty did not alter Afghanistan's official position of neutrality, but it marked the end of the country's policy of isolation and total dependence on Britain and the beginning of a permanent presence of German traders, diplomats and military personnel in Afghanistan. More-over, it fuelled the zeal of Afghan nationalist-modernists who were convinced that Afghanistan must sever its ties with Britain before any modernization programmes could take hold.[25] The Amir Habibullah refused to be swayed from his cautious foreign policy and pursued the 'usual Afghan game of positive neutrality – waiting to see which side would win …'.[26]

At the war's end, Habibullah attempted to parlay his policy of neutrality into international recognition of Afghanistan's independent status at the Paris Peace Conference. Britain refused to discuss independence, granting only an increase in the Amir's annual monetary subsidy. On 20 February 1919, an unknown assailant assassinated Habibullah, which brought to power his son Amanullah. Amanullah believed his first task was to restore the independence of Afghanistan – a task that would bring him into close contact with the newly victorious Bolsheviks in Soviet Russia.[27] Amanullah, in an attempt to consolidate his own somewhat tenuous position among the tribes and to gain Afghanistan's independence from Britain, launched the Third Anglo-Afghan War in May 1919. This short-lived affair, although a military defeat on the battlefield, was politically successful for the Afghans. In August 1919 the Treaty of Rawalpindi was signed between the war-weary British and the Afghan Amir. This treaty left Afghanistan free to conduct its own foreign affairs and marks the date of formal Afghan independence from British political control.[28]

Early Soviet–Afghan relations

The most important Soviet policies affecting early relations with Afghanistan centred on the Bolshevik attitude toward the Muslims of Central Asia. The

Bolshevik Revolution had released an abundance of nationalistic forces in Central Asia that had been repressed under the Tsarist regime. While attempting to consolidate power in Russia, the Bolsheviks faced the urgent nationalist demands and desire for independence by Muslims, who populated some of the most-recently conquered territory of the former Tsarist empire. At the time of the 1917 Revolution the entire fringe of the Russian empire, from Outer Mongolia to the Crimea, was peopled by approximately thirty million Muslims, a number that constituted about 14 per cent of the Russian empire's population.[29] These areas had been forcibly annexed by the Tsars, and resentment of Russian messianism and 'Russification' ran deep among the Muslim subjects.

Bolshevik policy was designed initially to pacify Muslims with promises of independence or autonomy until the new leadership in Moscow was able to finish dealing with more severe problems related to the civil war. Then, adopting the policies of the Tsars, Muslim nationalist separatism would be crushed by a combination of diplomatic manœuvring and outright force. Lenin was aware of the potential for using the nationality issue in helping to consolidate the Bolshevik position during the Russian Civil War, as well as the need to pacify Muslim nationalists temporarily with promises of autonomy. The Bolsheviks organized a Commissariat for Nationalities headed by Joseph Stalin. In December 1917 Lenin and Stalin issued a joint letter entitled 'To All the Toiling Moslems of Russia and the East', which was used to gain Muslim sympathy for the Bolshevik cause:

> Comrades! Brothers!
> Great events are taking place in Russia! ... The empire of capitalist plunder and violence is falling in ruins. The ground is slipping from under the feet of the imperialist robbers ... In the face of these great events, we turn to you, toiling and disinherited Moslems of Russia and the East ... Henceforward your beliefs and customs, your national and cultural institutions, are declared free and inviolable! Build your national life freely and without hindrance. It is your right. Know that your rights, like those of all the peoples of Russia, will be protected by the might of the revolution, by the Councils of Workers', Soldiers', and Peasants' Deputies ...
> Moslems of Russia!
> Moslems of the East!
> We look to you for sympathy and support in the work of regenerating the world.[30]

This revolutionary manifesto clearly expresses the Bolshevik intent to incite revolution in the Muslim-populated areas controlled by pro-Tsarist forces, and in other eastern areas such as India which were dominated by the West

European powers. However, after consolidating its hold in European Russia during the Civil War, by 1922 Moscow's active interest in the East faltered. Still, an awareness of the potential importance of these areas lingered on. Of all the early Bolshevik leaders, only Stalin remained continually involved in Asian affairs prior to Lenin's death.

Stalin managed to nullify the influence of the greater part of the Muslim leadership through bureaucratic manipulation. He did so by gathering the more moderate Islamic intellectuals under his direct control in Moscow. These leaders were promised power over all policies regarding Soviet Muslims. Most of these Muslim leaders were members of a group that sought to modernize Muslim communities and saw an alliance with communism as compatible with liberal Islamic thought. They had emerged largely from the reform movement known as *Jadists*.[31] In the end, none of the promised freedoms was granted, and all attempts to gain autonomy were forcefully repressed. Gradual Russification in the 1920s and 1930s using a combination of economic and political incentives and a liberal application of brute force served to suppress the strong cries of Islamic nationalism. Despite reports of Soviet mistreatment of Muslims in Soviet Central Asia, the Afghan King, Amanullah Khan, established relations with the new Soviet government shortly after gaining the throne in 1919. Amanullah was impressed by the revolutionary nature of the Soviet regime and was encouraged by Soviet promises of Muslim autonomy.

Amanullah's foreign relations

As mentioned earlier, Amanullah came into power after the assassination of his father Habibullah in February 1919. After some initial confusion and indecision, Amanullah's foreign policy followed three distinct paths: he established diplomatic relations with Soviet Russia, gradually normalized Afghanistan's relations with Britain, and strove for Pan-Islamic solidarity. More importantly, Afghanistan's new freedom, which had resulted from the recent upheavals in Russia and the British retreat from Afghanistan after the Third Anglo-Afghan War, allowed him to check both great powers by playing one off against the other.[32]

Even before Afghanistan had gained its independence, Amanullah had communicated his desire to establish 'permanent and friendly relations' with Russia. On 17 April 1919, two letters were sent to Moscow, in which Amanullah stressed the fact that Afghanistan was free and independent, and pointed out that the Afghan 'psychology had always contained in it ideas of equality, humanity and liberty'.[33]

Lenin replied on 27 May 1919, congratulating the king and the Afghan people for their heroic defence of liberty, and accepting the proposal to establish diplomatic relations. The Soviets saw great possibilities in an alliance with Afghanistan against Britain. Lenin gave special consideration to Afghanistan's strategic position and the potential of using it as a base for fomenting revolution in India. Lenin encouraged Amanullah to continue pursuing Pan-Islamism as a goal. In a letter to the Afghan ruler dated 27 November 1919, Lenin wrote that Afghanistan was the only independent Muslim state in the world, and fate had set before the Afghan people the great historic task of leading all the Mohammedan peoples to freedom.[34]

Lenin was playing a classic game of duplicitous diplomacy with Amanullah. His letter to the Amir contains direct contradictions with Lenin's statements directed toward the Second Congress of the Communist International in 1920. In one of his speeches regarding the role of the Comintern in more backward nations, Lenin declared, '... it is necessary *to combat Pan-Islamism* and similar trends, which strive to combine the liberation movement against European and American imperialism with the strengthening of the positions of the Khans, the landlords, the mullahs, etc.'[35] Amanullah probably was unaware of Lenin's deception, or simply chose to continue dealing with the new Russian leaders on the assumption that any anti-British regime served Afghanistan's best interests.

The two countries finalized a treaty of friendship in 1921. This treaty called for the establishment of regular diplomatic relations and respect for each other's independence (Article 1). The Afghans were given free and untaxed transit through Soviet territory of all goods (Article 6) and were promised financial and material aid (Article 10). The disputed areas of Bukhara and Khiva in Soviet Central Asia were recognized as independent and autonomous regions (Article 8). This provision was a concession to the Afghans and greatly enhanced Amanullah's position as a champion of Islamic solidarity (however, both regions actually remained under Soviet control). For their part, the Afghans agreed not to enter into military or political agreements that might be construed as contrary to the interest of either party (Article 3), and they gave the Russians permission to open five consulates in Afghanistan in exchange for permission to open seven consulates in the Soviet Union (Article 4).[36] The treaty placed Afghanistan in a much stronger bargaining position in its relations with Britain. The Afghans would no longer be forced to rely on British India as their sole conduit for trade.

The Comintern in Afghanistan

One of the important elements in early Soviet foreign policy was the Communist International – the Comintern. The Comintern was organized to function as the operational spearhead for the spread of worldwide revolution. Revolution was to be instigated by local communist parties in various nations under the guidance of the Soviet Union. Soviet policy used the Comintern for two basic purposes: to exploit antagonisms within the capitalist world in order to breed dissent among the working class; and to safeguard the security of the Soviet Union by keeping capitalistic nations off balance in suppressing their own internal disorders.[37]

The 'Manifesto of the Communist International', written by Leon Trotsky in 1919, reflected the optimism of Lenin and the rest of the Bolshevik leaders. The concept that the nations dominated by imperialism could be transformed directly from the precapitalist stage of development to socialism was an integral part of early Comintern philosophy. This transformation in South Asia would take place within the context of a European social revolution in which the once dominant colonial powers would aid the newly independent former colonies. Trotsky wrote:

> The emancipation of the colonies is possible only in conjunction with the emancipation of the metropolitan working class. The workers and peasants of Annam, Algiers, and Bengal, and also of Persia and Armenia, will gain their opportunity for independent existence only when the workers of England have taken state power in their own hands ... If capitalist Europe forcibly dragged the backward section of the world into the capitalist whirlpool, a socialist Europe will come to the aid of liberated colonies with its technology, its organization, its spiritual forces, in order to facilitate their transition to a planned organized socialist economy.[38]

The only manifestation of the early Comintern policies relating to Afghanistan was the 'First Congress of the Peoples of the East', held in Baku in 1920. After the 1921 peace treaty between the Soviets and Amanullah, and similar agreements with the leaders of Turkey and Persia, the Comintern's activities in the East were primarily focused on China, and the Arab states were left to their own devices.[39]

However, the presence of a small number of communist organizers in Afghanistan dates back to King Amanullah's reign. The Comintern had made some futile attempts in 1919 to generate revolutionary cadres in the country. Afghanistan had been one of the targets of a general propaganda campaign that the Comintern had launched from Germany. As part of that effort, lithographed pamphlets written in native languages and calling for national and social liberation movements had been widely distributed in South and East Asia. An Afghan representative had attended an Eastern Communist Central Committee meeting in Berlin in 1919, and Afghans had participated as well in the Comintern-sponsored Congress of Eastern Peoples in Baku in 1920. Some reports also indicate that a few communist agitators were active in Herat and in Mazar-i-Sharif, one of the sites chosen by the Comintern Executive Committee in the 1920s as a propaganda centre. However, there were few Marxists in Afghanistan before the formation of the People's

Democratic Party of Afghanistan (PDPA) in 1965. Historically, Afghan governments energetically resisted the dissemination of Bolshevik propaganda on Afghan soil, even as they sought to maintain friendly diplomatic relations with the Soviet Union.[40] Ideological penetration of Afghanistan was not a coveted goal of the early Soviet leaders, and neither did Marxist ideology find many interested ears among the tribal nomads and Islamic clerics of the country.

Internal strife and Soviet intervention

Amanullah considered himself a revolutionary who would lead Afghanistan into the modern world and was the first of many leaders who attempted to modernize Afghan society through extensive central government reform measures. Amanullah faced his first serious internal problems in 1924, when tradition-bound tribal opponents who opposed his policies and the right of the central government to dictate behaviour to the local authorities rose in rebellion. The Soviets came to Amanullah's rescue with warplanes, which bombed the rebels into submission. The Soviets also provided Amanullah with other military aid and established telephone and telegraph lines connecting Kabul with Moscow.[41] In August 1926 the Soviets and the Afghans signed a treaty of neutrality and non-aggression. The most important element of this treaty was Article II, which was later cited by the Soviets in the Second World War as justification for their demand that Afghanistan expel all German nationals from Afghan territory.[42] Prior to the Soviet invasion of 1979, Soviet troops had moved into Afghanistan on three separate occasions. The first and third Soviet 'invasions' were small-scale military incursions in 1925 and 1930. Both of these operations were directed against Afghan tribal insurgents who had made repeated raids across the border into Soviet territory and then fled to the safety of Afghan territory. On both occasions the Soviets withdrew their forces after requests from the Afghan and British governments.[43] However, the second invasion presented the Soviets with a dilemma that pitted traditional concepts of national interest against ideological consistency.

In response to Amanullah's social reform programmes, a growing body of revolutionaries, consisting of Islamic fundamentalists and anti-government tribal groups, took root in Afghanistan. In January 1929 Amanullah was forced to flee Kabul as rebels, led by peasant leader Bacha-i-Saquo ('Son of the Water Carrier'), invaded and took control of the city. The Soviets were forced into choosing between the pro-Soviet autocratic king and the 'poor, oppressed masses'. The Soviets, doubting that a peasant revolution could last long in a country that had been traditionally ruled by monarchs of the Pathan tribe, decided it was more prudent to support the King.[44] Interest overrode ideology as Ghulam Nabi, Amanullah's ambassador to the Soviet Union, convinced the Soviet government to aid Amanullah's cause by permitting him to raise a force in Russia equipped with Russian arms and aided by Soviet advisers and Central Asian Muslims. Nabi's plan envisioned that such a move would bring about a 'spontaneous' rising in northern Afghanistan in support of Amanullah, and Bacha-i-Saquo would be overthrown. In other words, the Soviets were persuaded to support a Bay of Pigs type operation. It was no more successful.[45] During the struggle Amanullah had apparently lost the stomach for revolution and hardship. He abdicated the title of Amir and fled to India. The Soviets withdrew their army in order to appease the British, who at that time were considering the re-establishment of diplomatic relations with the Soviet Union.[46] After a series of tribal battles one of King Amanullah's clan relations, Nadir Khan, defeated Bacha and regained the throne with British military aid in October 1929.[47]

Despite British alarmists who had distrusted Amanullah's early relations with the Soviets, Afghanistan's foreign policy remained largely independent of Russian influence, even though it was definitely anti-British. The Afghan Amir had insisted throughout his reign that all Russian arms sent to Afghanistan for eventual use in a national liberation movement in India be transported by the Afghan government, and that all Indian revolutionaries be disarmed upon entering Afghan territory. According to the famous Indian communist M.N. Roy, the Afghans made it clear that they had no intention of permitting any Soviet force to enter their territory to conduct operations against India.[48] For Moscow's part, the decision to aid Amanullah in 1929 can be compared with earlier actions in Turkey and Iran. In all three countries the communist organizations were either weak or nonexistent, and the prospects for communist revolutions were correspondingly poor. Each of these countries was ruled by men who wished to reduce British influence in the region – an aim shared by the Bolsheviks. In the face of these realities, the Soviets postponed the goal of exporting revolution to their Muslim neighbours and normalized relations with the existing regimes. The cause of world revolution was subordinated to the national interests of the Russian state.[49] Soviet policy during the early years of the regime was conditioned not by any altruistic interest for the welfare or independence of Afghanistan, but rather by the need to suppress the nationalistic aspirations of Soviet Muslims and the potential for using Afghanistan as a bargaining chip in the Anglo-Soviet power struggle. The importance of Marxist–Leninist ideology in foreign policy toward Afghanistan was curtailed until after the Second World War.

Nadir Khan and quiet neutrality

After his accession to the Afghan throne, Nadir Khan pursued a policy of diplomatic neutrality. During his reign only minimal attempts were made by the central government to pursue internal reforms at home. In taking a more

pragmatic and traditional position than Amanullah's, he thought the government should not impose upon the Afghan tribes new ideas and institutions.
He also thought that any new programmes ought to develop 'naturally', and
he was careful to avoid conflict with the Islamic community and urged all
Afghans to be good Muslims.[50] As Nadir pursued a very limited modernization programme at home, he followed an equally delicate foreign policy
based on traditional Afghan attitudes toward Britain and Russia. His most
difficult task was to make secure Afghanistan's hard-won independence and
to convince all elements, including the Soviets and the Muslim nationalist-
modernists, that he was not a tool of British imperialism. Unlike Amanullah,
he adhered to a policy of non-involvement in both India and Soviet Central
Asia. He saw 'positive neutralism' as the best means of survival. Such a policy
made it essential for him to remain on friendly terms with both the Soviets
and the British.[51] The Soviets responded in a positive manner to Nadir's
newly won position as Amir of Afghanistan and recognized his government
on 19 October 1929.[52]

In 1931 the two nations signed a new Treaty of Neutrality and Non-
Aggression, which essentially renewed the provisions of the 1926 accord. The
Afghan government, in an effort to demonstrate its goodwill, showed a
marked sympathy for the Soviet viewpoint at the International Disarmament
Conference in 1932. More importantly, from the Soviet point of view, the
Nadir administration not only prevented any anti-Soviet activities but also
expelled the last tribal insurgents that had caused the first and third small-
scale Soviet invasions of Afghan territory.[53] On 13 September 1932, the Afghan
government agreed to a Soviet proposal that called for appointing a number
of border control officers to help prevent the recurrence of such incidents.
These officers would be responsible for patrolling their own sides of the
frontier, but any incidents would be investigated jointly.[54]

Soviet influence was greatly diminished in Afghanistan by 1933 as Stalinist
Russia turned toward 'building socialism in one country'.[55] Efforts to instigate
revolutions in other nations were given low priority as the Soviets struggled
with the initial five-year plans. Maintenance of the international status quo
was seen as the Soviet Union's primary national interest. Karl Radek, editor
of *Izvestiia* and member of the Central Committee of the Communist Party,
declared the non-expansionist ethic underlying Soviet foreign policy in 1934:

> The attempt to represent the foreign policy of the Soviet Union as a
> continuation of Tsarist policy is ridiculous. Bourgeois writers who do
> so have not grasped even the purely external manifestations of this
> policy. It used to be an axiom of Tsarist policy that it should strive by
> every available means to gain possession of the Dardanelles and of an
> ice-free port on the Pacific. Not only have the Soviets not attempted
> to seize the Dardanelles, but from the very beginning they have tried

to establish the most friendly relations with Turkey ... The Soviet Union takes no part in the struggle for the re-distribution of the world.

The words of Stalin at the Sixteenth Congress of the Communist Party of the Soviet Union – 'We do not want a single bit of foreign land; but at the same time not an inch of our land shall ever be yielded to anyone else' – these words are the exact expression of the policy of the Soviet Union ...[56]

Soviet actions in this period generally validate Radek's characterization of Stalin's foreign policy at this time. However, despite its proclamations, the Soviet regime had demonstrated that it was willing to use military force to back its interests in Afghanistan. Yet at the same time the Soviets also had exhibited a large degree of restraint in dealing with Afghan border raiders and had attempted to ameliorate future problems through diplomatic agreements and bilateral cooperation.

Nadir Khan was assassinated on 8 November 1933, while attending a soccer game in Kabul and was succeeded by his son, Muhammad Zahir. The Soviets reacted with standard diplomatic condolences and accepted the change in government without further comment. Anti-British sentiment was at a peak in Afghanistan at this time, as was fear of Russian imperialism, and so the Afghan government approached Germany to provide military and development aid. From the Afghan point of view Germans were welcome foreigners. Germany had no history of imperialism in the region and was on unfriendly terms with both the Soviet Union and Britain.[57] By the mid 1930s Germany was the third most powerful foreign influence in Afghanistan. Japan's development into a major military and commercial power also had an impact on Afghanistan. As the number of Japanese commercial interests in Afghanistan grew, so did its ability to support the Afghan strategy of diluting British and Soviet power. In 1934 the Afghan foreign minister, Faiz Muhammad, privately stated that the usefulness of Japan to Afghanistan lay in the fact that Japan was the natural enemy of Russia.[58] At the same time, the Afghans sought to avoid provoking the Soviets. In Moscow the Afghan foreign minister signed a ten-year extension of the Soviet–Afghan Non-Aggression Pact of 1931. Also in Moscow, the preliminary talks for the 1937 Saadabad Non-Aggression Pact among Afghanistan, Turkey, Iraq and Iran took place. This Pact represented a small but decisive step toward the resurgence of Islam in regional politics in general, and the consolidation of Islamic policy along the southern borders of the Soviet Union in particular.[59]

When relations between Germany, the Soviet Union and the British grew increasingly hostile, Afghanistan became concerned that cooperation with Germany might draw the country into these looming international conflicts. In an effort to avoid possible violations of Afghan territory by either the British or the Soviets, King Zahir issued a decree on 6 September 1939, officially proclaiming Afghan neutrality in foreign affairs. The decree also restricted the activities of belligerent powers on Afghan soil. Soviet–Afghan relations were strained until mid 1940, when Soviet troops were withdrawn from their stations on the Afghan border and moved into the European theatre.[60]

The United States and Afghanistan

After the British retreat from Afghanistan in 1919, the Amir Amanullah sought to establish diplomatic relations with various countries. Amanullah's diplomatic mission was received in the United States by President Warren G. Harding on 26 July 1921, a meeting that granted *de facto* recognition of the legitimacy both of the new Amir and of Afghanistan's independence from Britain's control of its foreign policy. Harding agreed to consider Amanullah's offer to establish official relations, but no action was taken on this matter.[61] In 1922 Cornelius Engert, an American diplomat who was stationed in Persia, made an unofficial visit to Amanullah's court in Kabul and wrote a report that strongly recommended *de jure* recognition of the Afghan regime. Once again, for no apparent reason other than simple neglect, the United States took no action regarding Afghanistan.[62] In 1925 the Afghan minister to France, Nadir Khan, who later ruled Afghanistan after Amanullah's abdication following civil strife in 1929, discussed a treaty of friendship with the US ambassador in Paris. A draft of the treaty was sent to Secretary of State Frank Kellogg, who promised to study the proposal. For a third time, the United States failed to take action on Afghanistan's diplomatic overture.[63]

In 1930 the chief of the State Department division of Near East Affairs, Wallace Smith Murray, effectively blocked Congressional attempts to establish relations with Afghanistan. His opposition was articulated in a vivid (if not spurious) condemnation of the country: 'Afghanistan is, without doubt, the most fanatic, independent, hostile country in the world today ... the British ... have for years forbidden any white British subject to enter Afghanistan ... no foreign lives can be protected and no foreign interests guaranteed ... there would be no way for any foreign aggrieved power to bring pressure on Afghanistan, a landlocked Asiatic country accessible only through India or Soviet Russia.'[64] Although Murray's view was parochial and tinged with racist overtones, there was some degree of truth in his words – Afghanistan is a hostile land for unwanted foreigners, as both the British and later the Russians learned at a high cost. The pattern of US neglect and Murray's geopolitical view also foreshadowed US foreign policy during the Cold War, which will be discussed more fully in the next chapter.

The United States continued to withhold official diplomatic recognition to Afghanistan until the advent of the Franklin D. Roosevelt administration, when both the Soviet Union and Afghanistan joined the League of Nations and were recognized by the US government. However, the United States and Afghanistan did not sign a treaty of friendship until 1936.[65] Because of both countries' long histories of isolationism, British dominance in Afghanistan, and America's anticolonial ethic, the relationship between the United States and Afghanistan can best be described as negligible until after the Second World War.

THE FOUNDATIONS OF POLITICAL LEGITIMACY IN VIETNAM

Vietnam's political history of warfare is as long and traumatic as Afghanistan's. However, unlike Afghanistan, Vietnam went from colonialism to independence only to be recolonized by the French and occupied by the Americans. According to legend, present-day Vietnam originated in a kingdom called Van Lang (or Van Tang, 'Country of Tattooed Men'), ruled by the Hong Bang dynasty from 2879 to 258 BC. This ancient, semi-mythical dynasty was conquered by the King of Thuc, a northern invader who merged Van Lang with his own dominion to form the second Vietnamese Kingdom, Au Lac. Au Lac was to survive for only fifty years, and in 207 BC it was overrun by the Chinese general Trieu Da. Shortly thereafter, during a leadership crisis in China's Ch'in dynasty, Trieu Da revolted against the inner kingdom and declared himself ruler of a new independent state, Nam Viet. Nam Viet was able to survive as an independent state for approximately one century, but in 111 BC it was overrun by the armies of China's powerful new dynasty, the Han. The Han victory marked the beginning of a period of Chinese domination over the Vietnamese that continued for approximately a thousand years.[66]

Chinese rule was not without periods of unrest and revolution in Vietnam. The first uprising by the Vietnamese occurred in AD 39 and was led by two Vietnamese noble women, the Trung sisters. Both committed suicide by drowning after their forces were overrun by a Chinese army in AD 40, making the two heroines national martyrs and symbols of the anti-Chinese spirit that imbues Vietnamese society. Despite the brevity of their revolution, Vietnamese historians have always treated the Trung sisters as the forerunners of latter-day revolutionaries, and they are seen as the leaders of the first Vietnamese nationalist movement.[67] The Trung rebellion was the first in a dozen or so anti-Chinese uprisings between the years AD 39 and 939. These generally short-lived rebellions were an important component in the development of a separate Vietnamese political culture that was able to survive ten centuries of Sinization. Heroic figures in Vietnamese history such as Trieu Au (AD 248) and Ly Bon (AD 542), became enduring symbols of resistance to outside domination.[68]

Vietnam was able to free itself of Chinese control and became an independent state in AD 939, and it would remain independent for over 900 years until 1883, when France was able to solidify its colonial authority.[69] Much like Afghanistan, during this period Vietnam was characterized by constant changes in dynastic rule, internal strife and partition, wars of defence against the Chinese and wars of defence and aggression against the Cambodian empire. Unlike Afghanistan, whose present territorial boundaries were primarily determined by Russian expansion from the north and British expansion from the south in the nineteenth century, Vietnam's borders slowly expanded southward for approximately 700 years as the Vietnamese played the role of regional aggressor.[70] The Cambodian empire, which at its zenith stretched from the South China Sea into Burma, began in the thirteenth century to crumble under constant encroachments by the Vietnamese. This northern onslaught continued through the eighteenth century when Vietnamese expansion had advanced to the Gulf of Siam. The state of Champa, a tributary of the Cambodians, was completely overrun and incorporated into the Vietnamese state in the fifteenth century. In 1471 the Vietnamese razed the Champa capital of Indrapura, slaughtering 40,000 of its inhabitants. Little remains of the Champa culture today, apart from a few scattered stone sculptures and the enduring memory of its fate by Cambodians and Laotians, who regard Vietnam as the major aggressive force in Southeast Asia.[71]

For Vietnam, as for Afghanistan, in the sociology of Weber, traditional and charismatic authority were of greater importance than the legal/rational legitimacy of the central government. For the people of Vietnam the political legitimacy of the ruling monarch was firmly grounded in the adopted Chinese concept of the Mandate of Heaven. The most important duty of any Vietnamese ruler holding the Mandate of Heaven is the preservation of Vietnamese identity. Unlike the Afghans, for whom political loyalty was imbedded within the family/clan/tribal hierarchy with the 'national' identity of 'Afghan' being of secondary importance, the Vietnamese had a more unified and homogeneous national identity that coexisted with local and tribal affiliations. According to Timothy Lomperis, 'The Vietnamese have always been borrowers from other cultures, but the borrowing has had to be, in some way or other, Vietnamized by the ruling establishment so that the people would not lose their identity as Vietnamese. More tangibly, it has always been the almost sacred charge of Viet Nam's rulers to rid the country of foreign invaders and meddlers.'[72] In addition to the task of protecting Vietnamese culture from foreign influences and the territory of the nation from occupation, the holder of the Mandate of Heaven also gained legitimacy by ensuring justice and domestic welfare. In an agrarian society, cultivable land was the key economic variable to the personal success (and political loyalty) of the average peasant family. A just ruler was one who ensured an equitable and fair distribution of land among the peasants. This was similar to Afghanistan's nomadic tribesmen, whose main economic concern was with fodder for their flocks, and who looked to the central regime to adjudicate conflict over grazing rights. Land also held crucial religious significance among the Vietnamese because of the Confucian practice of ancestor-worship. Local burial grounds, in which were interred the bones and ashes of one's forebears, were the focal point of spirituality for the individual Vietnamese citizen.[73]

The European conquest

Vietnam's own successful colonial expansion toward the south coincided with the early penetration of the territory by European explorers. However, the earliest recorded contacts go as far back as AD 166, when Chinese records reveal the visit of a Roman representative of Emperor Marcus Aurelius Antonius, who ruled from AD 161 to 180.[74] The Portuguese are known to have explored the east coast of Indochina as early as 1516. Catholic missionaries are said to have visited Vietnam in 1527, and the first verifiable military expedition arrived in 1535 under the command of Captain Antonio da Faria. He established the first Portuguese trading centre at Faifo, a few miles south of present-day Da Nang. In 1615 Jesuits from the Portuguese colony at Macao were allowed to enter Vietnam after being expelled by the Japanese. The Jesuit mission at Faifo was staffed by Portuguese, Spanish, Italian and French priests.[75] Catholic indoctrination by French missionaries was closely connected with efforts to establish trade with Vietnam. One of the French apostolic vicars for Vietnam, François Pallu, was openly blunt in stating the need for cooperation between Church and business interests. Pallu wrote to the French East Indian Company in 1664 that the company would have full support of the Church and that the number of priests, bishops and converts would equal the number of pro-business advocates in Vietnam.[76]

Despite some early penetration by most of Europe's mercantile nations, Vietnam proved to be a difficult nation from which to profit. Initial missionary activity was tolerated by the leaders of Vietnam's various competing local factions, who were most interested in acquiring modern weapons to use against each other. However, when the country was internally unified in 1672, the Vietnamese mandarins began to impose a number of economic and religious restrictions on foreigners. As a result, the British withdrew in 1697 after twenty-five years of effort, the Dutch closed their trading centre in Hanoi in 1700, and French economic interests were also shut down. After 1700 only the Portuguese were able to maintain their trade centre at Faifo.[77]

The initial failure of Western colonialism in Vietnam during the eighteenth century was in large part determined by Anglo-French rivalry in India. Vietnam was given a long respite while France attempted to protect its position in India. After Britain's decisive victory over other European rivals in India, France ceded most of its Indian possessions and turned its attention back to Vietnam. Colonial advocates in Paris wanted to exploit France's foothold in the region in order to prevent the British from getting there first.[78] In a fashion similar to the Anglo-Russian rivalry in Afghanistan, French interest in Vietnam was based in part on its imperial aspirations as manifested in the centuries-old conflict with Britain. In the mid 1800s, in the subsiding wake of the French Revolution and the Napoleonic Wars, Vietnam once again became an object of France's renewed search for national glory and prestige.

While France's direct involvement in Vietnam waned during the eighteenth century and the Napoleonic Wars, Catholic missionaries kept alive dreams of a French colonial empire in Southeast Asia. Some of Vietnam's emperors allowed trade and religious contacts, usually in an attempt to gain a military advantage over local political rivals. Others saw the Jesuits as a threat and imposed sporadic pogroms to eradicate both foreign and native Catholics in the realm.[79] In 1820 Vietnam's new emperor, Minh-Mang, pursued a firm anti-Western policy and instituted a harsh persecution of all Christians.[80] He dismissed all of his father's French advisers and unceremoniously rejected the three trade missions sent by the French Crown in 1825, 1827 and 1831. In 1839, after the Opium War had broken out between Britain and China, resulting in the occupation of Chinese ports, Minh-Mang began to rethink his anti-Western stance, realizing that isolationism was not an effective protection from 'barbarian aggression'. He died in January 1841 before implementing a policy shift, and his successor Thieu-Tri (1841–47) increased the level of repression against missionaries and native converts.[81] During the 1830s, after decades of futile effort, France abandoned its attempt to infiltrate Vietnam strictly through diplomatic channels, and from 1840 onward Catholic propaganda openly agitated for military intervention in order to prevent the persecution of missionaries. Thieu-Tri further provoked the French toward intervention by ordering all missionaries out of Vietnam and condemning to death those who refused to depart.[82] In France religious zeal was increasing as a reaction to the secular spirit of the Revolution and the Napoleonic era. The navy, the most conservative branch of the French military establishment, was determined to re-establish France's global foreign influence after two decades of defeat and humiliation at the hands of the British.[83]

French intervention in Vietnam was part of the wider European and American desire to establish trading precedence in the region after Britain's seizure of Hong Kong in 1842. After obtaining trade and religious rights from the Chinese government in 1845, a French naval squadron sailed to Vietnam upon learning from the captain of the USS *Constitution* that he had failed to gain the release of a condemned French missionary bishop.[84] After negotiations, Bishop Lefebvre was rescued by the French fleet. Lefebvre, a true fanatic, re-entered Vietnam, was captured and condemned, and was re-rescued by either French or British authorities on at least three occasions. In France, Catholic writers generated such publicity of his devotion to Church and state that the king was persuaded to issue a royal decree demanding the release of imprisoned missionaries and permitting the free exercise of Christianity on Vietnamese soil. The decree, delivered by French naval authorities in April 1847, precipitated a diplomatic deadlock that ended with French warships attacking the harbour defences in Tourane (Da Nang). The result was one French casualty and more than a thousand dead Vietnamese.[85] This incident would set the tone of French policy over the next century: what could not be obtained through negotiations would be taken by force. In an angry response to the French attack, Thieu-Tri denounced the missionaries as accomplices to his foreign and domestic enemies, placed a bounty on their heads, and authorized the killing of all Europeans on sight. These orders were not fully implemented before Thieu-Tri died from illness in November 1847.[86] His successor, Tu-Duc, proceeded to intensify anti-Western policies, again ordering foreign priests to be slain. Vietnamese Catholics were treated as victims duped by the barbarians and were 'charitably' branded on the left cheek and their property confiscated.[87] The period of Tu-Duc's reign (1848–83) marks the beginning of the final stage of French colonial expansion in Vietnam. His quest to eliminate all European influence increasingly clashed with France's growing interest in expanding its overseas possessions. Tu-Duc's policies of brutally persecuting all Christians provided French imperialists with a pretence for intervention.[88]

The fate of Vietnamese independence was directly connected to the political circumstances in Paris. After the failure of the now-famous 1848 social revolution and the subsequent retrenchment of the traditional ruling classes, Louis Napoleon proclaimed himself emperor at the end of 1852. His successful *coup d'état* was staged with the help of the Catholic Church, whose leaders were committed to the missionary project in Asia. The Church's goals fitted into Napoleon III's vision of resurrecting French grandeur and re-capturing some of the glory of his renowned uncle, Napoleon Bonaparte. In 1857, after strong lobbying by Church and naval authorities, Napoleon III endorsed the idea of sending a military expedition to seize the harbour at Tourane, the site of the devastating French attack a decade earlier. The fleet reached Vietnam in the summer of 1858, and on 31 August it overwhelmed the outgunned Vietnamese defenders. Despite the easy victory, the French were unable to hold the port. The promised uprising of local Catholics never materialized, and the ravages of heat, disease, monsoon rains and constant guerrilla attacks forced most of the French to board their vessels and depart later that year, leaving only a small garrison behind. The naval commander, Admiral Rigault de Genouilly, then sailed to the small fishing town of Saigon, which showed excellent potential as a deep-water port. Without official authorization by Paris he attacked and seized Saigon, and after initial success, was forced to withdraw most of his forces under circumstances similar to the fiasco in Tourane.[89]

Despite this blow to French national prestige, France's quest for imperial power remained unshaken. Embarrassingly, the Vietnamese emperor, who laid claim to the Mandate of Heaven, was seen as being ineffective in resisting the 'barbarian' aggression when his military forces proved incapable of opposing the technologically superior French. Even though French policy was fragmented by personal power struggles among Church and naval dignitaries, and amplified by the disruptive centrifugal forces of Parisian politics, the Vietnamese emperor remained in a precarious position. As in many other colonial situations, certain factional leaders were willing to pledge temporary allegiance to the French in the hope of achieving local political victory. Such was the situation when in 1860, toward the end of the joint Anglo-French war with China, France was able to turn its attention back to Vietnam. In October 1860 Admiral Charner, the commander of French forces in the Far East, was ordered to Saigon to renew the failed mission of his predecessor. After a series of bloody battles in 1861 the French had taken all strategic points in the three provinces between Saigon and the Cambodian border. When Charner was replaced by Admiral Bonard, in November 1861, the violence of the French assault increased as the new commander expanded the territory under French control. However, by April 1862 the French had again overextended themselves, and Bonard attempted to negotiate a victory when it became apparent that a complete military conquest was beyond his means.[90]

To the surprise of the French authorities, the usually intransigent Tu-Duc agreed to negotiate. The besieged emperor was facing an internal rebellion in the north by a pretender of the old Le dynasty, and he decided that giving in to French demands in the south would enable him to solidify his control in the north. On 6 June 1862 a treaty was signed in Saigon giving France the following:

(1) possession of the three provinces adjacent to Saigon and the island of Poulo Condore;

(2) the opening of three Vietnam ports for trade with the West;

(3) freedom of action for French missionaries and free passage for French warships up the Mekong to the Cambodian border;

(4) veto power over any decision by Vietnam to cede any part of its territory to other states;

(5) indemnity payments of four million piastres.[91]

The Vietnamese emperor's expedient decision was matched by the French, and the northern rebels gained the support of the Church. However, Admiral Bonard agreed to withhold French aid after Tu-Duc agreed to cede Saigon and the three southern provinces to France. In consolidating his position,

Bonard was unsympathetic to the missionaries' plight, and he simply abandoned the pro-French rebels in the north. The missionaries' real value to the French government was finally made obvious: they had served as a cover for secular intervention.[92] From 1863 to 1867 Napoleon III's interest in Vietnam declined while he was embroiled in an attempt to place the Austrian Archduke Maximilian on the throne of Mexico. Between 1867 and 1872, despite defeat in the Franco-Prussian War, the French forces in Vietnam made much progress in subduing resistance, organizing an effective administration, and preparing the colony for large-scale economic exploitation. After Napoleon III's fall from power, French nationalism was strongly behind enlarging national territory. However, the public's attention was focused on Alsace-Lorraine rather than on the Far East. French authorities in Vietnam circumvented inaction in Paris by taking matters into their own hands. Without authorization, the local naval commanders often initiated offensive action and, after victory, would present Paris with *faits accomplis* that would force it to act. Such actions, conducted in haphazard and uncoordinated fashion, eventually led to the complete capitulation of Vietnam.[93]

In 1873 a French Navy lieutenant, Frances Garnier, was sent to Hanoi with a landing party of 110 marines with orders to expel a rogue French trader, Jean Dupuis. Once in Hanoi, however, Garnier joined forces with Dupuis and, after repeated attacks against local forces, established French military control in the area surrounding Hanoi. Garnier's adventure came to an abrupt end when he was killed in an ambush by Chinese mercenaries employed by Tu-Duc. Paris also was working against the local French authorities in Vietnam and did not wish to jeopardize its rule in the south by rash actions in the north. In January 1874 Paris ordered the remaining French forces out of Hanoi.[94]

Less than a decade after Garnier's ill-fated northern expedition, France renewed its imperial drive in Vietnam. Social, economic and political factors, including the continuation of Catholic missionary agitation and propaganda, the search for new overseas markets, and the intensification of international competition for colonies with Britain were the primary motivating forces behind France's resurgent interest in Vietnam. French pride would not concede that the rise of Bismarck's Germany on the Continent meant the eclipse of France's leading role as 'civilizer' of Africa and Asia. By 1880 imperial proponents had successfully linked the recovery of France itself with patriotism and colonialism.[95]

In April 1882 the Saigon administration sent another expedition to Hanoi, this time with the consent of Paris, then under the Republican administration of the outspoken imperialist, Jules Ferry. Twenty-five years after the ill-fated storming of the harbour at Tourane, the final French conquest of Vietnam had begun. The Vietnamese imperial court at Hue, under French bombardment, decided to submit. On 25 August 1883 it signed the Treaty of the

Protectorate, effectively terminating 900 years of Vietnamese independence. The last free Vietnamese emperor, Tu-Duc, died only weeks before his country's final capitulation.[96] In a proclamation that captured the spirit of both the mandarins and the people, the imperial household stated that Tu-Duc 'was killed by sorrow over seeing foreigners invade and devastate his empire, and he died cursing the invader, keep him in your hearts and avenge his memory'.[97]

France's ability to break Vietnam's steadfast resistance to colonialism did not produce an easy or secure peace. The 1883 treaty sparked an immediate protest from China and resulted in an undeclared war between the French and the Chinese. Under the treaty provisions, Vietnam recognized the French protectorate and surrendered to France control over its external affairs. French garrisons with unlimited local authority would be assigned to all major towns. The French were to occupy all the forts of the Hue River and all other strategic points deemed necessary for the preservation of peace. Vietnam ceded to France the province of Binh-thuan as well as all of its warships, and it agreed to pay the cost of French occupation.[98] Also, the name 'Vietnam' ceased to exist in French and other Western documents with the creation of the French administrative districts of Tonkin in the north, Annam in the centre, and Cochina in the south.[99]

By the end of 1883 there were more than 20,000 French troops in Tonkin engaged in fighting a combined force of Chinese and Vietnamese troops. The conflict dragged on until May 1884, when a draft convention was signed in which France agreed to guarantee China's southern border in exchange for the withdrawal of Chinese troops from Vietnam.[100] Fighting resumed before the terms could be fulfilled, and in early 1885 a French naval squadron under Admiral Courbet attacked the cities of Fuzhou on the Chinese coast and Keelung on the island of Formosa (Taiwan). Inland, the French commander in Tonkin, General de Negrier, attacked the Chinese troops in the Langson area, a town strategically located near the border. After months of hard fighting, both French contingents were successful in defeating the Chinese forces. However, before the French were able to exploit their victories, disaster struck. On 28 March General de Negrier was wounded, and his second-in-command, Captain Erbinger, decided (reportedly while intoxicated) to evacuate the town.[101] His troops panicked, abandoned all their supplies and military equipment, and fled into the mountains.[102] The news of this débâcle caused such a sensation that, as in the fall of Lord Melbourne's government after the First Anglo-Afghan War, the government of Jules Ferry was ousted by parliament after an aggressive verbal attack by Clemenceau, who accused Ferry of 'high treason' for bogging France down in Vietnam.[103]

Despite Clemenceau's spirited attack on his rival's colonial policies, French policy in Vietnam did not change after Ferry's departure. Clemenceau too was a nationalist. Notwithstanding his attack on Ferry, he maintained

France's Indochina imperial policy. China's inability to sustain resistance to widespread European imperialism in the region culminated in its recognition of France's protectorate over Vietnam in the June 1885 Treaty of Tientsin.[104] Even though France restored Formosa and the Pescadores Islands to China, Beijing's capitulation on its southern border reinvigorated the imperialist camp in Paris and spurred the intensification of the Vietnam conquest. The Treaty of Tientsin ended the debate over which imperialist power, China or France, would hold suzerainty over Vietnam. But, practically speaking, Vietnam would not be 'pacified' by the French until 1897, and sporadic outbreaks of nationalist rebellion would continue through the French period before the Second World War. The major obstacle facing the French in Vietnam was a lack of cooperation by the indigenous mandarin bureaucracy and the lack of an effective administrative structure to replace the corrupt and recalcitrant local authorities. This lack of a firm administrative base prevented the formulation of sound economic policy for French Vietnam. Furthermore, French business interests in Southern Vietnam had done very well exploiting the region without centralized control, and they resisted any attempts to regulate the Vietnamese economy under a strong central administration.[105]

A significant change in this situation came about with the arrival of Governor-General Paul Doumer in 1897 – the year in which the last major Vietnamese resistance movements of the nineteenth century were suppressed. Doumer disregarded the treaty conditions of protectorate status, under which France had hitherto governed by using local Vietnamese puppet-leaders. He established direct French rule over the entire country, including those regions already controlled by his freewheeling countrymen. Although the imperial court at Hue remained intact, it was deprived completely of real power. Officials at all levels of administration, from the emperor to the lowest level of local mandarin, had to serve the new French governor or face losing government employment status altogether. Doumer imported thousands of French bureaucrats to staff his new administration while employing Vietnamese personnel to serve as fronts to obscure the growing absolute power of the foreign officialdom.[106] This practice continued as late as 1930, and even though several more 'liberal' governors-general had made concessions to local sentiment and tradition, all major administrative positions remained monopolized by French nationals.[107]

Doumer's tenure as governor-general, which lasted until 1902, effectively determined the character and emphasis of important economic and social policies during the remaining period of French rule in Vietnam. His basic task was to enhance France's home economy by preparing Vietnam for systematic economic exploitation. The majority of Doumer's policies focused on creating an effective infrastructure. Railroads, harbours, highways, canals, bridges and other public works were built to facilitate the exploitation of

Vietnam's natural resources. The gem of Doumer's public works programme was the railroads, and he committed the bulk of local tax revenues and subsidies from Paris to advance their completion. In 1899 France complied with his request for a 200 million franc loan. However, the railroad construction project was a huge failure. Human errors, construction delays, lack of supplies and faulty materials were magnified by pervasive mismanagement and rampant corruption. In three years of nearly superhuman effort, less than 300 miles of the Yunnan-Fou line was completed, at the cost of over 25,000 workers who perished in the horrendous working conditions. The railroads never paid for themselves, and they became a huge drain on the annual budget. The trans-Indochina railroad was not completed until 1936, thirty-five years later.[108]

Doumer's successors followed his policies of promoting the export of raw materials and ignoring the development of local industries. The guiding principle of French economic policy in Indochina was to maximize immediate profits at the expense of any long-term economic considerations. The railroad boondoggle served to epitomize French economic policy. Neither the French at home nor the Vietnamese people profited from the railroads and other public works. The only beneficiaries were the companies that built them and the banks that granted loans for their construction. In essence, French colonial policy served to exploit Vietnam for the gain of a few individuals without facilitating internal economic development.[109] The reality of this injustice was not lost on the Vietnamese population, many of whom, in traditional fashion, began to see their foreign 'friends' as their worst enemies.

Post-Doumer Vietnam: the roots of rebellion

The Doumer regime was notable for establishing the tone and direction of French policy in Vietnam, and in doing so it became the catalyst for a resurgent Vietnamese nationalist movement that slowly gained momentum over the next four decades. To some extent the eventual success of the Vietnamese nationalists can also be attributed to the domestic political instability of their colonial masters. According to Bernard Fall,

> ... it may be considered an axiom of colonial administration that no colonial government can export a better administrative system than it possesses at home ... In the case of Indochina in general, and Viet-Nam in particular, the French system took hold with a vengeance ... In Paris, French governments fell with incredible speed, and colonial governors in Indochina followed the political fortunes of their backers at home, when they were not removed at the behest of influential Frenchmen in Indochina. During the forty-three years of French civil administration in Indochina, from October 1902 to March 1945, no

less than twenty-three governors or acting governors had ruled the area! Several times, there was no chief executive at all in Indochina for more than a year, and some governors general lasted no more than eight months before being recalled. It was obvious that under such conditions the pursuit of a consistent colonial policy was almost impossible – the more so as there was no French colonial policy.[110]

In essence, colonial policy after Doumer was placed on autopilot, sometimes with a competent administrator, yet routinely without strategic direction or structural innovations. Paul Beau, Doumer's immediate successor, and others who followed, often arrived with plans for reform. But policy innovations were generally resisted by local French interests, or later aborted when a new administration took over. Thus throughout the colonial period Doumer's basic policies remained intact, even when subsequent French authorities began to realize that local resistance movements were being spawned and sustained by unjust practices.

Upon his arrival in Vietnam, Beau was the first of Doumer's successors to face a growing number of nationalist revolutionary movements. The first major group to resist the French was headed by Phan Boi Chau, a highly talented mandarin who rejected French offers to enter the colonial adminis-tration, choosing instead to go underground and organize a movement of national resistance. Chau's resistance activities would span a twenty-year period and result in varying degrees of success. Chau, like other Asian scholar-patriots of his time, violently opposed colonial rule but was open to the progressive ideals and technological achievements of the industrialized West. Chau represented the new generation of Vietnamese intellectuals, who, though reared under the Confucian system, were destined to mould Vietnam's political future in the transitory phase between tradition and modernity.[111] In 1906 Chau, constantly on the run from French agents, travelled regularly between Vietnam, China and Japan (the latter served as a Mecca for Asian revolutionaries after its defeat of imperial Russia in 1905). In Japan he devoted his time to writing agitational propaganda and organizing the resistance movement, the members of which launched a military revolt in June 1908. However, the French intelligence network had warned the military authorities of the insurrection, enabling them to defeat it.[112]

International events also helped to weaken Chau's rebellion against France. In July 1908 the Japanese government, feeling the immense cost of its victory over Russia, decided to accommodate Western imperial powers in Asia. Japanese plans for hegemony in Asia were deemed best served through cooperation with the strong European states while it rebuilt its overstrained military forces and domestic economy. France and Japan signed an agreement barring Vietnamese anticolonial forces from operating out of Japan in exchange for major financial concessions. After this change in Japan's policy and the ensuing eviction of Vietnamese nationalists from Japanese soil, Chau was forced to turn to the Chinese for patronage.[113] He was eventually imprisoned by a Chinese warlord during the period 1914–17. After his release, in an accurate analysis of regional power dynamics, Chau predicted that Imperial Japan would soon be the greatest threat to Vietnam's independence. He even suggested that the French and the Vietnamese should cooperate in opposing Japanese encroachments in Asia. Chau, when accused by many of his followers of selling out to the French, repudiated his new plan and claimed to have been duped by the French. Whatever the truth of the incident (made doubly ironic by the accuracy of his view on Japan's ambitions), Chau's role as the pre-eminent leader of the Vietnamese resistance slowly declined, and he died in obscurity in 1940.[114]

Despite these setbacks, Chau and other Vietnamese leaders aspiring toward the Mandate of Heaven continued to resist the French and were able to build a substantial mass of support at the grass-roots level. However, in the 1920s some important nationalist leaders, enticed by minor administrative reforms instituted by the French, began advocating Franco-Vietnamese collaboration. Although this cooperative movement had declined by 1925 because there had been no significant change in French policy, it was a setback for the growth of the nationalist movement. The subsequent resurgence of clandestine groups, including the emergence of Vietnamese communists, instituted a period of steadily increasing revolutionary violence. All anti-colonial activities were ruthlessly repressed by the French authorities, who in 1930 authorized aerial bombardment of suspected rebel villages, a practice to which the Vietnamese peasants would be subjected for the next four and a half decades.[115]

Although Chau and his fellow revolutionaries were effectively neutralized by the French, they succeeded in laying the foundation of the modern nationalist movement in Vietnam. Their revolutionary élan was later adopted by Ho Chi Minh to defeat both the French and the Americans. Fuelling the nationalists was the reality that under the supposed 'benefits' of the colonial regime, the economic and social conditions of the average Vietnamese had deteriorated by the eve of the Second World War. The peasants were squeezed by a regressive system of taxation under which the poorest Vietnamese were required to pay a tax equal to that of the richest Frenchman. Even though the area of land involved in rice cultivation increased dramatically from 1880 to 1930, the per capita rice consumption of the Vietnamese peasant declined markedly in this period and was not supplemented with alternative nutritional sources. Rice was exported in increasing quantities to ensure French profits even though peasants went hungry. In these conditions it is of little wonder that Chau and other nationalists were continually able to foment revolution among the distressed masses, despite numerous failures and humiliations.[116]

The beginnings of communism in Vietnam

One of the many underground political movements in Vietnam formed in the interwar period was the Revolutionary League of Youth of Vietnam, commonly referred to as the Thanh Nien. Formed in 1925 as a result of efforts by the French Communist Party under orders from the Communist International, the Revolutionary Youth League would eventually become the leading nationalist force under the leadership of its founder Nguyen Ai Quoc. Nguyen Ai Quoc, better known after 1943 by his pseudonym, Ho Chi Minh, organized a specific programme for capitalizing on popular discontent with colonial rule among peasants and workers. In February 1930, under direction from the Comintern, Ho negotiated a merger of various competing Marxist factions into the Viet Nam Cong San Dang (Communist Party of Vietnam). Later that year, this name was changed to the Indochinese Communist Party (ICP) in order to include organizations in Laos and Cambodia.[117]

Ho Chi Minh was one of the first Third-World nationalist leaders to embrace Marxism–Leninism as the guiding doctrine for freeing their countries of colonial domination. However, his early writings clearly reveal indigenous nationalist roots that predate Marxist dogma. At the French Socialist Party Congress in 1920, Ho, an accredited delegate from the colonial areas, stated, 'I don't understand a thing about strategy, tactics, and all these other big words you use, but I understand very well one single thing: The Third International concerns itself a great deal with the colonial question. Its delegates promise to help the oppressed colonial peoples to regain their liberty and independence.'[118] Ho's connection with the Soviet Union began in 1922 when he attended the Fourth Comintern Congress in Moscow. As a Comintern member, Ho was noted for his energetic and vocal leadership, and in 1923 he was elected the Colonial Representative to the Executive Committee of the Krestintern (Peasants International). In 1924 he studied at the University of the Toilers of the East, participated in the Fifth Congress of the Comintern as a member of the French Communist Party delegation from the colonial areas, and was sent to China to serve with the Soviet liaison mission to Chiang Kai-shek. While operating out of China, Ho organized the Revolutionary Youth League, the Communist Party's forerunner. However, Chiang Kai-shek's decimation of the communist wing of the Kuomintang sent Ho fleeing to the Soviet Union in 1928. In 1929 he travelled through Thailand disguised as a Buddhist monk, setting up two newspapers that were smuggled into Vietnam, and finally returning to Hong Kong in 1930 to reorganize and consolidate the Vietnamese communist factions.[119]

The formation of the ICP in 1930 came at a crucial time in the history of Vietnam. The social stresses brought on by the global economic depression had led to growing unrest in both urban and rural areas. Economic disorder was combined with disastrous floods, urban unemployment, and a drastic reduction in the price of exported rice. These conditions magnified popular discontent with the French regime. In September 1930 strikes and riots throughout the country peaked with an outburst of violence. On 12 September a riot broke out in the provincial capital of Vinh. In response the French authorities dispatched troops and bombed the crowds from the air, reportedly killing 174 people and wounding hundreds.[120] The ICP used these disturbances to foment peasant unrest in areas threatened by starvation and organized peasant councils (soviets) in several provinces. In these new soviets a range of relatively moderate new policies were pursued, including the elimination of taxes and a reduction in rents. In some cases rich peasants and landlords were expelled and their property confiscated or destroyed. However, the ICP was ill-prepared for overthrowing existing state apparatus and proved unable to instigate a general uprising against the French. As a result, the colonial authorities were able rapidly to imprison the majority of ICP leaders, and suppressed the uprising by forcing the submission of the last communist 'soviet' by the summer of 1931.[121] Despite this setback and the subsequent years of persecution, isolation and near-extinction, the ICP survived. Ultimately the harsh experiences of 1930–31 would prove beneficial in later strategy, and the organization emerged more united, better disciplined, and with a greater understanding of the people's sentiments in Vietnam. A decade later the communists would turn to the untapped revolutionary potential of the millions of peasants and would not deplete itself in an ineffectual attack against superior forces.[122]

Some major changes did occur in the last three or four years of French rule before the Second World War. The Popular Front government in Paris appointed a new governor-general for Indochina who forced through a number of fiscal and political reforms. The new appointee, Brevie (1936–39), reduced the number of political prisoners by 70 per cent and altered the regressive tax system to the benefit of the poorest Vietnamese. In addition, he liberalized political laws, allowing most political parties and their press organs to operate openly. Although the Communist Party was officially banned, the 'Indochinese Democratic Front', led by Pham Van Dong and Vo Nguyen Giap, was allowed to operate until September 1939, when Germany and the Soviet Union invaded Poland, thus inspiring anticommunist sentiment throughout France and its colonies.[123] The future of Vietnam was in part decided on the battlefields of Europe. In Vietnam, the French were as unprepared for the outbreak of the Second World War as they were at home. When Hitler's blitzkrieg overran France in the spring of 1940, French Indochina was protected by only fifteen modern combat aircraft and one light cruiser. France's abrupt military collapse in Europe made resistance in the colonial possessions futile. Germany's ally Japan moved quickly to consolidate its position in Indochina, and on 30 August 1940, the Vichy regime signed an accord with Japan that recognized Japan's dominant position in the Far East.[124]

The United States and Vietnam

Unlike Afghanistan's continual association with Tsarist and Soviet Russia, Vietnam had had few dealings with the United States before the Second World War. In July 1787 Thomas Jefferson, while serving as minister to France, expressed an interest in importing varieties of Vietnamese rice seed that did not require an abundant supply of water. Jefferson's interest never found fruition, according to historian Robert Hopkins Miller, who aptly describes American–Vietnamese relations in the eighteenth and nineteenth centuries:

> Fifteen years would pass before an American merchant ship actually sailed into a Vietnamese port … and three decades would pass before an American merchantman would return with a little silk and sugar and a small cargo of rice that unfortunately succumbed to weevils and other vermin. That second voyage encountered a xenophobia, a disinterest [*sic*] in trade with America, a provincialism, and a range of exotic diseases, all of which were discouraging to American interest in the area for yet another decade.[125]

The Vietnamese accorded Americans a welcome similar to that they gave other European traders. Contact between Americans and Vietnamese over the course of the next century dealt almost exclusively with trade issues. In the 1830s there were a number of trade delegations from America, which were rebuffed by the Vietnamese. The Vietnamese were further alienated by the Western 'barbarians' in 1845, when the commander of the USS *Constitution* caused a minor incident by holding a number of mandarins hostage in an attempt to gain the freedom of a French Catholic zealot. By the 1880s US relations with Vietnam would be contingent on relations with other powers, primarily Japan.[126]

The US defeat of the Spanish fleet in Manila Bay in 1898 and Japan's victory in the war with Russia in 1905 marked the beginning of both nations' entry into imperialist global politics. Although direct confrontation between the two countries was avoided during the First World War, both sides had invaded Russian soil during the Russian Civil War (1918–21) primarily to check each other's expansion in the Pacific theatre with a secondary interest in stopping the Bolshevik 'red menace'.[127]

When Japanese forces annexed parts of Manchuria in 1931 and 1932, the United States began nearly two decades of military, economic and political assistance to China, first against the Japanese, and later the communists. Vietnamese ports were important to the US effort as logistic points for shipment of war supplies. Arms shipments through Indochina into China created tensions in US–French relations throughout the 1930s. Although American diplomats warned of Japanese expansionism, there was little commitment in Washington to acting in concert with other European powers to impede Japanese encroachments. In 1937 the French sought a commitment from the United States to protect Indochina from Japan in exchange for allowing arms shipments to China. When the United States refused, French authorities interdicted military supplies heading north because of Japanese retaliatory threats.[128]

In 1938 French policy vacillated on the arms shipment issue; at times weapons were allowed to move north, but shipments were routinely delayed or blocked altogether. Like the United States, France supported the Chinese war effort but continually feared Japanese reprisal. American diplomatic communiqués reflected an apprehension that American trade might be stopped by the French, with little indication that Japanese attacks in China or Indochina were a major concern. In October 1938 Japan landed troops on the South China coast in an attempt to block the ongoing arms shipments, and in February 1939 it occupied the island of Hainan, effectively gaining strategic control of access to the Gulf of Tonkin in the South China Sea. Irregular American and French arms shipments through Vietnam continued to reach China during 1939. However, with the collapse of the French military forces in Europe in July 1940, and Japan's occupation of Vietnam, American involvement in Vietnam was severely limited.[129]

SETTING THE STAGE: THE COMPARATIVE HISTORY OF VIETNAM AND
AFGHANISTAN

Despite the many miles that separate them and the vast differences in language, religion, culture and politics, the histories of Vietnam and Afghanistan share some remarkable similarities. In comparing Vietnamese and Afghan history, two closely related and interwoven elements are especially useful in setting the stage for analysis of the superpowers' defeat. First, the importance of imperialist ideological doctrine as an integral component of geopolitical decision-making; and second, how the wider superpower rivalry also impacted issues of political legitimacy and rebellion in Vietnam and Afghanistan. As we will see in the coming chapters, history has a way of both repeating itself with uncanny similarity and exhibiting new outcomes hitherto unforeseen.

Ideology and geopolitics

At the heart of all effective foreign policy, for good or ill, lies a strategic plan that is grounded in some sort of ideological doctrine. Policies that lack the support of the amalgam of the ideas and ideals that make up doctrinal mandates will eventually give way to those that are more cohesive. Similarly, foreign policies without a philosophy of action do not prevail. The lack of doctrinal support and consistency in France's policy towards Vietnam was in part responsible for the success of the latter in resisting French encroachments. For a number of decades, despite French 'interest' in Vietnam, because of the absence of a well-organized and sustained French imperial plan the Vietnamese successfully blocked French penetration. Time and again, France's Vietnam policy was neglected as Napoleon III pursued more grandiose designs in Europe and in Mexico. Unlike London's commitment to its South and East Asia imperial mission (which remained strong despite changes in governments), France's imperial adventures were as much an *ad hoc* product of insubordinate, glory-seeking naval officers and Christian zealots as a coherent national programme emanating from Paris.

This factor reveals a second important analytical consideration – the differing nature of British, Russian and French imperialism. The British expanded into areas of the globe where they could project naval dominance and extend political control with a minimum of ground forces. The Russians were not equipped to challenge the Royal Navy's dominance, and so they concentrated their expansion in contiguous land areas that could be overrun, absorbed and assimilated into mainstream Russian culture through administration devices and the settlement of Russian colonists. The French colonial drive suffered from a lack of naval power, and after the failure of Napoleon's efforts France could not expand its power in continental Europe without the risk of major war loss (witness the Franco-Prussian War of 1870). As a result, France was limited to areas where the British, Russians and other imperial powers with comparative advantages were uncommitted (a similar problem faced Germany in its imperial ambitions after the country was unified in 1871). Politically, French colonialism lacked a consistent, internally expressed imperial rationale, with colonial policy being used by domestic critics to displace their political opponents in Paris. The basic motivations behind French imperialism were thus more politically volatile than those originating in London. Imperial possessions were seen by some in France as enhancing its great-power status; however, no domestic consensus regarding Vietnam was ever sustained over time.[130]

In terms of administration, the general approach of French colonialism was more similar to the methods of the Russians than those of the British, who pursued a policy of association rather than assimilation. The British in India governed indirectly through native institutions with a comparatively small number of personnel. For instance, in 1925 approximately 5,000 British officials governed 300 million Indians, a ratio of 1:60,000. Yet it took an equivalent number of French nationals to govern an Indochinese population only one-tenth that size. Fully half of the French colonial budget went to administrative wages in 1925.[131] As a result, the British were able to maintain fairly cordial ties with a large number of their colonial possessions after emancipation, and during their various occupations the British paid enough respect to local customs of religion and politics to ensure their ability to cultivate some political allies, even as they threatened opponents with military force.

In Afghanistan the British pursued policies that were purely geopolitical in motivation, largely leaving the Afghans to dictate their own internal affairs. In London's eyes, Afghanistan served as a buffer state against the Tsars and later the Commissars, but it was not seen as an economic prize in the manner of other British possessions in Asia. As a result, as long as the Afghan government was seen as not cultivating contacts with the Russians, Britain maintained a hands-off policy. The French, however, continual losers in the overall competition with Britain for overseas possessions, required much more of their few colonial conquests to satisfy desires for economic, political and cultural pre-eminence. As a result, like the Russians, the French pursued messianic policies of cultural assimilation, contending that their imperial subjects were being enlightened under the benevolent guidance of a superior culture. Developments in French colonial policy after 1880 illustrate a persistent need to enhance national prestige and to vindicate French cultural superiority. Even after an intellectual shift in Paris favouring a change from assimilation to association beginning in 1909, tangible policies in Vietnam changed very little. The administrative and economic policies of the Doumer regime became the *modus operandi* of all subsequent governor-generals. Despite their public rhetoric about reform, only minor tinkering with the colonial administration actually took place. As will be discussed in the coming chapter, even after the Second World War French politicians resisted the surrender of their colonial empire, seeing the granting of independence as a repudiation of French ideals. Unlike the Americans, who eventually viewed the emancipation of the Philippines as the expression of government by the consent of the governed, and the British, who could begrudgingly rationalize that the independence of India and its commonwealth status represented the final fruition of their imperial patronage, the French had no such politically palatable options.[132]

Geographic realities also determined a major difference in the fates of Afghanistan and Vietnam. Because of their proximity to nations with greater military power, both Vietnam and Afghanistan became logical targets of imperial opportunity as determined by the aspirations of their neighbours. Afghanistan's unique position as a buffer state between the outer frontiers of the British and Russian empires allowed it to maintain a modicum of independence even in the peak era of European colonial expansion. Vietnam's exposed coastal position, and the absence of any similar balance of power, eventually led to its complete subjugation. Throughout history Afghanistan has been at the crossroads of all the major trade and invasion routes in Asia and the subcontinent. As Arnold Toynbee points out, a serious student of global history must 'always give Afghanistan a central place in his picture'.[133] The prime concern of Afghan leaders in relations with foreign powers has been to keep them at arm's length, preventing any country from becoming too influential in Afghan affairs, and to play rivals against each other to Afghanistan's own advantage.[134] To a certain extent, the Afghans were successful in doing this during the nineteenth century despite the overwhelming power of both the British and Russian empires. The British and the Russians viewed Afghanistan (under nominal British control) as a neutral buffer state separating their respective spheres of influence, but as a result of ongoing mutual distrust, both empires continued to interfere with Afghan affairs. Unlike the French, the British had no pressing national need to augment their already enormous overseas empire in terms of economic exploitation. National pride and national interest could be best served through maintaining Afghanistan as a buffer state between the Russian and British empires. The British and the Russians had no regard for the wishes of Afghanistan's rulers, and thus Afghanistan was merely an unwilling pawn caught in the Anglo-Russian power struggle. The many Anglo-Russian diplomatic agreements regarding Afghanistan clearly show that the most important factors influencing Afghan affairs were external and took place in London and St Petersburg. Similarly, Paris showed little concern for respecting Vietnamese sovereignty, and the pace of colonialism in Vietnam was determined by the intermittent interests of the French government. When, in the latter part of the nineteenth century, the French leaders finally decided to subjugate Vietnam through military conquest, traditional Vietnam was incapable of effective resistance.

For their part, the Russians exhibited continual interest in the political fortunes of Afghanistan. Despite numerous potential threats to Afghanistan's territorial integrity by Russian aggression, as reflected by its expansion into Central Asia, the fact remains that Tsarist Russia did not break its diplomatic agreements to regard Afghanistan outside of its sphere of influence. In general, Russia's involvement in Afghanistan resulted more from Anglo-Russian competition in other regions of the world than from direct Russian involvement south of the Amu Darya River. The Tsars, ever stretched by their existing commitments to the huge expanse of Eurasia that they occupied, were willing to consolidate their empire without attempting to annex Afghanistan. Like the French, the Russians were in competition with the British for national glory. However, Afghanistan's main value was in keeping the two empires from direct contact by serving as a neutral zone. Soviet policies toward Afghanistan, through the beginning of the Cold War, were basically a continuation of those begun by the Tsars. The Russians did not foment revolution in Afghanistan because positive relations with Britain in the 1920s and 1930s were contingent on maintaining the status quo.

Communist ideology functioned more as a rhetorical device than as a foreign policy guideline toward Afghanistan. Vietnam did not enjoy a similar luxury. The British were willing to concede French dominance in Vietnam, and they focused their attention on India, China and elsewhere. Vietnam could not play China against the French, because China itself was being carved up by foreign powers and was convulsed by internal strife. Vietnam was forced to go it alone against French aggression. Vietnam's approachable border on the South China Sea enabled the technologically superior French to attack at any chosen beachhead with overwhelming firepower. Despite difficulties with the rugged terrain and thick jungle, the French were able to resupply their forces more easily than the British garrisons could in the remote Hindu Kush. Afghanistan's geography deterred attack and occupation to a degree unmatched in Vietnam.

The relationship between the Soviet Union and Afghanistan was distinctly different from that of the United States and Vietnam before the Second World War. The Soviet Union, despite its revolutionary political character after 1917, was faced with a world in which little had changed outside its borders. Thus the traditional foreign policy considerations that had influenced Tsarist foreign policy also dictated Soviet foreign policy. Like the Tsars, the leaders of the Soviet Union remained interested and involved in Afghan affairs and viewed Afghanistan as a minor part of the larger global power struggle with the British empire. Historically, Soviet policy toward Afghanistan is clearly characterized by continuity rather than change.

In comparison, the United States had only minimal contact with Vietnam before the Second World War. The United States was primarily interested in developing trading relations with Asian countries, of which Vietnam was viewed as a lesser player. Vietnamese xenophobic isolationism and the US anticolonial foreign policy combined to produce a situation in which the Vietnamese, unwilling to distinguish Americans from other white Europeans, shunned all diplomatic overtures. The United States, although frustrated by the Vietnamese position, was unwilling or unable to force the issue by military means; and with the final success of French imperialism, the United States was excluded from direct involvement in Indochina. Later US involvement in Vietnam was somewhat similar to that of the Soviet Union in Afghanistan, at least from the perspective of great-power politics – both small countries were pawns in a larger struggle. Vietnam was seen as unimportant in itself but, because of its geographic position, it was a useful arms conduit for furthering US policy in China in the 1930s. Afghanistan's role in great-power politics was that of a buffer state between empires, and Vietnam was useful in US competition with Japan for dominance in the Pacific. During the Second World War Vietnam's importance to the United States would grow after direct conflict with Japan began. In contrast, Afghanistan's role as a neutral buffer state between the British and the Soviets was virtually guaranteed after Hitler's attack on the Soviet Union in June 1941 and the subsequent alliance of the USSR and Britain. As a whole, there is very little comparison between the bilateral relations of the Soviet Union and Afghanistan and those of the United States and Vietnam before 1940. One could characterize US policy toward Vietnam in terms of a continuous absence of significant interaction, with major changes occurring in the years following the Second World War.

Legitimacy and rebellion

At the foundation of any state, legitimacy is best understood as a mixture of various ideal forms. For any given society, the number of possible historical mixes is infinite; however, in comparing Afghanistan and Vietnam we do find a number of similarities that can be usefully characterized using Max Weber's three-part typology. Accordingly, rulers in both countries made legitimacy claims on the basis of some combination of charisma, tradition and legal/rational elements. One useful method of differentiating these categories is to look at three important variables in the polity of any state: (1) the position of the rulers, (2) that of the ruled and (3) that of the ruler's staff who implement the ruler's decisions. In charismatic authority, the rulers are leaders, the ruled followers, and the staff composed of those followers most closely affiliated with the person of the ruler, otherwise known as disciples. In traditional authority, rulers are masters, the ruled subjects, and the staff composed of retainers or vassals. In legal/rational authority, the rulers are functional superiors, the ruled are legal equals, and the staff are bureaucrats.[135] It should be emphasized that these categories do not correspond directly to historical reality in any country: indeed, in both Afghanistan and Vietnam we find claims to authority in all three categories; however, the relative importance of each can be determined for comparative utility.

In both countries, elements of legal/rational authority were important components of the domestic polity. In Weber's framework, of course, legal/rational authority is rooted in Western positivism, or law derived from secular sources. Nonetheless, it must be acknowledged that Confucianism and Islam are religious philosophies that have produced a significant canon of both legal and bureaucratic principles, practices and statutes. An important element of Weber's legal/rational authority was expressed in the Confucian practice of merit-based competitive examinations. Government officials in Vietnam were granted the official title of Mandarin and promoted within the bureaucracy on the basis of their examination scores. Similarly, religious leadership in Afghanistan gained increasing authority on the basis of scholarship rather than apostolic charisma. However, in both cases these elements of legal and bureaucratic behaviour can be subsumed under the categories of tradition. For instance, in Afghanistan, modernization in any form was seen as a violation of honoured tradition, in both tribal practice regulating social relations and in the interpretation of Islamic doctrine. Part of why the British succeeded in maintaining nominal allegiance of the Afghan government was that they did not attempt to 'modernize' Afghanistan. That country's own leaders ran into trouble with the affiliated tribes when they made their own attempts to modernize the political, economic and cultural institutions. The most legitimate 'law' in Afghanistan was the law of tradition. Similarly (though with dissimilar results), the laws of the Confucian order were based on ancient texts. Laws and bureaucratic practices were meant to be learned and implemented by the imperial mandarins. However, change was slow in coming to a society in which Vietnamese tradition was held in such high esteem. Unlike nineteenth-century Japan, which responded in dynamic fashion to Western intrusions by successfully modernizing social, political, economic and military structures (thereby enabling it to maintain political independence), China and Vietnam remained tradition-bound and were eventually overwhelmed by superior European technology and political organization. As such, in Vietnam and Afghanistan, traditional law was simultaneously a strength and a weakness.

The most important factor overall in the comparison of early colonialism in Vietnam and Afghanistan is the depth of the tenacity and will of the Vietnamese and the Afghans in resisting foreign intervention in defence of tradition and culture. Indeed, the early French experience in Vietnam had befallen the Chinese 900 years earlier. China, despite nearly a millennium of colonial domination, had ultimately failed to fully assimilate the Vietnamese into Han culture. Over the centuries, the Vietnamese adopted the Confucian code of law and ethics, Chinese characters for reading and writing, the Chinese system of government administration, and Chinese technology and social institutions, most notably, the concept of the Mandate of Heaven. In spite of it all, as a society the Vietnamese refused to 'become Chinese', while managing to retain and nurture a distinct national identity. In this regard, Afghan society developed somewhat differently by remaining less influenced by the outside world. Because Afghanistan survived relatively free of British and Russian domestic political influence, the culture in Afghanistan was more unchanged than that of Vietnam. Whereas the Vietnamese adopted different attributes of their colonial masters while retaining the idealism of a unique national identity, Afghanistan's various tribal cultures retained a higher degree of monocultural purity, while at the same time adhering to a similar anti-foreigner ethic when threatened by the British.

Over the centuries various aspirants to the Vietnamese Mandate of Heaven continually challenged Chinese domination, and eventually Viet-namese patriots won the freedom of their nation. The Vietnamese rulers of Vietnam were seen as legitimate because they defended tradition. As such, the revolutionary leaders of Vietnam exhibited a combination of primarily charismatic and traditional sources of authority, with tradition being the most important variable. Rebellion could be fomented by a charismatic warlord, but only if he or she made an appeal to the traditional values of Vietnamese identity and anti-Chinese nationalism. During the French period a similar social dynamic emerged. A portion of the Vietnamese population converted to Christianity, and other elements of French culture made some inroads in Vietnam. However, during the period in which the last emperors struggled to block Western cultural infestations, they successfully nurtured a hatred of foreigners that would outlast France's efforts to assimilate Vietnamese culture. Likewise, the leaders of Afghanistan embodied a combination of charismatic and traditional sources of authority, once again with tradition holding more power. Like political leadership in Vietnam, a charismatic tribal leader of Afghanistan could foment rebellion and unify the tribes when the British sent in military occupation forces by calling on anti-foreign tradition. However, once the foreign threat was withdrawn, the charismatic appeals of a single leader gave way to traditional tribal-based identity and loyalty. The tribes of Afghanistan exhibited a somewhat unified 'Afghan' nationalism only when threatened by a significant outside force. Although British and Russian diplomats in the nineteenth century continually haggled over who would control Afghanistan, the question arises as to what degree these discussions and decisions were actually related to realities in Afghanistan. The Afghans continually negotiated out of respect for British power or fear of Russian domination, but when they decided to resist, the British paid a high price. On three occasions the British and the Afghans fought wars – and it can be argued that the Afghans emerged victorious in all three. Britain retained nominal control of Afghan foreign policy, but could not maintain military occupation forces in the country proper. The British were able to 'control' Afghanistan only from the safety of India. Once foreign troops were sent in, the Afghans were willing to set aside their own internal disputes and fight the common enemy, whose very presence was a violation of the traditional culture and Islamic law that lay at the heart of Afghanistan's loosely-knit national polity. In similar fashion the Vietnamese people have a long and celebrated history of resistance to foreign intervention. The symbolic importance in the Vietnamese national psyche of such heroes as Van Lang, Trieu Da, the Trung sisters and Ly Bon cannot be underestimated. All of these figures gained fame by defiance and revolt against the Chinese, and despite more than a thousand years of Chinese cultural domination and attempted assimilation, the Vietnamese retained and cherished a collective memory of independence. This national aversion to Chinese control eventually was entrenched by 900 years of independence. The resistance to French intrusion by Vietnam's last three independent emperors, Tu-Duc and his father and grandfather, was a continuation of this time-honoured Vietnamese national ethic. In order legitimately to rule the peasant farmers of Vietnam, the

Mandate of Heaven required the rejection of foreign encroachments on the Vietnamese national identity and culture.

For a thousand years before the arrival of American troops, Vietnamese nationalists had been bent but never completely broken by the Chinese and the French. Likewise, despite the zenith of British imperial power during the nineteenth century, the Afghan tribes had managed to prevent the military occupation of their country. As the coming chapters will show, this was a reality of history of which decision-makers in Washington and Moscow were either tragically ignorant, or which they chose to ignore when afflicted by the myopic hubris of superpower.

NOTES

1. Richard S. Newell, *The Politics of Afghanistan* (Ithaca: Cornell University Press, 1972) p. 34.
2. The Turks are primarily responsible for introducing Islam into the region. Their most significant accomplishment was the creation of the Muslim state of Ghazni in AD 961. Under the leadership of the Sultan Mahumud, Ghazni became the centre of an empire that dominated most of central and western Asia and northern India for the next 300 years.
3. Newell, *The Politics of Afghanistan*, pp. 35–8.
4. T.A. Heathcote, *The Afghan Wars 1939–1919* (London: Osprey Publishing, 1980) pp. 7–8.
5. Vartan Gregorian, *The Emergence of Modern Afghanistan: Politics of Reform and Modernization, 1880–1946* (Stanford: Stanford University Press, 1969) pp. 13–14.
6. Donald N. Wilber, *Afghanistan* (New Haven, CT: Hraf Press, 1962) p. 175.
7. Louis Dupree, *Afghanistan* (Princeton: Princeton University Press, 1973) pp. 367–9.
8. Wilber, *Afghanistan*, p. 175.
9. Dupree, *Afghanistan*, p. 389. The British experience in Afghanistan has become part of history, legend and popular culture. The resolute Dr Watson of Sherlock Holmes fame was a casualty of an Afghan tribesman's bullet before meeting the famous detective.
10. Joseph J. Collins, *The Soviet Invasion of Afghanistan: A Study in the Use of Force in Soviet Foreign Policy* (Lexington: Lexington Books, 1986) p. 6.
11. Dupree, *Afghanistan*, p. 404.
12. William Habberton, 'Anglo-Russian Relations Concerning Afghanistan (1837–1907)', *University of Illinois Studies in the Social Sciences*, 21 (1937): 32–4.
13. Dupree, *Afghanistan*, p. 408.
14. W.K. Fraser-Tytler, *Afghanistan: A Study of Political Developments in Central and South Asia*, 2nd edn (London: Oxford University Press, 1953) pp. 137–9.
15. Cited in Habberton, 'Anglo-Russian Relations Concerning Afghanistan', pp. 42–3.
16. Dupree, *Afghanistan*, pp. 408–9.
17. Ibid.
18. Collins, *The Soviet Invasion of Afghanistan*, p. 7.
19. Wilber, *Afghanistan*, pp. 176–7.
20. Dupree, *Afghanistan*, pp. 426–8.

21. Fraser-Tytler, *Afghanistan*, p. 179.
22. Dupree, *Afghanistan*, p. 433.
23. Ibid., pp. 434–5.
24. Ludwig W. Adamec, *Afghanistan, 1900–1923: A Diplomatic History* (Berkeley: University of California Press, 1967) p. 82.
25. Alfred L. Monks, *The Soviet Intervention in Afghanistan* (Washington: American Enterprise Institute for Public Policy Research, 1981) p. 7.
26. Dupree, *Afghanistan*, p. 434.
27. Collins, *The Soviet Invasion of Afghanistan*, pp. 7–8.
28. Dupree, *Afghanistan*, p. 443; Adamec, *Afghanistan*, p. 135.
29. Leon B. Poullada, *Reform and Rebellion in Afghanistan, 1919–1929* (Ithaca: Cornell University Press, 1973) pp. 223–4.
30. 'Appeal of the Council of People's Commissars to the Moslems of Russian and the East', in *Soviet Documents of Foreign Policy, 1917–1924*, ed. Jane Degras (London: Oxford University Press, 1951) pp. 15–17.
31. Poullada, *Reform and Rebellion in Afghanistan*, pp. 224–5.
32. Gregorian, *The Emergence of Modern Afghanistan*, p. 231.
33. Ibid.
34. Ibid., p. 232.
35. Cited in 'Preliminary Draft Thesis on the National and Colonial Questions', *V.I. Lenin Selected Works*, 12 vols (New York: International Publishers, 1943) 10: 236.
36. 'Treaty Between the RSFSR and Afghanistan Signed in Moscow', *Soviet Documents of Foreign Policy, 1917–1924*, pp. 233–5.
37. Alvin Rubinstein (ed.), *The Foreign Policy of the Soviet Union*, 2nd edn (New York: Random House, 1966) pp. 51–2.
38. Leon Trotsky, 'Manifesto of the Communist International', *The Communist International, 1919–1943*, ed. Jane Degras (London: Oxford University Press, 1951) pp. 42–3.
39. Richard L. Levengood, 'The Soviet Doctrine of National Self-Determination in Theory and Practice' (MA dissertation, Montana State University, 1964) p. 97.
40. Gregorian, *The Emergence of Modern Afghanistan*, pp. 237–8.
41. Dupree, *Afghanistan*, p. 451.
42. 'Treaty of Neutrality and Non-Aggression between the USSR and Afghanistan, and Final Protocol', in *Soviet Documents of Foreign Policy, 1925–1932*, ed. Jane Degras (London: Oxford University Press, 1951) p. 131.
43. Thomas Hammond, *Red Flag Over Afghanistan: The Communist Coup, the Soviet Invasion, and the Consequence* (Boulder, CO: Westview Press, 1989) pp. 12–18.
44. Ibid., pp. 13–18.
45. Poullada, *Reform and Rebellion in Afghanistan*, pp. 184–5.
46. Hammond, *Red Flag Over Afghanistan*, pp. 13–14.
47. Poullada, *Reform and Rebellion in Afghanistan*, pp. 194–5.
48. Gregorian, *The Emergence of Modern Afghanistan*, p. 238.
49. Hammond, *Red Flag Over Afghanistan*, pp. 15–18.
50. Gregorian, *The Emergence of Modern Afghanistan*, p. 293.
51. Ibid., p. 322.
52. 'Reply from Karakhan to the Afghan Foreign Minister on the Formation of the New Afghan Government', *Soviet Documents of Foreign Policy, 1925–1932*, pp. 400–1.
53. Gregorian, *The Emergence of Modern Afghanistan*, p. 332.
54. 'Note From Stark, Soviet Envoy to Afghanistan, to the Afghan Foreign Minister, on

the Appointment of Frontier Commissioners to Settle Frontier Incident', *Soviet Documents of Foreign Policy, 1925–1932*, pp. 535–41.

55. Jan F. Triska and David D. Finley, *Soviet Foreign Policy* (New York: Macmillan, 1968) p. 3.
56. Karl Radek, 'The Bases of Soviet Foreign Policy', *Foreign Affairs*, 12 (Jan. 1934): 193–206.
57. Arnold Fletcher, *Afghanistan: Highway of Conquest* (Ithaca: Cornell University Press, 1965) pp. 233–6.
58. Cyriac Maprayil, *Britain and Afghanistan in Historical Perspective* (London: Cosmic Press, 1983) p. 74.
59. Ibid., pp. 74–5.
60. Ludwig W. Adamec, *Afghanistan's Foreign Affairs to the Mid-Twentieth Century* (Tucson: University of Arizona Press, 1974) pp. 243–5.
61. Gregorian, *The Emergence of Modern Afghanistan*, p. 233.
62. Leon B. Poullada, 'The Road to Crisis 1919–1980: American Failures, Afghan Errors and Soviet Successes', in *Afghanistan: The Great Game Revisited*, ed. Rosanne Klass (New York: Freedom House, 1987) p. 40.
63. Gregorian, *The Emergence of Modern Afghanistan*, p. 233.
64. Cited by Adamec, *Afghanistan's Foreign Affairs*, pp. 235–6.
65. Fletcher, *Afghanistan*, p. 237.
66. Joseph Buttinger, *A Dragon Defiant: A Short History of Vietnam* (New York: Praeger, 1972) pp. 26–8.
67. For an excellent recent history of ancient Vietnam from the third century BC to the end of Chinese domination in the tenth century AD see, Keith Wellor Taylor, *The Birth of Vietnam* (Berkeley: University of California Press, 1983).
68. Joseph Buttinger, *Vietnam: A Political History* (New York: Praeger, 1968) pp. 32–4.
69. The one interruption of Vietnam's independence occurred during 1407–27 when the Chinese reconquered its troublesome southern tributary. Vietnamese sovereignty was restored after a ten-year war of liberation which concluded in the founding of the greatest of all Vietnamese dynasties, the Later Le, which retained possession of the throne for more than three centuries. Cited ibid., pp. 36–9.
70. Ibid., p. 51.
71. Stanley Karnow, *Vietnam: A History* (New York: The Viking Press, 1983) pp. 98–103.
72. Timothy J. Lomperis, *The War Everyone Lost – and Won: America's Intervention in Viet Nam's Twin Struggles*, rev. edn (Washington, DC: CQ Press, 1993) p. 15.
73. Ibid., pp. 15–19.
74. Bernard Fall, *The Two Viet-Nams: A Political and Military Analysis* (New York: Praeger, 1963) p. 19.
75. Buttinger, *A Dragon Defiant*, p. 49.
76. Ibid., p. 50.
77. Ibid.
78. Buttinger, *Vietnam*, p. 66.
79. The number of Catholics killed in Vietnam is a topic of dispute among scholars. Citing French sources and figures provided by the Catholic Church, Bernard Fall claims that 30,325 Catholics were put to death by Vietnamese authorities prior to French colonial domination. Joseph Buttinger and Stanley Karnow both cite figures that total no more than a few score deaths. Apparently this wide discrepancy is a result of Fall's view that native Catholics should be counted, while Buttinger and Karnow limit their analysis to the number of European Catholics put to death. See

Joseph Buttinger, *The Smaller Dragon: A Political History of Vietnam* (New York: Praeger, 1958) p. 333; Karnow, *Vietnam*, p. 67; and Fall, *The Two Viet-Nams*, p. 23.

80. Despite his hatred for Westerners and Christians, Minh Mang would take no chances. After ordering the death by strangulation of a French Jesuit, the emperor had the priest's corpse exhumed three days later to determine the veracity of the Christian canon of Jesus's resurrection. See Karnow, *Vietnam*, p. 67.

81. D.G.E. Hall, *A History of Southeast Asia*, 4th edn (New York: St Martin's Press, 1981) pp. 686–7.

82. Buttinger, *A Dragon Defiant*, pp. 56–7.

83. Karnow, *Vietnam*, p. 67.

84. The captain of 'Old Ironsides' was John Percival, who was engaged in entertaining three or four mandarins when the news of the missionary's predicament arrived. Percival held his guests hostage while demanding the European priest's release. The Vietnamese adopted a position remarkably similar to late-twentieth-century US policy regarding hostages and refused to bargain for their release. Percival was left with no alternative but to free the dignitaries and sail away, thus ending the first thoughtless US intervention in Vietnam with a small loss of face but the peace intact. See Karnow, *Vietnam*, p. 69.

85. John F. Cady, *The Roots of French Imperialism in East Asia* (Ithaca: Cornell University Press, 1954) pp. 73–5.

86. Ibid.

87. Karnow, *Vietnam*, p. 71.

88. Hall, *A History*, p. 688.

89. Karnow, *Vietnam*, pp. 74–5.

90. Buttinger, *Vietnam: A Political History*, pp. 85–7.

91. Ibid., p. 87.

92. Ibid., p. 89.

93. Ibid., pp. 90–93.

94. Fall, *The Two Viet-Nams*, p. 24.

95. Cady, *The Roots of French Imperialism*, pp. 289–90.

96. Buttinger, *Vietnam*, pp. 97–8.

97. Quoted ibid., p. 98.

98. Hall, *A History of Southeast Asia*, p. 702.

99. Karnow, *Vietnam*, p. 86.

100. Hall, *A History of Southeast Asia*, p. 703.

101. See Karnow, *Vietnam*, p. 86.

102. Hall, *A History of Southeast Asia*, p. 704.

103. Karnow, *Vietnam*, p. 87.

104. Hall, *A History of Southeast Asia*, p. 704.

105. Buttinger, *A Dragon Defiant*, p. 64.

106. Ibid. Even after Doumer's departure, when the French policy of cultural assimilation gained momentum and Vietnamese were appointed to a variety of career posts, French partiality was transparent. A French janitor at the University of Hanoi received a base pay that was higher than that of a Vietnamese professor with a PhD from the University of Paris. After 1927, when reformers attempted to eliminate some of these gross inequalities, the most fervent opponents were French colonials. See Bernard Fall, *The Two Viet-Nams*, pp. 32–3.

107. Buttinger, *A Dragon Defiant*, p. 66.

108. Buttinger, *Vietnam*, pp. 114–15.

109. Ibid., p. 65.
110. Fall, *The Two Viet-Nams*, p. 31.
111. William J. Duiker, *The Rise of Nationalism in Vietnam, 1900–1941* (Ithaca: Cornell University Press, 1976) pp. 31–2.
112. Ibid., p. 50.
113. Ibid., pp. 65–6.
114. Ibid., pp. 78–100.
115. Buttinger, *The Smaller Dragon*, pp. 434–7.
116. Ibid., pp. 431–2.
117. Duiker, *The Rise of Nationalism in Vietnam*, pp. 191–216. See also Buttinger, *A Dragon Defiant*, pp. 72–3.
118. In Fall, *The Two Viet-Nams*, pp. 89–90.
119. Ibid., pp. 90–95.
120. Duiker, *The Rise of Nationalism in Vietnam*, pp. 222–3.
121. Ibid., pp. 222–9.
122. Ibid., p. 223.
123. Fall, *The Two Viet-Nams*, p. 38.
124. Ibid., pp. 39–43.
125. Robert H. Miller, *The United States and Vietnam 1787–1941* (Washington, DC: National Defense University Press, 1981) p. xvi.
126. Ibid., pp. 17–65.
127. See George Kennan, *The Decision to Intervene* (Princeton: Princeton University Press, 1961). For an analysis that correlates European and Asian motivations behind US intervention policy in the First World War, see Betty Miller Unterberger, *The United States, Revolutionary Russia, and the Rise of Czechoslovakia* (Chapel Hill: University of North Carolina Press, 1989).
128. Miller, *The US and Vietnam*, pp. 154–61.
129. Ibid., pp. 175–91.
130. Cady, *The Roots of French Imperialism*, p. 295.
131. See Karnow, *Vietnam*, p. 113.
132. Ibid.
133. Arnold Toynbee, 'Afghanistan as a Meeting Place in History', *Afghanistan*, 25 (April–June, 1960): 59.
134. Wilber, *Afghanistan*, p. 174.
135. This analysis is adopted from J.G. Merquior, *Rousseau and Weber: Two Studies in the Theory of Legitimacy* (London: Routledge & Kegan Paul, 1980) pp. 99–103. This framework is also very similar to Reinhard Bendix's, *Max Weber: An Intellectual Portrait* (London: Methuen, 1966) pp. 294–5.

2

The Origins of Superpower Intervention, 1940–55

The Second World War profoundly altered the global distribution of international power. At the end of the war the traditional masters of global politics, Britain, France and Germany, were superseded by the United States and the Soviet Union. However, despite great hopes to the contrary and the initial promise of new international institutions such as the United Nations, the world did not enter a more peaceful era. The centuries-long struggle for hegemony among European imperial powers was replaced by a new global hegemonic conflict between the United States and the USSR. This new struggle was qualitatively different from previous great power confrontations for two reasons: the dominant influence of ideology in foreign policy and the emergence of nuclear weapons. At its foundation, the Second World War was a struggle for supremacy between the dominant twentieth-century political ideologies: fascism, communism and liberalism. Historically, not since the signing of the Peace of Westphalia in 1648 had ideology been such an important cause of contention between global actors. However, with the defeat of Germany and Japan, at the end of the Second World War only fascism had been vanquished, and the strange bedfellows of the alliance between communism and liberalism turned their energies from cooperative partnership toward destroying each other. The struggle between liberalism and socialism was unique in that the emergence of strategic nuclear weapons and advanced delivery systems had created the first inescapable condition of security interdependence among sovereign great powers. Even as each side constructed vast arsenals in a desperate attempt to enhance national security, each new technological wonder actually increased mutual vulnerability and interdependence. Paradoxically, the two greatest military powers in world history were secure only by one another's leave.

This unique combination of competing ideologies and security interdependence produced a bipolar world in which direct military confrontation would systematically escalate into a nuclear war, in which mutually assured destruction (MAD) would result. However, instead of producing a more logical peace, military conflict was shifted to proxy theatres where traditional forms of war could be orchestrated with a lower risk of total nuclear destruction. Vietnam and Afghanistan were, along with Korea, among the most important and influential of these new theatres for superpower confrontation. Any useful analysis of the Vietnam and Afghanistan wars therefore must include a basic review of the core issues that motivated the Cold War and that subsequently provided the contextual setting and policy rationale for the superpowers' interventions in both Vietnam and Afghanistan. The Cold War was not only a struggle for power in the international system but also a conflict between the highly incompatible ideological principles that lay at the heart of each superpower's claim to domestic political legitimacy. The Cold War thus pitted the legitimation principles of Western liberalism as defined by the US government against the legitimation principles of socialism as defined by the Soviet leadership in Moscow.

Dating from the end of the Second World War to the collapse of the state-socialist regimes in Eastern Europe in 1989 and the subsequent disintegration of the Soviet Union in 1991, the Cold War can now be seen as a period when international power relations were dramatically shaped by the imperatives and perceptions that attended the highly militarized ideological rivalry between the United States and the Soviet Union. While some scholars characterize the Cold War as a 'long peace', to do so betrays a narrow Atlantic-centred perspective.[1] Northeast Asia, Southeast Asia and South Asia each represented a particularly important and far less peaceful arena of the Cold War. During the Cold War, Northeast and Southeast Asia were the site of at least four full-scale wars: the Chinese Civil War (1945–49), the Korean Civil War (1950–53), and the complex colonial and civil wars in Vietnam, Cambodia and Laos, known as the First Indochina War (1946–54) and the Second Indochina War (1965–75). The Afghan War (1979–89) witnessed the spread and intensification of the Cold War to South Asia. While all of these conflicts originated from localized legitimacy crises that had erupted into civil war, each local war was systematically embraced by the United States and the Soviet Union as part of the geopolitical legitimacy struggle on the global level. In retrospect it seems that the Cold War was inevitable. From the very beginning, the relationship between the United States and the Soviet Union seemed doomed because of the irreconcilable differences at the core of each political system. However, even though their political, social and economic systems were profoundly unalike before they attained superpower status at the end of the Second World War, until that time both countries were constrained by a combination of external and internal variables that kept them from significant direct interaction and, by default, from confrontation and conflict.

In this chapter the roots of superpower intervention in Vietnam and Afghanistan are compared, starting with a brief overview and comparison of the politics of legitimacy in the United States and Soviet Union. The comparison will incorporate a discussion of the crucial linkages between the politics of domestic legitimacy and the decisions of key individual policy-makers in the realm of foreign policy. The chapter will take us through 1956, by which time the United States had supplanted France as the dominant foreign interest in Vietnam and the Soviet Union had sown the seeds of its eventual invasion of Afghanistan. While the evolution of superpower involvement in Afghanistan was markedly peaceful during this period, Vietnam was torn by continuous warfare. In the following pages, I will trace the creation and early evolution of the containment doctrine, showing that in the process of its implementation in countries like Vietnam, containment as a global strategy served to corrode the foundations of legitimacy in US domestic politics. After nearly a decade of failing to inspire the interest of the United States in a strategic partnership, the Afghans turned in 1956 to the Soviet Union for economic development aid, thus marking one of the forgotten yet most critical failures of US containment doctrine in South Asia.[2]

LEGITIMACY IN THE UNITED STATES AND THE SOVIET UNION

In general terms liberal democracy in the United States can be described as a polity in which the application of state power is limited by certain restraints. One important limit on political power is the separation between the public and private realms. Using one's political office for private gain (usually for the enrichment of one's self, family or friends) is considered illegitimate. Political power is regulated by a routinized pattern of fair elections which includes open competition between two or more parties. In American democracy, the application of state power must be sanctioned in law, and all citizens are judged before the law on an equal basis. Basic freedoms exist, including the right of all individuals to speak freely without fear of government sanction, and the fundamental right to criticize the governing order. In the economic realm the role of government is limited supposedly to protecting the health and civil rights of individuals; the market is the primary allocator of goods and services, and the government's role is focused on ensuring that contractual obligations are upheld. American democracy is a mixture of the often contentious philosophies of pure liberalism (which holds the individual in highest regard), and pure democracy (which holds the collective or community in highest regard).[3] For instance, in the United States, one of the fundamental tensions in society is caused when the rights of the individual are pitted against the collective voice of representative government. One of the founding principles of the US Constitution is to ensure that the basic rights of the individual are not infringed upon by a tyranny of the masses, and, at the same time, the branches of representative government (the presidency and Congress) have the mandate to create and execute legislation. Furthermore, one of the cornerstones of the political order is the dispersion of political power into three supposedly equal branches of government: the executive, legislative and judicial branches, with the latter having assumed the function of ensuring the constitutionality of legislation enacted by the other two branches.

In American democracy, then, political legitimacy is rooted in two of Weber's categories: the first, traditional authority, consisting of cultural factors, includes political norms, moral standards, and/or societal values; and the second, legal–rational authority, consisting of procedural factors and legal rights delineated in the US Constitution and laws. Weber's third category – charismatic authority – also figures in American politics, especially among religious interest groups such as the Christian Coalition or the Moral Majority. However, while the personal charisma of an individual national political leader is important, the charismatic authority flowing from religion is rarely of fundamental importance and is certainly less important than American tradition more broadly conceived. Likewise, American tradition, although something all politicians aspire to represent, is clearly secondary to legal–rational sources of political authority and legitimacy. Indeed, one could safely summarize American 'traditional authority' as being rooted in the tradition of the Constitution and positive law. Crises of legitimacy occur when either of these is denigrated or transgressed by political leaders. For instance, a substantive breach in morality, ethics, or norms can often lead to a procedural/legal crisis of legitimacy when any sort of political cover-up is attempted. The war in Vietnam, beginning with early American involvement, produced a series of normative and procedural transgressions, which over time served to undermine public faith both in the war effort and in the US government itself, eventually claiming the careers of two American presidents.[4]

In comparison, political order, political legitimacy, and societal unity are based on very different foundations in socialist states like the Soviet Union. In basic terms totalitarian socialist regimes consist of a polity in which the application of state power has virtually no limits. The separation between public and private realms is extremely limited, and all individual behaviour is open to public scrutiny, governmental regulation and state control. In theory, in a socialist state individuals cannot use their political office for private gain, as private gain has presumably been eliminated from the realm of possibility in socialist society. Also in theory, political power flows from a mandate of the ruling working class, which has emerged triumphant through a series of macro-level economic power struggles in the historical-evolutionary process. By the time global economic structures have evolved to an advanced state of capitalism, socialism is achieved when the working class or the proletariat unite to overthrow capitalism's ruling class, the bourgeoisie. In the economic realm, the state is the sole allocator of goods and services, with each individual supporting the collective good of society by maximizing and contributing his or her natural skills and talents to the communal order, and the state redistributing these collective goods on an equal basis to all.

Like liberalism, socialism is an attempt to achieve an egalitarian albeit classless society; however, because the process of achieving socialism occurs through conflict and struggle, according to Leninist thought extraordinary measures must be taken to ensure that the working class succeeds in the seizure of power and that the survival of the socialist polity is guaranteed in a hostile capitalist world. Instrumentally, the success and survival of socialist ideology becomes the responsibility solely of the Communist Party, which is the locus of all political morality and legitimacy in society. In the Soviet Union a defining characteristic of the political order was the unity of powers. The executive, legislative and judicial branches existed in form, but in function all three branches were subservient to the political dictates of the Communist Party of the Soviet Union (CPSU). Totalitarian socialist states, as seen first in the Soviet Union, are thus characterized by the contradictory mandates of an egalitarian political ideology and a state that is intolerant of any form of political opposition. The stated foundation of legitimacy and authority of the Soviet regime was its claim to have discovered a superior ideology in the writings of Marx and Lenin. In addition, the leading role of the Communist Party was to propagate, enforce and ensure the survival of that ideology and the state that gave it substance. In theory, Weber's categories of charisma and tradition here have given way entirely to the rational/legal conclusions of the 'science' of socialism. Indeed, charismatic and traditional authority are seen as characteristics of presocialist phases in the global class struggle. Therefore, they are the enemies of socialism, and only 'reactionary' capitalists would use tradition or charisma as a source of ruling authority.

However, like many other political systems (including the US), the reality of politics in the Soviet Union was significantly different from the professed rhetoric of the ruling regime. In fact the foundations of political legitimacy in the Soviet Union were characterized by a great deal of both charisma and tradition, which merged together with rational/legal rule. Procedural mandates and the rule of law as stated by the various Soviet constitutions were clearly subordinate to the doctrinal dictates of the CPSU. The Soviet leadership based its political legitimacy on its guardianship of truth, in essence claiming ideological infallibility. In this respect Marxism–Leninism was analogous to Weber's charismatic authority, with the CPSU serving the organizational role of the state's officially recognized religion and the party members serving as high priests of the faith. In the case of Lenin and of Stalin, charismatic authority of the individual was expressed in the form of the 'cult of personality' that developed around their persons. The cult of personality as an expression of charismatic authority was a component of most other totalitarian socialist states as well (Mao Zedong and Kim Il Sung are excellent examples). Like great religious prophets, the top leaders in socialist orders were seen as being divinely inspired. These leaders were given credit for great works of science, literature, war, education, psychology and philosophy; and even (in the case of North Korea) the ability to control geophysical and astral phenomena.

On a more official level (and falling within Weber's framework of traditional authority) the fundamental guiding tenet of socialist ideology was that the Communist Party could do no wrong, and only the Party could judge the Party and its members. Thus, the organic Party (or more accurately its leadership cadre) could not break laws because they were the source of law; only Party members could interpret the law as it related to members of the Soviet polity. The logic of this legitimacy claim actually has deep cultural roots in Russian tradition. The legitimacy claim of the pre-Soviet Tsarist state maintained that the Tsar could do no wrong – simply because he or she was Tsar. Thus in Russia under the Tsar or commissar, the expression of political opposition of any sort was seen as an attack on truth and righteousness. When challenged by internal dissent, both Tsarist and Soviet regimes remained in power through the extensive use of military force and state violence, justifying repressive measures by claiming the moral high ground.[5] Concurrently, crises of legitimacy in the Soviet state were the result of two types of challenges to this infallibility claim. The first originated internally during periods when various individual actors and factions struggled for power within the Party. These internal factional power struggles occurred primarily during the change of leadership following the death of a paramount leader, or when significant doctrinal disputes were being contested.[6] The second type of legitimacy crisis originated from external sources during periods when the state proved itself to be fallible *vis-à-vis* the outside world. Historically, the most severe legitimacy crises in Russian politics – those that resulted in significant changes in the structures of politics and society – occurred after defeat in war.[7] As I will show in later chapters, the downfall of the Soviet Union occurred when both types of legitimacy crisis occurred at the same time.

THE ORIGINS OF SUPERPOWER INTERVENTION IN VIETNAM

The United States turned its attention toward Vietnam during the Second World War because of Japan's expansion in the Pacific, which threatened US interests. In the spring of 1940, partially as a result of the Western powers' weakened position in Europe, Japan became more aggressive in Indochina. After the capitulation of France in July 1940, the Vichy administration reluctantly agreed to the stationing of Japanese troops in Vietnam. Between September 1940 and August 1945, Vietnam was a *de facto* Japanese possession – administered by the French under Governor-General Decoux, but occupied and used by Japanese military forces.[8] Before Japan's attack on Pearl

Harbor, there was little the United States could do to block Japanese advances. However, Washington did become more concerned with Vietnam because of Japan's growing threat to other US interests in the region. According to historian Robert Miller,

> ... it was Indochina's progressive subjugation by Japan in 1940 and 1941 that triggered a sudden turnabout in Washington's strategic assessment. Indochina was still unimportant in itself to the United States – it had few natural resources and US commercial interests were minimal. But removed from friendly control, it offered an unfriendly power a springboard for threatening areas of real concern to the United States: China ...; the commodity rich Dutch East India ...; the sea lanes from the Indian Ocean to the Pacific; and the entire South Pacific area.[9]

In July 1941, after Japanese occupation of Vietnam's airfields and harbours, the United States imposed economic sanctions on Japan and demanded that Japanese troops be withdrawn from Indochina as a condition for lifting the sanctions. However, as Miller points out, these sanctions had no positive effect and may have accelerated Japan's imperialist plans: 'As the American economic measures against Japan tightened, Southeast Asia's resources became more important to Japan's objectives and thus made expansion southward inevitable. Thus, American and Japanese interests in the region clashed and Indochina became the focal point for that clash.'[10] Still, short of war there was little else the United States could have done to stop Japan, and it is highly doubtful that US passivity would have reduced Japanese aggression. President Franklin D. Roosevelt continued to negotiate with Japan in the months leading up to the Pearl Harbor attack, and on 6 December 1941 he sent a final message to the Emperor Hirohito, stating that 'Japanese military, naval and air forces have been sent to Southern Indo-China in such large numbers as to create a reasonable doubt on the part of other nations that this continuing concentration in Indo-China is not defensive in its character.'[11] One day later the surprise Japanese attack on Pearl Harbor confirmed Roosevelt's concerns over Japanese threats in Vietnam as being applicable on a much wider scale and closer to home.

During the Second World War Vietnam was not a scene of conflict between the major powers. However, US policy during and after the war was shaped by two contradictory goals: the desire to support the Free French claims as the legitimate government of France (which included France's prewar colonial areas); and US support for the ideal of national self-determination as outlined in the Atlantic Charter. In keeping with America's traditional anticolonial world-view, President Roosevelt was clearly disturbed by Vichy's collaboration with Japan and frequently cited French rule as a telling example of oppressive and exploitative colonialism. Roosevelt often talked about his determination to turn Indochina into an international trusteeship after the war.[12] However, despite his well-recorded views, at the time of his death on 12 April 1945, US policy toward its allies' colonial possessions was in disarray. It was clear that the territorial possessions of the Axis powers could be more easily dealt with than those of the Allies. In Vietnam, despite Roosevelt's often direct criticism of their rule, the need to mollify the French eventually triumphed as the political endgame regarding the postwar world began to gain momentum. Accordingly, the official policy of the US government was that the territories of Allied powers would only be placed under UN trusteeship as a result of voluntary measures by the mother country.[13]

Under President Harry S. Truman, the United States grew less ambivalent over the return of French forces to Vietnam, and there is no evidence that Truman gave the region as much attention as did Roosevelt, leaving US policy largely in the hands of military planners. At the Potsdam conference it was decided that Japanese troops north of the 16th parallel would surrender to the forces of the Chinese Nationalist leader Chiang Kai-shek, and those south would surrender to a small contingent of British troops. However, events on the ground in Vietnam itself did not collude with the great powers' master-plan. In mid August 1945, after the sudden Japanese surrender following the dropping of the atomic bombs, Viet Minh forces under Ho Chi Minh's command took over administrative control in Vietnam, and on 2 September 1945 Ho declared the independence of the Democratic Republic of Vietnam (DRV). The new republic existed as a unified state for only twenty days, after which newly arrived French troops, with the sanction of the local British commander, seized control from the DRV regime and declared French sovereignty restored in Vietnam. Despite the French return, the seeds of rebellion had again sprouted in the local polity, and Vietnam's struggle for independence entered a new phase.[14]

From 1945 to 1949 the United States remained officially neutral in the Franco-Viet Minh War. Beginning in October 1945 the official policy of the United States was not to oppose the re-establishment of French control in Indochina, and no official statement by the US government questioned even by implication French sovereignty over Indochina. However, it was also not the official policy of the US government to actively assist the French in re-establishing their political control over Indochina by the use of military force. Officially, the US willingness to see French control re-established was predicated on the assumption that future events would bear out the French claim to have the support of the population of Indochina.[15] Thus in reality the US decision to take no action in regard to France's return to Vietnam was of great significance, considering the position of the United States as the dominant power at that moment of history. If the United States had followed through with its own traditional anticolonial idealism, the Vietnam War as we now know it would likely never have happened. In the end, however, the idealism of freedom and self-determination had been supplanted by the new idealism of America's increasingly strident anticommunist crusade.

By March 1946 the French had re-established effective control in Vietnam after Ho Chi Minh agreed to a compromise solution. In agreeing to the temporary recognition of French sovereignty, Ho reasoned that Vietnam would gain from the removal of Chinese forces, which still occupied the northern parts of the country. In addition, both sides agreed to hold negotiations on the future of the country, with the French promising to withdraw their troops after a five-year interval. Despite the promise of a delayed independence, Ho was greatly criticized for this agreement, which many nationalists dubbed a sell-out to French imperialism. In response, Ho revealed his understanding of the ancient relationship between Vietnam and China in stating, 'You fools! Don't you realize what it means if the Chinese stay? Don't you remember your history? The last time the Chinese came, they stayed one thousand years! … if the Chinese stay now, they will never leave … I prefer to smell French shit for five years than Chinese shit for the rest of my life.'[16] However, as history has shown, Ho Chi Minh's belief in the good faith of the French authorities quickly proved to be naïve. Within six months the French were able to increase their military presence while concurrently provoking the nationalist forces, eventually causing peaceful negotiations to fail, and civil war returned to Vietnam. Because of the irreconcilable mix between national interests and ideals of American global anticommunism, French imperialism and Vietnamese nationalism, war would remain the basic condition of life for the people of Vietnam for the next three decades.

Containment, Vietnam and US global perceptions

From 1947 to the end of the Cold War in 1991, a single litmus test dominated US policy decisions in global politics: 'How were the communists involved?' This 'red test' was a result of the US perception of a growing rivalry with the Soviet Union and the threat posed by socialism and the 'Soviet model' as a potentially viable alternative to US-led liberalism. In the United States, the perception of the Soviet threat was driven primarily by two interrelated political and economic factors. The initial promise of a cooperative 'democratic' postwar Europe was quickly erased by fears of Soviet aggression, a fear that developed concurrently with Stalin's manipulation of elections in Eastern Europe, and the imposition of Soviet-model single-party dictatorships in those countries occupied by the Red Army. As a result, during the Cold War the long-standing politico-military effort of the United States was to 'contain' the territorial expansion of the Soviet Union as well as to prevent the spread of communism as the governing ideology of any state, which presumably would be allied with Moscow. At the same time, the projection of US power was also directed at ensuring the continued existence of a relatively open capitalist world economy, which benefited US-based corporations and transitional capital generally.[17] Against the backdrop of the rise of communist China and the Korean War, the United States accelerated its support in Asia for the economic reconstruction and political stabilization of Japan (as well as South Korea and Taiwan), at the same time as Washington's assistance to the beleaguered French effort to hold on to their colonial empire in Indochina increasingly became the focal point of a wider commitment to containing communism in Southeast Asia.[18] By late 1953 President Dwight D. Eisenhower was particularly concerned about the economic and political impact of a French collapse on Japan, which was seen by then as the linchpin in US efforts to contain communist China and the Soviet Union in East Asia.[19]

The concept of containment was first articulated by George Kennan in his famous 'X' article, which appeared in *Foreign Affairs* in July 1947. A handful of Kennan's seemingly innocuous words, buried in the middle of his thoughtful essay, were destined to shape the face of world politics for decades to come: 'In these circumstances it is clear that the main element of any United States policy toward the Soviet Union must be that of a long-term, patient but firm and vigilant containment of Russian expansive tendencies. … Soviet pressure can be contained by the adroit and vigilant application of counter-force at a series of shifting geographical and political points …'[20] Despite Kennan's later claims that his opinions and proposals for dealing with the Soviet Union were often misunderstood or erroneously applied, it was not long before his 'containment' metaphor had become synonymous with US foreign policy.

President Truman acted quickly to incorporate Kennan's concept of containment as the cornerstone of US policy. 'I believe', he stated, 'that it must be the policy of the United States to support free peoples who are resisting attempted subjugation by armed minorities or by outside pressures.'[21] Truman's declaration, which became known as the Truman Doctrine, was based on the perception of international politics as a zero-sum struggle for world domination, with the Soviet Union as an aggressive power bent on conquering the world. Containment was a policy that sought global military, political and economic alliances that could achieve the goal of blocking Soviet expansion. One of the most important countries in Europe was France, which, like Germany and other continental states, seemed vulnerable to the appeals of Marxist philosophy. Maintaining a communist-free Western Europe was a major priority for the United States, both in terms of geopolitical interests and as a market for US-manufactured goods. In order to assure France's cooperation in the anticommunist security system in Western Europe, the United States signalled its willingness to sacrifice the democratic rights and national aspirations of the citizenry of the developing world. As a result, the age-old aspirations of the Vietnamese for national independence were sacrificed to achieve US interests in Europe; and the leading Vietnamese nationalist Ho Chi Minh was an avowed communist. Combined, these factors ensured US neutrality in the Vietnamese civil war through 1949.

In 1949 the United States became more concerned with Vietnam as a result of the communist victory in China. Because America envisioned a monolithic communist effort directed and controlled by Moscow, European containment policies were applied to Asia as well. A National Security Council (NSC) study clearly delineates Indochina's importance to the evolving global East–West antagonism:

> ... it is now clear that southeast Asia is the target of a coordinated offensive directed by the Kremlin. In seeking to gain control of southeast Asia, the Kremlin is motivated in part by a desire to acquire southeast Asia's resources and deny them to us. But the political gains which would accrue to the USSR from communist capture of southeast Asia are equally significant. The extension of communist authority in China represents a grievous political defeat for us; if southeast Asia also is swept by communism we shall have suffered a major political rout, the repercussions of which will be felt throughout the rest of the world ...[22]

American fears of a Kremlin-controlled, Chinese-inspired expansion of communism in Asia were seemingly confirmed in 1950 when North Korean troops attacked South Korea. At the time, Washington's policy-making was dominated by the perception that all communists – Soviet, Chinese, Korean, Vietnamese – pursued common interests and goals. This strategic perception of the nature of the communist threat was espoused in terms of the domino principle: the loss of a single nation in Southeast Asia to communism would inexorably lead to the complete subjugation of Asia by communists, and the eventual direct intervention by Chinese troops in Korea was regarded in Washington as confirmation of the validity of the domino theory. After the Korean armistice was signed in 1953, the possibility of increased Chinese intervention was feared as weapons and warriors became available for duty in Indochina. The Eisenhower administration, which had come to office in part by its successful attack on the Democrats for 'losing China', made it clear that the Republican administration would not permit a similar 'loss' of Indochina and warned the Chinese communists not to intervene.[23]

American involvement in the Franco-Viet Minh War

Beginning in 1950 the United States began to increase its support for the French in Indochina. Analysts in the State Department justified US investment in France's war effort against the Viet Minh as the result of a zero-sum cost-benefit equation. 'Drawing the line' in Vietnam would be expensive, but not in comparison to the greater costs if Vietnam were lost. Accordingly,

> ... the choice confronting the United States is to support the French in Indochina or face the extension of Communism over the remainder of the continental area of Southeast Asia and, possibly, farther westward. We then would be obliged to make staggering investments in those areas and in that part of Southeast Asia remaining outside Communist domination or withdraw to a much-contracted Pacific line. It would seem a case of 'Penny wise, Pound foolish' to deny support to the French in Indochina.[24]

However, after the outbreak of hostilities in Korea in June 1950, such support was limited to financial and material assistance. Before the Chinese intervention in Korea, the US perception of a communist domino principle was first implicitly articulated in a memo by the Pentagon's Joint Strategic Survey Committee. In response to the debate over direct US involvement in Indochina, however, the committee determined that the United States should not commit its military forces to Indochina in order to assist the French in defeating the Viet Minh. It based this recommendation on reasoning emblematic of 'domino' logic:

(1) Involvement of US forces against Viet Minh forces would be likely to lead to a war with Communist China;

(2) A general war with Communist China would, in all probability, have to be taken as a prelude to global war;

(3) Our major enemy in a global war would be the USSR;

(4) Our primary theater in the event of a global war would, in all probability, be Western Europe; and

(5) The forces of the Western Powers are insufficient to wage war on the mainland of Asia and at the same time accomplish the pre-determined Allied objectives in Europe.[25]

As a result of this reasoning, which concluded that direct US involvement in Vietnam would lead to World War Three in Europe, the Pentagon committee recommended finding a political solution to the problems of Indochina, stating:

> It appears that, in view of the unrest in Southeast Asia generally and in Indochina specifically, military victory in Indochina over the communists would be temporary in nature. The long-term solution to the unrest in Indochina lies in the sweeping political and economic

concessions by France and in the ultimate self-government of the three Associated States within the French Union or their complete independence of France. From the viewpoint of the United States, pressure on France to provide the much needed leadership to initiate these reforms and to grant self-government will prove less expensive in United States lives and national treasure than military commitments by us.[26]

The commitment of Chinese forces to the Korean War fundamentally altered Washington's perception of the possibility of finding a peaceful political solution to the communist–nationalist–colonial dilemma in Vietnam. Two basic schools of thought existed at the State Department: the pessimists, who worried that the United States was taking the place of France as the primary Western belligerent in Vietnam; and the optimists, who believed that US power was up to any task, and, once tendered, US commitments could not be withdrawn without serious damage to American prestige. John Ohly, deputy director of the Mutual Defense Assistance Program, pessimistically concluded:

> ... the demands on the US for Indochina are increasing almost daily ... sometimes imperceptibly, by one step after another, we are gradually increasing our stake in the outcome of the struggle there. We are, moreover, slowly (and not too slowly) getting ourselves into a position where our responsibilities tend to supplant rather than complement those of the French, and where failures are attributed to us as though we were the primary party at fault and in interest. We may be on the road to being a scapegoat, and we are certainly dangerously close to the point of being so deeply committed that we may find ourselves committed even to direct intervention. These situations, unfortunately, have a way of snowballing.[27]

Despite these perceptive and logical warnings, the optimists, led by Secretary of State Dean Acheson, reasoned with metaphoric imagery that 'having put our hand to the plow, we could not look back'.[28] The United States, while still fighting the communist assault directly in Korea, increased commitment of aid to France for its war against the Viet Minh. By 1951 military aid shipments to Indochina were given second highest priority, just behind those designated for the Korean War.[29]

The impact of the Korean War on US policy

The Korean War had a number of direct effects on US policy toward Indochina. Primarily it motivated and solidified both the executive and legislative branches' determination that the best way to resist communist expansion was through increases in defence spending and military assistance programmes. A second effect was to harden the idea that the United States should not become unconditionally committed to a major ground war in Asia. China, with its vast human resources, was seen as a force which could not be defeated by traditional military means. The Korean War had fostered the idea that, even with superior firepower and air supremacy, the United States could not indefinitely sustain combat against the sheer mass of troops that China could contribute to a regional conflict. Future policy in Vietnam would later be greatly influenced by China's assault across the Yalu River to repel the US forces that had approached its southern borders. A third effect was the formation of the erroneous perception that communist aggression would spring primarily from external sources. As a consequence, US military aid to French efforts in Vietnam was designed to counter a conventional attack from the North. Hence the South Vietnamese military was largely unprepared to counter the guerrilla tactics employed by the communists when fighting intensified in the late 1950s.[30]

A fourth serious consequence of the Korean War was on the policy-making system of the United States. The decision to enter the Korean War was made by President Truman on his own claim of authority, without a declaration of war. Thus intervention in Korea and later in Vietnam were defined as 'police actions' or 'limited wars', with Congress relegated to the role of providing or withholding funds to maintain the war effort. Serious constitutional questions were ignored in Washington until after Chinese troops had forced the Americans to retreat southward in the Korean War. However, despite many dissenting voices over subsequent years, the precedent of presidential authority to send troops without a declaration of war was established by the Korean experience.[31] The fifth consequence of the Korean War was that China replaced the Soviet Union as the principal source of communist aggression in Asia according to US policy-makers. Although the war with China in Korea had not precipitated a wider global war with the Soviet Union in Europe, the domino theory was not abandoned and communism was still perceived in Washington as a worldwide monolithic threat.

A final consequence of Korea was its impact on American domestic politics. In 1952 the election victory of the Republican Party, led by Dwight Eisenhower, intensified America's acceptance of the domino principle and more firmly entrenched Washington's political commitment to draw the line of containment at China's border with Vietnam. In his first State of the Union Message, on 3 February 1953, President Eisenhower promised a 'new, positive foreign policy' that would actively oppose the linked communist aggression in Korea, Malaya and Indochina.[32] When the Korean armistice was signed in April 1953, American anxiety over Indochina actually increased, because China might turn its attention from indirectly aiding the Viet Minh to direct military intervention with its own troops. Secretary of State John Foster

Dulles warned, 'Communist China has been and now is training, equipping and supplying the Communist forces in Indochina. There is a risk that Red China might send its own Army into Indochina. The Chinese Communist regime should realize that such a second aggression could not occur without grave consequences which might not be confined to Indochina.'[33] Clearly, the Eisenhower administration was publicly threatening its willingness to use atomic weapons if China became too aggressive in aiding the Viet Minh. The underlying assumption of US policy was that without direct Chinese assistance, Ho Chi Minh could not overthrow the French in Vietnam. However, in staking out this new position, by the virtue of his success in the election, Eisenhower became the role model for future US presidential candidates during the Vietnam War. His increasingly hard line, together with his anti-communist rhetoric, proved to be a political winner with the American people. Later presidents feared being attacked by their domestic critics and opponents as 'soft on communism' – a fear which would raise the anticommunist rhetoric in domestic politics and in so doing draw the United States ever more deeply into Vietnam. Likewise, using the threat of nuclear weapons raised Vietnam's profile from that of a distant region few Americans had ever heard of, to that of a region in which the US president appeared willing to employ the country's most powerful weapons of mass destruction. In sum, Eisenhower's policies in Vietnam increased the political stakes in Vietnam, welding the ideals of domestic American politics to foreign policy in Vietnam. After Eisenhower, in the minds of key decision-makers from Kennedy to Nixon, the credibility of the American system was put on the line in Vietnam.

The French experience: a prelude

As history has shown, the basic US understanding of the military and political realities of Vietnam was fundamentally flawed, although these realities had been exposed by the French defeat at Dienbienphu. France's bitter experience in Vietnam in the first decade after the Second World War can be seen as a prelude to the equally disastrous US experience ten years later. The French, and later the Americans, greatly misjudged the rapidly changing political situation in Vietnam, especially the staying power of Vietnamese nationalism. While the Americans gave vocal support to the aspirations of nationalist movements opposing colonialism, they refused to accept the reality that a legitimate nationalist movement could also be Marxist-oriented but autonomous from Kremlin direction. According to Vietnam historian, Joseph Buttinger:

> It is impossible to overemphasize the importance of certain unique aspects in the political evolution of Vietnam immediately after World

War II. The Communists were able to seize power in Hanoi without meeting opposition, and they were on the way to gaining control of the entire country a few weeks later – all of this more than four years before the victory of Communism in China. Unlike the Communists in Poland, Rumania, Bulgaria, and Hungary, the Vietnamese Communists were capable of gaining power without the presence of a single soldier of a foreign Communist army in their country ... Like Tito in Yugoslavia, Ho Chi Minh directed a political and military movement more powerful than his combined enemies ... To obstruct the rise of a Communist Vietnam required political and military interference from abroad.[34]

The French were determined to re-establish their control over Vietnam regardless of the political character of the Vietnamese nationalist forces. It took them almost two months to gain control of the major cities and highways in Northern and central Vietnam after fighting broke out in November 1946. The slow pace of the French reconquest was a prologue of what was to come. Over the next four years, the Viet Minh opposed the French with locally recruited guerrillas, holding in reserve and building its regular army divisions in the mountainous North. The Viet Minh controlled the entire countryside because of the active support of the vast majority of the rural population, who supported the historic dreams of an independent Vietnam.[35]

As the United States had feared, the communists were able to take the offensive against the French colonial forces after Mao's victory over the Chinese nationalists. In 1950 an ample supply of weapons reached the Viet Minh, enabling them to engage French forces on a more regular basis. In spite of the increasing aid from the United States, the French were driven out of all their strategic strongholds along the Chinese border, and they were in danger of losing Hanoi until a skilled commander, Jean de Lattre de Tassigny, stabilized the military lines in 1951. The French, like the Americans later on, were always confident that a military solution could be achieved. For a number of years they ignored the political reality that the Vietnamese people and their Viet Minh leaders were determined to unify the country and obtain total independence. National independence, not communism, was the unifying force among all Vietnamese factions.[36]

Eventually the French made efforts to undercut the Viet Minh's political base by installing native governments in Laos, Cambodia and Vietnam. In Vietnam, Emperor Bao Dai, who had served as a figurehead puppet under both the French and the Japanese in the Second World War, was recognized by the United States as the head of the Vietnamese government in 1950. By recognizing Bao Dai, the United States attempted to avoid the appearance of being an accomplice of French imperialism. Bao Dai, an archetype of the playboy figurehead in a token royalty, was himself sceptical of the 'Bao Dai

Solution', sardonically acknowledging that it 'was just a French solution'.[37] Under the agreement between the two parties France retained control over Vietnam's foreign, military, trade and financial affairs. In other words, Bao Dai remained a puppet leader. His government was made up of wealthy landowners and members of the small social and economic elite, a group whose social profile helped to strengthen the Viet Minh's popular appeal among the poverty-stricken masses and assisted them in recruiting soldiers.[38]

By the end of 1953 French sovereignty had been reduced to enclaves around major cities in Hanoi, Haiphong and Saigon. Under intense pressure from internal dissent in France and US demands that the French do more in Vietnam, the French government appointed General Henri Navarre to command its forces in Indochina. Shortly thereafter, the 'Navarre Plan', which had been tailor-made to meet many of the recommendations of the United States, was implemented with the assistance of $785 million from the United States. This plan called for the consolidation of French forces from their scattered garrisons, an increase in force structure of nine additional battalions of French troops, and the creation of a Vietnamese National Army (VNA). The Navarre Plan, by offering a format for victory which avoided the direct involvement of US forces, incrementally deepened the US commitment to finding a military solution to the rapidly deteriorating French political and military position in Vietnam.[39]

The Navarre plan proved to be a failure within six months. The Viet Minh, recognizing the need to strike a decisive blow before the expanded US aid could have an impact, invaded Laos and intensified guerrilla activity. As a result, Navarre was forced to scatter the very forces he had concentrated in order to counter the new offensive. By early 1954 both sides were concentrating forces around the village of Dienbienphu in northwest Vietnam, close to the Laotian border. In adopting a battle plan reminiscent of that of General George Custer at the Battle of the Little Big Horn, Navarre envisioned an order of battle whereby French forces were garrisoned on the low ground in the broad valley surrounding Dienbienphu, heavily fortified with barbed wire and bunkers and supported by aircraft and artillery. He hoped to draw the Viet Minh into attacking his fixed positions, where the superior firepower of his 12,000 elite troops presumably would decimate the communist forces.[40]

Within France itself there was mounting public sentiment to end the seemingly interminable and costly war. The Korean armistice served as an example that many French citizens hoped could be replicated in Vietnam. Widespread disenchantment among the French public was reflected in the statements of Prime Minister Laniel that an 'honourable solution' would be acceptable to Paris. Peace feelers by Ho Chi Minh were repeated publicly on numerous occasions and had a significant impact on 'dovish' sentiments in France. Laniel's government acknowledged that Ho's peace moves had produced a widespread sensation within France, even to the extent of influencing President Vincent Auriol to order Laniel to open negotiations with Ho Chi Minh. At the Berlin Quadripartite Foreign Ministers' meeting in February 1954 the French insisted that Indochina be included on the agenda at the upcoming Geneva conference on Far Eastern problems.[41] One month later the siege of Dienbienphu began, and it would continue until the opening of the Geneva meetings in May 1954.

The United States was opposed to any negotiated settlement of the French–Viet Minh struggle. The subject of possible negotiations was discussed in NSC (National Security Council), following the observation that internal political pressures in France could force it to seek a negotiated settlement. It was feared that any negotiated solution in Vietnam would lead to a communist victory as soon as French forces withdrew. The NSC decided that the United States should use every possible means to prevent the French government from concluding the struggle on terms 'inconsistent' with basic US objectives.[42] However, the Americans were forced to acquiesce to France's insistence that Indochina be discussed at Geneva. France was swayed by the more sedate Soviet position after Stalin's death in 1953, and it had still refused to be a signatory of the US-planned European Defense Community. Like Dean Acheson before him, Secretary of State Dulles feared pressuring France too greatly on Indochina. He did not wish to goad them into splitting the Western alliance, thereby playing into the hands of the Kremlin.[43] Containment was to be pursued on all fronts, but protecting the Western European states was of primary importance to the United States.

In the early spring of 1954, just before the Geneva talks were to convene, the French position at Dienbienphu rapidly deteriorated. Defying all predictions of their battlefield capabilities by American and French 'experts', the Viet Minh had managed to transport heavy artillery pieces on to the ridge tops overlooking the French forces in the valley surrounding Dienbienphu. The heavy guns quickly isolated the battlefield by knocking out the airstrip, thus making resupply of the French garrison impossible except by random and inaccurate parachute drops. The success of the communist forces in seizing the high ground raised the real possibility that without direct American intervention the French would face a humiliating defeat.[44] Various proposals for aiding the besieged French garrison, including the use of tactical atomic weapons, were debated in Washington. Mistakenly, the French were led to believe by Admiral Radford, Chairman of the US Joint Chiefs of Staff, that the United States would provide direct air support if the French formally requested it. However, after intense deliberations, President Eisenhower decided not to support the proposal for unilateral American intervention, choosing instead to press for multilateral intervention by a coalition of forces primarily from Britain, France, Australia, New Zealand, the United States, and possibly the United Nations.[45]

Because the United States did not want to shoulder the entire economic and political burden, which was combined with a low probability of success, the cautious Eisenhower preferred the idea of multilateral intervention similar to the Korea model. The president did not wish to risk American prestige until France had made firm commitments to remain involved in Vietnam and Paris had made real progress toward granting independence to the Vietnamese. However, as revealed in a discussion with the British prime minister, Winston Churchill, the president was not without a certain flair for the dramatic in trying to convince Churchill to join with the United States and its 'United Action' plan, stating, 'If I may refer again to history; we failed to halt Hirohito, Mussolini and Hitler by not acting in unison and in time. That marked the beginning of many years of stark tragedy and desperate peril. May it not be that our nations have learned nothing from that lesson?'[46] The British, however, did not perceive these historical situations as comparable, and Churchill opposed any collective military intervention before the Geneva Conference, believing that an increase in military activity would undermine the chances for a peaceful solution and that escalation might inspire direct Chinese intervention. The British also rejected the American domino principle, and judged that a negotiated settlement leading to a North–South partition would be the best possible outcome to a complex political–military situation in Indochina.[47] France also rejected the 'United Action' approach, but for other reasons, preferring that the Americans intervene unilaterally with air support at Dienbienphu. They feared that a multilateral coalition would lead to an internationalization of the war, a situation that would take control out of their hands and undercut French sovereignty in the colonial areas. Echoing British concerns, the French also feared that a large-scale intervention beyond the level of air strikes in support of Dienbienphu would undermine the Geneva talks and increase public sentiment in France for getting out of Indochina at any cost.[48] Furthermore, although the French wanted American air strikes and logistical support, they were unwilling to accept increased American advice on how to conduct the war and find a workable political solution. France's prestige, like America's own, must be protected.

Faced with a negative reaction from the Congressional leaders of both political parties when consulted on the idea of unilateral intervention to assist Dienbienphu, President Eisenhower reaffirmed his decision that the United States would not intervene on France's behalf. Making the political discussions largely moot, the Geneva Conference opened with the announcement that the last defenders of Dienbienphu surrendered on 7 May 1954, after fifty-five days of stubborn but doomed resistance. As a result, the bargaining position of the French delegation was severely undercut at Geneva. On 12 June the French military disintegration in Vietnam was paralleled by a major political shake-up in Paris. The Laniel government fell on a 306–293 vote on the Indochina problem. On 17 June Laniel was replaced as premier by Pierre Mendes-France, who publicly vowed to reach a settlement at Geneva by 21 July.[49]

As promised, Mendes-France was successful in forcing a settlement at Geneva. On 21 July a cease-fire was concluded and a 'Final Declaration' was issued. The Geneva Accords of 1954 had two primary components: Vietnam would be temporarily partitioned at the 17th parallel, and nationwide elections on reunification would occur two years later, in 1956. Because France was still the legal sovereign of Vietnam, the South Vietnamese government that would later form was not a party to the Geneva Accords; nor was the US government. However, the United States maintained that it was committing itself to refraining from using force to disturb the cease-fire, that it stood behind 'full freedom of action' for the South Vietnamese, and that it would support the democratic principle of 'free elections' as outlined in the Geneva agreement.[50] The subjectivity of these apparently objective statements will be revealed shortly. In order to deflect criticisms from Democrats attempting to turn Eisenhower's own 'loss of China' accusations against him for the 'loss' of Vietnam, the president placed the blame on France. Eisenhower stressed that 'the United States has not been a belligerent in the war', and 'the primary responsibility for the settlement in Indochina rested with those nations which participated in the fighting'.[51]

The Geneva Accords of 1954 were a product of compromise on many fronts, and the agreements reflected the influences of the convention's major participants: France, Britain and the United States on one side, and the Viet Minh, Soviet Union and China on the other. France had finally extricated itself from the bloody civil war in the north yet retained a foothold in South Vietnam. Its valued colonial empire remained intact, if battered, and French honour had been marginally protected by the legal fig-leaf provided by the Accords. The Accords served momentarily to satisfy the United States, thereby allowing the British to avoid the difficult choice of joining with the Americans in a venture they believed was politically wrong and militarily foolish; or breaking with the Americans with the possible negative impact on the Anglo-American alliance in Europe. The Eisenhower administration viewed the Accords with mixed feelings. On the negative side, the communists had gained international diplomatic prestige at Geneva in addition to inflicting painfully real political and territorial defeats. On the positive side, the southern part of Vietnam had been preserved, and the two-year time lag before elections gave the United States time to formulate a defence of the South.[52] In addition, the United States was more free to manœuvre after the French capitulation. As George Herring noted,

> … from the start, the Franco-American partnership in Indochina had been marked by profound mutual suspicion and deep-seated tensions. From 1950 to 1954, the United States had provided France more than

$2.6 billion in military aid, but its efforts to influence French policies by friendly persuasion and by attaching strings had failed ... Eisenhower and Dulles had attributed France's failure primarily to its attempts to perpetuate colonialism in Indochina, and they were confident that without the problems posed by France the United States could build a viable non-Communist alternative to the Vietminh.[53]

Perhaps more important for Eisenhower was the fact that he was able to deflect domestic criticism of being soft on communism. In doing so, however, he drew the United States ever closer to the Vietnam conflict by implicitly committing US credibility to the defence of a regime in the South that had yet to be created.

The communist governments too had agreed to a compromise at Geneva. Both China and the Soviet Union were worried about the possibility of renewed fighting in Vietnam, which could bring the Americans into the war. Both communist powers remained stressed internally, with the Chinese trying to build a new economic and political order in a country still devastated by two decades of warfare with Japan, the nationalist government, and the US–UN coalition in Korea. Likewise, despite its public image as a powerful industrial and economic force, the Soviet Union had yet to recover from the ravages of the Second World War, and the political fall-out from the recent death of Stalin had yet to stabilize. The Eisenhower administration's sabre rattling, punctuated by the high-stakes rhetoric of Dulles's 'massive retaliation' speech in January 1954, sobered both the Chinese and the Russians. In putting national interest before ideology, both communist countries revealed their hesitancy to be drawn into a direct war with the Americans over Vietnam.[54] In 1979, after their own falling out, the Vietnamese government released a 'white paper' on Vietnamese–Chinese relations that confirmed Western suspicions of China's ability to pressure the Viet Minh. The Vietnamese white paper claimed that China had forced them to settle for partition in 1954 because of its fear of American intervention.[55] Furthermore, both the Soviets and the Chinese had helped themselves in the global ideological struggle. By engaging in dialogue and diplomacy they had improved their international status at Geneva in the eyes of third parties. Likewise, by avoiding war with the United States, they could claim to be the agents of peace, and it was expected that the final Viet Minh victory would be achieved by default in the 1956 unification elections, again bolstering their egalitarian credentials. The Viet Minh were forced to compromise by the reality that they could not sustain the war without assistance from the Chinese and/or the Soviets, and that the Americans would probably intervene if an agreement were not signed. They were able to use the next two years to prepare for war if necessary, and could publicly proclaim victory in defeating the French imperialists.[56]

From 1954 to 1956 the steady French withdrawal from Vietnam was paralleled by increasing degrees of US involvement. In June 1954 Ngo Dinh Diem was named premier of the State of Vietnam by Emperor Bao Dai. Diem was unknown to most young people, but he was known by older Vietnamese for his anticolonial credentials, having resigned as Minister of the Interior in 1933 because of his refusal to play the part of a French puppet minister. France, still smarting from its own wounded pride, criticized the United States as a result of Washington's direct involvement with the new South Vietnamese government of Diem. Even though many American officials who dealt directly with him were highly sceptical of his political base and governing abilities, President Eisenhower pledged full US support for his regime, primarily because Diem was one of the few staunch nationalist leaders in Vietnam who strongly opposed both the French and the communists. In doing so, the United States was staking its international credibility on a politician who had only minimal domestic support among his fellow Vietnamese.[57] In order to help support Diem, in September 1954, the Southeast Asia Treaty Organization (SEATO) was created, and its protection was extended to Vietnam by a special protocol to the pact. SEATO was designed by the United States as the primary organizational framework for blocking further communist expansion in Southeast Asia. By supporting the Diem regime and promoting 'nation-building' in South Vietnam, the United States was drawing the new line of containment at the 17th parallel. In late September 1954 the United States began dealing directly with Diem's government and armed forces, completely bypassing French involvement. Despite France's recent failures, in seeking to build a politically sound, economically viable, and militarily capable regime, the United States was further committing itself to creating political legitimacy in a faraway country of which it had little understanding.[58]

In the late 1950s, France was plagued by domestic political troubles as the United States was to be during the 1970s. France had rejected the European Defense Community in August 1954; it was bogged down with a similar colonial rebellion in North Africa; it suffered the humiliation of Suez in 1956 along with Britain and Israel; and it was displaced in South Vietnam by the United States. Just before the Suez crisis, general elections in France produced a government headed by the socialist Guy Mollet. The socialist government was sharply critical of US policy in Vietnam as being contrary to French interests, and condemned both the United States and Britain for stirring up dissent in the Arab world against France's interests in North Africa. On 26 April 1956 France fulfilled its obligations under the Geneva Accords and dissolved its military command in South Vietnam. On the date set for general elections to unify Vietnam, no French military forces remained in Vietnam. By late summer of 1956 France's long imperial experience in Vietnam had come to an ignominious conclusion.[59]

The Diem regime and Geneva betrayal

In the wake of the Geneva Accords, ever certain of its own capabilities, the United States was confident that it could succeed in Vietnam where France had failed. American assistance enabled Diem to foil a series of military plots to overthrow him. In violation of both the spirit and the letter of the Geneva Accords, the United States directly aligned itself with the Southern regime and engineered covert operations to undermine the Viet Minh in both the North and the South. After some initial hesitation, the Eisenhower administration strongly backed Diem after he successfully defended himself against a number of powerful sects in the South.[60] American backing helped Diem consolidate his power by arming loyal military forces against his various opponents. Also with American approval, Diem 'legitimized' his regime in a hastily arranged national referendum in October 1955 that pitted him against Bao Dai, the last puppet emperor of both the hated Japanese and the French. American advisers suggested that a 60 per cent margin of victory would be adequate to make the stage-managed affair appear real, and the 40 per cent going to Bao Dai would make it a legitimately contested election. At this juncture Diem and his brother Ngo Dinh Nhu first expressed what was to become a pattern of stubborn resistance to American advice: they 'won' the election with 98.2 per cent of the vote, including 605,000 votes from the 405,000 registered voters in Saigon.[61] Also with American backing, Diem refused to proceed with the all-Vietnam elections as stipulated in the Geneva Accords. It was clear that both the United States and South Vietnam believed that free elections that involved communists would be impossible. Hypo-thetically, if such an election could be held, no rational person would vote to be governed by communists. Secretary of State Dulles explained the rationale behind the US backing of Diem's refusal to adhere to the Geneva Accords: 'Neither the United States Government nor the Government of Viet-Nam is, of course, a party to the Geneva agreements. We did not sign them, and the Government of Vietnam did not sign them and, indeed protested against them ... We also believe that, if there are conditions of really free elections, there is no serious risk that the Communists would win ...'[62]

Thus the roots of the American legitimacy crisis that would explode onto the domestic political sphere a decade later had been firmly established, not only by the first of many rigged elections in South Vietnam but also by President Eisenhower's candid public estimate that Ho Chi Minh would receive 80 per cent of the vote in any all-Vietnamese election. The government of the United States had determined that communism and democracy were incompatible, especially when such a free election would have produced a communist victory. In doing so, the Eisenhower administration established a pattern of US policy that was fundamentally flawed by an irreconcilable paradox, for in order to preserve democracy and stop communism the United

States committed itself to the support of an increasingly anti-democratic regime, South Vietnam.

The Soviet Union in Vietnam, 1940–56

Soviet politics, both domestic and international, were shaped and guided by Lenin's overall philosophical world-view, which was grounded in Marx's perception that all history was the history of class struggle. Thus, as leaders of the Soviet Union, Lenin, Stalin, Khrushchev and Brezhnev all viewed foreign affairs as a zero-sum game played out between the capitalist and the socialist camps. According to sovietologist Walter Clemens, 'Lenin taught that the fundamental question of politics is "Kto kovo" – Who, whom? Which side will destroy the other? Armed with this view, he and his successors built a system that could seize and hold power but not one that interacts optimally with other states and systems or even with its own subjects.'[63] The use of military force and the application of coercive power enabled Lenin and his successors to survive against both domestic and foreign enemies. Whatever one side gained was at the corresponding expense of the other. Until the arrival of Mikhail Gorbachev in 1985, Soviet leaders believed that mutual, or positive-sum gains were impossible.[64] Soviet policies in Vietnam flowed from this zero-sum thinking. Any loss for the French or the Americans in Vietnam was seen as a gain in the overall position of the Soviet Union *vis-à-vis* its capitalist rivals.

In the three decades spanning the birth of the Soviet state in 1917 and the beginning of the Cold War, the Soviet Union had supported various revolutionary movements throughout the world. However, in the case of Vietnam, Moscow's early material assistance to the Indochinese Communist Party (ICP) was minimal. However, Ho Chi Minh and other Vietnamese communists primarily benefited intellectually from the lessons taught by Lenin and his contemporaries, especially those lessons on how to seize and hold power in an environment ripe for revolution. Leninism provided an organizational model that successfully taught mobilization, motivation, leadership and discipline in party cadres. However, just as Lenin had been forced to adapt orthodox Marxism to the realities of Russia, Leninist tactics and strategies had to be recast and fitted to Vietnam. According to Douglas Pike, '[t]he important point to be made here is that there was a great sea change in communism's passage to Asia. Emptied of much of its intellectual content, communism became more an instrument and less a philosophy. Moreover, although many outsiders consider Vietnamese communism to be a pale carbon copy of Soviet communism, there are many dissimilarities.'[65] The United States based its policies in Vietnam after the Second World War on the assumption that Ho Chi Minh was part of an international communist conspiracy in which all communists were in league against the United States and its allies. However, a closer analysis of the historic relationship between the Soviet Union and Vietnam largely refutes this perception. As noted in Chapter 1, before the Second World War the ICP was so nebulous an organization that its members were seen as only minor players in the Communist International (Comintern), and in the 1930s Stalin largely suppressed the activities of the Comintern in order to establish and maintain peaceful relations with the capitalist states. Stalin's *kto kovo* world-view concluded that the Soviet Union would be strengthened by maintaining a temporary peace with the capitalist order. In doing so, Stalin's strictures on the Comintern in the 1930s actually increased the level of independence of many communist parties outside the Soviet Union, especially outside of Europe. According to Alan Cameron, 'the early Communist movement in Vietnam was only on the fringes of Soviet control, even at the height of the Comintern period. Although Ho Chi Minh was indeed a Comintern functionary ... Moscow's attempts at control were only sporadically effective and often encountered serious obstacles in the factiousness of both individuals and groups within the ICP.'[66] And during the Second World War Stalin dissolved the Comintern to placate the USSR's Western allies, an act that forced Ho Chi Minh and his comrades to survive entirely on their own.

Unlike the scenario in most of the Eastern European communist states, Ho Chi Minh established a communist government in Vietnam in 1945 without Moscow's assistance via the Red Army. Much like the Chinese communists of the 1920s who had been sold out by Stalin to the nationalists, as a result of Stalin's decisions in the Second World War the Vietnamese communists felt isolated and somewhat betrayed by the lack of support from Moscow. According to journalist-historian Harold Isaacs, who conducted interviews with Vietnamese communists, Ho Chi Minh and his comrades were conditioned to expect no help from the USSR. One interviewee stated, 'The Russians are nationalists from Russia first and above all.' Another stated, 'They would be interested in us only if we served some purpose of theirs.'[67] The primary Soviet interest in Vietnam at the end of the Second World War was contingent on how events in Vietnam could influence politics in France and France's role in the Western alliance. Shoring up the political position of the French Communist Party (FCP) was higher on Stalin's agenda than the success or failure of Ho Chi Minh's revolution. When it became clear that the majority of the French proletariat (which would be voting in the elections) supported the re-establishment of the French empire, the FCP urged Ho Chi Minh to restrain himself. In September 1945 Harold Isaacs was shown an FCP document that 'advised the Annamite [Vietnamese] Communists to be sure, before they acted too rashly, that their struggle meets the requirements of Soviet policy. It warned that any premature adventures in Annamite independence might not be in line with Soviet perspectives. These perspectives might well include France as a firm ally of the USSR in Europe, in which case the Annamite independence movement would be an embarrassment.'[68] Clearly the FCP was towing Moscow's line, but because of Stalin's actions during the Second World War the Vietnamese communists were making decisions on their own. In retrospect, Ho Chi Minh's decision to defy the FCP recommendation and go ahead with the August 1945 declaration of independence suggests that he was operating without any overriding concern for Soviet policy preferences, acting as a nationalist rather than simply as a communist. Stalin's focus on Europe actually had a negative impact on the Vietnamese communists' view of their putative allies. According to Douglas Pike, 'the party cadres believe that the revolution would not have been destroyed [in 1945] had the USSR chosen to block the return of the French military forces – an option, it is held, Moscow easily could have exercised. A second legacy from this period, closer to reality, is the conviction among Vietnamese Communists that the DRV [Democratic Republic of Vietnam] was created largely without appreciable assistance from the USSR.'[69] However, as the Cold War intensified, the Vietnamese communists were forced by the powerful logic of Lenin's *kto kovo* rationale, which both the Soviet Union and the United States had adopted as the philosophy behind their rules of engagement. Even though they might not trust Moscow or Beijing because of past betrayals, when faced with the United States pouring billions of dollars into maintaining France's foothold in South Asia, the Vietnamese revolutionaries were forced to rely more heavily on the material support of their Chinese and Soviet patrons.

During the period of Stalin's rule, Moscow's ties with the Viet Minh and its support in the anti-French war effort were kept largely hidden. Ho Chi Minh was regarded as overly independent and a likely candidate to become an Asian Tito. The strange nature of Stalin's relationship with Ho Chi Minh is revealed in the memoirs of Nikita Khrushchev. In recalling a meeting in Moscow in the early 1950s attended by Ho, Khrushchev and Stalin, at which Ho asked the Soviets for aid, Khrushchev wrote, 'I remember once he [Ho] reached into his briefcase and took out a copy of a Soviet magazine ... *The USSR Under Construction* – and asked Stalin to autograph it ... Stalin gave Ho his autograph but shortly afterward had the magazine stolen back from him because he was worried about how Ho might use it ...'[70] Although it would be a mistake to conclude that the Soviet Union was only nominally involved in Vietnam, there is little evidence to suggest that Stalin had a great deal of interest, and therefore influence, in Vietnam. Stalin's interest in Vietnam was almost entirely derivative, and Soviet action (or inaction) was contingent on events occurring outside of Indochina. After Stalin's death, the Vietnamese hoped that the USSR under Khrushchev would take a more active interest in their struggle against the French and the Americans.[71]

Khrushchev's emergence as Stalin's successor in the mid 1950s was clearly marked by changes in Soviet foreign policy. Because of US nuclear superiority, direct confrontation with the United States could result in the destruction of the Soviet Union; however, the global struggle for power must continue. Under Khrushchev, Soviet policies in the Third World were initiated in order to help neutralize the dominant position of the United States in the industrialized world after the Second World War. Policy innovations in Asia could accelerate a strategic shift that had begun in China, and successes there would improve the Soviet Union's bargaining position against both the United States and its forces in Europe.[72]

Much like the United States, the Soviet position at Geneva was dependent on that of its allies. The Soviets, the Chinese and the Vietnamese apparently viewed the final Geneva agreements as possibly the best deal to be had under the given conditions. In his memoirs Khrushchev recalls the pre-conference discussions between Ho Chi Minh, Chou En-lai and himself, stating: 'The situation was grave. The resistance movement in Vietnam was on the brink of collapse. The partisans were counting on the Geneva Conference to produce a cease-fire agreement which would enable them to hold on to the conquests which they had won in the struggle of the Vietnamese people against the French occupation. Hanoi was securely in the hands of the French ... North Vietnam was pockmarked with enclaves which had been captured and occupied by the French.'[73]

The Soviets viewed the French retreat from the North, which resulted from the Geneva Accords, as a diplomatic victory. However, the compromises made by the communist side were also shaped by their perception of the Korean War. The Chinese position was revealed by Khrushchev to be similar to that of the Americans.

> Chou En-lai buttonholed me and took me into a corner. He said, 'Comrade Ho Chi Minh has told me that the situation in Vietnam is hopeless and that if we don't attain a cease-fire soon, the Vietnamese won't be able to hold out against the French. Therefore they've decided to retreat to the Chinese border if necessary, and they want China to be ready to move troops into Vietnam as we did in North Korea ... We simply can't grant Comrade Ho Chi Minh's request. We've already lost too many men in Korea – that war cost us dearly. We're in no condition to get involved in another war at this time.'[74]

In the early years after Geneva, relations between the Democratic Republic of Vietnam (DRV or North Vietnam) and the Soviet Union were less than intimate. The Soviet Union remained committed to the Vietnamese, but overt involvement in Indochinese affairs from 1954 to 1956 was downplayed with a mind to influencing anti-American sentiments in France and throughout Europe. The two countries signed a number of economic assistance treaties, and Ho Chi Minh visited Moscow in 1955, albeit without the degree of fanfare that accompanied the visits of other world leaders. While the Americans were building closer ties to the Diem regime in South Vietnam in the two years before the final French withdrawal, the North Vietnamese slowly became less important to their Soviet partners, a relationship that would change only after the final Sino-Soviet split and when US combat troops later became heavily involved in Vietnam in the late 1960s.

THE SUPERPOWERS IN AFGHANISTAN

Like Vietnam, the situation in Afghanistan during the period from 1940 to 1956 was largely dependent on the dynamics of great-power politics outside of Afghanistan's borders. Unlike Vietnam, Afghanistan was not a concern of the major actors in the Second World War, and its relations with the United States and the Soviet Union were very different from those of Vietnam the opening decade of the Cold War.[75] However, Afghanistan's domestic politics and its eventual pro-Soviet tilt were intricately tied to the Cold War, and its decisions were especially influenced by the containment policies of the United States in South Asia. In part, the growing level of Soviet influence in Afghanistan after 1955 was a direct result of American policy decisions in the first decade following the Second World War.

US–Afghan relations, 1941–56

During the war, Cornelius Engert, who had become the US resident representative in Kabul, organized a relief effort to help shore up the Afghan economy. Both exports and imports had been strangled in landlocked Afghanistan, and Engert's relief efforts resulted in generating a sizable degree of goodwill for the United States in Afghanistan among the population and in governing circles.[76] In 1941 the Afghans proposed that the two nations sign a more comprehensive treaty that would expand US–Afghan economic ties, including the US granting of a modified most-favoured nation clause. However, the United States declined to enter such a treaty during the Second World War.[77] No diplomatic mission was placed in Kabul until 1942; even then, it was done only as a wartime measure to prepare the way for the possible transit of Lend-Lease supplies to the Soviet Union.[78] In 1945 Afghanistan, which had maintained a strict neutrality during the war, faced immense social and economic challenges if it wished to enter the 'modern' world order. The war had demonstrated how weak the political independence of the landlocked country was when its economic lifelines to the outside world (the Soviet Union, India) were all but cut off by the outcomes of battles fought on distant lands and waters. Although Afghanistan had not suffered Allied occupation as had its neighbour Iran, the weakness of its position in the region was obvious to the Afghan leadership. In order to lessen its economic and political dependence on the Soviet Union and British India, Afghanistan returned to its historic policy of cultivating relations with powerful states outside of the region. Two countries that had been useful in the past, Germany and Japan, in 1945 could no longer be played against Russia and Britain in Afghanistan's traditional balance-of-power foreign policy. Therefore, the United States was seen as the most desirable (and capable) country that could help to maintain Afghanistan's political independence and provide the economic means for both modernization and development.[79]

From the outset of the postwar era, the United States was prepared to give material aid to Afghanistan, albeit limited and conditional in form. The rationale behind the US position on aid to Afghanistan was symptomatic of the practical limitations of implementing the stated ideals of communist containment. Afghanistan's primary importance for the United States, as it had been for its British predecessor in the leadership role in global power politics, lay in its geographic location bordering on the Soviet Union, Iran and Pakistan. American policies toward Afghanistan were therefore contingent on Washington's overall strategy in the region.

The pattern of postwar Afghan overture toward the United States began in 1946. Prime Minister Shah Mohammed Khan stated in August of that year that he was convinced that the United States could ensure Afghanistan's security, adding, 'For the first time in our history we are free of the threat of great powers using our mountain passes as pathways to empire.'[80] This statement was made despite the fact that the United States had earlier that year flatly rejected Afghan economic development proposals as being too vague. The Afghan government decided to proceed with its own economic development plans through private means in conjunction with American industrialists. It signed a $17 million contract with the Morrison-Knudsen Company of Boise, Idaho, to build roads and repair irrigation canals in the Helmand River Valley in southwest Afghanistan.[81] In 1947 Afghanistan renewed its attempt to tap American development funds in the form of a request for a $118 million loan, which was justified both in economic and political terms. Afghan officials presented the request to the US delegation in Kabul by mentioning Soviet offers of assistance. However, the officials of the then less politicized United States Export-Import Bank were unconvinced that the Soviet Union was a serious factor in determining the validity of the request, and it rejected the loan as being economically nonviable. Eventually, after intense lobbying by special interests, the bank would approve a mere $21 million of this loan, doing so only to ensure Morrison-Knudsen's profits in the Helmand Valley construction projects.[82]

Although 1947 was a fairly uneventful time in US–Afghan relations, it proved to be a watershed year in twentieth-century South Asian and superpower politics. The British withdrawal from India and the subsequent bloody partition of the country during the creation of the independent state of Pakistan changed the face of South Asian politics. By 1947 the fragile two-year period of postwar detente between the new superpowers was rapidly eroding into the first stage of the Cold War, and the first strategies of containment were being formulated in Washington to block the advance of world communism.

The implementation of the US policy of containment proved to be less simplistic than the idealistic public statements of the Truman administration, as the case of Afghanistan clearly illustrates. In July 1948 a National Security Council position paper outlined the broad criteria for supplying arms to non-communist nations in declaring:

> Certain free nations the security of which is of critical importance to the United States require strengthened military capabilities, if they are to present effective political resistance to communist aggression now, and military resistance later if necessary. Therefore, the United States should assist in strengthening the military capabilities of these nations to resist communist expansion provided they make determined efforts to resist communist expansion and such assistance contributes effectively towards that end.[83]

Afghan leaders realized that the withdrawal of Britain from the subcontinent had tipped the traditional balance of power in the region and placed Afghanistan in a vulnerable position *vis-à-vis* the Soviet Union. In order to restore the balance, and encouraged by the declared US policy on aid to nations seeking to resist communism, the Afghans began attempted to solicit economic and military aid from the United States.

Late in 1948, while continuing to pursue the aforementioned $118 million loan proposal, the Afghan representative, Abdul Majid Khan Zabuli, also requested US military assistance for Afghanistan. He presented his request in terms of both internal and external security requirements. As outlined in Chapter 1, Afghan leaders had been perpetually confronted with tribal revolts and now feared the ever-present danger posed by their powerful northern neighbour. Zabuli stated that the reason for seeking US weapons was to make a positive contribution in the event of a war with the Soviets. When war came Afghanistan would undoubtedly be overrun and occupied; however, in what can now be seen as prophetic, Zabuli also informed State Department officials that the Russians would be unable to pacify the country and the Afghans would pursue guerrilla warfare for an indefinite period.[84]

Zabuli's portentous analysis is a clear statement of the awareness on the part of Afghan officials of the potential threat to Afghan sovereignty posed by Soviet expansion. Afghanistan's desire to remain independent of Soviet dominance necessitated an alliance with the United States. Therefore,

Afghanistan apparently presented the United States with an ideal case for aiding a Third World nation seeking to defend itself from communist aggression or internal rebellion. However, Afghanistan was frustrated in its attempts to solidify new ties to the United States. The Truman administration paid little attention to Afghan requests and focused its energies on other Middle Eastern affairs such as the newly emerging Arab–Israeli struggle, the expanding rift between India and Pakistan, and the consolidation of political control in Iran.[85]

Undeterred, the Afghans were resolved to persist in their arms requests despite US indifference, and they adopted a more politically charged approach. In 1949, after repeated requests for arms had been denied by the United States, Afghan officials suggested that they might reassess Afghanistan's traditional position of neutrality in favour of whatever side agreed to provide weapons. A cable from the US embassy in Kabul reported that the Afghans had indicated that 'unless the US gave Afghan more assistance the Afghans might turn to the USSR'.[86] Despite this political gamesmanship, however, the Afghans had also indicated that they preferred to orient themselves more closely with the Western alliance. Some US officials voiced their support for the Afghan requests. Assistant Secretary of State George McGhee was one such official who realized that, in the wake of the British withdrawal from India, Afghanistan's willingness to abandon its traditional neutrality and associate openly with the United States was a significant change in policy. He recommended that 'in view of these and other considerations, our failure to extend some form of procurement assistance or token aid at this time would very seriously jeopardize our effort over the past two years to orient these countries to the West and away from Communism ...'.[87]

McGhee's viewpoint at the State Department reflected the basic concepts of containment and the Truman Doctrine; however, his opinion, while concurring with publicly stated US policy objectives, conflicted with that of strategic military planners. A study by the Defense Department concluded that Afghanistan was of little or no strategic importance to the United States. Its geographic location, coupled with Soviet capabilities, presaged Soviet control of the country whenever the international situation so warranted. In fact, the military report stated that any overt Western-sponsored military activities or aid might precipitate a Soviet move to take control of the country.[88] The Defense Department report reveals one of the inherent problems of containment: the conflict between ideological political goals and strategic military reality. The ability of the US military to fulfil its designated role within expansively defined goals of containment – supporting those states opposing communism with military aid – was challenged by the non-ideological logic in this report. Here it was argued that providing such military aid could actually provoke a Soviet counterstrike. This analysis would suggest that in certain instances the application of the military component of containment may in fact produce what it was meant to deter – Soviet expansion.

The internal debate between various political and military analysts in the State and Defense departments continued. The US embassy in Kabul endorsed the sale of arms in January 1950, hoping 'to exclude Soviet influence, cement Afghan–American friendship, maintain internal security, and promote settlement of differences with Pakistan'.[89] However, the US military again vetoed the recommendation. The decision not to arm Afghanistan may have been based on Washington's fears of further Soviet activity in Asia after the start of the Korean hostilities. A National Security Council report in August 1950 had concluded that

> ... the Kremlin might be prepared to accept in varying degrees the risk of a general conflict by launching local armed attacks in order to attain objectives regarded as being of importance to the Soviet Union ... the principal areas where actual Soviet forces could be employed for a local purpose are Iran, Turkey, Yugoslavia, Greece, Afghanistan, Pakistan, or Finland ... In the event of overt attack by organized USSR military forces against Finland or Afghanistan: the United States should itself take no military action in these to oppose the aggression ...[90]

Again Afghanistan had fallen outside the perceived bounds of practicality in the US attempt to apply the political ideals of containment in South Asia. It would appear that as early as 1950 Afghanistan had been conceded to the Soviet sphere without the bootprints of a single Red Army soldier having marked Afghan soil.

The Afghans, however, were still reluctant to become a permanent fixture within the Soviet sphere of influence. In April 1951 the Afghan prime minister, Shah Mahmud, visited Washington. The State Department briefed President Truman that Afghan arms requests were being ignored rather than refused. The president was advised to tell the prime minister that the US, heavily strained in Korea, had limited means to furnish arms and that the Afghans should rely on the collective security of the United Nations.[91] The Afghans nevertheless went ahead with a formal arms request in August 1951. In an apparent change of policy, the United States conditionally agreed to supply arms to Afghanistan if the following terms were met: (1) the $25 million price tag would have to be paid in hard currency; (2) the Afghan government would have to arrange its own transportation through Pakistan; and (3) the sale would be made public. On the face of it the persistent Afghans had finally won their battle to obtain weapons. This was not, however, the case, since they themselves considered the terms to be unacceptable and to amount in fact to a 'political refusal'.[92] In order to understand the Afghans' reasoning for rejecting the US arms proposal we must delve more deeply into the regional politics of South Asia. The Afghans' rejection of the terms of the proposed arms sale was interwoven with the intricate and convoluted relationships existing between the United States, India, Pakistan and their own country.

Regional politics

In terms of regional power capabilities, by far the most important nation in South Asia is India. After the withdrawal of Britain in 1947, India had the largest territory and population, it had inherited the largest army, it had established democratic institutions, and its leaders were admired in parts of the West. Therefore, in terms of a traditional realpolitik conception of power, India was the most logical and desired country for the United States to align itself with in the struggle to contain Soviet expansion in the region. However, the choice was not the Americans' to make. India's leaders considered Washington's analysis of the global communist threat to be in error and felt that the policy of containment was likely to cause more conflict than was necessary, insisting on remaining neutral in the East–West struggle.[93] At this juncture, US military planners made a major blunder. Instead of acknowledging India's crucial strategic importance in the region, they blindly turned to Pakistan in order to obtain any sort of military foothold in South Asia. This decision would have dramatic, long-term repercussions on relations between the United States and Afghanistan. The Pentagon reasoned that Pakistan, in spite of its conflict with India over the trauma of the partition, had some valuable strategic assets. Its geographic position commanded the second stage of the classic invasion route from Central Asia on to the Indian plains, and its western border reached the strategic oil region of the Persian Gulf. Washington perceived that a close working relationship with Pakistan, unlike Afghanistan, could make a significant contribution to securing these interests. Hence Pakistan was seen as a worthwhile candidate for partnership in containment.[94]

The evolution of US–Pakistan ties took place at a gradually accelerating pace from the partition of India in 1947 to the signing of a Mutual Defense Agreement in 1950, which was further strengthened in 1954. The United States remained neutral over the Indo-Pakistani dispute concerning the Kashmir Valley and urged cooperation between India, Pakistan and Afghanistan to promote collective security in South Asia. By 1949 US defence planners had begun to view Pakistan with more interest, noting that 'from the military point of view, the countries of South Asia excepting Pakistan have, under present and prospective conditions, little value to the United States. ... While the countries of South Asia, excepting Pakistan, are of negligible positive strategic importance to us, encroachments by the USSR would endanger our national policy of Communist containment ...'[95] It is unclear from this document why Afghanistan and India did not also interest the Joint Chiefs of Staff as being of 'positive strategic importance'. However, the key phrase in this document may in fact be 'under present and prospective conditions'. The rift between Pakistan and India, and India's solid stance on remaining neutral, explain why military planners were seeking alternative solutions to the problems of implementing containment in South Asia. However, it is unclear how an alliance with Pakistan would strengthen the US position in the region if such an alliance would push India into the arms of the Soviet Union.

The most important factor blocking Afghanistan's involvement in the US containment strategy in South Asia – and increasing US reluctance to provide arms – was the ongoing dispute between Afghanistan and Pakistan over the area known as 'Pushtunistan'. The history of this issue reaches back to the days of British domination in the region, and it is worthy of some detailed consideration given that the dispute has never been resolved and may even cause discord between Afghanistan and Pakistan during the twenty-first century. The Pushtunistan problem dates to the establishment of the Durand Line as the border between Afghanistan and the northern territory of British India in 1893. The border was drawn both for reasons of administrative convenience and strategic utility. However, the border survey that determined the basis for the Durand Line failed to consider the ramifications of artificially dividing the indigenous ethnic groups that populated the region. Subsequently, both the Baluch and Pushtun tribes were split in half by the arbitrary decisions of British nineteenth-century surveyors.[96]

The issue of Pushtunistan became one of the major planks in Afghanistan's postwar foreign relations. Afghanistan's leadership circles, dominated by men of ethnic Pushtun stock, began to press for the formation of a separate state of Pushtunistan shortly before the British withdrawal from India in 1947. The proposed state would extend from the Wakhan corridor in the northeast (bordering China) to the Arabian Sea in the south, covering the two provinces of North-West Frontier and Baluchistan as well as the free tribal territory (an area not defined by the Durand Line) and parts of Kashmir Valley. Its population in 1950 would have been approximately seven million (including 5.5 million Pushtuns) and would have covered an area of 190,000 square miles.[97] The new government of Pakistan adamantly refused to discuss any proposal that would have further eroded its already weak position in relation to India. In 1951 the US State Department took the ambiguous position of encouraging Afghanistan to settle its border dispute with Pakistan while promoting regional cooperation between India, Pakistan and Afghanistan in order to counter 'international communist gains'.[98] Simultaneously the United States condemned Afghanistan's demands regarding Pushtunistan, yet it conceded that negotiations were necessary. Furthermore, the United States added to the confusion by never publicly clarifying its position on Pushtunistan, even when requested to do so by the government of Pakistan.[99] However, the United States indicated to Pakistani officials its 'unofficial' view that the Durand Line constituted the legal boundary between Afghanistan and Pakistan.[100]

While stating its desire for negotiations on the Pushtunistan dispute, the 'unofficial' US position removed any real pressure on Pakistan to compromise with Afghanistan on the border issue. Realistically, it gave Pakistan no incentive to pursue sincere negotiations, and even encouraged the termination of negotiations when it became clear that the United States would support Pakistan's position if negotiations failed. The United States was hoping in vain for peace between the Afghans and the Pakistanis, who seemed more interested in their own national interests than the US anticommunist crusade. American diplomats were doubly hindered because the excessive idealistic rhetoric of containment had served to paint the United States into a diplomatic corner. Both Afghanistan and Pakistan were friendly toward the Americans and hostile toward the Soviet Union, and when the United States proposed on three occasions to help mediate the Pushtunistan dispute, Afghanistan accepted the offer. Pakistan, which contended that the matter was an internal one and not subject to mediation, rejected negotiations. The Americans were unable to pressure the Pakistanis on the issue of Pushtunistan, because they feared that Pakistan, if pushed too far, might follow India's policy of nonalignment, thereby threatening the military encirclement of the Soviet Union. In the end, Pakistan was simply thought to be a more important ally than Afghanistan, and the Afghans were left to conclude that the lofty ideals of containment were nothing more than hollow American rhetoric.

The United States also believed that any military assistance it might give to Afghanistan was more likely to be used against Pakistan than against the Soviet Union. Although this may have been an accurate assessment, it is also clear that Afghanistan could never have seriously threatened Pakistan with a small quantity of US arms. In retrospect, containment was revealed to be inadequate as a functional guidepost for strategic policy in the region. When complex problems such as Pushtunistan arose, the United States was forced to resort to classical balance-of-power thinking, in this case alienating Afghanistan, which saw US policies as being hypocritical, misleading and contradictory. It is now clear why the Afghan government condemned the terms of the 1951 arms sale as being a 'political refusal'. When Pakistan became aware of the publicly announced sale, it would certainly not have allowed the arms to be transported through its territory. There was the added indignity of requiring Afghanistan to pay cash for the weapons at a time when most US allies were receiving outright grants for arms or lenient repayment terms. Louis Dupree, the leading Western scholar on Afghanistan, summarizes how the Afghans viewed this situation:

The Afghans refused to participate in the Baghdad Pact, but asked the Americans once again for arms assistance to correct the upset 'balance of power' in the region. 'Why should America arm Pakistan?' government officials asked. 'Who will the Pakistanis use the arms against? Surely not the Russians, since Pakistan and the Soviet Union have no common boundary.' India had similar objections, and, in truth, Pakistan always considered India more an enemy than either the Soviet Union or the People's Republic of China.[101]

While continually hoping that some sort of cooperation could be formulated among the nations of South Asia, the United States blindly pursued its own military alliances with Pakistan, further alienating Afghanistan and India, both of which were more concerned with their own national interests and regional security matters than with the US fascination with a world communist threat.

Fundamentally, US policy toward Afghanistan in this period remained contingent on how Washington viewed the Soviet Union's ability to project power into Afghanistan. Despite Afghanistan's apparent willingness to increase ties with the West even to the point of abandoning neutrality, analysts in the United States decided that overt military aid to Afghanistan would increase the likelihood of a Soviet response. In such an event, the United States would not have been able to aid Afghanistan because of the immense logistical problems posed by the country's geographic isolation. For instance, in 1952, during a dispute between the Soviet Union and Afghanistan over the presence of a UN oil exploration team in northern Afghanistan, the US ambassador in Kabul told Washington that even if the US were to offer arms, Afghanistan's borders could not be guaranteed.[102]

In addition to its policy of denying weapons to the Afghan government, the United States provided only a meagre amount of non-lethal aid to Afghanistan from 1945 to 1955. Apart from financing Morrison-Knudsen's profits on the problematic Helmand Valley project, America limited its aid to foodstuffs and some technical assistance.[103] Thus, in addition to its frustration over the spurned arms requests, Afghanistan resented the amount and kinds of assistance it was receiving in comparison to Pakistan and Iran. By 1954 Pakistan had received $97 million in grain and $37 million in development assistance (fertilizers, mining and construction equipment, iron and steel materials, industrial machinery and railway equipment), while Afghanistan had received only $2.1 million in technical assistance and $2.6 million in grain. Technical assistance was concentrated in the provision of agricultural experts, foreign study for Afghans, vocational education, and teacher training.[104] In 1955 the US Congress authorized increased development assistance for the Third World, but Afghanistan was again passed up for political reasons regarding its border troubles with Pakistan.[105] After ten years of frustration, the Afghans had had enough. By 1955 it was clear from their perspective that Turkey, Iran and Pakistan would constitute the only valued assets in America's southern-tier strategy to contain the Soviet Union. Afghanistan was considered to be expendable.

Into the Soviet fold: Soviet–Afghan relations, 1939–56

The Soviet Union's temporary alliance with Germany before Hitler launched Operation Barbarossa caused tension in Soviet–Afghan relations because of the possibility of Soviet designs on British India – a possibility magnified by the large numbers of Soviet troops stationed along sections of the Afghan border. However, after Germany's attack on the Soviet Union the Soviet threat was greatly reduced. In the autumn of 1941 the Soviet and British governments sent urgent requests to the Afghan government for the expulsion of all Axis nationals except those on diplomatic missions. The Soviet minister in Kabul justified the Allied demands on the basis of the Afghan–Soviet Treaty of 1926. The Afghans were angry at the joint Anglo-Soviet request, knowing that they had in fact maintained strict neutrality and that their neutrality tended to favour the Allies. The Afghans felt that the abrasive treatment they were receiving was undeserved, and they did not appreciate being told what to do by their neighbours, regardless of how powerful they might be. However, the Afghan prime minister knew too that his country was in no position to challenge the British and the Russians. He decided that Afghanistan had no choice but to comply with the requests, whatever the eventual outcome of the war in Europe might be.[106] By the closing months of 1943 this had proved to be a wise decision; it was becoming evident that the Allies were slowly gaining an upper hand against the Axis powers. The Afghans, never ones to back a losing side in a political fight, began to regard the Soviet Union, Britain and India in a more favourable light. During the course of the war Afghanistan became increasingly dependent on British India, which, at considerable cost to its own limited resources, did everything possible to provide Afghanistan with supplies. Britain thus managed to keep Afghanistan neutral and out of the war.[107] Afghan neutrality during the war served the purposes of all parties, and in retrospect it seems that there was little that the Afghans could have accomplished in supporting the Axis powers, and they could have lost a great deal by confronting the British and Russians.

Like the growing interests of the United States in Vietnam after the Second World War, Soviet involvement in Afghanistan was directly related to the East–West power struggle. From the Soviet viewpoint, the United States initiated competition over Afghanistan by providing aid in 1945 for the construction of an extensive water management system in the Helmand Valley.[108] Peter Franck notes in his analysis of Afghanistan that '[i]n the wake of Western involvement in Afghanistan through growing aid programs, normalcy in Afghan–Russian relations did not prevail long. To the Soviet

Union, economic commitments in Afghanistan and elsewhere had political overtones as well. Certainly, in Soviet eyes, the rebuilding in 1947 by an American contractor of a modern high-speed road from the Pakistan border to the second-most-important business center of its neighbors had strategic importance.'[109] Franck's opinion of the motivation behind Soviet aid to Afghanistan was confirmed by the major architect of postwar Soviet policies toward the Third World: Nikita Khrushchev. In his memoirs, Khrushchev describes the rationale underlying Soviet foreign policy goals in Afghanistan:

> In its desire to encircle us with military bases, America threw itself all over a country like Afghanistan ... The Afghans asked us to help build several hundred kilometers of road near the Iranian border ... However, because Afghanistan didn't have railroads, such a highway would be a main artery, carrying the economic lifeblood of the country. The road also had great strategic significance because it would have allowed us to transport troops and supplies in event of war with Pakistan or Iran ... The amount of money we spent on gratuitous assistance to Afghanistan is a drop in the ocean compared to the price we would have had to pay in order to counter the threat of an American military base on Afghan territory ...[110]

It is important to note how Khrushchev's statement reveals the degree to which the motivations underlying Soviet policies actually mirror those of the United States. The primary impetus behind both sides' foreign aid policies was to deny the other influence and control over strategic nations of the Third World – in this case, a country that directly bordered on the Soviet homeland. Lenin's guiding *kto kovo* ethic was actively being engaged by Washington's policy of containment. Both national policies were expressions of zero-sum thinking, with Afghanistan being one of many prizes on the global chessboard.

Soviet influence in Afghanistan increased in the 1950s partly because of its support for Afghanistan on the issue of Pushtunistan. In 1950, when Pakistan denied Afghanistan transit rights for goods entering and exiting the country, the Soviet Union offered free transit rights and started supplying the Afghans with essential items under embargo by Pakistan.[111] The Soviet position was further enhanced by the US rejection of Afghan arms requests in 1948, 1951 and 1954.[112] Another flare-up of the Pushtunistan problem in 1955 again led to a closing of the Pakistan border, at which time the Soviets again provided essential imports such as gasoline and construction materials. However, even before the death of Stalin and the advent of new policies toward the Third World under Khrushchev, the Soviets and the Afghans were moving slowly ahead on economic relations. In July 1950 they signed a four-year barter agreement under which the Afghans agreed to exchange raw cotton and wool for Soviet petroleum, cloth, sugar and other commodities.

The Soviets also guaranteed a much higher rate of exchange than any Western nation for Afghanistan's limited variety of exports. The 1950 agreement was augmented by an offer to construct several large gasoline storage tanks and to take over oil explorations in northern Afghanistan from a Swedish company. By 1952 Soviet–Afghan trade had doubled, and for the first time the Afghans permitted the Soviet Union to establish a trade office in Kabul.[113]

In 1953 the Soviets advanced Afghanistan a $3.5 million credit for the construction of two grain silos, a flour mill, and a bakery under generous terms bearing a modest 3 per cent interest rate.[114] This effort was followed in July 1954 by a technical aid and credit agreement of $1.2 million for construction of a gasoline pipeline across the Amu Darya River, which served as the natural border with the Soviet Union. Both of these projects had clear implications for Afghanistan's ability to sustain itself (with Soviet assistance) in the event of future discord with Pakistan over Pushtunistan. In August 1954 the Soviets increased their popularity among the Kabul masses by agreeing to finance the paving of the capital city's streets. This project, which had previously been rejected twice by the US Export-Import Bank, turned out to be a major, low-cost public-relations victory for the Soviets.[115] In most instances the Soviet Union provided aid for the various projects that the United States had earlier denied.

In December 1955 Khrushchev and Premier Nikolai Bulganin stopped in Kabul as part of their tour of Asia. The Soviet leaders publicly supported Afghanistan for the first time: 'We sympathize with Afghanistan's policy on the question of Pushtunistan', said Bulganin. 'The Soviet Union stands for an equitable solution of this problem, which cannot be settled correctly without taking into account the vital interests of the people inhabiting Pushtunistan.'[116] During this visit the two governments signed a ten-year extension of a 1931 Afghan–Soviet Treaty of Non-Aggression.[117] In May 1956, six months after the Khrushchev/Bulganin visit, Soviet–Afghan relations entered a fundamentally new phase of increased diplomatic, economic and military relations. Afghanistan became one of the first Soviet targets of opportunity in the East–West competition for clients in the developing world. In a major escalation in the emerging aid war with the United States, the Soviets announced the gift of a 100-bed hospital, an Il-14 transport plane for King Zahir, and a loan of $100 million – with low interest and a thirty-year repayment schedule. This loan, which amounted to a tremendous sum for its day, produced three irrigation projects, one military and one civilian airport, two hydroelectric plants, a road maintenance plant, and a road over the rugged Hindu Kush with a tunnel that would connect northern and southern Afghanistan for the first time. By 1956 there were over 460 Soviet technicians in the country.[118]

After the final US rejection of Afghan arms requests in December 1954, Afghanistan, frustrated and with wounded pride, finally turned to the Soviet

Union. Military assistance from the Eastern bloc, mainly in the form of arms transfers, advisory support and training, began in 1955, with an agreement between Afghanistan and Czechoslovakia for $3 million in weapons. The first direct Soviet–Afghan arms agreement, signed in 1956, provided for the sale of $25 million-worth of military equipment, including MiG-15 jets. By 1965 the value of military equipment would stand at approximately $275 million, under repayment terms that required only 50 per cent reimbursement by the Afghans. This military equipment included 100 tanks and 100 airplanes. Over 200 Afghan military cadets had been sent to the Soviet Union for training by 1962, and during the period from 1953 to 1963 the Soviets had built or were building military airfields in Bagram, near Kabul; Mazar-i-Sharif in northern Afghanistan; and at Shindand in the central part of western Afghanistan.[119]

The US response

The Soviet–Afghan weapons agreement in 1955 caused significant concern in Washington over what appeared to be a changing balance of forces in the region. In 1956 the National Security Council agreed to 'encourage Afghanistan to minimize its reliance upon the Communist bloc for military training and equipment, and to look to the United States and other Free World sources for military training and assistance'.[120] Henry Bradsher, a noted journalist and author specializing in Soviet and Afghan affairs, provides a poignant critique of the US's change of heart: 'There was no detectable sense of irony in the secret NSC study, no reference to the repeated American spurning of Afghan military aid requests before the Soviet deal, no recognition of the effects of America's arming Pakistan, apparently no institutional memory of what had gone before.'[121] The United States also increased its economic development aid to Afghanistan in an attempt to compete with the massive Soviet aid package presented by Khrushchev in 1955. However, belated aid programmes could not compensate for the mismanagement and neglect that US relations with Afghanistan had suffered over the course of the previous decade. The Soviet Union had gained the upper hand in Afghanistan by 1956, and would slowly increase its dominant position over the next twenty-three years. As we will see in later chapters, in 1979 the Soviets invaded Afghanistan in order to prop up a faltering communist regime made up of political leaders and officers in the Afghan military who had been trained and equipped by the Soviet Union ever since 1955. Although the failure of US policy toward Afghanistan in the 1950s arguably cannot be directly blamed for the Soviet action in 1979, it is clear that US containment policy (or in this case the lack thereof) failed to restrain the growth of Soviet influence and power in Afghanistan at a time when the Afghans were virtually begging the Americans for help.

THE ORIGINS OF INTERVENTION: A FIRST COMPARISON

By 1956 the United States and the Soviet Union had both established relationships with Vietnam and Afghanistan that would eventually lead to the start of their respective military interventions in 1965 and 1979. Politics in both Vietnam and Afghanistan reflected generalized global trends of the postwar era, including competition and intervention on the part of the superpowers, the turbulent devolution of the European colonial system, and the rise of nationalist and national-liberation movements. However, in all of these elements events in Vietnam unfolded very differently from in Afghanistan. Although the Soviet Union's relationship with Afghanistan was enmeshed in a much deeper historical framework than that of the United States in Vietnam, the superpowers' policies toward Vietnam and Afghanistan in the first decade after the Second World War were shaped and motivated by the ideological superstructure of Cold War rivalry as it was manifested in the geopolitical world. Vietnam became important to the United States only in the context of the global power struggle between the communist East and the capitalist West, with issues related to France's role in the European security order and Japan's role in Asia the key motivating factors. Likewise, it should not be forgotten that US economic interests were of the utmost concern in the minds of policy-makers in Washington. Maintaining the growth of the US economy, already in a difficult transition away from the superheated military production of the Second World War, could only be achieved over the long term if there were export markets for the finished goods emerging from American factories. Because these goods (and the accumulated capital derived from the profit of their sale) could not be absorbed indefinitely at home, it was determined that US economic prosperity could only be achieved in a relatively free and open global trading order managed in Washington. Likewise, many of the resources needed to fuel the domestic industrial machine could only be obtained from abroad in the developing world. While it seems plausible that the United States did not wish to replace the Europeans in the role of imperialists, the economic rationale rooted within the containment doctrine was undeniably similar to that which had motivated the traditional colonial powers. Even though the US leadership seemed sincere in its anticolonialist rhetoric, the worst-case scenario would be the arrival in the ex-colonial areas of communists, who could then deny the Americans critical resources and markets, using those elements of power to their own advantage, thus threatening America. In sum, from the US perspective, its interwoven military security and economic security were threatened by the spread of what was then perceived as a monolithic socialist camp. With each territorial gain made by the communists, the United States, because of the political incompatibilities of the two systems, would lose both militarily and economically.[122]

Oddly, even though it was not perceived as such in Moscow, in making the final cost-benefit analysis the United States was willing to concede Afghanistan to the Soviets while at the same time it was willing to fight in Vietnam, where it was believed that with US power and leadership something akin to the Korea stalemate could be salvaged after the French withdrawal. The Soviet role in Afghanistan in the early phases of the Cold War was also driven by the wider global struggle over ideology, but because of its location as a border state on the Soviet frontier, Afghanistan was a higher-priority issue to the Kremlin than other more distant countries in the developing world. In this respect, Soviet national security interests in Afghanistan were driven more by geography than ideology, with the reverse being true for the United States in Vietnam. The Kremlin, which was well aware of the US plan to isolate it geographically by means of an extensive international military alliance network, took great pains to draw the Afghans away from the Americans. Ironically, the American decision to abandon Afghanistan to the Soviets was made with the hope that it would strengthen South Asian security. However, by focusing on Pakistan as its strategic partner, the United States drove both Afghanistan and India from their positions as true neutrals into postures of neutrality that were clearly slanted in the pro-Soviet direction. Even more ironic is the fact that the Soviets achieved their national interest objectives in Afghanistan by abandoning a public rhetorical strategy based purely on Marxism, succeeding instead by emphasizing the importance of the right of all peoples to national independence and freedom from colonialism – two issues that the United States thought itself to embody. In other words, the Soviets were able to seize the moral high ground in relations with Afghanistan after the United States had refused to accommodate Kabul within the stated rhetoric of containment.

Vietnam was marked by violence and civil war primarily because the solution to the European colonial question had not been determined. As discussed in Chapter 1, Afghanistan had established and maintained its nominal independence because of its unique geographic location as a buffer state between the British and Soviet empires. Thus, unlike in Vietnam, in Afghanistan the postwar debate had gone beyond concerns of political sovereignty to include discussion of the country's economic development, and how an independent and neutral Afghanistan would position itself in the newly emerging bipolar world after Britain's withdrawal from the sub-continent. Because of French insistence on re-establishing its prewar empire, the struggle for national independence in Vietnam was merged and later submerged with the growing global power struggle between East and West. Japan's wartime occupation of Vietnam had focused American attention on the region as being important to Asia, but France's importance to American containment plans in Europe had made Vietnamese independence expendable regardless of American distaste for colonialism. However, by the time the French colonial question in Vietnam had been settled at Dienbienphu, the politics of the Cold War had instigated a new form of struggle in Vietnam – the battle between the legitimation principles of American liberalism versus the legitimation principles of Soviet socialism.

In contrast, Afghanistan's national independence movement had triumphed at the end of the First World War, and unlike many national independence movements after the Second World War, Afghanistan's revolution against British domination was free of ideological factors. Vietnam, from the US perspective, was not simply a country seeking independence from colonial rule; it was also seen as a battleground between communism and democracy, where Vietnamese national independence under Ho Chi Minh was unacceptable because of his communist orientation. Because the colonial and national independence questions in Afghanistan had been settled before the beginning of the Cold War, initial superpower involvement was marked by peaceful economic and political competition. Put simply, there was no internal struggle in Afghanistan that the superpowers could easily exploit for their own gain. Ironically, the United States was willing to pour billions of dollars into a risky venture to stop communism in Vietnam, but ignored Afghanistan's pro-Western appeals, thereby providing Moscow with a relatively cheap and easy victory in the South Asian theatre of the Cold War.

During the period from 1945 to 1955 the United States and the Soviet Union perceived each other in markedly similar fashion. Both pursued foreign policies in terms of a zero-sum struggle in which one side's gain was automatically the other side's loss. The United States saw Vietnam as a crucial element in its global strategy of containment; Afghanistan clearly was not of equal importance. One useful explanation for this difference is that during the Cold War both superpowers perceived national interest primarily in terms of a reaction to the opposing side's actions. The United States viewed Vietnam as important only because communists were involved there. Before 1945 the United States had no overriding 'national interest' in Vietnam, yet after the Second World War, US national interests were believed to be threatened anywhere that the communists might be lurking (including Vietnam). Because communists were not involved in Afghanistan, the country was largely ignored by Washington. Only after the Soviet Union began its massive aid programme to Afghanistan in 1955 did the United States become concerned with the country. Likewise, the Soviet Union viewed Vietnam as important only because of French and American involvement. Both China and the Soviet Union urged the Viet Minh to compromise at Geneva because their own national interests would be served short of the goal of full independence. China could not afford another Korea-like war with the United States, and the Soviet Union was concerned with reducing France's involvement in the Western European alliance. As we will see in the coming chapters, the consequences of this approach to foreign policy were eventually harmful to different degrees to both superpowers. In essence, both the United States and the Soviet Union transferred to each other control over how they would define their national interests. As John Lewis Gaddis states, 'to define interests in terms of threats is, after all, to make interests a function of threats – interests will then expand or contract as the threats do'.[123] As a result, the Cold War in the Third World would be a battle over 'protecting' what turned out to be largely illusory interests.

NOTES

1. John Lewis Gaddis, *The Long Peace: Inquiries into the History of the Cold War* (New York: Oxford University Press, 1987). This criticism is made in Bruce Cumings, 'The Wicked Witch of the West is Dead: Long Live the Wicked Witch of the East', in Michael J. Hogan (ed.), *The End of the Cold War: Its Meaning and Implications* (Cambridge: Cambridge University Press, 1992) p. 87.
2. Douglas A. Borer, 'The Genesis of a Forgotten War: Containment in Afghanistan 1947–1956', *Comparative Strategy*, 11, 3 (July–Sept. 1992): 343–56.
3. Andrei S. Markovits and Mark Silverstein, 'Introduction: Power and Process in Liberal Democracies', in Andrei S. Markovits and Mark Silverstein (eds), *The Politics of Scandal: Power and Process in Liberal Democracies* (New York: Holmes & Meier, 1988) pp. 4–5.
4. This analysis was adopted from Theodore J. Lowi's synopsis of domestic political scandals. See 'Foreword', pp. vii–xii, in Markovits and Silverstein (eds), *Politics of Scandal*.
5. It should be noted that Party members could be judged by other Party members as having broken the law; however, no such judgemental power existed outside of the Party.
6. The exceptions were the transition from Khrushchev to Brezhnev in 1964, and Gorbachev to Yeltsin in 1991.
7. Douglas A. Borer, 'War Loss and Political Reform: An Ongoing Pattern in Russian History', *Studies in Conflict and Terrorism* 20, 4 (Oct.–Dec. 1997): 345–70.
8. Joseph Buttinger, *A Dragon Defiant: A Short History of Vietnam* (New York: Praeger, 1972) pp. 74–5.
9. Robert H. Miller, *The United States and Vietnam 1781–1941* (Washington, DC: National Defense University Press, 1981) p. 234.
10. Ibid.
11. US Department of State, *Foreign Relations of the United States*, Vol. IV, *The Far East* (Washington, DC: US Government Printing Office, 1941) pp. 723–5 (hereafter *FRUS*).
12. *The Pentagon Papers*, Gravel Edition (Boston: Beacon Press, 1971) Vol. 1, p. 9 (hereafter *PP*).
13. Ibid., pp. 14–15.
14. Ibid., p. 17.
15. Telegram from Acting Secretary of State Dean Acheson to Chargé Walter Robertson in China, 5 Oct. 1945. In Gareth Porter (ed.), *Vietnam: A History in Documents* (New York: Meridian, 1979) p. 38.

16. *PP*, Vol. 1, pp. 49–50.
17. Mark T. Berger and Douglas A. Borer, 'Introduction: The Rise of East Asia: Critical Visions of the Pacific Century', in Mark T. Berger and Douglas A. Borer (eds), *The Rise of East Asia: Critical Visions of the Pacific Century* (London: Routledge, 1997) pp. 3–9.
18. Andrew J. Rotter, *The Path to Vietnam: Origins of the American Commitment to Southeast Asia* (Ithaca: Cornell University Press, 1987); Lloyd C. Gardner, *Approaching Vietnam: From World War II Through Dienbienphu, 1941–1954* (New York: W. W. Norton, 1988).
19. Berger and Borer, 'Introduction: The Rise of East Asia', pp. 3–5. See also Gabriel Kolko, *Anatomy of A War: Vietnam, the United States, and the Modern Historical Experience* (New York: New Press, 2nd, expanded, edn, 1994; first published 1985) p. 545.
20. George Kennan, 'X', *Foreign Affairs*, 54 (July 1947): 566–82.
21. 'The Truman Doctrine', in *Documents of American History*, Vol. 2, ed. Henry S. Commager (New York: Appleton-Century-Crofts, 1968) pp. 524–6.
22. *PP*, Vol. 1, pp. 37–8. This quotation comes from NSC/48, 23 Dec. 1949.
23. Ibid., pp. 54–5.
24. *FRUS (France) 1950* (Washington, DC: Government Printing Office, 1976) Vol. 6, pp. 711–15.
25. William Conrad Gibbons, *The US Government and the Vietnam War: Executive and Legislative Roles and Relationships*, Part I: 1945–1960 (Princeton: Princeton University Press, 1986) pp. 82–3.
26. Ibid., p. 83.
27. Ibid., p. 84.
28. Ibid., p. 85.
29. *PP*, Vol. 1, p. 83.
30. Gibbons, *The US Government and the Vietnam War*, Part I, pp. 73–4.
31. Ibid., pp. 74–8. Despite the passage of the War Powers Resolution after the American defeat in the Vietnam War, American presidents have continued to send troops into combat without a declaration of war. Examples include President Reagan's invasion of Grenada (1983) and bombing of Libya (1986); President Bush's invasion of Panama (1990) and war against Iraq (1991).
32. *PP*, Vol. 1, p. 85.
33. Ibid., pp. 85–6.
34. Buttinger, *A Dragon Defiant*, p. 79.
35. Ibid., pp. 89–90.
36. Ibid., pp. 90–91.
37. Robert Shaplen, *The Lost Revolution: The US in Vietnam, 1946–1966* (New York: Harper & Row, 1966) p. 64. Cited in George C. Herring, *America's Longest War: The United States and Vietnam 1950–1975* (New York: John Wiley & Sons, 1979) pp. 14–15.
38. Ibid., p. 15.
39. *PP*, Vol. 1, pp. 86–7; Herring, *America's Longest War*, pp. 25–6.
40. Herring, *America's Longest War*, pp. 26–7.
41. *PP*, Vol. 1, pp. 95–6.
42. Ibid., p. 87.
43. Herring, *America's Longest War*, pp. 27–8.
44. Ibid., pp. 28–9.
45. Ibid.
46. *PP*, Vol. 1, p. 99.
47. Ibid., pp. 101–3.

48. Ibid., p. 103.
49. John P. Burke and Fred I. Greenstein, *How Presidents Test Reality: Decisions on Vietnam 1954 and 1965* (New York: Russell Sage Foundation, 1989) p. 93.
50. Ibid., p. 97.
51. Ibid.
52. *PP*, Vol. 1, pp. 174–8.
53. Herring, *America's Longest War*, p. 41.
54. *PP*, Vol. 1, pp. 166–72.
55. 'SRV (Socialist Republic of Vietnam) Foreign Ministry's White Book on SRV–PRC Relations, 4 Oct. 1979', in *Foreign Broadcast Information Service Daily Report: Asia and the Pacific*, Vol. 5, no. 204, 19 Oct. 1979. Hereafter cited as *FBIS*.
56. *PP*, Vol. 1, pp. 172–3.
57. Peter A. Poole, *The United States and Indochina from FDR to Nixon* (Huntington: Robert E. Krieger, 1976) pp. 39–41.
58. Ibid., p. 181.
59. *PP*, Vol. 1, pp. 180–84.
60. These included the Binh Xuyen, an organized crime syndicate; the Cao Dai, an eclectic religious sect that controlled much of the territory west of Saigon; and the Hoa Hao, a reformed Buddhist sect that was strong in the southern tip of Vietnam. See Poole, *The United States and Indochina from FDR to Nixon*, p. 40.
61. Herring, *America's Longest War*, pp. 47–55.
62. *PP*, Vol. 1, pp. 245.
63. Walter C. Clemens Jr, *Can Russia Change? The USSR Confronts Global Interdependence* (Boston: Unwin Hyman, 1990) p. xix.
64. Ibid., pp. 24–5.
65. Douglas Pike, *Vietnam and the Soviet Union: Anatomy of an Alliance* (Boulder, CO: Westview Press, 1987) p. 22.
66. Allan W. Cameron, 'The Soviet Union and Vietnam: The Origins of Involvement', in W. Raymond Duncan (ed.), *Soviet Policy in Developing Countries* (Waltham: Ginn-Blaisdell, 1970) p. 178.
67. Harold Isaacs, *No Peace for Asia* (Cambridge, MA: MIT Press, 1947) pp. 172–3.
68. Ibid., p. 173.
69. Pike, *Vietnam and the Soviet Union*, p. 31.
70. Nikita Khrushchev, *Khrushchev Remembers*, trans. and ed. Strobe Talbott (Boston: Little, Brown, 1970) p. 481.
71. Pike, *Vietnam and the Soviet Union*, pp. 34–5.
72. Ibid., p. 38.
73. Khrushchev, *Khrushchev Remembers*, pp. 481–2.
74. Ibid., p. 482.
75. Much of this material appeared in Borer, 'The Genesis of a Forgotten War', pp. 343–56.
76. Leon B. Poullada, 'The Road to Crisis 1919–1980: American Failures, Afghan Errors and Soviet Successes', in Rosanne Klass (ed.), *Afghanistan: The Great Game Revisited* (New York: Freedom House, 1987) p. 40.
77. Vartan Gregorian, *The Emergence of Modern Afghanistan: Politics of Reform and Modernization 1880–1946* (Stanford: Stanford University Press, 1953) pp. 390–91.
78. Poullada, 'The Road to Crisis 1919–1980', p. 40.
79. Gregorian, *The Emergence of Modern Afghanistan*, pp. 390–92.
80. *New York Times*, 9 Aug. 1946: 5.

81. Henry S. Bradsher, *Afghanistan and the Soviet Union*, 2nd edn (Durham: Duke University Press, 1985) p. 19.
82. Ibid., p. 18.
83. NSC/14/1: 'The Position of the United States with Respect to Providing Military Assistance to Nations of the Non-Soviet World', 10 July 1948 (Extract). *US–South Asian Relations 1947–1982*, Vol. 2, ed. Rajaendra K. Jain (Atlantic Highlands: Humanities Press, 1983) p. 11. Hereafter cited as *US–SA*.
84. *FRUS, 1948*, Vol. 5, p. 491–3.
85. Bradsher, *Afghanistan and the Soviet Union*, p. 19.
86. *FRUS, 1949*, Vol. 6, p. 777.
87. 'Memorandum from Assistant Secretary of State McGhee to Lloyd Berkner, Co-ordinator for Foreign Military Assistance Programmes, 16 August 1949' (Extracts). Cited in *FRUS*, Vol. 6, pp. 45–7.
88. *The Declassified Documents 1979 Collection* (Washington, DC: US Government Printing Office, 1979), no. 33A. Cited in Bradsher, *Afghanistan and the Soviet Union*, p. 20.
89. Leon B. Poullada, 'Afghanistan and the United States: The Crucial Years', *The Middle East Journal*, 35 (1981): 186.
90. 'The Position and Actions of the United States with respect to Possible Further Soviet Moves in Light of the Korean Situation', Report by the National Security Council, 25 Aug. 1950. Cited in *FRUS, 1950*, Vol. 1, *National Security Affairs: Foreign Economic Policy* (1977) pp. 376–87.
91. Bradsher, *Afghanistan and the Soviet Union*, p. 20.
92. Poullada, 'Afghanistan and the United States', pp. 186–7.
93. W. Howard Wriggins, 'US Interests in South Asia and the Indian Ocean', in Lawrence Ziring (ed.), *The Subcontinent in World Politics: India, Its Neighbors, and the Great Powers* (New York: Praeger, 1982) p. 208.
94. Ibid.
95. Memorandum of the Joint Chiefs of Staff, 24 March 1949. Cited in *FRUS, 1949*, Vol. 1, pp. 30–31.
96. G.S. Bhargava, *South Asian Security after Afghanistan* (Lexington, MA: Lexington Books, 1983) pp. 69–70.
97. Ibid., pp. 25–7.
98. Department of State Policy Statement with regard to Afghanistan, 21 Feb. 1951. Cited in *FRUS, 1951*, Vol. 1, part 2, *Asia and the Pacific* (Washington, DC: 1977) pp. 2008–9.
99. Acheson's telegram to the Embassy in Pakistan on Afghan–Pakistani differences, 28 Nov. 1950. Cited in *FRUS, 1950*, Vol. 5, p. 1455.
100. Ibid.
101. Louis Dupree, *Afghanistan* (Princeton: Princeton University Press, 1980) p. 510.
102. Joseph J. Collins, *The Soviet Invasion of Afghanistan: A Study in the Use of Force in Soviet Foreign Policy* (Lexington, MA: Lexington Books, 1986) p. 19.
103. Technical cooperation was extended to Afghanistan under President Truman's Point Four programme. An agreement was signed between the two countries in Kabul on 7 February 1951. See Nake Kamrany, *Peaceful Competition in Afghanistan: American and Soviet Models for Economic Aid* (Washington, DC: Communication Service Corp., 1963) pp. 24–5.
104. Peter Franck, *Afghanistan Between East and West* (Washington, DC: National Planning Association, 1960) pp. 43–4.

105. Ibid., p. 44.
106. Cyriac Maprayil, *Britain and Afghanistan in Historical Perspective* (London: Cosmic Press, 1983) pp. 82–3.
107. Ibid., pp. 84–5.
108. Dupree, *Afghanistan*, pp. 482–5.
109. Franck, *Afghanistan Between East and West*, p. 9.
110. Khrushchev, *Khrushchev Remembers*, pp. 298–300.
111. Donald N. Wilber, *Afghanistan* (New Haven, CT: Hraf Press, 1962) p. 184.
112. Bradsher, *Afghanistan and the Soviet Union*, pp. 19–20.
113. Dupree, *Afghanistan*, pp. 493–4.
114. Franck, *Afghanistan Between East and West*, p. 37.
115. Anthony Arnold, *Afghanistan: The Soviet Invasion in Perspective*, 2nd edn (Stanford: Hoover Institution Press, 1985) p. 34.
116. N.A. Bulganin, and N.S. Khrushchev, *Speeches During Sojourn in India, Burma and Afghanistan, November–December 1955* (New Delhi: 1956) p. 175, cited in Bradsher, *Afghanistan and the Soviet Union*, p. 25.
117. Wilber, *Afghanistan*, p. 185.
118. Collins, *The Soviet Invasion of Afghanistan*, p. 21.
119. Ibid., p. 23.
120. 'Note by the Executive Secretary to the National Security Council on U.S. Policy South Asia', 7 December 1956, *Declassified Documents Quarterly Catalog* 5 (Jan.–March, 1979): 44B. Cited in Bradsher, *Afghanistan and the Soviet Union*, p. 28.
121. Bradsher, *Afghanistan and the Soviet Union*, p. 28.
122. With the benefit of hindsight in the 1990s, we can see that this rationale was incorrect. The territories occupied by the Soviet Union in Eastern Europe were more burden than boon, and Soviet support for allied regimes in the developing world were more costly than its economy could bear.
123. John Lewis Gaddis, *Strategies of Containment: A Critical Appraisal of Postwar American National Security Policy* (New York: Oxford University Press, 1982) p. 98.

3

From Containment to Detainment:
The United States in Vietnam (1956–65) and
the Soviet Union in Afghanistan (1956–79)

From 1956 to 1965 the American commitment in Vietnam steadily increased to the point where President Lyndon Johnson decided that only direct involvement by US combat troops could save the South Vietnamese government from being overthrown by the communist forces of Ho Chi Minh. Likewise, in 1979 the Soviet intervention in Afghanistan was designed to protect a fledgling pro-Soviet communist regime in Kabul that had seized power less than a year earlier. In both interventions the superpowers blamed 'outside' aggression for undermining the stability of their clients, and both superpowers publicly claimed that without such interference their allies could govern independently. In doing so they asserted that the governments on whose behalf they were intervening were legitimate governments and thus legally entitled to and morally worthy of military and political assistance.

This chapter will compare the similarities and differences in how direct military intervention came to pass in Vietnam and Afghanistan. In Vietnam, the United States provided ever-increasing economic, military and political support to the South Vietnamese government from 1956 to 1965. Despite massive US assistance, totalling over $3.6 billion[1] from 1953 to 1965, the political stability of the southern regime remained fragile throughout the Eisenhower, Kennedy and Johnson administrations. On 6 March 1965 President Johnson ordered 3,500 Marines to Da Nang to defend a US air base there. It was the beginning of Johnson's fateful decision to make Vietnam's civil war America's own. In Afghanistan, a highly different sequence of events led to the Soviet invasion in December 1979. From 1956 to 1978 both the Soviet Union and United States provided a substantial amount of economic aid to Afghanistan. However, the country was not in a condition of a civil war, and it was not considered to be an active theatre in the Cold War. In April 1978 a Marxist-led palace coup toppled the traditional ruling family in Afghanistan. Less than two years later the Soviet politburo had decided that its newest brethren in the 'Socialist Commonwealth' would not survive without direct assistance from the Red Army. On 24 December 1979 General Secretary Brezhnev ordered 5,000 paratroopers into the Afghan capital. It was a decision which, when reversed a decade later by General Secretary Gorbachev, would signal the beginning of the downfall of the Soviet empire.

In this chapter the analysis of American involvement in Vietnam will be broken down along lines of the presidential administrations of Eisenhower, Kennedy and Johnson. Likewise, the Soviet involvement in Afghanistan will be separated into the Khrushchev and Brezhnev years. The policy decisions of the two superpowers will be analysed both in the focused context of events in Vietnam and Afghanistan, but also in the context of the wider international environment in which the Americans and the Soviets were operating. In this chapter I will focus the analysis on the concept of containment, arguing that it is a useful term for capturing the motivation of both superpowers' foreign policies. Just as the United States sought to contain what it perceived as communist aggression in Vietnam, the Soviet Union sought to contain what it viewed as capitalist aggression in Afghanistan. However, using the concept of political legitimacy as a tool for evaluating the superpowers' rationale for intervention, I will argue that in both cases, containment is a misnomer. Vietnam and Afghanistan, rather than being true candidates for assistance under the moral and legal rationale of containment, were more the targets of superpower policies of 'detainment' – a term I use to reconceptualize the Cold War in Vietnam and Afghanistan more precisely.

THE SUPERPOWERS IN VIETNAM, 1956–65

The Eisenhower years

In 1956 the United States had assumed total responsibility from France for the survival of a non-communist state in South Vietnam. The period from 1956 to 1958 was characterized by cautious optimism about President Diem's chances for building a new nation in partitioned Vietnam, similar to Syngman Rhee's success in South Korea. In both North and South Vietnam the process of 'nation-building' proved to be a formidable task, and so the struggle between Hanoi and Saigon was deflated in this period as the new governments attempted to stabilize their new positions and create new and loyal polities on opposite sides of the 17th parallel. The outwardly positive side of Diem's early rule was a result of a massive infusion of American aid. American assistance prevented an economic collapse in the South, but it did little to promote basic economic development or to improve the living standards of the average rural peasant. In both the North and the South a successful programme of land reform was the key to winning the support of Vietnam's agrarian people, who constituted 90 per cent of the population. In the North agriculture was forcibly collectivized, and although brutal and ineffective in its early years, by the end of the 1950s the North had begun to progress economically and had gained relative independence from its communist patrons in the People's Republic of China (PRC) and the Soviet Union. In the South, Diem's regime became increasing dependent on US economic assistance, and American aid created an illusion of economic vitality. The aid programme that was instituted was based on the relatively successful US containment policy in Europe and Korea. However, applying a similar containment strategy in Vietnam was a transfer of incompatible policy analogy. In Europe, where containment was conceived and first implemented, the economic, social and political systems were already established, even though they needed massive rebuilding aid. Containment in Europe thus could be a workable mixture of military security (as manifested in the North Atlantic Treaty Organization (NATO)) and economic assistance (as provided by the Marshall Plan), both of which would help to create and foster legitimacy for pro-US regimes. In Korea, where there had been a traditional cross-border military invasion by Northern communist forces, the primary role of UN–US intervention was to provide military security, with the domestic political base largely stable and policeable by South Korean authorities. In Vietnam, however, the circumstances were entirely different from those in Western Europe or Korea. French colonial rule had prevented the development of indigenous economic and political institutions that could be protected through military force. The real battle for Vietnam, then, was never easily defined by such targets as borders, invasion routes, or cities; rather it was the struggle for the loyalty of the Vietnamese population and for who would hold the Mandate of Heaven of Vietnamese nationalism.[2]

In order to maintain domestic support in the United States, the politics of nation-building in the South during the Eisenhower years were marked by illusory democratic reforms in South Vietnam. In March 1956 the South Vietnamese selected an assembly to write a constitution for the Republic of Vietnam (RVN). The election was largely a repetition of Diem's first bogus foray into democracy, and all candidates with any support outside of the ruling government were disqualified from running. While some Americans naïvely assumed that Diem shared their political values, many agreed with Secretary of State Dulles's opinion that it was enough for Diem to be 'competent, anti-Communist and vigorous'.[3] This proved to be absolutely wrong, not only in regard to the governance of Vietnam but also in the façade of lies that the US government would present to its own people for the next decade – a façade that would eventually be blown down by domestic protest and turmoil in America.

Thus, the RVN was a democratic state in name only. Diem and his close circle of family advisers ruled an authoritarian regime every bit as repressive as that of the communist North, and they conceived of themselves as founders of a new Vietnamese dynasty laying claim to the Mandate of Heaven. With the assistance of his brothers Nhu and Ngo Dinh Can, President Diem dominated all branches of the decision-making process and ruled through a network of agents, informants and assassins. By the spring of 1956 approximately 20,000 people had been arrested as communist sympathizers. The only significant 'reform' enacted by the government in the 1950s further alienated the regime from the rural population, which traditionally governed itself on matters of local concern. In an attempt to centralize political power Diem abolished local elections for village leaders and appointed loyal outsiders to govern the countryside. Newspapers that dared criticize the government were shut down, and any anti-government activity was countered with government violence.[4]

Diem's success at imposing a police state in the South was a direct result of American collusion. Ironically, in October 1954 President Eisenhower had offered direct aid to South Vietnam on the condition that Saigon institute a programme of economic, social and political reforms. However, when these reforms failed to materialize in Diem's government, and when political conditions in fact worsened, the Eisenhower administration chose not to enforce its demands for reform. This was due in part to Washington's view that stability was more important than reform, seemingly unaware that Diem's 'reforms' were planting the seeds for rebellion rather than simply keeping order. Diem's building of an authoritarian state was made possible in that the bulk of American assistance to the RVN was in the form of military equipment and training. From 1956 to 1960, 78 per cent of US aid went into the RVN's military budget, and this figure did not include direct equipment transfers and police training. In this period only two per cent of American aid went into health, community development and housing programmes.[5]

Internally in South Vietnam, the war never truly ended for the anti-French peasants despite the agreement by the great powers at the Geneva conference, though in the countryside peace did prevail as the domestic insurgency was greatly reduced until the latter half of 1957. Faced with constant pressure by Diem's agents, however, the Viet Minh slowly reconstituted itself and resumed the armed struggle, this time against a repressive Vietnamese regime that was not perceived to hold the Mandate of Heaven. The renewal of civil warfare in the South was by most accounts (including that of the US government) undertaken without direction or coordination from the communist North. Peasants who made up the bulk of the former Viet Minh were acting on their own initiative with the immediate goal of self-preservation. As reported in the *Pentagon Papers*, the Government of Vietnam (GVN) was responsible for the rebellion in the territory south of the 17th parallel:

> First, with respect to the stay-behinds [Viet Minh who did not go north in 1954] themselves, by no means were all dedicated communists ... Many reported that they feared the communists ... and apparently

might have been willing to serve the GVN faithfully had it not hounded them out of society ... Second, with regard to the peasants in general, the Viet Minh were widely admired throughout the south as national heroes, and the GVN committed a tactical error of the first magnitude in damning all Viet Minh without qualification as communists. Third, the GVN created by its rural policy a climate of moral indignation which energized the peasants politically, turned them against the government, sustained the Viet Cong, and permitted 'communists' to outlast severe GVN repression and even to recruit during it.[6]

This is a telling document which accurately foreshadows the fundamental legitimacy problem that rotted the core of Diem's regime. Diem indeed claimed the Mandate of Heaven, but he could never convince the true source of traditional legitimacy, the Vietnamese people, that he deserved to hold that title.

Using the same tactics that had enabled them to succeed against the French during the first Indochina war, the Viet Minh formed a new coalition of anti-government forces, which the Diem regime labelled with the pejorative term 'Viet Cong' (Vietnamese Communists). The Viet Minh were encouraged by widespread support in the countryside, and in 1958 they increased the level of political agitation and began a vigorous anti-government terror campaign.[7] In contrast to subsequent US government statements to the American public that the South was a constant victim of northern aggression, in truth the insurgency in the South was not given public support by Hanoi until 1959 – a fact recorded in secret US government documents that would later help to delegitimize the war in minds of Americans. By 1959 it was clear to the Viet Minh that Diem would never hold democratic elections to reunify the country as agreed in Geneva, and that the indigenous rebellion in the South was at serious risk of being crushed by the onslaught of US-armed government forces. In 1960 the leadership in North Vietnam organized the National Liberation Front (NLF) to coordinate military operations between North and South. Like the Viet Minh, the NLF leadership was composed mostly of communists, but it sought to unify all anti-Diem forces by playing down ideology and emphasizing a nationalist-independence call to arms with the goal of unifying the country.[8]

By the end of 1960 Americans in Saigon were greatly alarmed by the strength of the insurgency and the growing inability of the South Vietnamese government to cope with the political crisis. Diem had reacted to the rebellion with policies that further eroded his position in both the cities and the rural areas. Peasants were forced to relocate to areas where government troops could 'protect' them from the NLF. After being provided with a small sum (US $5.50) that did not cover the replacement cost of their land, peasants were forced to work on community projects without compensation. The primary damage, however, lay in the deep resentment created in the peasants by being forced to abandon the villages that contained the sacred tombs of their ancestors.[9] A final point that underscores the reality that Diem's regime was in danger of collapse from its own erroneous policies is the change in US military training programmes. Before 1960 US training had focused on preparing the South Vietnamese to counter a conventional cross-border attack from the North. However, by 1960 it was clear that troops infiltrating from the North were a minor problem compared with the indigenous Southern rebellion. New programmes for counter-insurgency and anti-guerrilla operations were formulated by the Pentagon, and ongoing training programmes were reoriented. Simultaneously, Diem was gently (and unsuccessfully) urged to reform his policies and open his government to more democratic means.[10] Hence it is clear that by 1960 the underlying motivation of US involvement in Vietnam – the 'containment' of communist aggression from the North – had been altered. In 1960 US policy began to be transformed from one of assisting an allied regime to repel outside aggression by an ideological enemy, into one of propping up a dictatorial regime that had little popular support.

During much of its last year, the Eisenhower administration was also concerned with other pressing regional and international matters. Events both in neighbouring Laos and the Cold War in general were considered to be more pressing than Diem's recalcitrance in Vietnam. In 1960 US–Soviet relations were under heavy strain. After Fidel Castro's successful pro-Soviet revolution in Cuba, the U-2 incident involving Gary Powers, which caused an abrupt ending of the Paris summit meeting between Eisenhower and Khrushchev, and a new flare-up over Berlin, all combined to intensify America's singularly rigid Cold War mentality. In Laos, as in Vietnam, the United States used covert action in an attempt to stymie the implementation of the Geneva Accords. The neutralist regime of Souvanna Phouma resigned after US aid, on which the Laotian government had become highly dependent, was cut off. To the United States, any dealings with the communist Pathet Lao were unacceptable, even though the coalition government (including right, left and centre factions) was pro-Western. With the backing of the CIA, General Phoumi Nosavan, the right-wing leader of the Royal Army, assumed power and began a programme to combat communism. Phoumi jailed the leader of the Pathet Lao, Prince Souphanouvong, and denounced the Geneva Accords while seeking unrestricted US military aid. Both the Chinese and the Soviets denounced the United States as civil war erupted in Laos in May 1960, and both began to supply aid to the Pathet Lao. The State Department issued public warnings about the crisis, and the Pentagon announced that troops were being readied in case intervention was ordered by the president.[11]

The convoluted Laotian situation was one of the many Cold War foreign policy problems that President Eisenhower turned over to his successor, John F. Kennedy. In a pre-inaugural briefing Kennedy was warned that the fall of Laos would threaten the rest of the vulnerable 'dominoes' in Southeast Asia – Thailand, Cambodia and South Vietnam. The Eisenhower legacy was a mixed one indeed. The president, conditioned by his experience of the Second World War and the Korean War, had continually drawn the bottom line in Vietnam at the level of multilateral intervention. And history will always show that Eisenhower had kept the United States out of direct military intervention in Vietnam. Nevertheless, he warned Kennedy that if the SEATO allies could not be convinced to participate, then the United States might have to go it alone in combating communism in the region.

Despite the lack of a military commitment to Vietnam, the Eisenhower legacy was one whose importance is more perceptual than tangible, a legacy 'rich in rhetoric and momentum' that made it difficult if not impossible for future American politicians to deviate from the course he had established.[12] Eisenhower's repeated use of the domino images became the foundation of an accepted and unduly simplified mindset in which all communists came from the same mould, all communists were fundamentally evil, all communists were implacably hostile, and all communists were a direct threat to the American people. In consequence, the domestic politics in Vietnam became part and parcel of a worldwide US national-interest commitment to blocking communism everywhere. Backing away from such a commitment in the rice paddies of Southeast Asia would be seen as a green light for aggression by communists in Japan and Europe – areas conceived of as vital American interests. As a result of these domino-imagery linkages, the areas now vital to American interests were broadened to a scope never before seen in US foreign policy. Any future US president would face two options: either accept and perpetuate the symbolic imagery of the domino theory – which, to judge from Eisenhower's two terms in office, the American electorate had accepted as truth, in large part because of the public's fundamental trust in their president's veracity; or attempt to argue against this powerful imagery by using a more sophisticated, less emotive and more ideologically compromised verbal strategy. However, from the time of the Truman administration through the last intense period of the Cold War during the Reagan administration, those who would argue with logic instead of simplistic imagery proved time and again to be on the losing side in American domestic politics. In short, by the end of his administration, Eisenhower had staked America's international credibility on fighting communism in Vietnam, even though he had not committed troops there. Any future US president who failed to uphold that commitment would be vulnerable to the criticism of 'losing Vietnam' and being 'soft on communism'.

On a more structural level the Eisenhower legacy was important to future events in three areas, two of which were internal to Vietnam. First, the South

Vietnamese economy and armed forces had become totally dependent on US assistance programmes. The communist's pejorative label for the Southern regime as 'My-Diem' (translated as US-Diem) was not only descriptively accurate but also a politically effective tool in undermining support for the Southern regime. Because of his close association with the Americans, Diem was seen by many Southerners as the latest in a long line of puppets controlled by foreigners. In contrast, Ho Chi Minh, the Viet Minh and the Viet Cong were all seen by the rural masses as nationalist patriots rather than communists, and hence as having a far more legitimate claim to the Mandate of Heaven than did Diem. Second, the Eisenhower administration had created the administrative framework that would allow for rapidly expanded levels of US commitment. In direct violation of the Geneva Accords Eisenhower had doubled the permitted number of military personnel in the Military Assistance Advisory Group (MAAG). The command structure created on the ground by MAAG would continue to grow as Eisenhower's successors used it to funnel increasing numbers of American advisory and support personnel into Vietnam. Third, with the creation of SEATO, the Eisenhower administration had created the international institutional rubric to make the case for direct US military intervention under international law. The NATO model was apparently serving European containment well and therefore was seen to be applicable to Southeast Asia. SEATO was created to 'deter aggression', but it would later serve as the mechanism for intervention in what was primarily a civil war in Vietnam.[13]

The Kennedy administration

Upon taking office in January 1961, John F. Kennedy inherited both the problems and the growing momentum toward US intervention in Vietnam established by his predecessor. In his inaugural address, Kennedy signalled the beginning of a more aggressive and activist US foreign policy that would raise the likelihood of military actions against communism everywhere. The new president promised, 'We shall pay any price, bear any burden, meet any hardship, support any friend, oppose any foe to assure the survival and success of liberty.'[14] In doing so the Kennedy rhetoric recommitted the power of the United States to worldwide containment of communism, making Vietnam a likely battleground for American resolve. However, building on the momentum established by President Eisenhower, Kennedy seemed even more willing to escalate the US commitment to Vietnam in pledging: 'To those new states whom we welcome to the ranks of the free, we pledge our word that one form of colonial control shall not have passed away merely to be replaced by a far more iron tyranny.' American assistance to those trying to 'help themselves' would continue 'for whatever period is required, not because the Communists may be doing it … but because it is right'.[15] In making this pledge Kennedy was speaking to the hearts of the American nation, with its myths and traditions of egalitarian idealism, democratic values and commitment to justice. In doing so he added an additional layer of simplifying obfuscation to the more complex realities of politics in the developing world, reducing any rationale for American commitments abroad to a simple matter of the forces of good doing battle with the forces of evil. Since communism had already been equated with evil, any regime pledging itself to anticommunism was by definition conceived of as good, just and democratic – or at least this was the message the US government would feed to its masses. Thus the seeds of the coming legitimacy crisis first planted by Eisenhower in Vietnam were given further nourishment by President Kennedy.

Kennedy's involvement with Vietnam predated his presidency. As a US senator in 1955 he joined the influential organization American Friends of Vietnam (AFV). His initial perception of the country was laid out in a 1956 speech to the AFV entitled 'America's Stake in Vietnam', which contained the following major points:

(1) Vietnam represents the cornerstone of the Free World in Southeast Asia, the keystone in the arch, the finger in the dike. Burma, Thailand, India, Japan, the Philippines and obviously Laos and Cambodia are among those whose security would be threatened if the red tide of Communism overflowed into Vietnam.

(2) Vietnam represents a proving ground for democracy in Asia. However we may choose to ignore it or deprecate it, the rising prestige and influence of Communist China in Asia are unchangeable facts. Vietnam represents the alternative to Communist dictatorship. If this democratic experiment fails ... then weakness, not strength, will characterize the meaning of democracy in the minds of still more Asians. The United States is directly responsible for this experiment ... We cannot afford to permit that experiment to fail.

(3) Vietnam represents a test of American responsibility in Asia. If we are not the parents of little Vietnam then surely we are the godparents ... This is our offspring, we cannot abandon it ... And if it falls victim to any of the perils that threaten its existence – Communism, political anarchy, poverty and the rest – then the United States, with some justification, will be held responsible; and our prestige in Asia will sink to a new low.

(4) America's stake in Vietnam, in her strength and security, is a very selfish one – for it can be measured, in the last analysis, in terms of American lives and American dollars ... the key position of Vietnam

in Southeast Asia, as already discussed, makes inevitable the involvement of this nation's security in any new outbreak of trouble ...[16]

Clearly, Kennedy's views were very similar to his predecessor's. He believed in containment as a policy applicable on a global scale, he supported the validity of the domino theory, and he was convinced that US credibility in Asia was contingent on holding the line in Vietnam. Thus, the ghost of 'losing China' echoed loudly in the new president's assessment of Vietnam. However, Kennedy also was willing to go much further than his predecessors in stating that Vietnam was already essentially a democratic country and that the future of democracy itself was at stake. By forsaking Vietnam, the United States would be guilty of abandoning its own ideals in a country for which the president believed America was responsible. In portraying Vietnam as blood-kin to the US 'family', Kennedy further aggregated the emotional bonds while simultaneously obscuring the vast gulf separating the two nations' cultural and historical experiences. Finally, Kennedy entrenched the notion that the security of the United States itself was tied directly to that of Vietnam: US security was the same as Vietnam's security. Therefore, if communist aggression increased in Vietnam south of the 17th parallel, America was morally obligated to protect its child. In very publicly espousing the position that renewed civil war in Vietnam would inevitably mandate American involvement, Kennedy had further committed US prestige and credibility to the outcome of Vietnam's civil war.

With these basic perceptions entrenched in his mind, President Kennedy acted to expand US involvement in Vietnam only days after taking office. However, at the time, compared to other areas, Vietnam was not seen as a high-priority trouble spot on the president's foreign-policy agenda.[17] Like Eisenhower before him, at the time Kennedy considered ongoing events in Laos and their relation to the high-stakes game with the Soviet Union to be of greater concern on the regional and global level than the situation in Vietnam. In one of the first major decisions of his administration, Kennedy announced in March 1961 that the United States was willing to negotiate a settlement on Laos that would guarantee its neutrality. The minimum aim in Laos was defined as preventing communist forces from controlling the heavily populated lowland areas in western Laos, thus preventing the Laotian communist domino from subsequently toppling into Thailand. Kennedy's policy, which amounted to a *de facto* partition of the country, was intended to convince Soviet leaders that the US government could be both firm and reasonable, and that further steps might be taken to reduce Cold War tensions.[18] Soviet Premier Khrushchev's January 1961 speech declaring the Soviet Union's policy of supporting 'wars of national liberation' among peoples in the colonial areas had greatly intensified American fears of communist subversion in Indochina (and everywhere). Khrushchev's militant speech, which many analysts have suggested was aimed more as a warning to the Chinese than to the Americans, made a 'conspicuous impression' on President Kennedy.[19] Combined with increased Soviet aid to Cuba and to insurgents in the Congo and Laos, the speech created a lasting suspicion among Americans of all indigenous rebellions. Holding the line in Vietnam was also given higher priority after the Bay of Pigs fiasco in April 1961.

Kennedy's Laotian gambit quickly crumbled. Like Afghanistan, Laos, as a landlocked country bordering on China and North Vietnam, was judged to be a poor choice for an American military commitment. At the time, any US effort to save Laos was made doubly problematic by the political difficulty in explaining why communism on America's doorstep in Cuba did not justify sending American forces, while a remote country in the jungles of Southeast Asia was worth fighting for. However, after acquiescing to communist gains in both Cuba and Laos, containment policies in Vietnam were moved up on Kennedy's agenda. Events in Germany also stiffened the president's resolve to escalate events in Asia when in August 1961 the Soviets constructed the concrete wall that sealed off East Berlin from the western zones. Under increased domestic pressure from hard-line Republicans, any consideration to negotiate on Vietnam was shelved. While admitting the dangers of increased commitment in Vietnam, Kennedy concluded that in cases in which the United States had shown strength and determination it had 'come home free'.[20]

Despite his apparent willingness to escalate American involvement, Kennedy, much in the mould of Truman and Eisenhower, chose a middle ground between advisers calling for direct military intervention and those recommending withdrawal. On the political front in Vietnam, Kennedy decided that Diem should be pressured to reform his family oligarchy, and tactical military changes would be emphasized to counter the domestic insurgency. As a result, increased numbers of American advisers were sent to train Vietnamese forces, and American aid was to be tied to political reform in Diem's government. In addition, Diem was informed that the United States would 'expect to share in the decision-making process in the political, economic and military fields as they affect the security situation' – an indication that Vietnamese sovereignty would be further adulterated.[21]

Unwilling to surrender any of his absolute decision-making power, Diem called Kennedy's bluff, strongly protesting the new American policy as an intrusion in Vietnam's internal affairs. After an unsuccessful search for a possible replacement for Diem, the State Department concluded that Diem was the best of a bad lot. In his half decade of rule, taking a leaf out of Stalin's book, Diem had imprisoned or executed all potential political rivals who retained nationalist prestige. Having no good alternative puppet, the

Americans caved in on political reform, and the status quo remained intact. The American fence-straddling in 1961 was one of the determining factors leading to direct military intervention in 1965. The most critical mistake Kennedy made in Vietnam was the same mistake Eisenhower had made – that of deciding not to act on tough policy decisions that might have salvaged the situation, yet at the same time deciding not to withdraw, thereby increasing the risk to American prestige. The key to success in Vietnam – real political reform that could build solid support for the government among the people of South Vietnam – was never achieved. Combined with a growing American military commitment, this lack of political will on Kennedy's part increased Diem's intransigence and moved the United States closer to war. It is true that Diem might never have been convinced to modify his behaviour. However, if the Americans had drawn a clear line and maintained it, the issue could have been resolved before American prestige and power became thoroughly committed to one side in a civil war that had ever decreasing levels of public support and legitimacy.[22] According to historian Robert Miller:

> At the political level US policy-makers followed this gradualist, measured approach, at least in part, because they could not conceive of failure; at the same time, they did not consider abandoning the enterprise because they could not countenance further communist encroachments anywhere. This led the political leadership of successive administrations, Republican and Democrat alike, to discount professional and diplomatic judgments that did not square with what were perceived to be political imperatives: to win and stop communism. Yet, that leadership was unwilling to take early decisive action that might have made it possible to achieve that goal while maintaining domestic political support.[23]

In 1962, having decided erroneously that a military solution would solve what was essentially a political problem, the United States again increased its involvement in Vietnam. The Military Assistance Advisory Group (MAAG) was restructured into the Military Assistance Command (MAC), a change that included raising the number of American advisers from 3,205 in December 1961 to more than 9,000 by the end of 1962.[24] American advisers performed an ever-increasing array of tasks, the most serious of which included combat sorties in Vietnamese aircraft supplied by the United States. However, the United States denied that US troops were in combat, and when on 15 January 1962 President Kennedy was asked directly if they were, the response was an emphatic 'no'. Two days earlier US pilots had begun combat support missions that would total over 200 sorties by the end of the month.[25] Kennedy's direct lie to the American public was one grain in the quicksand of deception leading the United States into the Vietnam quagmire, and later undermining public faith in the republic and the presidency.

The administration's official denial of US involvement was an attempt further to conceal violations of the 1954 Geneva Accords. Earlier in 1961 the State Department had released a 'white paper' outlining North Vietnamese violations of the Geneva Accords in order to justify American violations. Even Guenter Lewy, one of the strongest supporters of American involvement in Vietnam, regards the report as an exaggeration. Using documents in the JFK Library, Lewy reveals that in October 1961

> ... the CIA estimated that about 10–20 per cent of the VC [Viet Cong] full-time strength of 16,000 consisted of infiltrated cadres. Despite North Vietnamese help, 'the VC effort is still largely a self-supporting operation in respect to recruitment and supplies'. More basically, the preoccupation with infiltration from the North diverted attention from the political and social grievances on which the insurgency thrived, and it fed the illusion that mere military measures – increases in border controls and in the strength of the South Vietnamese armed forces – would be sufficient to defeat the VC.[26]

Throughout 1962 Vietnam remained a second-order problem on Kennedy's global foreign policy agenda. The new infusion of American men, materiel and combat tactics appeared to be helping to stabilize the government. Helicopters, which the Soviets would also use effectively in Afghanistan, proved to be a formidable battlefield weapon when first introduced in 1962. American optimism was also focused on the 'strategic hamlet' programme. The idea, modelled on a British plan that had worked well in Malaya, centred on physically walling off villages from Viet Cong infiltration and attack. However, like earlier 'agro-village' programmes, the rural peasants resented being herded into fortified enclosures where corrupt officials had siphoned off the economic aid and social services that were designed to build peasant support. In what became typical of US projects in Vietnam, although conceived with the best intentions, the programme was poorly implemented, and in reality many 'secure' villages only existed on paper to please American advisers and ensure that more aid would be forth-coming. Those areas deemed insecure were declared 'open zones' and were randomly bombarded by air and ground artillery to force uncooperative peasants into the government hamlets. This programme further solidified villagers' hatred for the government and increased the Viet Cong's political stature.[27]

In the spring of 1963 American officials began to reconsider the US commitment to Vietnam. After the intense stand-off with Khrushchev over missiles in Cuba, and the signing in 1962 of a fourteen-nation agreement that officially neutralized Laos, Kennedy and the Joint Chiefs of Staff sought to balance US commitment in Vietnam with America's other global strategic interests. A plan was produced for a phased withdrawal of US troops, based on the premise that by 1965 the South Vietnamese would be able to continue improving the ongoing counterinsurgency efforts.[28] The Pentagon's optimism was quickly erased by a new explosion of civil unrest in South Vietnam. On 8 May 1963, in response to a new law outlawing the display of any flags other than that of the government, nine Buddhists celebrating the 2,527th birthday of their patron were killed by government troops firing into the celebrating crowd. Diem's implausible claim that the Viet Cong were responsible only aggravated tensions, and two days later 10,000 Buddhists marched in protest of the government action. Diem responded by arresting thousands. On 11 June the crisis deepened and the world was shocked by the televised public self-immolation of Quang Duc, an elderly monk protesting against Diem. While he burned, Quang Duc sat stoical until dead after having set a match to his own gasoline-soaked robes. His action fomented additional anti-government protests among high school and university students throughout the South.[29]

Diem was able to repress the protests by mass arrests. However, in Washington a search was on for a replacement of Diem. The US government could no longer stomach its creation. Henry Cabot Lodge, the new US ambassador, indicated in a cable to Secretary of State Dean Rusk in late August that, in his view, the war could not be won with Diem in charge and that the United States should support the ouster of Diem. Within days of Diem's severe crackdown on the Buddhists a number of South Vietnamese generals opened secret talks with US officials. The generals wanted to know what the US attitude would be if a change in government were to occur. Officials in Washington, outraged over Diem's continuing crackdown on Buddhists despite his pledges to the contrary, signalled that although they would not support the generals in event of failure, the generals could be assured of US support if they succeeded in removing Diem. Even though the coup-plotters lost their nerve at the end of August, President Kennedy had clearly given the go-ahead for a US-supported coup. When it was learned in October that the generals were once again plotting Diem's overthrow, the United States indicated to the leading generals that it would not intervene on Diem's behalf and would support such an effort if the new regime appeared capable of increasing both popular support and military effectiveness. On 1 November 1962, while Diem was talking to Ambassador Lodge, key military and communication systems around Saigon were seized. Later in the day, after learning of the coup, Diem phoned Lodge, but received no assurances of US support from the ambassador. Fearing for his life, Diem fled with his brother Nhu, and both were quickly captured and executed by the plotting generals' forces.[30]

The Kennedy legacy

The Kennedy administration's decision to sanction the coup against Diem sealed America's fate in Vietnam. In the name of democracy and American national interest, President Eisenhower had condoned the South's abandonment of an international treaty that had ended French colonialism and would have allowed the Vietnamese people to decide their own fate. Completing the circle, the Kennedy administration continued to support Eisenhower's dictator, and then fully abandoned the American ideals of democracy and justice by supporting a plot to overthrow Diem. In a stark critique, George Herring concisely summarizes the Kennedy legacy:

> Kennedy and most of his advisers accepted, without critical analysis, the assumption that a non-Communist Vietnam was vital to American interest. ... His cautious, middle course significantly enlarged the American role and commitment in Vietnam, and with the coup, the United States assumed direct responsibility for the South Vietnamese government. Although apparently troubled by growing doubts, Kennedy refused, even after the problems with Diem had reached a crisis point, to face the hard questions ... He bequeathed to his successor a problem eminently more dangerous than the one he had inherited from Eisenhower.[31]

Like Truman and then Eisenhower, Kennedy was confident that American power would succeed in Vietnam. Diem's murder by the American-backed generals, though perhaps abhorred on a personal level, was welcomed on a tactical level. Kennedy believed that with Diem finally out of the way, US policies would succeed in stopping Vietnam's long slide into the communist camp. In reality Diem's death only succeeded in further destabilizing Vietnam, and by default accelerated America's decade-long slide into war. As fate (or poetic justice) would have it, Kennedy was assassinated in Dallas three weeks later. Kennedy's assassination rocked American society to its core, a society which pledged itself to fulfilling what were perceived to be his wishes, thus adding pressure to fulfil the president's commitment to saving America's 'child' in Asia.

The Johnson administration

Like his predecessors, Vice-President Lyndon Johnson believed in containment and in the domino theory in Asia, and he believed that the United States had vital interests in Vietnam. Unlike Vice-President Truman, who was generally ignorant of President Roosevelt's policies and plans, Johnson was fully aware of, and involved in, Kennedy's domestic and foreign policy agendas at the time of the assassination. He made it clear from the start of his tenure in office that he would continue Kennedy's policies in Vietnam, but that he intended to put his personal stamp on foreign policy.[32] After a brief burst of euphoria in Saigon following Diem's death it became apparent that the political and military situation in the South was rapidly deteriorating. Diem's death had created a political vacuum that could have been filled only by another leading anticommunist nationalist leader, all of whom had been liquidated by Diem. In retrospect, as Ambassador Maxwell Taylor noted, 'Diem's overthrow set in motion a sequence of crises, political and military, over the next two years which eventually forced President Johnson in 1965 to choose between accepting defeat or introducing American combat forces.'[33] By 1965 Johnson believed that he had no other choice, once again looking at Vietnam through the larger lens of the Cold War. Two days after Kennedy's murder, presidential aide Bill Moyers reported Johnson as saying, 'They'll think with Kennedy dead we've lost heart ... the Chinese. The fellas in the Kremlin. They'll be taking the measure of us ... I told them to go back and tell those generals in Saigon that Lyndon Johnson intends to stand by our word.' To another aide Johnson stated that he 'was not going to be the president who saw Southeast Asia go the way China did'.[34]

Within Vietnam the new junta of supposedly pliant pro-American generals did not view the local situation in the same way that Washington did. According to General Duong Van Minh, the leader of the anti-Diem coup, the new government should seek a neutralist position, which was non-communist instead of anticommunist – an important distinction which recognized that not all anti-government forces were motivated by ideology. The new government sought to achieve a political solution by reaching out to the NLF and the various other dissenting groups (Buddhists, students, sects) that Diem had alienated. Thus, at the beginning of his term Johnson was presented with a window of opportunity either to withdraw from the war or at least to change the direction of US policy. Duong Van Minh's Military Revolutionary Council looked forward to American disengagement, and Johnson's friend and colleague in the Senate, Mike Mansfield, appealed directly to Johnson to pursue the possibilities of peace that were now available. However, others attempted to keep Kennedy's legacy burning brightly. They appealed to Johnson's fears of Asian dominoes and to Johnson's own political future. 'Don't even think about neutralization', Kennedy's former top aide, McGeorge Bundy, instructed the president. Neutralization would only mean unification on Communist terms; Japan, Thailand and the Philippines all would shift toward neutrality; US prestige would drop so low in South Korea and Taiwan as to 'require compensating increases in American commitment there – or else further retreat'. Furthermore, Johnson was told that he would lose the next election if he backed out of Vietnam. Adviser Walt Rostow stoked the rhetorical fire, claiming that neutralization of South Vietnam would be 'the greatest setback to US interests on the world scene'. The secretary of defense, the head of the CIA and the Joint Chiefs of Staff all agreed.[35]

The political upheaval in the South that accompanied Diem's ouster was seized upon by the Viet Cong and North Vietnamese. After being rebuffed in attempts to negotiate with the new government, Hanoi increased the level of infiltration and supplies into the South and encouraged the Viet Cong to launch a military offensive in order to exacerbate tension within the new Southern government, which was internally factionalized. On 29 January 1964 a second military coup, led by General Nguyen Khanh, successfully overthrew the military junta. General Khanh, a favourite of US military officers, received immediate support from the Johnson administration. He was entirely in favour of US advisers at all levels of civilian and military affairs. He even asked Ambassador Lodge for advice on whom to appoint to his cabinet. Robert McNamara described him as highly responsive to US advice, and Lodge believed that the United States did not have a better relationship with a government leader anywhere in the world.[36] In the minds of some in Washington, the United States had finally achieved the perfect instrument for its policies in Vietnam. In doing so, the Vietnamese civil war was fundamentally transformed from an American-supported effort to an American war with local supporters.

Sliding over the brink

Events on the world stage had shifted significantly by 1964. The Sino-Soviet split was judged by many to have created a 'polycentric' world. The CIA, however, concluded that communist powers, acting in unison or independently, would attempt to exploit anti-American sentiment in the Third World. The disorder and instability created by a world characterized by polycentric communism was no less a threat to the United States than a single monolithic movement controlled by Moscow. When a French diplomat observed that the stakes in Europe were significant, but in South Vietnam minimal, Secretary of State Rusk countered that Berlin would be in jeopardy if South Vietnam fell.[37]

Unlike the Soviet incursion into Afghanistan in 1979, the American military offensive in Vietnam was not an abrupt or spectacular incident that reverberated around the world. Direct US military involvement transpired in a gradual sequence of escalatory actions that culminated in the introduction of American combat troops in March 1965. These troops landed in Vietnam not as advisers to the Vietnamese armed forces: rather their mission was to protect American installations, and they operated with full independence from South Vietnamese forces. The steps leading to this first stage of the American military intervention began in January 1964 when Johnson approved increases in covert military action against the North. Although he rejected advisory recommendations calling for direct US bombing of North Vietnam, Johnson approved contingency plans that included such action if North Vietnam 'provoked' an American response. In other words, the United States would sanction South Vietnamese attacks on the North, but if the North retaliated, the United States would use the North's response as justification for selective bombing above the 17th parallel. The president's new contingency plans have been reported to be the penultimate step in the US military commitment. According to the *Pentagon Papers*, 'The active US role in the few covert operations that were carried out was limited essentially to planning, equipping and training the GVN (Government of Vietnam) forces involved, but the US responsibility for the launching and conduct of these activities was unequivocal and carried with it an implicit symbolic and psychological intensification of the US commitment. A firebreak had been crossed …'.[38] In March 1964 Johnson ordered the Defense and State Departments to prepare contingency plans for a sustained bombing campaign and increased US involvement. By May a detailed 'scenario' had been written which listed the important political and military steps required to Americanize the war. The much-debated Gulf of Tonkin 'crisis' in July 1964 provided the administration with the scenario it needed to act.[39]

On 2 August 1964 the US destroyer *Maddox* was attacked by three North Vietnamese torpedo boats in international waters twenty-eight miles off the coast of North Vietnam. The action against the *Maddox* was a North Vietnamese response to a skirmish the previous evening initiated by South Vietnamese vessels on two islands off North Vietnam. The North Vietnamese apparently assumed that the *Maddox* had been supporting the covert attacks. As in earlier incidents of attacks on US personnel, the president did not order retaliation, but the destroyer *Turner Joy* was ordered into the Gulf of Tonkin to support the *Maddox*. Two nights later both ships reported that they were under attack while cruising sixty miles off the North Vietnamese coast. Both ships fired upon what they thought were attacking torpedo boats. However, the captain of the *Maddox* would later acknowledge that no clear evidence of an attack existed and that freak weather conditions may have caused sonar operators to see nonexistent targets. Even though serious questions were raised in Washington about the alleged attack, the administration decided to retaliate. Acting on the advice of Secretary of Defense McNamara, on 5 August the president informed Congressional leaders of both parties that in response to unprovoked attacks on US ships he had authorized retaliatory air strikes against the torpedo boats' bases and on a nearby oil-storage facility.[40]

While of minimal military importance, the Gulf of Tonkin incidents had monumental political repercussions in the United States. The administration used the alleged attacks to secure a Congressional resolution that authorized Johnson to take 'all necessary measures to repel any armed attacks against the forces of the United States and to prevent further aggression'. The resolution, which was based on a draft prepared three months earlier as part of the administration's war contingency plans, passed in the Senate on a vote of 88–2 and received unanimous approval in the House. It was a broad grant of authority giving the president near-unilateral control over conducting the war in Vietnam.[41]

According to opinion polls, Johnson's handling of the Gulf of Tonkin incident was enthusiastically supported by the American public. His approval rating jumped thirty points overnight in a Louis Harris survey, and he was able to nullify the claim of his Republican rival in the 1964 presidential race, Senator Barry Goldwater, that he was soft on communism. The short-term gains for Johnson's presidency, however, had serious long-term implications for American policy in Vietnam as well as for American domestic politics. From a policy perspective, American prestige was even more highly committed to defending South Vietnam, but with the added risk of being more inclined to respond directly to North Vietnamese provocations. From a political perspective, Johnson was encouraged by the easy passage of the Gulf of Tonkin Resolution to ignore subsequent Congressional objections. However, when, in later years, it became apparent that the president had misled Congress on the US provocation that led to the Tonkin incidents, when questions arose as to the veracity of the 'attacks' themselves, and when the existence of carefully prepared contingency plans for such an incident as prelude to major US involvement became known, the credibility of the president's Vietnam policy in the minds of Congress and the American people began to erode.[42]

Despite its historical significance, in 1964 the Gulf of Tonkin Resolution did not signal the beginning of an all-out American escalation of the war in Vietnam, or a break in the continuity of US policy. Rather, it was one of many incremental steps during the Kennedy and Johnson administrations which slowly but steadily solidified America's entry into the war – steps that were often explained and justified by bureaucratic sophistry or even outright presidential lies. By late November 1964 a dual-phase programme had been formulated for intensifying air attacks in the North, which would be coordinated with political reforms in the South. The first phase would consist of raids against infiltration routes along the Ho Chi Minh trail in Laos, and tit-for-tat retaliation strikes in response to North Vietnamese aggression. The second phase would consist of a large-scale air offensive following improvements in the political order in the South. Johnson initiated phase one of the bombing but refused to begin phase two in December 1964 after Viet Cong operatives killed two American advisers in Saigon on a Christmas Eve attack. In his memoirs Johnson claimed to have feared that American reprisals might provoke additional enemy attacks, which could further destabilize the Southern regime.[43]

Johnson's fears were well founded. In the month of December political conditions in the South had deteriorated to their lowest level in years. Earlier that year a cycle of 'revolving door' governments began. In the face of massive student and Buddhist protests, General Khanh had turned over power to a civilian government (while retaining the post of military commander in chief). On 19 December Khanh and a number of other generals staged a coup against the civilian regime they had placed in power. Johnson administration officials publicly threatened that aid would be reduced even while plans for expanding American involvement were moving forward. As in the Diem years, American threats were ignored by Southern political rulers, and US credibility was undermined when no punishments materialized. In short, General Khanh was not a puppet whose strings were easily pulled. For approximately three weeks in January 1965 he shared power with the civilian Premier Huong, and then staged his third coup, once again taking sole possession of the reins of power. At the end of February Khanh (openly at odds with the US embassy) once again turned over power to a civilian regime, headed by Premier Phan Huy Quat. However, in less than a year, governing power had again shifted, this time into the hands of other leading military figures who deposed General Khanh as commander of the army and forced him into exile.[44]

In retrospect, the rapid turnover in governments during this period reveals that no single person or alliance of individuals could claim even a modicum of legitimate authority in the South. As a result, the population in the South had little interest, respect or sympathy for their so-called government, which seemingly changed with greater regularity than the relatively predictable seasonal weather patterns. The only consistent ruling authority recognizable to the average Vietnamese citizen was the ever growing number of American military forces; as foreigners, however, the Americans could never hold the Mandate of Heaven.

The last steps: sustained bombing and ground forces

In the early months of 1965 the United States decided to launch a programme of reprisal air strikes against North Vietnam. This programme evolved progressively into a sustained bombing campaign of rising intensity. The logic behind the attacks had shifted 180 degrees since November 1964 when air attacks were believed to have a destabilizing influence. However, it was believed in 1965 that things could not get worse. The air war was launched to boost Southern morale and unity and to convince North Vietnam that further infiltration of men and supplies into the South would be at a high cost. It was also believed that the bombing attacks could be used to induce concessions by the North in diplomatic negotiations. Operation Rolling Thunder was initiated in mid February without a major policy review or debate. It followed on the heels of Operation Flaming Dart, the reprisal plan implemented on 10 February 1965 immediately after an attack on the US Army barracks at Pleiku and a nearby helicopter base, in which nine Americans had been killed. A clear and important distinction must be made between Flaming Dart and Rolling Thunder. Flaming Dart (like earlier reprisals) was designed to counter specific acts of aggression by North Vietnamese and Viet Cong forces. Rolling Thunder reflected a conscious US decision to move from an event-specific reprisal policy to a new policy of reprisal justified on general strategic objectives.[45]

As in previous escalations, the president and his representatives publicly denied that a change of policy had taken place, stating that the new US air strikes were simply a response to the attack at Pleiku. It is clear from a review of the *Pentagon Papers*, however, that the Pleiku attack was not the cause for a change in policy but rather, like the Tonkin Gulf incident, a pretext for the implementation of a sustained bombing attack that had been planned months in advance. Presidential adviser McGeorge Bundy later admitted, 'Pleikus are like streetcars' – if one is missed, another would have followed soon enough to provide cover for the change in policy.[46]

The implementation of Operation Rolling Thunder in February 1965 was the last preamble decision in a series of incremental decisions leading to the full Americanization of the Vietnamese civil war. Spanning well over a decade and four American presidents, these decisions culminated in the introduction of US combat ground forces on 6 March 1965. In response to General William Westmoreland's request, President Johnson ordered 3,500 Marines to Da Nang to defend the American air base that was launching Rolling Thunder strikes into North Vietnam. It was a quiet American invasion, without fanfare, major press reports, or great debate among political leaders. On 4 May 1965 the president requested Congressional approval for an additional $700 million to meet the cost of the increasing US involvement. Three days later the bill was signed into law by the president, who stated, 'Let the meaning of this action be clear. To the brave people of South Vietnam, who are fighting for the right to choose their own way of life, this resolution says: "America keeps her promises. And we will back up those promises with all the resources that we need."'[47] By the end of 1965, American forces in South Vietnam numbered 184,314.[48]

The Soviet Union in Vietnam, 1956–65

Increased involvement on the part of the United States in support of the South Vietnamese regime virtually ensured the Soviet Union's involvement with the communist government headed by Ho Chi Minh. However, as discussed in the previous chapter, the relationship between the socialist brethren in Moscow and Hanoi was not always a cordial one. Historic experience had taught the leadership of the DRV not to trust either the Soviet Union or the People's Republic of China. However, without Soviet and Chinese material assistance to counteract US aid in the South, Ho Chi Minh's goal of unifying Vietnam could not have been achieved. In the post-Geneva years the Soviet Union considered North Vietnam as an important symbol of Moscow's commitment to the Third World. It poured a large quantity of developmental assistance into the country. According to Soviet documents, 'from 1955 to 1965, the Soviet Union and the Democratic Republic of Vietnam signed seven agreements providing for Soviet economic, scientific and technological assistance'. Under these agreements the Soviet Union extended credit to the sum of 320 million roubles, or 40 per cent of the total material assistance granted North Vietnam by socialist countries.[49] In 1957 the Soviets dumbfounded their DRV comrades by proposing that both Vietnams be admitted to the United Nations. This move, which would have undermined the DRV's claim to be the only legitimate government in Vietnam, was withdrawn after an irate Ho Chi Minh visited Moscow. In the latter 1950s the Soviet Union also supported the DRV's decision to renew the armed struggle toward unification.[50]

During his tenure, Khrushchev's policies toward Vietnam were shaped not only by the global struggle with the United States but also by the intra-communist feud with China. As the growing rift between Mao and Khrushchev widened after the latter's 1956 secret speech denouncing Stalinism, Khrushchev's Vietnam policy became a highly complicated exercise. The Soviet Union's objectives were primarily designed to prevent China from gaining such influence in Hanoi that it could shut out Moscow's influence – an objective best achieved by increasing its own influence over Hanoi. However, a total Viet Cong victory in South Vietnam was not necessarily a positive goal, since such a victory might be seen as a success for China and for Maoist thought. Likewise, the Soviet Union wanted to prevent peace and stability in South Vietnam because that would be seen as a victory for the United States. Moscow sought simultaneously to maintain amicable relations with the United States, though Khrushchev was careful not to behave in such a way as to open himself to a Chinese charge of conspiracy with the United States, thereby undermining Soviet leadership in the 'socialist common-wealth'.[51]

Eventually this maze of conflicting objectives would force the Soviet leadership to establish a hierarchy of priorities. By the early 1960s the war in Vietnam was becoming increasingly risky and expensive to the Soviet Union. North Vietnam began building defences against anticipated US air attacks, and such systems could only be effective if supplied by the Soviet Union, thus increasing the material cost and level of political commitment. There were also limited gains from such a commitment. The ground war was being fought along a Maoist 'peasant army' strategy, and if the war did go northward, Chinese troops, not Russian troops, would intervene, as they had in Korea.[52]

In 1963 and 1964 Khrushchev embarked on a policy of reducing Soviet involvement in Vietnam. Diplomatic exchanges and trade both dwindled, and in February 1964 Khrushchev was insulted by Hanoi when the DRV (like the PRC) refused to sign the limited nuclear test ban treaty. Later that year, Moscow responded in relatively muted fashion to the US air strikes during the Gulf of Tonkin incident. However, unlike the PRC, Hanoi could not openly condemn the Soviet Union while it still held out hope for advanced anti-aircraft technology. The Soviet Union's policy of disengagement in Vietnam was abruptly reversed in October 1964 with Khrushchev's departure from power.[53]

In 1965, after the sustained US air war against North Vietnam had begun, the Soviet Union and the DRV solidified what was to become an awkward yet enduring alliance. In February 1965 Soviet Premier Aleksei Kosygin made a historic trip to Hanoi to negotiate and sign a defence pact. During his stay, and apparently by coincidence, the United States undertook air raids against the DRV in retaliation for the Viet Cong attacks at Pleiku. Kosygin adroitly used 'being bombed by the Americans' to underscore the importance of the Soviet Union's new commitment to the DRV at a mass rally.[54] At the end of his visit the two countries signed a joint communiqué which was treated by the Soviet Union as a binding defense pact. The communiqué's more important points include:

- The Soviet Government again confirmed it would not remain indifferent to the safeguarding of the security of a fraternal Socialist State and would render the necessary assistance and support to North Vietnam.

- The two Governments reached proper agreement on the steps to be taken to strengthen the defensive potential of North Vietnam and agreed to hold regular consultations.

- The Soviet Union fully supports the South Vietnamese people's just heroic struggle for independence, democracy, peace and neutrality waged under the leadership of the National Liberation Front ...

- The unity of the Socialist camp and the international Communist movement is an imperative condition for the victory of the working class in the struggle against imperialism and for peace, national independence, democracy and Socialism.[55]

Over the next ten years Soviet policy in Vietnam would remain largely consistent with that established in the Kosygin visit. Moscow would supply all the necessary war materiel for the Vietnamese to continue the fight against the United States. Moscow would support any negotiated settlement that was acceptable to Hanoi, and it would use its own involvement to castigate the United States in the world press while simultaneously undercutting China's growing influence in the developing world.[56] After reaching approximate strategic nuclear parity with the United States by the late 1960s, involvement in Vietnam became a relatively low-risk, high-gain situation for the Soviet Union during the Cold War – a state of affairs that would reverse itself in Afghanistan a decade later.

THE SUPERPOWERS IN AFGHANISTAN, 1956–79

The Khrushchev years

Despite its apparent status as a relative nonentity in the bipolar world, tragically Afghanistan did not escape the ideological struggle and violence of the Cold War. While Vietnam was one of the first of many Cold War battlegrounds, Afghanistan was indeed the last. From 1956 to 1978 the ruling authorities in Afghanistan effectively balanced Soviet and American interests in their affairs, benefiting from the peaceful competition between the superpowers. In 1978 a communist-led palace coup overthrew the government in Kabul, setting in motion a sequence of events that inspired a countrywide revolt, the Soviet invasion and retreat, and the Afghan civil war, which continues into 1998 and the foreseeable future.

In 1956 the Soviet Union began to solidify its role as Afghanistan's primary benefactor in economic, political and military affairs. In regard to developing countries in general, Soviet policies were undergoing significant changes. Unlike Stalin, Khrushchev emphasized the importance of the developing nations. And the new Soviet tolerance for non-aligned or neutral nations was a clear rebuttal to Stalin's 'two-camp' thesis. Afghanistan was one of the primary targets of the new Soviet policies that followed the Twentieth Party Congress in 1956, and relations with Afghanistan would be used as a model for new Soviet policies toward the Third World. As in Vietnam, internal events in Afghanistan had a major effect on bilateral relations. Afghanistan had pursued its first democratic reforms in 1950. A free press was allowed, and three newspapers critical of governmental policies appeared. A leftist-oriented student union was formed, and student criticism of the government began in earnest. However, in 1951 the government closed the student union and in 1952 shut down the last opposition newspaper. In 1953 Prince Daoud was appointed prime minister by King Zahir. Daoud governed effectively through a relatively loyal, well-paid army. He may be characterized as an authoritarian reformer, much in the mould of King Amanullah at the turn of the century. His willingness to use police power enabled him to enforce reforms that would have been beyond the power of any 'liberal' progressive movement at that time. After the Soviet Union established itself as

Afghanistan's major arms supplier in 1955, Daoud's increasingly close relations with the Soviet Union earned him the nickname 'the Red-Premier' by US analysts. In 1959 his reforms included the enforcement of the tax laws and the encouragement of women to abandon the Muslim tradition of veiling their faces in public. In typical fashion, Afghans protested against these non-traditional practices. Daoud silenced any objections with jail terms, and the more zealous protesters were simply shot. However, the enforcement of government policies was largely limited to the few urban centres.[57]

In the 1950s and 1960s Afghan and Soviet representatives exchanged a series of visits. In 1958 Marshal K.Y. Voroshilov visited Kabul, and in 1960 Khrushchev followed up his 1955 visit by returning to Afghanistan. King Zahir travelled to Moscow in 1957; Prime Minister Daoud and Foreign Minister Naim made separate visits to the Soviet Union in 1959; and Daoud was back in Moscow in 1960 and 1961. During each visit Soviet leaders reiterated their support for Afghanistan's struggle over the Pushtunistan region.[58]

The Brezhnev years

Afghanistan's second attempt at democratic reforms began in 1963. Prince Daoud was forced to resign by King Zahir, who feared that his nephew was gaining too much control over Afghan affairs. King Zahir then deliberately abandoned 200 years of autocratic dynastic rule with the implementation of the 1965 Afghan constitution. This constitution barred most of the royal family (Daoud in particular) from both politics and government. The constitution set up a representative system that included a parliament consisting of directly elected as well as appointed members. The king, however, retained extensive reserve powers that severely limited the scope and power of the democratic reforms. Among his prerogatives were the dissolution and summoning of parliament, the appointment of the prime minister and other cabinet members, and the naming of the chief justice and senior civil and military officials.[59]

Problems arose immediately with the new parliament. In the true spirit of democracy, it rejected the king's appointment for prime minister, Dr Yussuf, and accused him and many other government officials of bribery and corruption.[60] Certain left-wing members led by Nur Muhammad Taraki continued to protest, and riots ensued in which three people were killed. Yussuf was forced to resign to quell the disturbances.[61] In 1968, after much delay and fierce debate, a bill legalizing political parties (but not the Communist Party) was passed by parliament. The king refused to sign the bill, and the elections of 1969 passed without legal political parties. These elections were to some extent rigged in favour of pro-government candidates, and the leftist faction in parliament was reduced from five to three seats. Among the leftists was a new member, Hafizullah Amin, who, along with

Nur Muhammad Taraki and Babrak Karmal, formed the leadership nucleus of Afghanistan's first Communist Party – the People's Democratic Party of Afghanistan (PDPA).[62]

Although the Soviets lost a valuable asset when Daoud was removed in 1963, relations between the two countries remained unchanged. High-level visits continued to facilitate normal relations. In 1963 Brezhnev visited Kabul, and in 1965 King Zahir visited Moscow. In 1966 and 1967 Afghan prime minister Muhammad Hashim Maiwandwal and Soviet president Nikolai Podgorny exchanged visits. Other exchanges continued through 1973, and both sides praised the quality of bilateral relations. The Afghans voiced support for the Soviet position on disarmament, the progress of decolonialization, the war in Vietnam and the Arab–Israeli conflict.[63] In Afghanistan the reforms instituted by King Zahir gave rise to various opposition forces. In urban areas leftist activities continued to increase, as did the concern of the nationalistic and religious circles in Afghan politics, which had significant support among the rural tribes.[64] Having run the country for ten years, former prime minister Prince Daoud probably found it frustrating to sit on the sidelines and watch the monarchy's power usurped by commoners. Daoud discussed rebellion for more than a year with various opposition elements, but he concentrated his plans among leftist military officers.

In Afghan society the military was by far the most important revolutionary element, and it supported Daoud for a number of reasons. He had obtained large quantities of modern arms from the Soviet Union. Daoud also fostered closer ties to the Soviet Union, which appealed to many Soviet-trained personnel in the Afghan officer corps. Daoud was a former army officer who had obtained the rank of lieutenant-general. In addition, progressive urban Afghans had been antagonized by the king's on-again, off-again reform programme. Having been promised change, many politically active Afghans were determined to have it.[65]

Daoud, with the aid of military officers, took control of the government in a near-bloodless coup on 17 July 1973. The king was out of the country at the time, and loyalist resistance was thus minimized. Daoud announced on radio that the monarchy was being replaced by a republican system of government. He became founder, president and prime minister of the new Republic of Afghanistan.[66] In Washington, it was Daoud's associates who caused speculation that the July coup in Kabul was a pro-Soviet affair, and Daoud's close relations with the Soviet Union as prime minister from 1953 to 1963 added to this speculation. The coup had been executed primarily by junior army officers trained in the Soviet Union.[67] On 19 July 1973 the Soviet Union became the first nation to recognize the new Afghan republic.[68]

Many of Daoud's backers were members of or associated with Afghanistan's fledgling Marxist organization – the PDPA. He appointed a number of cabinet ministers from the PDPA, yet the nature of the new republican regime was neither communist nor exclusively pro-Soviet. If the Soviets had aided Daoud in his coup, he soon demonstrated that lingering gratitude did not limit his independence.[69] Within a year Daoud began to reduce the power of the leftists in the government and to move his regime somewhat to the 'right'. Leftist officials, one by one, were either dismissed outright or assigned to distant diplomatic posts. The left-wing minister of the interior was replaced by a conservative. However, the president refrained from publicly taking an anticommunist stance. Daoud also disappointed the leftists by changing Afghan foreign policy. He lessened his dependence on the Soviet Union and strengthened ties with other countries, particularly Pakistan and Iran.[70]

Daoud's conduct in foreign affairs both pleased and disturbed the Soviet Union. Since 1968 Moscow's proposed formation of a collective security system in Asia had been received coolly by Soviet allies in the region. In 1974 Daoud pleased the Soviets by giving a qualified endorsement of the plan, but he also reaffirmed Afghanistan's policy of nonalignment and neutrality.[71] At the same time, Daoud increased his involvement with Arab states and reduced tensions with Pakistan over the Pushtunistan issue. The most troublesome aspect of Afghan foreign policy, from the Soviet perspective, was Daoud's increased contacts with Iran, which was the United States's single most important strategic partner in the region at that time.

A review of Daoud's Seven-Year Plan provides some interesting insights regarding the amount of foreign aid the Afghans expected to receive from the Shah. Official Afghan documents list the sources of expected moneys for specific new projects. The Soviet Union is listed as the source for over sixty projects, in comparison to fewer than twenty for Iran. However, the combined Iranian sources of aid amounted to approximately $634 million.[72] It is apparent from these documents that the Afghans had great faith in the Shah's ability to provide aid from the influx of petrodollars – a belief that would soon be dispelled. The vast majority of the Shah's money was designated for the construction of over 1,800 kilometres of railroads linking Herat and Kabul to Iran. The stated purpose of the railroad was to 'link important agricultural and industrial regions of the country and make it possible to exploit coal and other mineral deposits ... Furthermore, construction of important transport infrastructure will considerably facilitate the transit trade with neighbouring and other countries.'[73]

The plan for this railroad concerned the Soviets for two reasons. First, it would lessen Afghan dependence on the Soviet Union as a market. It had been the case in Afghanistan for many years that if the Russians did not buy Afghan goods, they would not be purchased at all. For decades the Soviets purchased Afghan goods at deflated prices and would look upon the possibility of competition with Iran, a state with vast amounts of petrodollars, with great disfavour. The trade calculation, however, was the least of Soviet concerns. The real problem was the strategic influence that an Iran–Afghanistan railroad might have had on Soviet–Afghan relations and on the balance of power in South Asia. Iran was closely aligned with the United States before the 1979 Islamic revolution. Any large-scale Iranian involvement in Afghanistan was viewed by the Soviets as having implications on the overall strategic balance in the region. A shift in Afghanistan's alignment in favour of the Iranians, and the construction of a significant infrastructure component in the form of a railroad, were seen as threats to the Soviet Union. The Soviets could only view the Shah's proposal as a threat to their economic and political ties with Afghanistan, and any policies put forth by the Shah were interpreted as an extension of US meddling in the region.

Under a new constitution in 1977, Daoud appointed a new cabinet composed of personal supporters and known anticommunists. The communists, along with other leftists, had been passed over in choosing the new government. Daoud had apparently abandoned earlier attempts to reform the Afghan government and was systematically reducing all potential sources of opposition to his rule. He removed Soviet military advisers from the lower levels of the Afghan military and cut their number slightly. He sent men to train on Soviet military equipment in India and Egypt to remove them from Soviet influence. All of these actions followed Daoud's visit to Moscow in April 1977. The official record of the visit, however, shows no sign of discord between the Soviets and the Afghans.[74]

A sampling of the more important aid projects should also be noted. One of the Soviet Union's most successful programmes in Afghanistan was the joint production of raw materials. After Soviet geologists discovered rich natural gas deposits in Afghanistan, an agreement was signed in 1965 for aid in extracting the gas and for the construction of a pipeline to the Soviet border. In May 1967, just before the pipeline was opened, Afghanistan agreed to supply the Soviet Union with gas through 1985 in exchange for debts incurred in this venture.[75] After Daoud's return to the helm of Afghan politics in 1973, Soviet aid steadily increased from $120 million in 1972 to $150 million in 1974. This aid, when coupled with a Soviet moratorium on debt repayments and increased earnings from exports, provided for favourable economic conditions in Afghanistan through the first four years of Daoud's regime.[76] Soviet aid to Daoud's regime increased every year until his overthrow in 1978. In 1975 the Soviets gave Afghanistan $425 million for Daoud's Seven-Year Plan (1976–83), and in 1977 a twelve-year agreement on economic cooperation was signed.[77] By the time of the communist coup in 1978, a total of more than $1.2 billion in Soviet economic aid had been extended to Afghanistan. An additional $110 million had been provided through East European countries as part of a coordinated Eastern bloc aid programme. In addition to aid, by 1979 some 7,600 Afghan students had been trained in Soviet academic and technical institutions.[78]

The impact of military assistance

As noted in Chapter 2, the Soviet bloc became Afghanistan's sole supplier of military hardware in the mid 1950s. Military assistance, mainly in the form of arms transfers, advisory support and training, was begun in 1955 with an agreement between Afghanistan and Czechoslovakia for $3 million. The first direct Soviet–Afghan arms agreement was signed in 1956, providing for the sale of $25 million-worth of military equipment, including MiG-15 jets. By 1965 the value of military equipment, which included 100 tanks and 100 airplanes, stood at approximately $275 million, under repayment terms that required only 50 per cent reimbursement by the Afghans. More than 200 Afghan military cadets had been sent to the Soviet Union for training by 1962, and during the period of 1953–63 the Soviets had built or were building military airfields in Bagram, near Kabul; in Mazar-i-Sharif in Northern Afghanistan; and at Shindand in the central part of western Afghanistan.[79] In 1969 the Soviet military newspaper *Krasnaya Zvezda* reported: 'In most cases the officers attending the classes reported to Marshal A.A. Grechko in Russian: many of them having studied in Soviet military schools', thus indicating the extent of Russian language skills in the Afghan officer corps.[80] Opinions regarding the effects of this training on Afghan officers are mixed. Many post-invasion analysts in the West regarded the training period as evidence of Soviet indoctrination and subversion of Afghan military personnel. They point to the fact that Soviet-trained military officers would later engineer the 1979 coup. However, many of these analysts overlook the fact many of these same officers also aided in seizing power in 1973. Louis Dupree foreshadowed this point in his classic book, *Afghanistan*, in 1973:

> Many Western observers worried about the political orientation of Afghan officers trained in the USSR and the fact that Soviet personnel served as advisors to Afghan military schools. The Afghan government, however, maintained its bi-tarafi ('without sides') pattern and dispatched some officers to the USA for training ... Afghan officers, trained in Russia and the United States, often compare their experiences and find them reasonably similar ... Neither the USA nor the USSR turned out to be the paradises painted by their respective propaganda. ... The end result of Soviet (and American) military training tends to make the military even more pro-Afghan than pro-Soviet ...[81]

Military assistance steadily increased with the return of Daoud in 1973. Arms transfers from the Soviet bloc grew from $66 million in 1971/72 to $137 million in 1973/74. These transfers included such relatively modern equipment as armoured personnel carriers, modern artillery, T-62 main battle tanks and MiG-21 aircraft.[82] From 1975 to 1977, during the years of increased flexibility in Daoud's foreign relations, Soviet arms transfers continued unabated with record deliveries of $127 million worth of equipment in 1977 alone.[83]

Roots of the Afghan civil war

The level of Soviet concern in 1978 over Afghanistan remains unclear. Daoud's independent actions would logically annoy the Kremlin, but Soviet–Afghan relations were satisfactory, and Daoud indicated that he looked to the Soviet Union as his primary ally. In April 1978 Daoud travelled to Moscow, where one account of the visit indicates that serious problems did in fact exist. A widely recounted story holds that Brezhnev addressed Daoud in a rude manner and presented him with a long list of complaints about Daoud's foreign and domestic policies. Daoud reportedly rose to his feet and replied, 'I want to remind you that you are speaking to the president of an independent country, not one of your Eastern European satellites. You are trying to interfere with the internal affairs of Afghanistan, and this I will not permit' – whereupon Daoud and his entourage marched out of the room. One associate said to Daoud, 'Did you see the look on Brezhnev's face when you said that? Mr President, you are a dead man.'[84] However, despite reports of personal friction between Daoud and Brezhnev, there is no evidence to suggest that official Soviet–Afghan relations were severely strained. From 1975 to 1978 no criticisms of Daoud appeared in the Soviet media, nor was there any reduction in trade, aid or military assistance. At the Twenty-fifth Party Congress in 1976 the familiar favourable reference to Afghanistan was repeated and in 1976 and 1977 a number of positive articles on Soviet–Afghan relations, which included personal praise of Daoud, were published in *International Affairs* (Moscow).[85]

On the home front Daoud received less positive reviews. His heavy-handed tactics and reform policies had alienated many of his closest supporters, and by 1978 his policies had played into the hands of potential rebellious forces, having incurred the displeasure not only of the leftists but also of Islamic fundamentalists and tribal leaders. In the realm of the central government's ruling authority, Daoud had indeed altered Afghanistan's internal politics. Using the capabilities provided by Soviet military transfers, he had steadily centralized the coercive power of the government *vis-à-vis* the regional tribes. With an armed force of approximately 90,000 troops, Daoud had the power to suppress firmly any dissenting Islamic groups, such as the Muslim League, that objected to the degree of his involvement with the Soviet Union.[86] However, in doing so he had also alienated students, intellectuals, army officers and some members of the middle and upper classes. There were also serious economic problems in urban areas; unemployment was high, and several hundred thousand Afghans were forced abroad to find jobs in Iran and other Gulf states. Daoud's government had trouble making payments on the many loans it had received from foreign countries. Meanwhile, dissent among the poorer population increased as a result of severe food shortages and increased taxes.[87] However, as long as the armed forces were loyal, Daoud's power base remained relatively incontestable. In the urban areas, the leading anti-government forces were directed by a small cadre of Afghan communists. These communists, taking a direct lesson from the Bolsheviks' successful *coup d'état* in 1917, focused their attention on the military as the crucial element in a successful rebellion.

The Afghan communists

On 1 January 1965 the People's Democratic Party of Afghanistan (PDPA) was formed.[88] Following Soviet organization and edict, PDPA members were identified as 'comrade', a seven-member central committee was chosen, and Nur Muhammad Taraki was elected as general secretary of the party. This body officially adopted orthodox Marxist–Leninist ideology as its guiding doctrine, and its organizational structure strictly imitated the Soviet model.[89] The largest problem facing the PDPA leadership was the lack of popular support drawn from the working class in Afghanistan. Approximately 20,000 people (only 0.07 per cent of the population), could be considered industrial workers in the mid 1960s.[90] A Soviet writer commenting later on problems facing the revolutionary movement in 1978, noted:

> The backwardness of pre-Revolutionary Afghanistan was also manifested in: the unequal development of the various regions of the country; the presence of numerous groups of the rural and urban population closely connected with pre-capitalist economic structures, and which retained many features of a traditional social organization; the small number and weakness of the modern industrial proletariat, which hardly reached 50,000; the traditions of communal and patriarchal (tribal) organization, especially among the Pushtuns and Baluchis living in the southern regions of Afghanistan, and the considerable influence of the so-called traditional leaders (Khans, maliks and sardars of tribes and Moslem dignitaries) on the local population.[91]

In 1967 the PDPA split into several factions, the two largest of which were *Khalq* (Masses), headed by Taraki, and *Parcham* (Banner), headed by Babrak Karmal. Taraki favoured a Leninist-type party based on the working class, while Karmal wanted to form a more broadly based national-democratic front.[92] The two other leftist factions were more Maoist than Marxist in character. *Shu'la-i-Jawed* (Eternal Flame) was a Parcham splinter group that accused Karmal of revisionist views. It was known as 'chup-i-chup' in Kabul, meaning 'left-of-left'. *Setem-i-Meli* ('against national oppression') was an outspoken Maoist organization that promoted the interest of all non-Pushtun ethnic minorities and worked to organize the peasant population.[93] The early breakdown of the PDPA is evidence of its weakness as a viable political organization. During this moment in Afghan history, Marxist–Leninist ideology appears to have been little more than an appealing anti-government platform for a small number of disgruntled urban civil servants to rally behind. Even among this group, Marxist understanding was rudimentary at best, with sophomoric ideological squabbles concealing more deeply entrenched ethnic animosities. In reality the split among the communist factions once again affirms the lasting power of traditional tribal and kinship affiliations, with the members of Khalq being drawn from the more rural-oriented Pushtuns, and Parcham's affiliates coming from the urban-oriented Persian-speaking intellectuals.[94]

Apparently the Soviets maintained ties with both major factions, keeping their options open. Moscow did not regard either faction as a full-fledged Communist Party. For over five decades before the 1978 revolution, no Afghan delegate was invited to any international communist conference, nor were statements by Afghan communists ever published or announced outside of Afghanistan. Perhaps the Kremlin did not take the PDPA seriously, and the Soviets perceived their best interests as lying with the traditional powers in Afghanistan. Nevertheless, the Afghan communists looked to the Soviet Union as their mentor, model and friend.[95]

After years of bitter rivalry, the two communist factions finally agreed to unite in 1978. This merger is believed to have resulted from Soviet pressure, which was exerted through other communist parties in the region, including the Communist Party of India.[96] Although Parcham had closer ties to Moscow, Taraki was chosen as leader of the unified party because the Khalqis had more supporters in the military at that time. It is unknown whether the Soviets intended the PDPA to seize power, or only to put more pressure on Daoud to modify his increasingly independent foreign policies. The best Soviet efforts, however, were not able to do more than paper over the differences between the rival PDPA factions for a short time.[97]

Apparently neither the communists nor anyone else expected Daoud's government to crumble as quickly as it did. The sequence of events leading up to the communist coup began on 17 April 1978. On this date Mir Akbar Khyber, a former leader of Parcham, was assassinated. The killer was never discovered, although the CIA, the KGB and the PDPA itself all came under suspicion. Khyber's death made him a martyr for the communist cause. A crowd estimated between 15,000–30,000 people turned out for the funeral on 19 April, which evolved into a PDPA-orchestrated anti-American rally. Taraki and Karmal both made strong speeches aimed at the US embassy. Daoud was alarmed at the unusually large crowd, and he ordered the arrest of PDPA leaders.[98] The following week Daoud's security police made a midnight raid that netted seven ranking PDPA Central Committee members, including Taraki, Karmal and Amin. All were jailed except Amin, who was loosely held under house arrest.[99]

The actual *coup d'état* began on 27 April, and Western experts have disputed who actually organized it. The official Afghan communist version holds that Amin was able to direct the coup while under house arrest. Others speculate that pro-PDPA military officers, namely Major Waranjar and Colonel Quadir – the same commanders that aided Daoud in the 1973 overthrow of King Zahir, planned the rebellion. Waranjar and Quadir knew that the combination of their roles in overthrowing the old regime, their falling out with Daoud over his failure to implement reforms, and their connections with the illegal PDPA put them at risk of being purged from the military and the government. They decided to move first. The general consensus among Afghan observers is that a combination of PDPA activists and dissatisfied junior military officers were responsible for the planning and execution of the coup.[100]

Unlike the 1973 action against King Zahir, the 1978 coup was far from being bloodless. A combination of daring, improvisation and sheer luck on the side of the rebel officers won the day against the significant number of troops that rallied to Daoud's defence. Far from having mass support in the army and airforce (as the post-coup propaganda claimed), the PDPA only controlled a few hundred members in the officer corps. They were well placed to be brought into action, however. Also helping the PDPA side was the general lack of commitment to the Daoud government, which served to paralyse a number of senior military officers commanding outlying garrisons when they were called on to bring their troops to support Daoud. Inertia by parts of the Afghan military eventually allowed the rebel troops to overcome those Daoud loyalists who chose to fight. Daoud and almost twenty of his relatives were killed after refusing to surrender.[101]

Analysis of the coup, even by most of the hard-line anti-Soviet writers, points to limited Soviet involvement at best. If the Soviets gave the PDPA orders or suggestions that they overthrow Daoud, they did not choose 27 April as the particular date. Little prior consultation with the Soviets could have occurred while the PDPA leadership was under arrest. It is possible, however, that the Kremlin had told the PDPA earlier to take power whenever a favourable opportunity presented itself. At the time there were 3,000 Soviet advisers in Afghanistan, and the KGB and Soviet military intelligence had extensive contacts in the Afghan military. The arrest of PDPA leaders, and not Soviet pressure, apparently caused the wary military commanders to initiate the revolt.[102] When the coup erupted, the Soviet embassy acted as surprised as other embassies. Soviet Ambassador Aleksander M. Puzanov was off trout-fishing in the Hindu Kush – hardly the most strategic position from which to direct a rebellion.[103]

Once they had ousted Daoud the revolutionaries immediately established a new government and started ruling by decree. Taraki was named both president and prime minister, and he retained the post of PDPA secretary-general. The cabinet consisted of eleven members of Khalq and ten Parchamis. Amin was named the deputy prime minister and foreign minister, and Karmal was named vice-president. The leading military figures, Waranjar and Quadir, were promoted and also given cabinet posts. Afghanistan's new leaders insisted that they were nonaligned and repeatedly denied to the foreign press that the PDPA was even Marxist.[104] However, the actions and statements of the new regime clearly defined its Marxist orientation. Afghanistan could be considered nonaligned only in the same sense as Castro's Cuba, as Taraki drew Afghanistan even closer to the Soviet Union. The Soviet Union was the first country to recognize the new regime, on 1 May 1978. Relations between the two countries soon exhibited 'fraternal' characteristics as Brezhnev sent his personal greetings to the new Afghan leader, Nur Muhammad Taraki.[105] The Soviet press explained the reasons for Daoud's downfall as resulting from the fact that 'contradictory tendencies of Afghanistan's political development in recent years ... left hopes for radical changes unfulfilled by Daoud'.[106]

The most significant diplomatic agreement between the Soviets and the new regime was the Treaty of Friendship, Good Neighbourliness and Co-operation signed in Moscow on 5 December 1978. Although there are few specifics in the treaty, Articles 4 and 8 contain implicit security commitments that would be used in 1979 to justify the legality of Soviet intervention:

> Article 4. The high contracting parties, acting in the spirit of the traditions of friendship and good-neighborliness, as well as the UN Charter, shall consult each other and take by agreement appropriate measures to ensure the security, independence and territorial integrity of the two countries. In the interests of strengthening the defense capacity of the high contracting parties they shall continue to develop co-operation on the military field on the basis of appropriate agreements concluded between them.
> Article 8. The high contracting parties shall facilitate the development of co-operation among Asian states and the establishment of relations of peace and good-neighborliness and mutual confidence among them and the creation of an effective security system in Asia on the basis of joint efforts by all countries on the continent.[107]

The new regime began a series of purges, imprisonments and executions. Thousands of Daoud's civil servants, diplomats, governors, police, professors and the like were jailed, and their positions were filled with party faithful who possessed little experience in government.[108] The honeymoon also ended between Parcham and Khalq. Most of the Parchamis were purged from the cabinet by Taraki in July 1978; some were demoted and assigned to diplomatic posts abroad. Karmal was one of Taraki's targets, but on his ordered recall as ambassador to Prague he refused to return to Kabul, choosing instead to flee to the Soviet Union. Apparently the Soviets kept him safe in Moscow in case he should ever be needed. Lesser members of Parcham, including hundreds of military officers, were also purged from important positions.[109] Along with the political purge, Taraki pursued an ambitious plan of rapid social and economic reforms. These reforms were pressed forward with revolutionary zeal. The first months of the PDPA regime appear to have gone relatively well, before resentment of change began to seep in. The mass of the rural population seemed to be adopting a cautious position toward the new policies, which included the positive measures of spreading educational and health opportunities and granting cultural rights to nationalities.[110]

However, in keeping with their strong love of tradition, the Afghans soon became weary of government officials interfering in their lives. The majority of the new PDPA reforms were seen as an affront to tribal heritage and culture. The attempt to impose rapid and arbitrary change by brute force, against the wishes of the people, produced not progress but chaos, bloodshed and civil war. Programmes addressing land reform, marriage laws and other social issues threatened the foundations of traditional Afghan society and were implemented by the new regime so quickly that even the Soviets later criticized them. Although the failed reform policies had been introduced under Taraki, for political reasons the Soviets would later place the majority of blame on Amin, claiming,

> Great harm to the revolution has been done by Hafizullah Amin who wormed his way to power by intrigues and deceit. H. Amin used impermissible methods in implementing such major transformations as the agrarian reforms and the liquidation of adult illiteracy, which distorted their progressive essence. People's traditions and religious convictions were ignored, there were crude violations of revolutionary legality, arrests and executions, without trial or investigation, of innocent people, including honest members of the PDPA.[111]

The single factor that probably did the most to create antagonism toward the communist regime was its lack of Islamic credentials and apparent adherence to atheism. To make matters worse, the Muslim green was replaced by the communist red in the Afghan flag. In a country consisting of virtually 100 per cent devout Muslims, atheistic leaders were bound to command very little respect. Like Diem's regime in South Vietnam, it almost appears that the Taraki regime planned systematically to alienate every segment of the Afghan populace by implementing radical policies in a society bound by tradition. In response to the endless string of indignities imposed by the new regime, the Afghans rebelled. By the autumn of 1978 the uprising had spread to all twenty-nine provinces, and the revolt cut across almost every segment of Afghan society. The opposition included not only religious leaders and landlords but also virtually all classes and occupations within the general population. In March 1979 the government's attempt to introduce education for women sparked a mob revolt in the city of Herat. Afghan soldiers joined in the carnage that followed, in which many government officials, including more than a hundred Soviet advisers and their families, were beheaded. Horrifically, their heads were stuck on poles and paraded around the city in triumph, with the final death total reaching 5,000. Much like those Americans who stereotyped Asians as having little respect for life, the Herat massacre implanted the stereotype among Russians that the Afghans were 'savages'. As a result, the later indiscriminate killing of civilians and combatants in both Vietnam and Afghanistan was justified as being morally acceptable. Afghan soldiers also mutinied in Kabul, and in all these instances brutal counter-measures were used by the government forces.[112]

The Herat incident proved decisive in stimulating contingency planning for intervention by the Kremlin. As the rebellion grew and the communist government showed itself less able to suppress it, the Soviets were asked repeatedly by the Afghan government to augment their role in the conflict. From April to November 1979 the Afghan government made at least a dozen requests for Soviet troops, ranging in size from single battalion to multiple divisions.[113] The Soviets responded to some but not all of these requests, and by November 1979 there were more than 4,500 military advisers in the country. As in the US response in Vietnam in 1965, increased supplies of modern military equipment were sent into Afghanistan, and Soviet pilots in helicopter gunships and jet aircraft began to fly combat missions against rebel positions. The Soviets sent troops to assume control of strategic airfields, roads and bridges. Step by step, Moscow was rapidly moving toward massive intervention.[114] The leadership in Moscow was clearly worried about the country holding together under PDPA leadership. In addition to offering weapons and ideological advice, like the United States in Vietnam, the Kremlin realized the importance of strengthening the PDPA government among the people. After being prodded by Soviet advisers, Taraki and Amin were seen attending prayer services, and they were pressed to patch up relations with the remaining Parcham cadres. As in the case of the Vietnamese elements who rejected Washington's suggestions, the Afghan leaders ignored the majority of Soviet suggestions.[115]

The Soviets focused their displeasure with the uncooperative Afghans on Amin, who was the real mover of Afghan policy. Apparently President Taraki had assumed more of a figurehead role while Amin actually controlled the government, and Moscow attempted to undermine Amin from within.

Taraki, after returning from a trip to Cuba, stopped in Moscow for informal talks with Brezhnev. He was apparently instructed to manœuvre Amin out of the Afghan government. Shortly after his return to Kabul a gun battle occurred at the presidential palace in which the target, Amin, escaped unharmed. Taraki, however, was not so lucky; he became the first Afghan communist leader to be deposed, and like many previous Afghan sovereigns, he met a violent death in the process. Amin was immediately proclaimed president and took over all of Taraki's duties.[116] The Soviets had been caught by surprise again. Unlike the results of the US-supported coup against Diem, the very leader that Moscow wished to have removed from power was now in complete charge – after having ousted the man so recently seen in the Soviet media cordially meeting with Brezhnev. Amin in turn did not trust the Soviets and went so far as publicly to accuse the Soviet ambassador of helping to plot against him. The Soviets were asked to replace Ambassador Puzanov, and they were further insulted by Amin's absence from a reception in celebration of the Great October Revolution at the Soviet embassy in Kabul.[117] Still, the Soviets decided, for the time being, to work with Amin, and Amin pacified the Soviets somewhat by carrying out one of the main policies that Moscow had been advocating: attempting to broaden the base of popular support. He also made efforts to blunt the rebellion by promising religious freedom, repairing mosques and referring to passages in the Koran in his speeches. However, most Afghans paid no attention to these feeble attempts by Amin to convince them that he was a good Muslim and the representative of Allah. In the eyes of the population, the government lacked legitimacy both in their eyes and in the eyes of God.[118]

Military intervention

The Politburo may have begun to consider the possibility of military intervention as early as the spring of 1979, and from April to August various officials conducted fact-finding missions. In August 1979 Lieutenant General Gorelov, the Chief Military Adviser in Afghanistan, counselled against any further Soviet deployments. His analysis was countered by the senior in-country KGB officer, Lieutenant General Invanov, who argued the opposite. Like the US government in Vietnam, the Soviets sent another fact-finding mission led by General Ivan G. Pavlovskii, the Commander of Ground Forces and a specialist on military intervention. Pavlovskii had made a trip to Czechoslovakia in 1968 before the Soviet invasion of that country and he had commanded the invading Eastern-bloc troops. During August–October 1979 Pavlovskii surveyed the Afghan situation, eventually advising against further Soviet involvement on the grounds that it lacked a clear military mission. Pavlovskii was overruled by the senior defence official on the politburo, Marshal Ustinov – a move which suggests that Brezhnev's politburo had already made the political decision. Personnel and equipment began to accumulate in Soviet Central Asia, reserve units were mobilized, and additional troops were transferred from the western Soviet Union.[119]

Statements appearing in Soviet military journals in early 1979 indicate that Soviet theorists were building their case for the containment of 'imperialist' aggression. Colonel K. Vorobiev stated, 'Experience shows that only by using armed force can one defend the revolutionary conquests from the attacks of imperialist interventionists, surprise the attacks of the enemies of social progress, and assure the development of a country proceeding along a socialist path.'[120] Like the American global Cold War view in Vietnam, Afghanistan's internal troubles were perceived as being fomented by the Soviet Union's enemies, namely the United States and China. Articles in the Soviet press spoke of increased infiltration by 'counter-revolutionary' forces and warned that the Soviet Union could not remain indifferent to Pakistani and Chinese cooperation directed against Afghanistan.[121] Soviet journalist Leonid Teplinsky would write, 'By the end of 1979 the situation in the Democratic Republic of Afghanistan had sharply aggravated. The imperialists and their henchmen had virtually started an undeclared war against the revolutionary Afghan people. Thousands upon thousands of rebels armed and trained abroad, whole armed units were sent over to Afghan territory. In 1979 alone, about 15,000 mercenaries were trained at 70 special centres in Pakistan.'[122] Despite the animosity between President Amin and the Soviets, the rapidly deteriorating internal situation forced the two sides to work together for a short time. Brezhnev and Kosygin publicly offered Amin their support with an additional $6.7 million in military equipment as well as KGB experts to help him improve the efficiency of the Afghan secret police.[123] As the tempo of Soviet involvement increased, the Afghan regime also faced steadily increasing internal turmoil and rebellion. By the end of 1979, it had become clear to the Kremlin that the Amin regime would soon be overthrown by forces opposing Marxist rule. Like the US presidential deceptions in Vietnam, though, as late as 23 December 1979, the Soviet news media was denying Western claims that Red Army troops were mobilized for intervention in Afghanistan. *Pravda* referred to these claims as 'pure fabrications', quoting Hafizullah Amin as saying, 'The Soviet Union has never infringed on our sovereignty ... is not doing so, and never will.'[124] One day later, on Christmas Eve 1979, Soviet forces began their invasion of Afghanistan.

There are no clear and consistent accounts of what actually occurred in the last days of December 1979. Western analysts were sceptical of Soviet claims that a desperate President Amin had called for Soviet assistance. In fact, however, both Taraki and Amin had been seeking greater troop commitments for months. What seems to have caused the confusion is the widely held Western view that 100,000 Soviet troops suddenly invaded the country all at once, assassinated Amin, and began their occupation. Actually, Soviet forces intervened in roughly two phases, with the first contingent of troops having the Afghan government's approval. Early in July, a battalion from the 105th Guards Airborne Division had been transferred to Bagram airfield near Kabul. It was these troops who seized control of the base, paving the way for the rapid infusion of Soviet forces beginning Christmas Eve 1979. As late as 26 December, Amin is reported to have told an Arab journalist that the Soviet Union respected Afghan independence and that Soviet forces were coming to help him put down the rebellion.[125] From 24 to 26 December, approximately 5,000 Soviet airborne troops landed in a steady stream of transport aircraft at the Bagram military air base north of Kabul, and mechanized forces moved across the Soviet–Afghan border. There was no reaction by Afghan ground forces to indicate that the Soviet troops were unexpected arrivals. The Afghan forces did not oppose the Soviet forces and apparently had received approval of the Soviet landing in advance. On the evening of 27 December Soviet forces seized all strategic points in the city, and special forces units attacked and killed Amin and his small contingent of personal supporters.[126]

In the early morning hours following Amin's death, Kabul Radio broadcast a message from Babrak Karmal announcing the formation of a new government under his leadership. On this date, 27 December 1979, he officially asked the Soviet Union for assistance:

> Because of the continuation and expansion of aggression, intervention and provocations by the foreign enemies of Afghanistan and for the purpose of defending the gains of the Saur [April] Revolution, territorial integrity, national independence and preservation of peace and security, and on the basis of the treaty of friendship, good-neighborliness and cooperation dated 5 December 1978, the Democratic Republic of Afghanistan earnestly demands that the Soviet Union render urgently political, moral and economic assistance, including military aid, to Afghanistan. The government of the Soviet Union has accepted the proposal of the Afghan side.[127]

Western sources claim that this message was broadcast from a powerful transmitter inside the Soviet Union operating on the Kabul radio frequency. Karmal would later claim that he had returned before the Soviet troops entered the country and had directed the coup against Amin.

Soviet media sources presented the coup against Amin as an internal Afghan affair that did not involve Soviet troops. Historian Ghulam Muradov tersely summarized events by stating,

> More and more people became convinced that only the liquidation of the Amin regime and rectification of his mistakes and crimes could open the road to realizing the ideals of the April revolution and improve

the situation in the party and country as a whole. H. Amin lost support in the party, among the people, and by the end of 1979 found himself completely isolated. On December 27, 1979, the patriotically minded majority of the PDPA, the Revolutionary Council and the armed forces of the DRA [Democratic Republic of Afghanistan] overthrew the criminal regime of H. Amin.'[128]

It was claimed that Soviet troops entered Afghanistan in large numbers only after Karmal's request, and Soviet forces already in Kabul had not taken part in the fighting until after Amin's death.

Within an hour of the Kabul Radio report announcing the formation of the new Afghan government, the Soviet news agency TASS reported that Brezhnev had sent Karmal a congratulatory message on his new position as Afghanistan's leader.[129] Brezhnev later justified the Soviet invasion by two sources of international law: first, Article 51 of the UN Charter, which guarantees all nations the right to individual or collective self-defence when threatened by outside aggression (in this case the Afghan communists accused the United States, Pakistan and China); and second, Article 4 of the Soviet–Afghan treaty of 1978, which called for military cooperation to ensure security and territorial integrity. In a statement on 13 January 1980, in *Pravda*, Brezhnev spoke of the 'forced nature' of the Soviet military aid to Afghanistan and its temporary character.[130] Brezhnev underscored the Soviet version of 'imperialist' (rather than communist) containment in stating

> It was no simple decision for us to send Soviet military contingents to Afghanistan ... But the Central Committee of the CPSU and the Soviet Government acted in full awareness of their responsibility and took into account all the relevant circumstances. The sole task of the Soviet contingent is to assist the Afghans in repulsing the aggression from without. They will be fully withdrawn from Afghanistan once the reasons for the Afghan leadership's request for them disappear.'[131]

The Soviets also distanced themselves from connections with the ouster of Amin, going so far as to claim, 'The fact that the removal of Amin took place concurrently with the beginning of the introduction of the Soviet contingent is a pure coincidence in time and there is no causal relationship between the two events. The Soviet troops had nothing to do with the removal of Amin and his accomplices. That was the doing of the Afghans themselves.'[132]

Motivations for the Soviet invasion

There is no single factor that can provide an adequate understanding or explanation of why the Soviet Union invaded Afghanistan. It is clear, however, that public justifications (as with US government statements on Vietnam) often obscured real policy goals and motivations. Regrettably, despite the opening of Soviet-era archives in Russia after 1991, there is no source of documents such as the *Pentagon Papers* which clearly outlines the decision-making process or reveals monumental new 'truths' about the Soviet invasion. On a number of occasions both General Secretary Mikhail Gorbachev and Soviet Foreign Minister Eduard Shevardnadze claimed that they (as candidate members of the Politburo in 1979) had no prior knowledge of invasion plans, and were informed by press reports of the Soviet action.[133]

Other information has revealed that select members of the Soviet politburo were briefed by various military experts beginning in August 1979. Despite ambiguities, these varying reports make it clear that: (1) the decision did not involve the entire politburo, though the exact make-up of the small circle remains unclear; (2) at a minimum, the decision-making body included General Secretary Brezhnev, Foreign Minister Andrei Gromyko, KGB Chief Yuri Andropov, Defence Minister Ustinov; and Ideology Chief Mikhail Suslov; (3) a variety of policy opinions, and arguments both for and against invasion, were provided by the KGB and military analysts; and (4) the majority of Soviet accounts emphasize the primary importance of Brezhnev, despite his enfeebled condition, in making the final decision.[134] Regardless of who made the decision, such as the American decision to send combat forces into Vietnam, the Soviet decision to send troops into Afghanistan was influenced by a combination of historic, immediate, ideological, regional and global factors.

Foremost among historic factors is geography. Even though the historical quest for warm-water ports[135] had largely been bypassed by advances in technology, Soviet interest in Afghanistan was heavily shaped by traditional considerations of border security. As noted in previous chapters, under both the Tsars and the Soviets, the Russian empire had always considered Afghanistan to be an important geopolitical entity. Territorial competition with the British had given way to competition with the Americans after the Second World War.[136] A particularly insightful observation is made by Robert S. Litwak, who states:

> The dynamic of imperial power, however, is governed by a self-perpetuating logic. For the empire, all territorial acquisitions in defense of the frontier are by definition defensive. This attribute makes the debate over whether Soviet action in Afghanistan was motivated by offensive or defensive considerations particularly unenlightening. The fact that Afghanistan is contiguous to the Soviet Union automatically placed it in a different category from other instances of involvement in the Third World.[137]

What then were the Soviet leaders defending? And what were the domestic, regional and global 'threats' that could cause a defensive reaction? On the domestic and regional level two crucial though quite separate ideological factors must be considered that were related to political legitimacy and stability in the Soviet order – socialism and Islamic fundamentalism.

As mentioned earlier, General Pavlovskii had spent some time in Afghanistan surveying the situation several months before the invasion, as he had done in Czechoslovakia before commanding the Eastern bloc troops in the 1968 Soviet invasion of that country.[138] Pavlovskii's involvement in the pre-invasion planning serves to highlight the continuity in theory and practice in Soviet foreign policy during the Brezhnev years. The political decision to invade Afghanistan was heavily influenced by Marxist–Leninist theory. In 1968 the Soviets had justified the Czechoslovakian invasion in writings that later became known as the Brezhnev Doctrine:

> There is no doubt that the peoples of the socialist countries and the Communist Parties have and must have freedom to determine their country's path of development. However, any decision of theirs must damage neither socialism in their own country, nor the fundamental interests of the other socialist countries, nor the worldwide workers' movement, which is waging a struggle for socialism. *This means that every Communist Party is responsible not only for its own people but also to all the socialist countries and to the entire communist movement* ... Just as, in V.I. Lenin's words, someone living in a society cannot be free of that society, so a socialist state that is in a system of other states constituting a socialist commonwealth cannot be free of the common interests of that commonwealth ... World socialism as a social system is the common achievement of the working people of all countries, *it is indivisible* ...[139]

This is the crux of the Brezhnev Doctrine: once a country is socialist – and aligns itself with the Soviet Union – it must always remain socialist. The primary 'common interest' of the socialist confederation is the loyalty of all its members. Ideological constructs are not declared frivolously by the leaders of a state who justify their own positions of authority on the basis of an infallible ideology. The Brezhnev Doctrine is thus more than simply a cursory *ex post facto* exercise in Soviet theory. Once incorporated into the publicly pronounced edicts of Marxist–Leninist thought and reaffirmed by successive Soviet regimes with the backing of state military forces, it became difficult for Soviet leaders to deviate from any important theoretical constructs that served to legitimize the regime. The supposed unerring 'scientific' correctness of Marxist–Leninist ideology was the very crucible from which coercive state authority emanated and justified the Communist Party's monopoly of power in the Soviet Union.

The Soviets acknowledged the Afghan communists as a legitimate ruling party in a revolutionary state. In 1978 they had thus accepted Afghanistan as part of the international socialist movement, making themselves responsible for the success of socialism in Afghanistan. Combined with the geopolitical reality of Afghanistan's location on the Soviet border, such ideological recognition provided precedent for the implementation of the Brezhnev Doctrine in times of crisis.[140] In the world outside of the Soviet Union, the Brezhnev Doctrine (a Western term) was perceived as having been extended beyond the boundaries of the Warsaw Pact, much in the same fashion that George Kennan's original proposal to stop the spread of Soviet-supported communism was expanded to include communism of all variations. By openly committing large numbers of non-advisory troops to combat outside of the lines drawn at Yalta, the West's policy of containment was being challenged by a new manifestation of the Soviet policy of socialist containment of what was perceived as 'imperialist' aggression.

The Kremlin was also concerned with the rising tide of Islamic fundamentalism in the Middle East. The Muslim population of Central Asia, then projected to reach eighty million by the year 2000, was the fastest demographic growth sector of the Soviet population in 1979. With a Soviet–Afghan border of over 400 miles adjacent to revolutionary Iran, the leadership was concerned about the possible spillover effect if socialism was defeated by Islamic fundamentalism in Afghanistan. The Soviet Union also believed that the United States was responsible for fomenting dissent in its Muslim population. A KGB general in Azerbaijan warned, 'In view of the situation in Iran and Afghanistan, the US special services are trying to exploit the Islamic religion – especially in areas where the Muslim population lives – as one factor influencing the political situation in our country.'[141] Thus, regime maintenance in Afghanistan served demands of both Soviet ideological legitimacy and realpolitik.[142]

A survey of Soviet officials showed that many were deeply concerned with America's potential role in Iran to support the return of the Iranian monarchy. 'A 1981 US International Communications Agency report, based on 160 proxy interviews of middle-level Soviet officials and analysts, reported that many Soviet analysts believed that the US build-up in the Indian Ocean presaged a full-scale invasion of Iran ... We had to gain a foothold to match the one the United States was going to obtain.'[143] The Kremlin leaders clearly miscalculated US policy in Iran. Yet, like the Americans in Vietnam, they worried about the possible negative results of not taking action in Afghanistan. Likewise, Soviet prestige in aligned socialist states in the developing world, including Angola, Ethiopia and Vietnam would be heavily damaged if 'reactionary forces' were able to overthrow a socialist-oriented state directly on the Soviet border. Brezhnev cited the loss of Chile in 1973 as an example of this line of thinking: 'To have refrained from intervention in Afghanistan would allow aggressive forces to repeat here what they were able to do, for example, in Chile ...'.[144]

The Soviets were also concerned with their place in the trilateral relationship involving America and China. In December 1979 Soviet fears were increased by NATO's evolving plans to deploy new medium-range ballistic missile systems, and their uncertainty regarding relations with America was magnified by the looming failure of the SALT II treaty in the US Senate. Moscow was also concerned with the growing relationship between America and China. In 1978 and 1979 there appeared to be little hope for improvement in relations with either America or China while the two were in the midst of their own detente. The Soviets had backed Hanoi during China's poorly executed invasion of Vietnam in December 1978 (in response to Hanoi's invasion of Cambodia). China's invasion had occurred only two weeks after Deng Xiao Peng returned from a Washington summit that had solidified the resumption of full diplomatic ties between the United States and China.[145] Bilateral relations with China hit a new low in April 1979 when Beijing refused to renew the 1950 Sino-Soviet Treaty of Friendship, and both sides reported yet another border clash in Central Asia. In October the pace of decay accelerated when the United States announced that Harold Brown, the Secretary of Defense, would visit China to discuss technology transfers. A senior Western diplomat in Moscow reported that Foreign Minister Gromyko was obsessed by the threat to Soviet security posed by the growing Sino-US accommodation.[146] Likewise, the conflict between Moscow and Beijing for influence among socialist states in the developing world remained keen. For their part, the Soviet Union was fighting two ideological cold wars, one against the United States, in which Western liberalism was pitted against Marxism–Leninism, and the second against China, in which the Moscow-centred Marxism–Leninism was pitted against the Beijing-centred Marxism–Leninism–Maoism.

The leadership in the Kremlin had been concerned that Hafizullah Amin, wary of Soviet attempts to dispose of him, might sell out to the United States. According to Andrei Gromyko, 'Brezhnev was simply shaken by the murder of Taraki, who not long before had been his guest, and who thought that the Amin group might cut a deal with United States.'[147] An additional factor in the decision to invade Afghanistan was what Joseph Collins describes as an 'absence of constraints'. In military, economic and political terms there was apparently little that the outside world could do in 1979 to counter the Soviet move. The United States could only counter through its nominal ally Pakistan, and US attention was focused on the ongoing revolution in Iran. China could do little in the remote Wakhan corridor region and had been embarrassed by its weak military performance against Vietnam the previous year. The United States had not reacted strongly to the invasions of Hungary and Czechoslovakia, both of which served as a guide and precedent for Soviet intervention in socialist states on its border. Moreover, the Afghans were divided and seen as easily cowed by the might of the Red Army, which had successfully subdued the Central Asian regions in the 1920s. Finally, unlike the United States, there was no domestic opposition or real potential for protest.[148]

The United States in Afghanistan, 1956–79

Beginning in 1956 the United States belatedly attempted to redress its failure to implement containment in Afghanistan during the previous decade. In order to counter Soviet successes, Afghanistan was included in a low-budget programme run for allied and neutral countries which placed foreign officers in US military schools. From 1958 to 1962 enrolment had risen from one to a peak of sixty-eight, though in 1978 (the last year of the programme) only twenty Afghans were enrolled in the programme. By 1978 over 3,700 Afghan officers had been trained in the Soviet Union.[149] As noted in Chapter 2, large-scale Soviet aid to the developing world caused a change in US containment policy. Before 1956 most US funds were awarded on both economic and banking (profit) criteria. After 1956, political concerns were factored in, and often became the overriding reason for granting aid. In 1959 the State Department designated Afghanistan an 'emergency action area', and it began studying ways to compete with Soviet programmes. While the Soviet Union focused on training military officers, the United States made a major effort to train important civilian personnel. Grants were made for education in Kabul and for Afghan students studying at US universities. In a cooperative effort, which characterized a number of superpower development projects, Soviet-built roads in the north and west were linked to American-built roads in the south and east.[150]

Altruistic cooperation was only one motivation behind US aid to Afghanistan. A case in point was the international airport in the southeast city of Kandahar. Construction on the airport continued even after its sole purpose for existence, to provide a refuelling base for propeller-aircraft, had been made obsolete by the development of longer-range jet aircraft. The airport was not, however, simply a case of an infrastructure project which once started, created a momentum of its own. The United States feared that if it shut the project down, the Soviets would take it over. Developmental funds for a needless airport were seen as necessary to prevent the Soviets from controlling Afghan civil aviation. In addition to the Cold War public relations boost, the airport was reported to have been designated as a potential recovery base where US strategic bombers could land after attacks in the Soviet east in the event of a nuclear war.[151]

Generally, however, before the communist coup in 1978 and the Soviet invasion the following year, the United States did not greatly concern itself with Afghanistan. Policy indifference in the first decade after the Second World War gave way to inconsistent and half-hearted competition with the

Soviet Union in the 1960s and 1970s. Leon Poullada summarizes the US programme as follows:

(1) It was inefficiently executed, cumbersome, burdened with red tape and plagued by long and unjustified delays ...

(2) It lacked steadfastness. As the global Soviet threat shaded off into detente, the program lost momentum and received declining appropriations.

(3) It could not compensate for bumbling American diplomacy, which mishandled the military aid and Pushtunistan issues. Soviet diplomacy, on the other hand, exploited these issues brilliantly.[152]

In 1978 the United States reacted cautiously to the overthrow of Daoud. American analysts were hesitant to classify the coup as 'communist' for three reasons. First, it was unclear that the Soviets had been involved in the coup, and many of the military officers involved had been supporters of Daoud in his 1973 revolt. Also the very idea of a 'communist' revolution seemed somewhat outlandish in the tradition-bound Islamic state of Afghanistan. Second, the Carter administration did not wish publicly to concede to another Soviet 'victory' in the Third World. Condemning the new PDPA leadership might have negative results, as any hostile US reaction might force the new regime even closer to the Soviet Union. Third, the US administration and its foreign policy experts were distracted by the civil unrest in Iran, the Camp David peace talks, the SALT II treaty, new relations with China and NATO missile negotiations. As had been the case during the previous forty years, Afghanistan simply did not have a priority for the decision-makers in Washington.[153]

The United States initially followed a policy of 'constructive engagement' and in May 1978 recognized the newly renamed Democratic Republic of Afghanistan. American aid continued through 22 February 1979, when the remainder of its $20 million commitment for that year was suspended. American aid was severed after the mysterious kidnapping and death of the US ambassador, Adolph Dubs. The kidnappers, whose motives remain shrouded, were killed along with Ambassador Dubs when Afghan police (accompanied by Soviet advisers) stormed a hotel room in Kabul in a hail of automatic weapons fire. The State Department responded with a formal protest to both the Soviet Union and Afghanistan. When the protest was rejected by both parties, the United States elected not to replace the ambassador, cut the US embassy staff, removed dependants and ended the Peace Corps' 22-year programme in Afghanistan.[154]

In the final months of the build-up before the Soviet invasion, US intelligence was well aware of military activity along the Soviet–Afghan border. On five occasions US diplomatic representatives expressed concern to Soviet officials over the activity, and they made it clear that US–Soviet relations would be jeopardized if the Soviets moved into Afghanistan.[155] However, no clear specifics of the possible US response were signalled to the Soviets, and US threats at that time lacked a certain credibility. Over the course of the previous year the Soviets had become anaesthetized to such routine warnings. The United States had failed to act on its protests after the stationing of Soviet combat troops in Cuba and the arrival of Soviet naval forces in Vietnam. The mildness of the US response to activities in these countries – which were of enough historical importance to America that Soviet involvement had seemed likely to invoke a strong reaction – logically led the Soviets to conclude that any US response to its policies in Afghanistan would also be relatively indulgent.

THE INTERVENTIONS COMPARED: FROM CONTAINMENT TO DETAINMENT

Having summarized the history of US and Soviet relations in Vietnam and Afghanistan leading to direct military intervention, it is now possible to begin to answer one of our primary questions: 'Was Afghanistan the Soviet Vietnam?' In the first two chapters a number of similarities in the political histories of Afghanistan and Vietnam were discussed, with especial attention to their dealings with neighbouring great powers and to the importance of traditional sources of political legitimacy. One critical difference, however, was the evolution and eventual elimination of direct European (British) colonialism in Afghanistan, and the continuing presence of European (French) colonialism in Vietnam at the beginning of the Cold War. The timing of events is of crucial importance to our understanding of the evolution of American and Soviet relations in Vietnam and Afghanistan. In Vietnam the United States had little or no history of relations before the Second World War. Intervention in Vietnam's internal affairs (both in support of the French, and unilaterally) from 1945 to 1965 was a marked change from a long historic US policy of isolationism. However, in the context of the Cold War, both in regional and global terms, American involvement in Vietnam was a logical extension of its containment policy. After China had been 'lost' the United States had managed a partial victory against communism in Korea. The Korean experience helped to condition the United States into making a binding commitment to containment in Asia as being fundamental to its worldwide national interests. However, as will be seen more clearly in the next chapter, the Korean War conditioned the United States to fear direct Chinese involvement. This fear led the United States to seek a compromise in Vietnam modelled on the partition of Korea, a plan that was based on the erroneous assumption that local political dynamics in one Asian country were similar to those in any another.

By contrast, the Soviet Union's history of relations in Afghanistan was markedly different. Dating back to Tsarist times, Moscow's policies toward Afghanistan were consistent to an unusually high degree – until 1979. Previously, changes in governments in Afghanistan were not challenged by Moscow, as long as border stability was maintained and Russia's foreign competitors in superpower politics did not appear to be seeking undue advantages. This policy rationale had been maintained into the Soviet era, showing that ideological purity was of secondary importance to national interest. In the early period of Soviet–Afghan relations, when the Bolsheviks actively promoted worldwide revolution, they chose to establish normal diplomatic contacts with the Afghan monarchy. As seen in the previous chapter, the Soviets did not promote revolution in Afghanistan, and they went so far as to aid the monarchy when faced with internal rebellion. Perhaps the best example of the Soviet Union's desire to uphold the status quo is its reaction to the peasant rebellion in 1929. Bacha-i-Saquo, the peasant leader, was the perfect, ideologically correct rebel as described by Leninist revolutionary theory. Instead of supporting a leader of the peasant masses, the Soviets chose to support the king, apparently viewing Bacha as an ally whose time had not arrived in tradition-bound Afghanistan. The Soviets decided that their national interest was best served by helping to perpetuate the Afghan monarchy. If the Soviets were planning to annex Afghanistan in the 1920s and 1930s, this situation had presented them with an ideal opportunity. However, maintaining good relations with Britain and building the state at home were higher priorities. Their decision not to support the peasant revolt refutes any claims of Soviet imperialism toward Afghanistan prior to the Cold War.

However, like the world-view in US policy toward Vietnam, by 1979 ideology had become entrenched as an important factor in all Soviet foreign policy, marking a distinct change in the continuum of Tsarist and Soviet policy toward Afghanistan up to that point. In the Cold War period, national security concerns had (in certain cases) become synonymous with the defence of ideological doctrine. By abandoning the Afghan socialists to what was perceived as aggression from capitalist imperialists, Soviet state security would be directly threatened. In some cases, as in Chile, little could be done. However, because of the contiguous border with Afghanistan the Soviets believed that they were protecting not only the socialist cause but also the Soviet Union itself. Thus traditional concerns of territory and geopolitics became juxtaposed with ideology – as in the rationale behind US policies in Vietnam. Vietnam itself was seen as vital to US security because abandoning the country to the communists would threaten more vital economic and political interests in Europe and Japan. Both superpowers perceived their actions as having major ramifications beyond the locus of actual events. In the global Cold War theatre, all stages, no matter how remote, were interconnected in the greater drama. Even though Vietnam and the United States are separated by approximately 7,000 miles of ocean, psychologically the border between the capitalist and communist world was contiguous.

The roads to superpower intervention had similar as well as dissimilar characteristics. In Vietnam, the United States managed to stave off direct intervention for over a decade by supporting the French efforts to destroy the Viet Minh. In Afghanistan, the Soviet Union intervened much more quickly, in a period of approximately one year. The United States had the convenience of supporting a close ally, whose importance to European security was the primary motivation for aid in Vietnam. The United States also moved slowly in its Vietnam policy because of the Korean War, which had been conducted with the support of Western allies. However, in Afghanistan the Soviets perceived an 'absence of constraints'. Its Eastern European interventions had not caused a direct confrontation with the United States, and so intervention in Afghanistan should have elicited a similarly mild response. Thus both superpowers had been conditioned by their previous interventions. The US experience in Korea conditioned decision-making in Vietnam, and the largely successful Soviet interventions in Eastern Europe were seen as the role model to be copied when defending socialism in Afghanistan, even to the extent of using the same military staff personnel to plan and command the operations.

Despite the differences in conditions and time-span, the reasoning and justifications for the two interventions were very similar. The superpowers viewed the survival of their client states as tied to their own national security. Both superpowers believed that if their treaty commitments and public pledges to Vietnam and Afghanistan were not upheld, then their international credibility and prestige would be undermined. In the case of the United States, domestic political concerns played a crucially important role, as the hyperbolic political rhetoric of containment made any failure to fight communism the Achilles' heel of American politics. Democrats and Republicans alike upheld the doctrine of containment; the debate was over which political party did it better. After the 'loss of China' in 1949, both parties believed that going 'soft on communism' was tantamount to political suicide. Thus, losing Vietnam was seen as losing the next election. Although public opinion was not as critical a factor in the totalitarian one-party rule of the Soviet Union in 1979, it should not be overlooked. Mistakes in foreign policy had cost Khrushchev his position in the party, and because the Eastern European states were considered important variables in the domestic politics of the Soviet empire, weakness on the part of the Kremlin might be interpreted as a loosening of the reins throughout the socialist camp. Likewise, if the Kremlin allowed its Afghan allies to fall, it opened itself to further criticism from its communist competitors in Beijing.

Throughout its history, US foreign policy has been rationalized simultaneously according to the often contradictory mandates of traditional

European-style balance-of-power politics and the utopian idealism of the Enlightenment. The distinction between traditional power politics and idealism in US foreign policy is often traced to President Woodrow Wilson. Wilson is the US president most identified with an institutional approach to idealism (which was expressed in his promotion of the League of Nations); likewise, vibrant idealism was conspicuous in his famous Fourteen Points plan for permanent peace in Europe at the end of the First World War. But the idealism in US foreign policy actually dates to the founding of the republic. Many of the influential political figures of the time, notably Thomas Jefferson and Tom Paine, believed that the United States and its revolution would serve as a universal model, that the principles of American democracy could be applied to the rest of the world.[156] Although early US political leaders avoided direct involvement in continental European affairs and largely rejected the use of military force and military intervention as amoral tools of European statecraft, the early Republic nonetheless clearly pursued its own version of a balance of power in such regional policies as the Monroe Doctrine. Similarly, the westward expansion across the North American continent illustrates well the duality of American foreign policy. Dating from the Louisiana Purchase, running through the Spanish–American War, the Mexican–American War and the purchase of Alaska, Jefferson, his peers and their successors were proponents of expansion on the North American continent and involved themselves deeply in the allocation of the state resources and the diplomatic necessities that were required to confront France, Britain and Russia for the territories west of the original thirteen colonies. However, American imperialism in North America was justified in terms of idealized democracy and 'manifest destiny', both of which had flowed from the original religious mythology of the first Puritans. From the founding of the republic, the success of the American Revolution was a sign that God had blessed the American people, that America was a 'special' place, and that it was America's destiny to lead the world.[157]

Throughout American history, this crusading spirit was evident in every instance of US intervention. However, like that of other states, US intervention was determined largely by its power capabilities. During the first century of its existence, the United States was largely incapable of intervening abroad. However, upon achieving the substantial financial and industrial foundations that are the critical precursors for the building of military power-projection capabilities, the United States entered its own era of international intervention – focused first on its neighbours of lesser power in Central America, South America, the Caribbean and Asia, and later in Europe with the world wars. Intervention in Vietnam was the latest in this sequence of ideologically based interventions.

Likewise, the roles of power and of ideology were crucial to the conduct of Soviet foreign policy. Before Gorbachev's revolutionary changes in the mid 1980s, Soviet politics, both internal and external, were shaped and guided by Lenin's overall world-view, as discussed in Chapter 2 – the *kto kovo* ('who will do in whom') understanding of politics as a zero-sum game. The invasion of Afghanistan, like previous Soviet invasions in Eastern Europe, was conditioned by this world-view. Military force was seen as necessary in order to prevent the loss of an allied Marxist government in 1979. Keeping with the time-honoured practices of 'scientific socialism', which dictated that policies be grounded in Marxist–Leninist theory, the Soviets justified the Afghan invasion along orthodox ideological lines. The model invoked was that of the Czechoslovakian invasion, under the guise of the Brezhnev Doctrine – the Soviet equivalent of America's 'Monroe Doctrine'.

The most glaring similarity, evident at the very beginning of both military interventions, was the worsening lack of domestic legitimacy of the regimes in Saigon and Kabul. In South Vietnam from 1956 to 1965, the Diem regime had systematically moved to eliminate possible political enemies and competitors. Although certainly not democratic, Diem's behaviour was not necessarily a violation of the Vietnamese tradition of authoritarian/imperial dynastic rule. However, even though he was successful at eliminating any competition by alternative elites south of the 17th parallel, he failed to generate a significant base of popular support among the masses. Many Catholics who had been driven out of the North by the communists in the mid 1950s supported Diem's regime; however, the more traditionally important and highly respected Buddhists, often viewed as the embodiment of morality in Vietnam, were some of his harshest critics. Diem was thus not just a dictator, but an unpopular dictator with little claim to the Mandate of Heaven – an honour which in the eyes of many Vietnamese was defended by Ho Chi Minh and the nationalist/communist forces. In Afghanistan, the ruling legitimacy of Taraki, Amin and the PDPA elite was even more tenuous than that of Diem in South Vietnam. The new regime had some support in urban areas, primarily in the small proportion of 'Westernized' and educated Afghans; however, its only real base of power was in the upper levels of the military officer corps. Among the enlisted troops, lower-echelon officers and many senior officials, support for the new regime was very weak, with over 50,000 members of the 90,000-strong armed forces joining in the anti-government rebellion, including entire battalions of troops that had changed sides altogether.

Both superpowers had difficulty in dealing with their allies before intervention. The superpowers' inability to control their respective allies had a number of serious repercussions. First, even though Diem was clearly operating outside of American control and often infuriated his 'handlers' by doing things his own way, his regime's total dependence on US economic and military aid undercut his standing as a true Vietnamese nationalist. This was also the case in the Soviets' dealings with their socialist brethren in

Afghanistan. The Afghan communists were factionalized along historical ethnic lines and generally refused to adhere to Soviet pressures to patch up their differences. They did manage to do so long enough to oust Daoud, but infighting returned shortly after the Saur (April) Revolution. President Taraki, a pliant Soviet puppet who was more inclined to take orders from Moscow, was removed by the Kremlin's least-favoured Afghan communist, Hafizullah Amin. As with Diem, Amin's reliance on Soviet assistance helped to debase his standing in the eyes of his tradition-oriented subjects, who were in the majority. The superpowers' inability to control Diem and Amin heightened the risks to their own prestige and credibility, as the rest of the world believed the two leaders were pliant puppets. This was especially troublesome to the United States because of the longevity of Diem's rule. The more time that passed without the institution of the political reforms needed to stabilize the South and build domestic support for the regime, the more the United States became committed to an unpopular leader and, short of massive intervention, the less it could do to halt the slide. Time and again Diem successfully called what he correctly perceived as the US bluff, yet US aid was never cut off. One can only conclude that the tail was wagging the dog. The Soviet case is somewhat different, for Amin's rule did not have the longevity of Diem's, and the systematic, long-term insurgency against Diem contrasts with the more spontaneous uprising against the PDPA regime in Afghanistan. As a result, the Soviets decided much more quickly than the United States that direct intervention was the only way to keep their ideologically compatible client from being defeated. However, unlike Diem's firmer faith in America's loyal commitment to his leadership, Amin distrusted his Soviet patrons, knowing that his abrupt removal of Taraki had placed him in a dangerous position. Thus in both countries the local puppets relied heavily on military and economic lifelines provided by their masters to survive, but neither acted in total compliance with the directives of the superpowers.

Another other important similarity was the equal willingness of the United States and the Soviet Union to resort to military coups when their clients had become too unreliable. In the case of Diem, his death resulted in the more rapid Americanization of the war and further committed the United States to Diem's numerous lesser nationalist successors. Furthermore, in later years, when the details of US complicity in the scheme became known by increasing numbers of American citizens, the legitimacy of the war effort was further undermined, as was the fundamental credibility of the US government. At that time the great majority of Americans could not conceive of their government's being involved in such a disgraceful and immoral enterprise – an act that violated the very core of their ideals. In the case of Afghanistan, the civil war was more rapidly Sovietized by the same forces that were responsible for the death of Amin. The conduct of Soviet troops after their arrival was a clear violation of international law, despite the technical validity of the Kremlin's claim of having been invited by the Afghan government. Clearly, Amin would not have invited Red Army forces into Afghanistan to kill him. In this regard the Soviet violation of Afghan sovereignty was more egregious than that of the Americans, who were not directly responsible for the death of Diem. Nevertheless, just as Diem was the creation of US containment policy in South Vietnam, his death was in large part the responsibility of the US government.

In both cases, the decision to resort to force revealed a similar problem-solving dynamic in the minds of superpower leaders. It was believed that policy objectives in Vietnam and Afghanistan could be achieved with the assistance of massive military power. The multiple failures of their clients' policies and their clients' lack of standing among the masses were serious deficiencies, but they could be mended under the protective cover of overwhelming military force. The Americans never really considered that the Vietnamese might not want capitalism and democracy if it meant being dictated to by foreigners, nor did the Soviets overly concern themselves with whether or not the Afghans really wanted socialism. Neither superpower questioned the essential propriety of its own guiding ideology, and both assumed that the Vietnamese and the Afghans who fought against them were either ignorant Third Worlders or the agents of their enemies. Military force would stabilize the situation long enough to convert a significant proportion of the unenlightened, to intimidate those who could be cowed, and to kill the rest. It was acknowledged by national leaders and advisers in both Washington and Moscow that intervention might be long and difficult, but both fundamentally believed that they were incapable of being defeated by the insurgent forces in Vietnam and Afghanistan.

Throughout this chapter I have argued that both superpowers pursued policies in Vietnam and Afghanistan that can be characterized as in terms of ideological containment. As I mentioned at the start of the chapter, however, I believe a more accurate term to describe these superpower policies would be *detainment*.

A majority of the domestic populations of both South Vietnam and Afghanistan clearly expressed their lack of faith in the governing authorities that ruled over them. In the case of Vietnam, the US government's own official history of the Southern insurgency (the *Pentagon Papers*), supports this assertion. Rather than acting to 'contain' the aggression of communist forces from the North, the United States was responding to a communist-led rebellion in the South. The Viet Minh, and later the National Liberation Front, were seen by many Vietnamese as the champions of national liberation because of their record of fighting the Japanese and the French. The NLF thus was perceived by its supporters to embrace the ultimate cultural goal shared by virtually all Vietnamese: national liberation and independence from foreign control. Likewise, rather than acting to 'contain' the aggression of imperialist forces based in Pakistan and China, the Soviet Union was responding to a countrywide rebellion in Afghanistan that was grounded in the combined rationales of Islam, Afghan tradition and historical tribal politics. In sum, the United States and the Soviet Union each attempted to *detain* a population against its will, and *detainment* rather than containment more accurately characterizes US and Soviet policy in these two cases.

This assertion is not simply an exercise in semantic play; rather, it is founded in the moral concepts and distinctions of just-war doctrine.[158] American intervention policies in Vietnam, which were mirrored by those of the Soviet Union in Afghanistan, were grounded in the traditional right of all states to protect themselves from outside aggression. Both the United States and the Soviet Union claimed to be assisting legitimate governments in responding to covert (and at times overt) military moves by other states.

The key word here is of course 'legitimate'. American intervention in Vietnam was premised on the idea that South Vietnam was ruled by a legal and legitimate government, which had been created in the South after the 1954 Geneva Accords. However, when the South Vietnamese regime refused to permit the 1956 elections as stipulated at Geneva, it clearly lost all the legal legitimacy that had been conferred temporarily by the agreements. Likewise, the Soviet legalist argument based on the 1978 Treaty of Friendship and Cooperation with Afghanistan and on the UN Charter is completely debased by the Red Army's murder of the legally recognized sovereign of Afghanistan, President Amin, and the installation of their own puppet dictator, Babrak Karmal.

Even so, the legal legitimacy of any government in the eyes of international law is of subordinate importance to the legitimacy of a government in the eyes of its own people. Political legitimacy can be defined and categorized in many ways, of which Weber's typology (as discussed in Chapters 1 and 2) is but a single model. Going beyond Weber, it is possible to argue that at its most reductionist level (devoid of ideals and morality), legitimacy can be conceived of as simply the ability of a state to control the population within its borders. Ironically, the contemplation of such an 'amoral' definition can be found in the work of two highly idealistic and moralistic writers on modern politics: the nineteenth-century philosopher John Stuart Mill; and the twentieth-century just-war scholar Michael Walzer. Mill argues that a modern state should be viewed as legitimate and self-determining whether or not the state apparatus is derived from popular sovereignty. Thus a state should be considered legitimate even if it lacks free institutions; however, Mill argues that any state that has had institutions (free or otherwise) imposed on it by an outside power cannot be considered legitimate. Legitimacy is thus culture-specific, and other than the important common denominator that legitimacy is determined by local factors, it has no consistently universalizable principles. Of course, Mill argues that democracy is the best form of government because it champions individual liberty; however, even democracy can be legitimate only if it is won by members of a society – it cannot be won for them.[159]

Michael Walzer makes a similar argument in his now famous analysis of just and unjust wars, and he clarifies the concept of legitimacy to a point from which a 'legitimacy test' can be derived. Like Mill, Walzer acknowledges that governments can be legitimate even if they do not conform to Western ideals of democracy. According to Walzer, 'What is crucial is the standing of that government with its own people.' In the case of the US support of the regime in South Vietnam, Walzer states:

> Had the new regime been able to rally support at home, Vietnam today would have joined the dual states of Germany and Korea, and Geneva 1954 would be remembered only as the setting for another cold war partition. But what is the test of popular support in a country where democracy is unknown and elections are routinely managed? The test, for governments as for insurgents, is self help … One assumes the legitimacy of new regimes; there is, so to speak, a period of grace, a time to build support. But that time was ill-used in South Vietnam, and the continuing dependence of the new regime on the United States is damning evidence against it.[160]

Thus in Vietnam the Southern regime could have been considered legitimate (and joined Korea as another partitioned state in Asia) if it had managed to engender enough popular support to survive. Likewise in Afghanistan the communists' task was to achieve some modicum of domestic legitimacy with Soviet assistance. Before intervention, the ruling power of the Afghan regime was heavily reliant on the 90,000 members of the Afghan military; however, when asked to serve the communist Afghans, approximately 50,000 troops rebelled, and the communist regime thereby lost a significant instrument of its ruling power. Therefore, it is unmistakably clear that when the United States and the Soviet Union initially intervened in Vietnam and Afghanistan, they did so on behalf of illegitimate governments. Neither regime was threatened primarily from outside aggression until *after* the United States and the Soviet Union intervened, thereby significantly altering the domestic balance of forces and driving many of the local regimes' opponents into sanctuaries abroad.

With the benefit of hindsight it is easy to criticize the superpowers for attempting what now seem futile quests; however, in the context of their own times, the initial interventions in Vietnam and Afghanistan were not inconsistent within the internal logic of the Cold War struggle for international legitimacy. In other theatres in the wider Cold War drama, both the

United States and the Soviet Union had successfully intervened on the behalf of governments involved in civil conflict, and both had succeeded in part by using military force to help their clients unify the domestic polity and to create some rudimentary form of political legitimacy. Our task, then, is to try to determine why the superpowers were unable to do so in Vietnam and Afghanistan.

NOTES

1. *US Overseas Loans and Grants and Assistance from International Organizations: Special Report Prepared for the House Foreign Affairs Committee* (Washington, DC: US Agency for International Development, 29 March 1968) p. 59.
2. David L. Anderson, *Trapped by Success: The Eisenhower Administration and Vietnam, 1953–1961* (New York: Columbia University Press, 1991) pp. 121–2.
3. George Herring, *America's Longest War: The United States and Vietnam, 1950–1975* (New York: John Wiley, 1979) pp. 62–3.
4. See ibid., pp. 63–5; and Anderson, *Trapped By Success*, p. 132.
5. Anderson, *Trapped by Success*, pp. 132–3.
6. *The Pentagon Papers*, Gravel Edition (Boston: Beacon Press, 1971) (*PP*), Vol. 1, pp. 329–30.
7. Peter A. Poole, *The United States and Indochina from FDR to Nixon* (Huntington: Robert E. Krieger Publishing Co., 1976) p. 54. See also Herring, *America's Longest War*, p. 66.
8. Poole, *The United States and Indochina*, p. 55.
9. Herring, *America's Longest War*, p. 68.
10. Ibid., pp. 68–9.
11. Leslie Gelb and Richard Betts, *The Irony of Vietnam: The System Worked* (Washington, DC: Brookings Institution, 1979) pp. 67–8.
12. Ibid., p. 67.
13. Ibid., pp. 67–8.
14. Cited in William Conrad Gibbons, *The US Government and the Vietnam War: Executive and Legislative Roles and Relationships*, Part II: *1961–1964* (Princeton: Princeton University Press, 1986) p. 3.
15. Ibid., pp. 3–4. The tragic irony of this statement is evident in hindsight. The Vietnamese people suffered far more in the period of American neocolonialism than they ever did under the French.
16. Ibid., pp. 5–6.
17. In the spring of 1961 Kennedy authorized an additional 100 advisers for MAAG and 400 Special Forces troops to train the Vietnamese in counterinsurgency techniques. Earlier in the year he had approved an additional $42 million to aid in support and expansion the Army of the Republic of Vietnam. See Herring, *America's Longest War*, p. 76.
18. Poole, *The United States and Indochina*, pp. 62–3.
19. Arthur M. Schlesinger Jr, *A Thousand Days* (Boston: Houghton Mifflin, 1965) p. 40.
20. See Herring, *America's Longest War*, pp. 82–3.
21. *PP*, Vol. II, p. 120.

22. Herring, *America's Longest War*, p. 85.
23. Robert H. Miller, 'Vietnam: Folly, Quagmire, or Inevitability?' *Studies in Conflict and Terrorism*, 5, 2 (April–June, 1992) pp. 114–15.
24. Herring, *America's Longest War*, pp. 86–7.
25. Gibbons, *The US Government and the Vietnam War*, Part II, p. 108.
26. Guenter Lewy, *America in Vietnam* (Oxford: Oxford University Press, 1978) p. 23.
27. Ibid., p. 25. See also Herring, *America's Longest War*, pp. 88–9.
28. *PP*, Vol. II, pp. 182–3.
29. Marilyn B. Young, *The Vietnam Wars, 1945–1990* (New York: HarperPerennial, 1991) pp. 95–6.
30. Ibid., pp. 98–9. See also Herring, *America's Longest War*, pp. 96–107. For various US documents on the coup planning, see *PP*, Vol. II, pp. 763–9, 780–93.
31. Herring, *America's Longest War*, p. 107.
32. Such is the pity. An ignorant and uninvolved vice-president might have been able to halt America's slide into Vietnam. Johnson's personal foreign policy stamp on the presidency was to magnify and consummate the errors of his predecessors.
33. Maxwell Taylor, *Swords into Plowshares* (New York: W.W. Norton, 1972) pp. 242–4.
34. Cited in Gibbons, *The US Government and the Vietnam War*, Part II, p. 209.
35. Young, *The Vietnam Wars*, pp. 106–7.
36. Ibid., pp. 108–9. See also Herring, *America's Longest War*, pp. 109–11.
37. Herring, *America's Longest War*, pp. 115–16.
38. *PP*, Vol. II, p. 106.
39. Poole, *The United States in Indochina*, p. 110.
40. Herring, *America's Longest War*, pp. 119–22.
41. Poole, *The United States in Indochina*, p. 125.
42. Ibid., p. 121. See also Herring, *America's Longest War*, p. 123.
43. Lyndon B. Johnson, *The Vantage Point: Perspectives on the Presidency, 1963–1969* (New York: Holt, Rinehart & Winston, 1971) p. 121.
44. Poole, *The United States in Indochina*, pp. 134–42.
45. See discussion of Operation Flaming Dart II (a precursor to Rolling Thunder) *PP*, Vol. III, p. 271.
46. Bundy, quoted in Herring, *America's Longest War*, p. 130. See also *PP*, Vol. III, pp. 684–91.
47. Johnson, *The Vantage Point*, p. 142.
48. *PP*, Vol. III, p. 417.
49. V.A. Sharov and V.A. Tyrurin, *Southeast Asia: History, Economy, Policy* (Moscow: Progress Publishers, 1972) pp. 52–3.
50. Douglas Pike, *Vietnam and the Soviet Union: Anatomy of an Alliance* (Boulder, CO: Westview Press, 1987) pp. 42–3.
51. Ibid., p. 44.
52. Ibid., pp. 45–6.
53. Ibid., pp. 47–8.
54. Poole, *The United States in Indochina*, p. 138.
55. TASS, 10 Feb. 1965. Cited in Pike, *Vietnam and the Soviet Union*, pp. 77–8.
56. Ibid., pp. 78–9.
57. John C. Griffiths, *Afghanistan: Key to a Continent* (Boulder, CO: Westview Press, 1981) pp. 159–61.
58. Donald N. Wilber, *Afghanistan* (New Haven, CT: Hraf Press, 1962) p. 185.
59. Griffiths, *Afghanistan*, pp. 162–3.

60. Yu V. Gankovsky, et al., *A History of Afghanistan*, trans. Vitaly Bashakov (Moscow: Progress Publishers, 1982) pp. 267–8.
61. Griffiths, *Afghanistan*, p. 166.
62. Ibid., pp. 168–70.
63. Joseph J. Collins, *The Soviet Invasion of Afghanistan: A Study in the Use of Force in Soviet Foreign Policy* (Lexington, MA: Lexington Books, 1986) pp. 34–5.
64. Syed S. Hussain, *Afghanistan under Soviet Occupation* (Islamabad: World Affairs Publications, 1980) p. 95.
65. Thomas Hammond, *Red Flag over Afghanistan: The Communist Coup, the Soviet Invasion, and the Consequences* (Boulder: Westview Press, 1984) pp. 35–6.
66. Anthony Hyman, *Afghanistan under Soviet Domination, 1964–1981* (New York: St Martin's Press, 1982) p. 64.
67. Ibid., p. 64.
68. 'Protocol Signed', *Pravda*, 21 July 1973, p. 1, cited in *Current Digest of the Soviet Press*, 29 (August 1973) p. 25. Hereafter *CDSP*.
69. Hyman, *Afghanistan under Soviet Domination*, p. 64.
70. Hammond, *Red Flag over Afghanistan*, p. 38.
71. 'In a Friendly Atmosphere', *Pravda*, 6 June 1974, p. 4, cited in *CDSP*, 23 (July 1974) pp. 11–14.
72. *Government of the Republic of Afghanistan: First Seven-Year Economic and Social Development Plan, 1355–1361*, Vol. II annex (Kabul: Ministry of Planning, 1355) pp. 39–140.
73. *Government of the Republic of Afghanistan: First Seven-Year Economic and Social Development Plan, 1355–1361*, Vol. I text (Kabul: Ministry of Planning, 1355) p. 195.
74. Henry S. Bradsher, *Afghanistan and the Soviet Union* (Durham, NC: Duke University Press, 1983) p. 65.
75. Elizabeth Kridl Valkner, 'Soviet Economic Relations with the Developing Nations', in *The Soviet Union and Developing Nations*, ed. Roger Kanet (Baltimore: Johns Hopkins University Press, 1974) p. 222. It is interesting to note that this agreement is not mentioned by those scholars who claim that one of the reasons for the Soviet invasion in 1979 was to exploit Afghanistan's rich resources. This agreement would indicate that the Soviets and the Afghans were working together to develop Afghanistan's fledgling petroleum industry, and any gas flowing to the Soviet Union through 1985 was legally justified by trade agreements decided twelve years before the Soviet intervention.
76. Collins, *The Soviet Invasion of Afghanistan*, p. 36.
77. Ibid., p. 41.
78. CIA, 'Communist Aid Activities in Non-Communist Less Developed Countries, 1979 and 1954–1979,' (Washington, DC: Government Printing Office, 1980) p. 17. Cited in Bradsher, *Afghanistan and the Soviet Union*, pp. 24–5.
79. Collins, *The Soviet Invasion of Afghanistan*, p. 23.
80. *Krasnaya Zvezda*, 28 Dec. 1969, p. 1, cited in *CDSP*, 52 (Jan. 1980) p. 25.
81. Louis Dupree, *Afghanistan* (Princeton: Princeton University Press, 1973) pp. 525–6.
82. Collins, *The Soviet Invasion of Afghanistan*, p. 36.
83. Ibid., pp. 40–41.
84. Hammond, *Red Flag over Afghanistan*, p. 42.
85. Collins, *The Soviet Invasion of Afghanistan*, pp. 39–40.
86. Griffiths, *Afghanistan*, p. 180.
87. Ibid., p. 182.
88. Hammond, *Red Flag over Afghanistan*, p. 30.

89. Gankovsky, *A History of Afghanistan*, pp. 273–4.
90. Bradsher, *Afghanistan and the Soviet Union*, p. 44.
91. Ghulam Muradov, 'The Democratic Republic of Afghanistan: The Second Stage of the April Revolution' in *Afghanistan: Past and Present* (Moscow: USSR Academy of Sciences, 1981) p. 179.
92. Hammond, *Red Flag over Afghanistan*, p. 32.
93. Hyman, *Afghanistan under Soviet Domination*, p. 59.
94. Mark Galeotti, *Afghanistan: The Soviet Union's Last War* (London: Frank Cass, 1995) p. 15.
95. Ibid., pp. 32–3.
96. Fred Halliday, 'Revolution in Afghanistan', *New Left Review*, 112 (Nov./Dec. 1978) p. 31.
97. Anthony Arnold, *Afghanistan's Two-Party Communism: Parcham and Khalq* (Stanford: Hoover Institution Press, 1983) p. 56.
98. Bradsher, *Afghanistan and the Soviet Union*, p. 73.
99. Arnold, *Afghanistan's Two-Party Communism*, p. 57.
100. Bradsher, *Afghanistan and the Soviet Union*, p. 75.
101. Hyman, *Afghanistan under Soviet Domination*, pp. 76–7.
102. Hammond, *Red Flag over Afghanistan*, p. 54.
103. Bradsher, *Afghanistan and the Soviet Union*, p. 83.
104. *New York Times*, 30 April 1981, p. 10.
105. Collins, *The Soviet Invasion of Afghanistan*, pp. 52–3.
106. 'Revolution's First Days', *Pravda*, 6 May 1978, cited in *CDSP*, 18 (June 1979) p. 20.
107. 'Treaty of Friendship, Good Neighborliness and Co-operation', 5 December 1978. Translated by Cyriac Maprayil, *The Soviets and Afghanistan* (New Delhi: Reliance Publishing House, 1986) pp. 100–1.
108. Halliday, 'Revolution in Afghanistan', pp. 37–8.
109. Hammond, *Red Flag over Afghanistan*, p. 68.
110. Fred Halliday, 'War in Afghanistan', *New Left Review*, 3 (Jan./Feb. 1980) p. 32.
111. Muradov, 'The Democratic Republic of Afghanistan, p. 183.
112. Hammond, *Red Flag over Afghanistan*, pp. 69–72. See also Galeotti, *Afghanistan*, p. 7.
113. Galeotti, *Afghanistan*, pp. 8–10.
114. Hammond, *Red Flag over Afghanistan*, p. 75.
115. Bradsher, *Afghanistan and the Soviet Union*, pp. 103–4.
116. Ibid., pp. 109–13.
117. Collins, *The Soviet Invasion of Afghanistan*, p. 68.
118. Hammond, *Red Flag over Afghanistan*, pp. 88–90.
119. Galeotti, *Afghanistan*, p. 9; Hammond, *Red Flag over Afghanistan*, p. 97.
120. Colonel K. Vorobiev, 'The Incarnation of Leninist Ideas on the Armed Defense of Socialism', *Kommunist Vooruzhnnykh Sil*, 1 (Jan. 1980) p. 22, cited in Alfred L. Monks, *The Soviet Intervention in Afghanistan* (Washington, DC: American Enterprise Institute, 1981) p. 42.
121. A. Petrov, *Pravda*, 1 June 1979, p. 5, cited in *CDSP*, 21 (July 1979) p. 20.
122. Leonid Teplinsky, 'Soviet–Afghan Cooperation: Lenin's Behest Implemented', in *Afghanistan: Past and Present* (Moscow: USSR Academy of Sciences, 1981) p. 218.
123. Hammond, *Red Flag over Afghanistan*, pp. 88–9.
124. *Pravda*, 23 Dec. 1979, p. 5, cited in *CDSP*, 51 (Jan. 1980) p. 4.
125. Arnold, *Afghanistan's Two-Party Communism*, p. 96.
126. Bradsher, *Afghanistan and the Soviet Union*, pp. 179–81.

127. Kabul Radio, 27 Dec. 1979, cited in Bradsher, *Afghanistan and the Soviet Union*, p. 181.
128. Muradov, 'The Democratic Republic of Afghanistan: Second Stage of the April Revolution', p. 185.
129. Cited by Bradsher, *Afghanistan and the Soviet Union*, p. 185.
130. Teplinsky, 'Soviet–Afghan Cooperation', p. 219.
131. *Pravda*, 13 Jan. 1980, cited in ibid.
132. *New Times* (Moscow), 17 (April 1980) p. 18, cited in Hammond, *Red Flag over Afghanistan*, p. 100.
133. Adam Michnik, interview with Eduard Shevardnadze in *Gaseta Wyborcza*, 27–29 Oct. 1989, pp. 4–5, trans. in *Foreign Broadcast Information Service* (Soviet Union) (31 Oct. 1989) p. 24. Hereafter *FBIS*.
134. See Cynthia Roberts, '"Glasnost" in Soviet Foreign Policy: Setting the Record Straight.' *Radio Liberty: Report on the USSR*, 50 (15 Dec. 1989) pp. 4–8.
135. Initially, the warm-water port theory was combined with perceived Soviet intentions regarding Afghan mineral resources and Middle East Oil supplies. For a compelling repudiation of the offensive analysis (warm-water port theory, annexation, oil and mineral aggregation), see Collins, *The Soviet Invasion of Afghanistan*, pp. 99–108.
136. Ibid.
137. Robert S. Litwak, 'The Soviet Union in Afghanistan', in Ariel Levite, Bruce W. Jentleson and Larry Berman (eds), *Foreign Military Intervention: The Dynamics of Protracted Conflict* (New York: Columbia University Press, 1992) p. 75. See also Edward N. Luttwak, *The Grand Strategy of the Soviet Union* (New York: St Martin's Press, 1983) pp. 82–3.
138. Hammond, *Red Flag over Afghanistan*, p. 97.
139. S. Kovalev, 'Sovereignty and the Internationalist Obligations of Socialist Countries', *Pravda*, 26 Sept. 1968, pp. 1–2, in *CDSP*, 39 (Oct. 1968) pp. 10–12. Note that Kovalev is a pseudonym for Brezhnev.
140. Robert F. Miller, 'Afghanistan and Soviet Alliances', in Amin Saikal and William Maley (eds), *The Soviet Withdrawal from Afghanistan* (Cambridge: Cambridge University Press, 1989) p. 104.
141. Yusif-Zade in *Baku Worker* (Bakinsky Robochy) (19 Dec. 1980) p. 3, cited in *FBIS* (Soviet Union-III-4), 7 Jan. 1981.
142. Litwak, 'The Soviet Union in Afghanistan', pp. 75–6.
143. Cited in Collins, *The Soviet Invasion of Afghanistan*, p. 129.
144. *Pravda*, 13 Jan. 1980, p. 1, cited in ibid., p. 130.
145. Collins, *The Soviet Invasion of Afghanistan*, pp. 130–33.
146. Ibid.
147. Roberts, '"Glasnost" in Soviet Foreign Policy', p. 7.
148. Ibid., pp. 133–5.
149. Bradsher, *Afghanistan and the Soviet Union*, pp. 28–9.
150. Ibid., pp. 29–30.
151. Ibid., p. 30.
152. Leon B. Poullada, 'Afghanistan and the United States: The Crucial Years', *Middle East Journal* 35 (1981) pp. 185–6.
153. Collins, *The Soviet Invasion of Afghanistan*, pp. 57–8.
154. Ibid., pp. 58–73.
155. Raymond Garthoff, *Détente and Confrontation: American–Soviet Relations from Nixon to Reagan* (Washington, DC: Brookings Institution, 1985) p. 924.
156. See Robert W. Tucker and David C. Hendrickson, *Empire of Liberty: The Statecraft of*

Thomas Jefferson (New York: Oxford University Press, 1990).

157. See David M. Fitzsimons. 'Tom Paine's New World Order: Idealistic Internationalism in the Ideology of Early American Foreign Relations', *Diplomatic History*, 19, 4 (1995) pp. 569–82.

158. The following argument closely parallels that provided in Michael Walzer's *Just and Unjust Wars: A Moral Argument with Historical Illustrations* (New York: Basic Books, 1977) pp. 97–101.

159. John Stuart Mill, 'A Few Words on Non-Intervention', in *Dissertations and Discussions: Political, Philosophical, and Historical* (Boston: William V. Spencer, 1868), Vol. III, pp. 238–63.

160. Walzer, *Just and Unjust Wars*, p. 98.

4

Detainment at War: The United States in Vietnam (1965–73), the Soviet Union in Afghanistan (1980–89)

Detainment by military force was imposed on the populations of Vietnam and Afghanistan by the superpowers for nearly a decade in both countries. The underlying need for detainment in Vietnam and Afghanistan had been firmly established at the onset of American and Soviet intervention – the governments in Saigon and Kabul were illegitimate in the view of many citizens, enough of whom were willing to engage actively in rebellion against the state. Without assistance from the superpowers, domestic opposition forces would have overthrown the governments of the Republic of Vietnam and the Democratic Republic of Afghanistan. However, because of the global struggle for power and legitimacy during the Cold War, both the Americans and the Soviets attempted to change this fundamental problem of legitimacy by using military force.

This chapter will sketch how the superpowers attempted to use their military might to create enough local stability that an effective indigenous governing apparatus could be created. In both cases superpower intervention created a complex paradox: without direct military support the regimes in Saigon and Kabul could not have survived; yet with superpower backing, both regimes were severely impaired in their ability to convince the people over whom they ruled that they were legitimate national governments. The civil war in South Vietnam was transformed into an international war that pitted primarily the United States and ARVN against North Vietnam and the National Liberation Front (NLF or Viet Cong) forces in the South. In Afghanistan, the conflict was transformed from a civil war pitting the PDPA regime against various rebel groups, to an international war pitting the Soviet Union and the PDPA against these same Afghan rebel groups. In these transformations, until the decision to abandon detainment and to withdraw, the South Vietnamese and Afghan regimes became secondary political actors, although they did make some inroads in creating a popular base of support while under the protection of their superpower patrons. However, despite some level of success, they were unable to establish a sufficiently broad domestic base to marshal enough mass support to defeat their more determined opponents. Combined with other military and political factors, this lack of domestic legitimacy would be their eventual undoing once the military forces of the United States and the Soviet Union were withdrawn in 1973 and 1989.

THE SUPERPOWERS IN VIETNAM, 1965–73

The United States

The introduction of American ground forces to protect the air base at Da Nang in March 1965 was soon followed by a massive increase in troop levels and changes in battlefield strategy. Troop increases were driven by General Westmoreland's shift from an enclave strategy (defending important bases and strategic locations) to a more traditional offensive doctrine that sought to engage and destroy the enemy. American escalation was also driven by the continued deterioration of the military situation in the South. Despite a constant increase in the level of US aid and the bombing of the North, the NLF/Viet Cong mounted a number of successful attacks against ARVN forces. The civilian government of Phan Huy Quat was dissolved in a coup in May 1965 led by Air Marshal Nguyen Cao Ky and General Nguyen Van Thieu. The new government was the fifth since the assassination of Diem. Most of President Johnson's advisers had little faith in the new leaders and pressed Johnson to expand the air war and ground combat mission; in July 1965 General Westmoreland, backed by Walt Rostow and the Pentagon, requested that the president send an additional 179,000 troops. Johnson sent Secretary of Defense McNamara to Saigon to investigate the need for the troops.[1] On his return McNamara advised Johnson to accede to Westmoreland's request, and he urged the president to ask Congress to permit the calling up of 235,000 reservists for active service, and to fund the call-up as well. McNamara's request sparked widespread discussion in the White House of the domestic political costs. The president's military advisers emphasized that it might take hundreds of thousands of men and several years to achieve the goal of defeating the communist forces. They urged Johnson to call up the National Guard and the reserves and seek public support on national security grounds. He rejected this bold action, asking, 'Do all of you think the Congress and the people will go along with 600,000 people and billions of dollars being spent 10,000 miles away?'[2] In doing so, the president made the fateful decision to deceive the American people regarding what was happening in Vietnam and what would be necessary to achieve victory. Johnson made the decision to go forward with the war, with full knowledge of the probable size of future commitments, but without any attempt to gain the support of the American people. It was a decision that would later haunt his presidency and would magnify the coming legitimacy crisis in the US domestic polity. In July 1965, by avoiding the hard task of engendering popular support among the American masses, Johnson had made the Vietnam War his own war.[3]

General Westmoreland was given virtual carte blanche for the level of American involvement over the next two years. In February 1966 the president agreed to another increase in US troop strength to the level of 429,000 by the end of the year.[4] The monthly cost of the war was running at approximately $2 billion, but the huge escalation of US involvement produced few tangible gains on the ground. The US strategy for achieving victory in Vietnam was never well defined. It suffered a great deal from Washington's perceptions of global-level political constraints, primarily the possibility of drawing Soviet or Chinese intervention. Washington's fear of generating a wider war if it launched an invasion of North Vietnam kept the American ground war limited to Vietnamese territory south of the 17th parallel and within the borders of South Vietnam – a restraint that was not reciprocated by the enemy. To compensate, the United States relied heavily on bombing, and the air war rapidly assumed massive proportions. By 1967 the United States had dropped more bombs in Vietnam than it had in all theatres in the Second World War; the 25,000 tons of bombs dropped on the North in 1965 had risen to 226,000 tons in 1967.[5] Other material costs to the United States were also high. Between 1965 and 1968, for example, over 900 aircraft worth approximately $6 billion had been lost.[6]

Leaving aside for a moment questions concerning the legality, legitimacy, or morality of the war effort, the question remains as to why the massive bombing and troop commitment did not enable the United States to prevail. Westmoreland's strategy of attrition was based on the notion that the combined air and ground offensive could kill the enemy faster than they could be replaced. This was an erroneous assumption, and it fundamentally contradicted the traditional American view of the inherent perils of Asian land wars – the huge populations of most Asian countries. According to Guenter Lewy, 'there was no evidence that these hardships had reduced North Vietnam's ability or willingness to continue the conflict or had demoralized the population to any appreciable degree. On the contrary, the bombing appeared to have engendered a psychological climate of common danger which aided the government in winning support for its demands of stern sacrifices and facilitated other measures of control. The bombing had also helped the regime cast the United States in the role of a cruel aggressor.'[7] In addition to strengthening the North's resolve, the bombing did little significant damage to the Northern war effort in economic terms. North Vietnam relied on support from China and the Soviet Union for war supplies, and its predominantly agricultural economy could not be bombed out of existence. In human terms, an estimated 200,000 North Vietnamese reached draft age each year. Thus, in human capital, the North could replace its losses faster than the United States could kill North Vietnamese soldiers, and any American troop escalation at the time could be matched or exceeded by Hanoi.[8]

Westmoreland's attrition strategy was thus doomed to failure, unless the Northern troops could be blocked from entering the battlefield. However, such a strategic blocking manœuvre would entail large numbers of US troops on three fronts: Laos, Cambodia and North Vietnam. The border with North Vietnam had been sealed to a high degree, but Laos (which had been 'neutralized' in the 1962 Geneva agreements) and Cambodia were used by the North as the lifeline for supplies and personnel entering the South, and as sanctuaries by the Viet Cong. When heavy US firepower generated unacceptable levels of pressure in the South, the Vietnamese could simply cross the border and choose the time and place of their next assault. In addition, Southern areas that were controlled by the Viet Cong and then 'taken' by American attacks were promptly abandoned as the American troops returned to their bases. In reality, because Westmoreland did not have sufficient troops to isolate the battlefield from excursions via Laos and Cambodia, his attrition strategy was fundamentally flawed. The ARVN forces, who should have taken over the role of policing the areas where communist forces had been destroyed or driven out, were at the time relatively small, poorly armed and ill trained. Thus, the Americans simply did not have enough troops on the ground in Vietnam both to take and to hold territory, and when American forces left a 'pacified' area, Vietnamese communist forces moved back in.[9] As a result, year after year, Westmoreland requested more troops. At the end of 1967 the general called for an additional 200,000 men to augment the approximately 470,000 Americans already in Vietnam.[10]

The Southern regime

The regime of Ky and Thieu was given a public display of support when Ky met President Johnson in Honolulu in early 1966. However, a number of familiar problems plagued the new leaders of South Vietnam. Buddhist demonstrators spearheaded the organization of various groups that were dissatisfied with the new government – students, labour unions, Catholics and disgruntled soldiers. The US consulate in Hue was torched by demonstrators demanding the end of foreign intervention and the establishment of a democratically elected civilian government. As before, the regime suppressed the rebellion with military force, this time with the direct support of US marines. Once again the fundamental problem in Vietnam was replayed: the Southern government was not seen as legitimate by a significant component of the population, and building genuine support was difficult when American forces were seen as the latest in a series of foreign interlopers.[11]

This was not a problem lost on the Americans either in Vietnam or in Washington, and it cannot be said that the Americans made no serious efforts to convince the Southern population that its future was best served by the generals in Saigon. New programmes were pursued in an attempt to build support for the government and undermine the NLF. One such programme that epitomized the continuing American 'nation-building' effort was the Rural Development Programme. Emulating the NLF's own political tactics, Rural Development teams would go to villages and live with the inhabitants, carrying out daily tasks along with education programmes. Eventually the programme failed for many reasons, including the lack of trained personnel, mistrust by local officials, mistrust by the population, lack of funds, poor administration, poor implementation and lack of security. Winning the hearts and minds of villagers often was under way when the shooting war intervened. Programme personnel were routinely harassed or killed by the NLF, and US aircraft often bombed villages while in pursuit of suspected combatants.[12]

The eventual failure of many American-designed development programmes was also due in part to the lack of credibility of the Ky and Thieu government. After meeting with Ky in Guam in 1967, President Johnson requested that the South Vietnamese hold a national election that would allow some image of democratic legitimacy on the part of its ally to be presented to the American public. The election was held after a screening of candidates, and those with 'pro-Communist' or 'neutralist' views were disqualified. Over 80 per cent of the South Vietnamese voters turned out, many of whom had been pressured by the government. In order to ensure turnout, as ballots were cast, each person's identity card was punched, thus allowing those who declined to participate to be arrested later for having complied with the NLF's appeal to boycott the election.[13] Forcing voter turnout, however, became a two-edged sword for Ky and Thieu, and the election itself revealed the fragile character of the regime. Before the election Thieu had decided to challenge Ky for the presidency, a move which threatened to split the South Vietnamese army. The generals arranged a partial compromise in which Ky would run for vice-president but after the election would be named chairman of the secret military council that would set government policy. Thieu also agreed to be the figurehead president, but later he would actually outmanœuvre his colleagues and concentrate power in his own person. The elections were contested in relatively free and open democratic fashion because of the presence of American observers. However, the results were an embarrassment to the government when Thieu received only 35 per cent of the vote, with the remainder shared among a field of candidates. Finishing second with 17 per cent of the vote was Truong Dinh Dzu, an obscure civilian with no political experience or visible group of followers. Apparently Dzu had been poorly screened, and after being validated as an official candidate, he had campaigned on a programme of peace with the North. The vote for Dzu was seen as a vote against the government by many, and Thieu promptly arrested him along with a number of other political dissenters. The election gave Thieu a legal façade to satisfy the Americans but also revealed the weakness of his support. Most Vietnamese viewed the election as a US-directed performance with a Vietnamese cast.[14]

By 1967 the war in Vietnam had spread to the streets of American cities. Lyndon Johnson had chosen to pursue both his 'Great Society' programmes and the war in Vietnam. It was an impossible burden, according to Vietnam historian Larry Berman:

> Nothing symbolized the potential bankruptcy of a guns-and-butter policy more than the outbreak of racial violence throughout urban America during the summer of 1967. Rioting in late July left 26 dead in Newark; 40 killed in Detroit, where for the first time in twenty-four years federal troops were needed to stop the rioters. Federal para-troopers ultimately restored order, arresting over 7,000 looters and snipers. In the words of Senator J. William Fulbright, the Great Society had become a 'sick society'. The president refused to abandon his guns-and-butter strategy, but his political coalition in Congress and credibility with the general public began unraveling.[15]

However, opposition to the war had begun years earlier in United States. In 1964 the Rolling Thunder campaign had inspired 'teach-ins' on a number of American university campuses. In April 1964 approximately 12,000 students had gathered in Washington to march in protest of the war. Antiwar protest slowly spread as the degree of American involvement intensified, and when little progress was reported to justify the growing number of dead and wounded Americans, the antiwar movement grew incrementally. By 1967, after three years of increasingly negative press reports from Vietnam, the antiwar movement had become a significant social force. Opposition arose from virtually every segment of the American populace, ranging from religious pacifists who saw the war as an immoral act, to members of the US military who saw the war as having a negative impact on US security.[16]

In Congress, the president was faced with growing dissatisfaction as well. Senator Fulbright, one of the most respected Congressional leaders and an early supporter of the war, spearheaded the opposition. Fulbright, angered by what he then saw as President Johnson's subterfuge beginning with the Gulf of Tonkin incidents, conducted a full-scale public debate on the underlying principles of US foreign policy. At one point in his rebuttal of the administration's arguments, Fulbright informed Secretary of State Dean Rusk, 'After all, Vietnam is their country. We are obviously intruders from their point of view. We represent the old Western imperialism in their eyes.'[17]

Opposition to the air war even penetrated to the highest levels of Johnson's cabinet. A Defense Department study prepared for Secretary McNamara concluded not only that Rolling Thunder had failed to meet its goals but also that after analysing nine different bombing strategies, 'We are unable to devise a bombing campaign in the North to reduce the flow of infiltrating personnel into SVN.'[18] The study had a heavy impact on McNamara, according to the State Department's Harry McPherson, who remembers, 'McNamara, obviously on edge, condemned the bombing ... He recited the comparative figures; so many tons dropped on Germany and Japan and North Korea, so many more on Vietnam. "It's not just that it isn't preventing the supplies from getting down the trail. It's destroying the countryside in the South. It's making lasting enemies. And still the damned Air Force wants more."'[19] By November 1967 McNamara was recommending the complete termination of bombing in the North and a levelling-off of ground force commitments. Having become a 'dove' in the eyes of the president, McNamara was soon replaced by Clark Clifford as Secretary of Defense.[20]

The Tet offensive: dislodging detainment

The unmistakable turning point of US involvement in Vietnam was the now famous Tet offensive in early 1968. The Tet offensive is arguably one of the greatest strategic victories in modern warfare. Likewise it is one of the most ironic, considering that those who 'won' the battle were mostly left dead on the battlefield. The growing criticism of the Vietnam War by the American public achieved critical mass after the Tet offensive, which was launched by the Viet Cong and the North Vietnamese on 30 and 31 January 1968. After the Tet offensive the key political problem faced by the Johnson administration shifted from winning the 'hearts and minds' of the Vietnamese to retaining the 'hearts and minds' of Americans at home. Ever since the beginning of detainment in 1956, when the United States supported the South's repudiation of the Geneva Accords, the Southern regime's legitimacy slowly eroded in the eyes of the Vietnamese people. This erosion of faith fed back into the United States, ultimately driving President Johnson from office and accelerating the political momentum for a US withdrawal from Vietnam.

Tet (the Vietnamese New Year) began with a poorly coordinated attack on 30 January. Approximately 80,000 North Vietnamese regulars and NLF forces attacked more than a hundred cities in South Vietnam. The goal was to achieve a popular uprising against the government of South Vietnam and to show the American public that the very idea of security in South Vietnam was a fantasy. Within twenty-four hours of the beginning of the offensive, thirty-six of forty-four provincial capitals, five of six major cities, sixty-four district capitals and fifty hamlets were under attack. The most symbolic and spectacular assaults took place in Saigon at the US embassy, the presidential palace, the main airport and the headquarters of the South Vietnamese general staff, where suicide bombers caused heavy damage. In addition, the city of Hue was overrun, and the ancient Citadel, the imperial seat of the traditional rulers of Vietnam, was taken by storm.[21]

Although surprised by the attack, the US and ARVN forces reacted well. The cities and towns captured during the offensive were all retaken. The price was often high, as revealed by the US commander in charge of retaking the provincial capital of Ben Tre, who stated, 'We had to destroy the town to save it.'[22] The liberation of the ancient capital of Hue was also a long and costly affair, taking three weeks of fierce fighting. Like Ben Tre, the ancient city was reduced to ruins; the US and ARVN forces lost approximately 500 men; the NLF lost as many as 5,000; close to 5,000 civilians were killed or missing; and over 100,000 refugees were driven from their homes. Overall, the NLF and North Vietnamese forces suffered huge losses, with estimates going as high as 40,000 killed. Most of the heavy casualties were among indigenous Southern forces, who were decimated and never fully recovered from their losses during Tet.[23]

To the American public, the Tet offensive was a decisive psychological victory for the communist forces and served as a reality check for how the war was actually progressing. According to Larry Berman:

> Tet revealed that despite the presence of 525,000 men, billions of dollars, and extensive bombing, the United States had not stopped the enemy from replacing its forces. The rate of the war and capacity to sustain it were controlled not by America's superior technology, but by the enemy. In effect, the United States faced stalemate in Vietnam … the United States was no closer to achieving its political objective than at the outset of Americanization in 1965. It was becoming increasingly evident that no amount of military power would bring North Vietnam to the conference table.[24]

From Tet onward, American public opinion rejected a long, drawn-out military campaign in the jungles of Vietnam, and more questions were asked regarding how the war had been presented in the first place to the American people. As a result the American people began to embrace the shocking idea that their leaders had actually lied about what was happening in Vietnam, why the United States was fighting there, and what the prospects for victory were. In March 1968 various polls reported a sharp increase in the number of Americans who believed that the United States had been wrong to get involved in Vietnam. Johnson's approval rating dropped to an all-time low of 26 per cent. The polls revealed no consensus for either escalation or withdrawal, only a growing conviction that a hopeless quagmire had developed and grave doubt about the president's ability to change the situation.[25]

Johnson's public standing was further undercut by the surprise showing of Senator Eugene McCarthy in the March 1968 Democratic Party primary election in New Hampshire. McCarthy had run on an antiwar platform and was known as one of America's leading 'doves'. Apparently, however, many self-proclaimed 'hawks' had voted for McCarthy in protest of Johnson's handling of the war, which they believed should be pursued more vigorously.[26] In combination, the Tet offensive, widespread popular disenchantment among both hawks and doves, and General Westmoreland's request for yet another 206,000 troops (which would require the mobilization of the US reserve forces) all combined to put heavy political pressure on Lyndon Johnson. He was faced with three basic options: withdraw from Vietnam, agree to Westmoreland's requests, or continue with more of the same. The first two options did not appear to be politically viable. Withdrawal from Vietnam would mean defeat for his policies, not only in Vietnam, but also his beloved Great Society. At the same time, however, Johnson believed that further escalation would be impossible because of increasing levels of Congressional opposition, which seemed more sensitive to public opinion, and which Johnson believed insurmountable if he chose to mobilize the military reserves to meet Westmoreland's request. The third option was hardly an optimal choice, but when politically caught between a rock and a hard place, Johnson essentially chose more of the same.

On 22 March Johnson rejected Westmoreland's proposals to escalate the war, in part because President Thieu had announced a major increase in the numbers of conscripted soldiers in the South, raising the ARVN's strength by some 135,000 men. Also, the military situation looked more favourable after NLF activities in the South were reduced in wake of the significant Tet losses. With an eye on public opinion, the president agreed to an increase of only 13,500 American troops, but General Westmoreland was recalled as commander of US forces and made Army Chief of Staff. He was replaced by General Creighton Abrams. During the last weeks of March, Clark Clifford, the new Secretary of Defense, began pressing the Johnson cabinet for a negotiated settlement, which would include a large reduction in the intensity of bombing. Clifford was partially supported by Secretary of State Rusk. However, Rusk did not believe that a bombing reduction would help the negotiations. Still, a bombing pause and subsequent failure of negotiations could be used to counter domestic critics.[27]

Johnson decided to take the Rusk approach. On 31 March 1968, in a televised address, he announced that the bombing of North Vietnam would be curtailed, and would actually cease if the American 'restraint' was matched by concessions from Hanoi. The most important and significant part of Johnson's speech, however, was his announcement that, 'I shall not seek, and I will not accept, the nomination of my party for another term as your president.'[28] It was a major turning point in US involvement in Vietnam: the war had claimed its most powerful casualty – the president of the United States.

Peace through war: the Nixon years, 1969–73

Johnson's decision not to run for a second term thrust the Vietnam debate into the forefront of the 1968 presidential campaign. Ending the war 'honourably' became a major issue for Richard Nixon on his way to winning the election. During Johnson's final year in office, however, he laid the groundwork for Nixon's negotiated withdrawal by the formulation and implementation of the 'Vietnamization' policy. Under the new policy, the American war in Vietnam would slowly evolve back into to a ground war between conflicting Vietnamese forces, with the United States maintaining its role as supplier of military and financial assistance and increasing the lethality of the air war.

In 1963 Lyndon Johnson had entered the Oval Office as the last US president faced with the choice of sending troops to South Vietnam, or standing by while Vietnamese nationalism achieved its goal of unification under a communist banner. In 1969 Richard Nixon was faced with a different problem, as the American flag had already been committed. However, it was clear that American society was being increasingly stressed by his predecessors' commitments. Nixon was faced with the dilemma of protecting US credibility while fundamentally altering the nature of the American commitment in Vietnam. He chose to pursue a strategy of gradual yet highly lethal disengagement, combined with a more complicated diplomatic gambit.

The Vietnamization programme begun by the Johnson administration was proceeding in orderly fashion as large numbers of South Vietnamese were conscripted into the armed forces; however, the diplomatic negotiations with Hanoi remained deadlocked in Paris. On 8 June 1969 President Nixon met with Thieu on Midway Island. Nixon announced that 25,000 American troops would be withdrawn from Vietnam in the next two months. As South Vietnamese forces assumed more of the fighting, additional American troops would be withdrawn: 100,000 in 1969 and 100,000–150,000 during 1970. In a nationally televised speech on 3 November 1969 Nixon announced that while previous administrations had Americanized the war, his administration was preparing the Vietnamese for a complete withdrawal of US forces. The rate of withdrawal, however, would depend on North Vietnamese behaviour, both on the battlefield and at the Paris Peace talks.[29]

By 1969 Nixon and National Security Adviser Henry Kissinger had moved from their earlier positions of defending the war effort to the necessity of ending it, not only for reasons of domestic politics but also to achieve new strategic goals. In a distinct departure from their predecessors, Nixon and Kissinger perceived the conflict in Vietnam as a less important, yet still significant, component of a new US global strategy that sought actively to exploit the communist rivalry between Beijing and Moscow. In this strategic view, Vietnam was not considered to be absolutely vital to US interests, but ending the war 'honourably' to preserve US credibility and respect globally was seen as critical. In the Nixon–Kissinger world-view, the Soviet Union remained the greatest threat because of its achievement of approximate parity in strategic (nuclear) force structure; however, they saw communism itself in less simplistic terms than had previous US presidents. Thus detente with the Soviet Union could be pursued as a tactical manœuvre, but more important was that the groundwork for normalization with China be initiated. Although Nixon and Kissinger did not abandon entirely the concepts of containment, by considering the potential benefits of better relations with China, they began shaping US security policy in keeping with more traditional balance-of-power reasoning and with a de-emphasis of ideology. However, the Soviet Union and China both had to be convinced that a US withdrawal from Vietnam did not mean that the United States was unwilling or unable to confront aggression elsewhere. According to Kissinger, 'However we got into Vietnam, whatever the judgment of our actions, ending the war honorably is essential to the peace of the world. Any other solution may unloose forces that would complicate the prospects of international order.'[30] Likewise, Nixon concluded that in Vietnam, '[t]he Communists were willing to continue fighting regardless of losses. They had a total commitment to victory. We had, at most, a partial commitment to avoid defeat. If this situation continued, in the end they would win.'[31]

Thus in Vietnam Nixon and Kissinger were faced with the same fundamental problem as every US administration from Truman's onward: How to counter Hanoi's relentless drive to unify the country? Using a more extreme 'carrot and stick' approach, they showed their determination to settle the war 'honourably' by expanding the war into Cambodia and Laos, renewing the air war against the North, and even spreading rumours about nuclear strikes in order to gain a more acceptable negotiated settlement. However, because the government in Hanoi was unwilling to bend, despite the heavy doses of punishment inflicted on the North, Nixon and Kissinger's approach ultimately proved to be a barren negotiating strategy. Furthermore, as more US troops were withdrawn from Vietnam, Hanoi's incentives to negotiate were systematically diminished. After sustaining their struggle for over thirty years against the military might of Japan, France and the United States, the nationalist/communist forces were not suddenly going to give up the struggle for national independence, especially when their most formidable opponent to date was withdrawing its troops. Nixon's strategy simply was not credible. In Saigon the new US policies also produced increasing resistance by President Thieu, who was unwilling to negotiate with Hanoi, knowing that his own position was becoming increasingly precarious as the

Americans departed. However, Hanoi rightly judged that, once started, the Americans could not easily reverse their decision to withdraw. Their total commitment to national independence made a negotiated settlement with the United States both unnecessary and essentially inconceivable.

Nonetheless, President Nixon was determined to punish the North for its defiance. In 1970 and 1971 he made two of the most controversial foreign policy decisions of his presidency – the military invasions of Cambodia and Laos. He had decided that the strategic advantages of directly attacking the Ho Chi Minh trail with ground forces outweighed the potential political backlash of widening the war without Congressional approval. Nixon hoped that Hanoi would be influenced to negotiate if faced with a US president willing to wage a wider war. In explaining the decision Nixon declared, 'I would rather be a one-term president, at the cost of seeing America ... accept the first defeat in its sound 190-years' history.'[32] In March 1969, more than a year before the ground invasion of Cambodia, Nixon had authorized the secret and illegal bombing of Vietnamese base camps close to the border. Over the next fourteen months 3,630 B-52 sorties would drop over 100,000 tons of bombs inside Cambodia. Like the bombing of the North, these raids had no significant effect on the NLF's ability to fight. A year later, when faced with large formations of American troops, the NLF simply moved deeper into the Cambodian interior, returning to their previous positions after US forces were withdrawn.

In terms of strategic doctrine, Nixon's new approach was arguably an improvement on his predecessors'. In taking the war into Cambodia and Laos, he clearly intended to relieve the pressure on South Vietnam by isolating the battlefield geographically. However, because American troops did not occupy the new ground that they routinely secured, Nixon's policies were more of the same, except that the war was now being fought by American troops on the soil of two additional countries. Of course, strategic doctrine on the battlefield can never be separated from its fundamental roots in politics. In political terms, Nixon's secret Cambodian policy was important for other reasons. According to historian Marilyn Young:

> Fearing a public outcry over what most people would take as blows against rather than for peace, the decision was made to keep the raids secret from Congress and the American public. Through an elaborate system of double reporting, even the secret records of B-52 bombing targets were falsified so that nowhere was it recorded that the raids had ever taken place. At the first hint of a leak to the press ... the White House exploded (behind closed doors) with anxiety and anger. An ever-expanding network of illegal wire-taps was put into place to trace the leaks. Indeed, the first tendrils of the Watergate conspiracy, and the beginning of Nixon's downfall, can be seen here, not in the actual bombing of a neutral country but in keeping it secret.[33]

In Paris the Cambodian ground invasion was met by a complete suspension of the peace talks by the North Vietnamese and NLF. In the United States mass antiwar protests erupted. College campuses across the nation were scenes of upheaval. National Guard troops shot and killed six students at Kent State University and Jackson State College. More than a 100,000 citizens marched on Washington in May 1970 to protest against the bombing of Cambodia and the killing of college students. Congress voted a symbolic protest by overturning the Gulf of Tonkin Resolution. The president was outraged. According to George Herring,

> Nixon struck back hard. He ordered intensification of a secret programme of domestic surveillance conducted by the FBI and CIA. ... There would be no more 'screwing around' with Congressional foes, he instructed his staff. 'Don't worry about divisiveness. Having drawn the sword, don't take it out – stick it in hard.' The president publicly blamed domestic opponents for prolonging the war, and he bluntly warned Congressional leaders that if 'Congress undertakes to restrict me, Congress will have to assume the consequences'.[34]

By the end of June 1970 Nixon ordered that the troops be withdrawn from Cambodia. However, without even waiting to see if the North Vietnamese had been influenced by his high-risk gambit to bring them to the bargaining table, the president increased the pace of US troop withdrawals. By the end of 1971 only 175,000 US troops remained in Vietnam, of which only 75,000 were combat forces. However, in 1971 US and ARVN units invaded Laos in an operation that mirrored the Cambodian incursion, with similarly futile results. The protests at home continued, the most dramatic staged by a group of decorated Vietnam War veterans who testified to their own war crimes and tossed their combat decorations on to the White House lawn. Washington was virtually shut down by roaming mobs and street riots.[35] Public trust was in shambles in the summer of 1971. The legitimacy of the US government and its Vietnam policy was under open attack as secret documents on Vietnam began being published by the *New York Times*. The *Pentagon Papers* confirmed the arguments of the long-standing government critics on how US intervention in Vietnam had been falsely presented during the Kennedy and Johnson administrations. Nixon became obsessed by the leak of Pentagon papers, and when the Supreme Court overturned the injunction preventing their publication, the president created a clandestine group of 'plumbers' to plug the leaks within the government. Public distrust was reflected in opinion polls, which showed that 71 per cent thought the decision to send troops had been a mistake, with 58 per cent viewing the war as immoral. The president's approval rating on the war dropped to a low of 31 per cent, and a near majority of Americans felt that all US troops should be withdrawn even if the South would fall to communists.[36] Nixon and Kissinger were fighting a two-front rearguard action, one in Vietnam and one at home. Their power to shape events was rapidly being eroded.

In March 1972 North Vietnam launched what it hoped would be the final offensive of the war. Over 120,000 troops poured across the border into Cambodia and South Vietnam. Initially the attack was a major success, and Saigon was seen to be under direct threat when Nixon struck back. The president authorized a massive air campaign code-named Linebacker, stating, 'The bastards have never been bombed like they're going to be bombed this time.'[37] The Vietnamese attack came at a critical time in US–Soviet relations. In a secret appeal, Kissinger met with Premier Brezhnev during preparations for the upcoming Moscow summit for the signing of the SALT treaty on strategic nuclear weapons. Kissinger warned that US–Soviet detente would be threatened if the North Vietnamese attack continued. Nixon was prepared to risk Soviet cancellation of the summit for the sake of his presidential credibility. He observed, 'If we were to lose in Vietnam there would be no respect for the American president ... because we had the power and didn't use it ... We must be credible.'[38] In order to maintain credibility, on 8 May 1972, the president announced that Haiphong Harbour would be mined, a naval blockade of the North would commence, and massive sustained bombings would continue. In both military and international political terms, Nixon's escalation was successful. The North's use of a conventional military assault with armour, convoys and concentrated troop formations was vulnerable to the unrelenting American air strikes, which previously had little impact on the guerrilla war. American air power enabled the ARVN to stabilize the front lines and to mount a small counterattack. Both the Chinese and the Soviets issued relatively mild protests, and the SALT summit proceeded in Moscow. In keeping with history, Vietnam was not seen to be important enough to jeopardize improving superpower relations.[39]

Despite the military and international political gains, on the domestic front, demonstrations once again erupted in the United States. Still, many Americans believed that the president's action was justified in light of the North's invasion. For the first time in many years, 'containment' of outside aggression seemed actually to be an accurate description of what was happening in Vietnam. However, continuing the pattern of domestic subversion, Nixon's agents forged thousands of letters and telegrams expressing the 'public's' approval of Nixon and his bombing campaign. For a short span, Nixon's decisive gamble had paid off on all fronts, and his 1972 re-election bid was strengthened.[40]

Although diplomatic contact between the United States and North Vietnam had been maintained since Johnson's last years in office, negotiations had continually deadlocked with both sides unwilling to compromise on key issues. In late October 1972 Kissinger raised public hopes by declaring, 'Peace is at hand', but Nixon decided to use his projected electoral victory as a bargaining tool. Nixon's landslide victory over the dovish George McGovern provided, in the president's mind, an American 'Mandate of Heaven'. During the holiday cheer of 1972, Nixon decided to press harder for a solution to US involvement in the war, launching the now infamous 'Christmas bombings' of the North. These air attacks were the most intense and devastating of the entire war. In twelve days more bombs were dropped on Hanoi and Haiphong than in the entire period from 1969 to 1971. Nixon also ordered more than $1 billion worth of military hardware to be delivered to the Southern government, and he gave President Thieu concrete assurances that if the North violated the agreements being negotiated in Paris the United States would retaliate; the United States would not abandon South Vietnam.[41] However, Nixon had decided to make peace. He threatened to cut off aid and to proceed with negotiations without the South if President Thieu continued to resist a negotiated settlement. Thieu disapproved of the US policy, but given the depth of his dependence on the United States he had little choice other than to go along with it. Thieu expressed a deep bitterness over what he perceived as a US sell-out, telling his cabinet,

> Kissinger treats both Vietnams as adversaries. He considers himself as an outsider in these negotiations and does not distinguish between South Vietnam, as an ally, and North Vietnam, as an enemy. The Americans let the war become their war; when they liked the war they carried it forward. Then they want to stop it they impose on both sides to stop it. When the Americans wanted to enter, we had no choice, and now when they are ready to leave we have no choice.[42]

The North also was apparently convinced that it was an appropriate time strategically to sign a diplomatic agreement if it would finally rid them of the Americans. On 28 December 1972 they agreed to resume negotiations, a day after US bombing ceased. In the week of 8–14 January, Secretary of State Kissinger and North Vietnamese Foreign Minister Le Duc hammered out an agreement that met Nixon's minimum 'peace with honour' conditions. All US prisoners of war would be returned in exchange for the withdrawal of US troops. Although Thieu's government would remain in power, North Vietnamese forces located on the soil of the South could remain, and their political body, the Provisional Revolutionary Government would be recognized. Like the French before them, the Americans were unable to impose a solution on who would rule the Vietnamese.[43]

Ironically, there is some evidence to suggest that in the period from 1965 to 1972 the domestic legitimacy of the government of Vietnam had strengthened, especially after the Tet offensive. Government legitimacy was further augmented during the Vietnamization programme that began during the Johnson administration and rapidly expanded under Nixon. In 1965 the arrival of US forces had a number significant influences on the average Vietnamese villager. First, the level of violence increased significantly with the massive firepower of US forces. Many a villager watched as their homes, fields, temples and ancestral burial sites were destroyed by napalm, rockets, machine guns, cluster bombs and other heavy weapons. At the same time, however, many an NLF guerrilla was annihilated, and often the villagers blamed the communists for bringing destruction into their lives. According to a former NLF political cadre, 'All of us agreed that the people were then very tired of war and that they were also very afraid of it. That is why all the policies of the Front have run into difficulties.'[44] The increased levels of violence that accompanied the Americans thus did not necessarily turn the villagers into NLF supporters and detractors of the South Vietnamese government. After the arrival of the Americans the NLF consistently failed to achieve tangible military victories that might prove that they held the Mandate of Heaven. According to an NLF platoon leader from Quang Tin province, 'In 1963 and 1964 the VC held the upper hand in my village, but since October 1965, the ARVN troops have been winning. If the VC had been able to win some battles the people would support them, but they'd not only failed to fight against the ARVN, they'd also dragged the people into the troubles. Therefore, the people became fed up.'[45]

In sum, many average Vietnamese civilians would support whichever side could provide security. According to James Trullinger, many villagers attempted to appease both the NLF and the US/ARVN forces 'during extended periods of political uncertainty about local balance of power, but when the balance shifted in favor of one side, there were corresponding shifts among the uncommitted – and among the committed, too. Many began to support the side which appeared stronger, sometimes abandoning support for the seemingly weaker side.'[46] Within the borders of South Vietnam, the weaker side was plainly evident after the Tet offensive, which severely damaged the NLF's ability to wage war against the government and US forces. Shortly after Tet, a senior US adviser in Tay Ninh province concluded:

> The change in attitude of the people during the past month has been dramatic. Many segments that earlier could be described as neutralist or, at best, lacking in full support to the government have now moved into the government camp. The basic cause of this change has been the viciousness of the Viet Cong actions within the province. The fact that the Viet Cong violated the Tet holidays, violated the 'sanctuary' of the area around the Cao Dai temple, and suffered defeats every time they met the GVN forces within the province have all contributed to this change of attitude.[47]

It is clear in retrospect, however, that the Tet offensive's most important political impact was on the attitudes and perceptions of the American people.

After Tet the NLF might have been emasculated as an effective fighting force, but when told this by military analysts and politicians, many Americans simply could not believe it, in part because they were beginning to learn that the war in Vietnam was much more complicated than they had been led to believe.

The Soviets in Vietnam 1965–73

From 1965 to 1973 the estimates of Soviet aid to Vietnam, both economic and military, range from US$4–6 billion.[48] The Soviet–Vietnamese relationship during the war was a relationship motivated by both common and divergent purposes, as Moscow and Hanoi pursued different (but not necessarily conflicting) national interests. During the Cold War the Soviet Union, like the United States, pursued a myriad of global interests that forced the Kremlin constantly to balance its obligations. Hanoi pursued a single-minded goal – to unify the country – and had a single criterion for its relations with Moscow – maintaining the flow of the war materiel that allowed the battle to be fought. As a result of shared goals *vis-à-vis* the United States, the Soviet Union pursued a strategy of low-profile but solid support. This support was low-profile in the sense that the Soviet Union did not deny its material support of the Democratic Republic of Vietnam, but it did not clearly link its aid to the DRV's goal of unification. The Soviets often took the middle ground, favouring negotiated settlement, which might postpone but eventually achieve unification. From Moscow's perspective, the middle-ground strategy was valuable in that it helped to perpetuate the war, which was seen as a political monster and significant economic drain for the United States.[49]

In the competition within the communist world, the military needs of North Vietnam also presented Moscow with the additional opportunity to detach the DRV from China. The American air war could only be countered by sophisticated military equipment, which the Soviet Union could provide but which was beyond the capacity of the Chinese. To the historically aware leaders in Hanoi, an alliance with the Soviets was also seen as politically preferable for the DRV because of Vietnam's long hatred for their powerful northern neighbour and sometimes occupier. Despite historical anti-Chinese sentiment, however, the DRV was forced to play a delicate balancing act that sought to gain maximum support from both its communist patrons. The Chinese supplied large quantities of food, ammunition and small arms, while the Soviets supplied tanks, anti-aircraft missiles and other heavy equipment. Both China and the Soviet Union supplied advisers, technicians and logistics personnel, many of whom became casualties of American air raids.[50]

For its part China was wary of becoming involved directly in Vietnam after its experience in Korea, which had cost the nation dearly. Ironically, the

US fear of Chinese intervention if the war were moved north was matched by the Chinese fears of the costs to themselves if a similar defensive action were deemed necessary. In 1980 Vo Nguyen Giap, the DRV's second most famous nationalist and the military strategist who is given credit for defeating both the French and the Americans, recollected:

> The Chinese government told the US that if the latter did not threaten or touch China, then China would do nothing to prevent the attacks [on Vietnam]. It was really like telling the United States that it could bomb Vietnam at will ... We felt that we had been stabbed in the back ... Later when the US began systematically to bomb North Vietnam, the Soviet Union proposed to send air units and missile forces to defend Vietnam. It was the Chinese leaders that prevented it from doing so. We had to resolve the situation in a way which would not affect our war of resistance against the Americans. For this reason we could not publicly denounce the Chinese, nor could we reveal the Soviet proposal ... After Nixon signed the Shanghai Communiqué, this showed that the Chinese leaders were clamoring for an American presence in Southeast Asia, even in South Vietnam. When we recount all these events and link them to the war in the southeast [Cambodia] we can see the treachery of the Chinese leaders.[51]

President Nixon's visit to Beijing in July 1971 was seen as both threat and insult to Hanoi. Vietnam's most hated enemy was being honoured by a supposedly close ally. The Vietnamese were further shocked and greatly concerned by Nixon's trip to Moscow in May 1972. Hanoi's memory of the 1954 betrayal at Geneva by its two communist allies remained in clear focus. The leaders of the DRV were determined never again to trust the fate of unification to the conference table and to their allies. By 1973 Moscow was clearly weary of the whole business, reacting with virtual indifference to the US blockade and mining of Haiphong Harbour.[52] In retrospect it is clear that the Soviet Union played a crucial role in the pace of Vietnam's successful unification. However, as Soviet diplomats continually asserted to US officials in private conversations, the Soviet ability to influence Vietnamese leaders was limited. The Vietnamese were determined to unify the country with or without Soviet aid, and they were willing to turn to the Chinese if the Soviets pressured them too greatly on a settlement with the Americans. Soviet policy during the Vietnam War was an equal mixture of pragmatic international politics and judicious self-interest. Assistance to the DRV was beneficial both on ideological grounds and in terms of realpolitik. Much like the US support for the Afghan rebels during the 1980s, the Kremlin leaders saw it as a relatively low-cost, high-benefit investment in the Cold War power struggle for global influence.

THE SUPERPOWERS IN AFGHANISTAN, 1979–88

The Soviet Union: the Brezhnev years

In January 1980, after the Christmas assassination of President Amin by Soviet special forces (Spetsnaz) units, the new Afghan regime under Babrak Karmal began to change the outward appearance of the PDPA in accordance with Soviet pacification policies. He sought to lessen the outwardly Marxist character of the regime in order to appeal to the greater masses of traditional Afghan society and gain legitimacy. Karmal emphasized moderation in the pace of reforms that were to be implemented, and he attempted to establish a broad-based national front that included noncommunist elements in his government. Karmal paid special attention to eradicating the perceived atheistic character of his government. According to Soviet documents, the following list includes some of the official political and social goals of the new administration:

- The strengthening of unity of all – big and small – peoples and tribes of Afghanistan; complete elimination of all discrimination of Afghan citizens connected with their nationality, language, race, tribe, sect, origin, education, sex, way of life, property status;
- the provision of all Afghan Moslems with the necessary conditions, complete freedom and reliable protection in performing the religious rites required by Islam; the rendering of assistance to the ulema (Moslem theologians) in discharging their duties;
- the development and consolidation of democracy on the principles of collective leadership and democratic centralism;
- strict adherence to the principles of peaceful coexistence, non-alignment, positive neutrality and international solidarity and cooperation with the Soviet Union, other socialist countries and revolutionary forces of our time.[53]

Karmal's greatest problem was to convince the people that he was a devout Muslim and that he respected Afghanistan's political traditions. His speeches opened with the traditional incantation, 'In the name of Allah, the compassionate and merciful'. Mullahs were brought to Kabul for conferences and were sent on free tours of Soviet Central Asia to convince them that the Soviet Union was not suppressing Islam.[54] Karmal also announced a total amnesty for all political prisoners who survived the Amin regime. Many of the prisoners were Parcham officials who had been jailed after Amin's rise to power and would take part in the new government. The government announced that it had released 15,000 prisoners by July 1980.[55] In spite of these efforts to put a new face on the communist regime, Karmal had little success in winning 'the hearts and minds' of the Afghan people. He was looked on as a weak tool of the Russians, a greater sin in the eyes of fiercely independent Afghans than either Taraki or Amin had committed. Taraki and Amin were hated for their policies and their atheism, but they at least were Afghans who had risen to power through their own devices. Karmal was viewed as a mere puppet of the Soviet invaders.[56]

The Kremlin leadership realized, as had the American leaders in formulating Vietnam policy, that some degree of domestic legitimacy had to be created for their wards in Kabul. One part of the Soviet plan to strengthen Karmal's regime was to end the bloody split between the Khalq and Parcham factions of the PDPA. However, just as the United States had little success in unifying factional interests in Vietnam, Karmal made only minimal efforts to engineer a reunion. Along with Amin, the Khalqi leadership cadre was all but eliminated in the new regime, though Khalqis still outnumbered Parchamis by a considerable number in the lower echelons of the PDPA, especially among the various branches of the armed forces. The remaining Khalqis resented Karmal's use of Soviet military backing, which had ensured Parcham's return to power; the Parchamis had not forgotten their persecution by the Khalqis – and neither side was inclined to forgive and forget. Although they were all members of the communist PDPA, the split between the two factions remained firmly grounded in historical tribal animosities.[57] In June, July and October 1980 three serious military mutinies occurred when Khalqi commanders were replaced by Parchami officers. These rebellions were suppressed by force. The Parcham faction attempted to increase its size through recruitment, and, by PDPA accounts, more than 40,000 new members were added. In 1983 a firefight broke out between Khalqi policemen and Parchami army officers in Herat that resulted in over a hundred dead.[58]

However, like the regime in South Vietnam after the Tet offensive, the new regime was able to engender some support, primarily limited to urban areas. The PDPA policy that was most successful was the formation of the National Fatherland Front (NFF) – although success is a relative concept here. The NFF was designed to appeal to the nationalistic sentiments of the Afghans and to supplement the PDPA organization by engaging the membership of those who were leery of communism. This was one of many attempts to broaden the base of popular support under the Karmal regime. By mid 1983 official claims placed NFF membership at 600,000 in 410 committees. A later news release may have mistakenly given the correct membership figures when it claimed 55,000 members in over 1,000 committees.[59] Despite the continued efforts of the new regime to heal its internal rift and appear less Marxist in character, these policies had little effect on the progress of the civil war. Although the Soviets dictated PDPA policy and maintained nearly complete control over Karmal, even they could not force an end to the factional blood feud within the PDPA. Still, the NFF formed a nucleus of urban supporters that helped to maintain the Afghan regime for three years after the Soviet withdrawal.

The Soviet war

From the landing of Soviet troops in Kabul on Christmas Eve 1979 until they left nearly a decade later, the only real source of power in Afghanistan was the Soviet Union. Although the Karmal regime attempted to make gains on the political front at the urging of its Soviet advisers, it soon became apparent from the lack of cooperation by the vast majority of the Afghan people and the fierce resistance put up by the Afghan freedom fighters (Mujahideen) that Soviet military forces were needed throughout the country for the regime to survive. By the end of the first week of January 1980, more than 50,000 Soviet troops were in Afghanistan. By the end of March, six full divisions, totalling 85,000 personnel, were in various positions around the country. By 1984 this number had steadily increased to approximately 115,000, where it remained through 1988.[60] As the Soviet forces increased in size, there was a corresponding decrease in Afghan forces. The Afghan army suffered huge numbers of desertions, which at times included entire divisions, shrinking it from an estimated 90,000 troops in 1978 to 30,000 in 1981. Mutinous Afghan units were credited as one of the best sources of rebel weapons in the early months of the war.[61] It is believed that during the planning of military operations the Soviet leadership surrounding Brezhnev anticipated a relatively quick incursion into Afghanistan. Like the United States in Vietnam, the Soviet Union perceived itself as capable of great deeds, and militarily the Russia-centred empire was at the peak of its power. Like the US plan in Vietnam, Soviet military power would stabilize the political situation by cowing any potential opposition and destroying any rebels foolish enough to challenge the firepower of the Red Army. Soviet hubris regarding its military prowess clearly mirrors that of the United States in Vietnam.

Soviet forces in Afghanistan included ground troops, air force personnel and support troops, numbering from 90,000 to 104,000. These forces were supported by 50,000 ground and air force personnel in the southern Soviet Union. Troops were deployed geographically with about one-third of ground forces in the Kabul area with other major deployments at Mazar-i-Sharif and Qunduz in the north, Herat and Farah in the east, Kandahar in the south and Jalalabad in the east. Major air bases are located in Jalalabad, Bagram, Kabul, Kandahar, Herat, Shindand and Farah.[62] Soviet strategy focused on holding the major centres of communication and transportation, while carrying out a limited war of attrition against the Mujahideen. Like the Americans in Vietnam, the Soviets sought to inflict as much damage as possible on rebel forces at the minimum cost to their own troops. They used their superior tactical mobility and firepower to make up for an insufficient number of troops and to hold casualties to a minimum. Control over territory remained more or less constant during the nine-year occupation. The Soviets had daytime control over the major cities and strategic garrisons, while the rebels had night-time control over virtually the entire country. The Soviets attempted to reduce rebel-controlled areas by pursuing a combined 'scorched-earth' and 'migratory-genocide' policy. The migratory-genocide policy was a plan to depopulate rebel-held territory and thus remove the Mujahideen's base of support. The Soviets forced huge numbers of people in the countryside to flee to Iran and Pakistan by deliberately burning crops. Reminiscent of US tactics in Vietnam, the Soviets used high-altitude carpet bombing and a 'free-fire zone' approach in rebel-infested areas where all people were considered targets.[63] On a more sinister note, the Soviets also used small antipersonnel mines in the form of watches, ballpoint pens, books and dolls. These devices caused enormous damage among the civilian population, and many women and children lost feet or hands as a consequence.[64] There were also reports by the US State Department that the Soviets used chemical weapons in at least fifteen provinces of Afghanistan.[65] The Soviets categorically denied such accusations. The immediate material and human costs to the Soviets were considerable. As of 1984 casualties were estimated conservatively at 30,000 killed and wounded. Over $12 billion had been spent, and over 3,500 vehicles, including tanks, armoured personnel carriers and trucks, had been destroyed. Over 600 aircraft were estimated to have been shot down.[66] These numbers grew in the final four years of the war as the Mujahideen received greater numbers of increasingly more effective anti-tank and anti-aircraft weapons.

In addition to attempting to increase membership in the PDPA and the NFF, the Soviets promoted increased economic and trade ties, as well as new policies with sociopolitical ramifications. All of these measures were designed to build long-term economic, political and social ties between the Afghans and Soviets. The economy in Afghanistan was devastated by the civil war, and in 1984 crop production was estimated to be at one-fifth of pre-1978 levels. As a result the Soviets were forced to import massive amounts of food, and rationing was implemented in Afghan cities.[67] Soviet investment in the Afghan economy also increased. More than 140 industrial facilities were being built (or repaired from war damage) with Soviet assistance. In 1984 total trade figures between the two nations doubled from 1977 levels, and the Soviets were responsible for more than 80 per cent of Afghan trade. The Soviets claimed to have trained over 60,000 Afghan workers of all vocations. There were more than 9,000 Afghan college students in Soviet schools.[68] A more subtle and possibly more important policy with long-range effects was the export of young children for educational purposes. In the late 1980s there were over 20,000 young Afghans being raised and educated in the Soviet Union. Before the Soviet withdrawal, it was feared in the West that after they returned to Afghanistan, these students would form the nucleus of a new military and party elite with particularly strong ties to the Soviet Union. Special Russian-language courses were developed in the Afghanistan school system, which was expanded to reach rural areas.[69]

Unlike the United States in Vietnam, from the war's beginning the Soviet Union had engaged in a relatively active diplomatic agenda with the international community over Afghanistan. The Soviets drew worldwide condemnation for their action, and relations with Third World countries, as well as superpower relations, rapidly deteriorated after the invasion. In each of six separate UN votes on the Soviet invasion, the Soviet Union received a total number of negative votes ranging from 104 to 123.[70] Despite their inability to defeat the Mujahideen on the battlefield and the failures in finding an internal political solution, like the United States prior to the Nixon administration in Vietnam, the Soviets did not exhibit much flexibility in their position through the first six years of occupation.[71] The Soviet negotiating position began to emerge in Brezhnev's speech of 23 February 1980 at the Russian Republic Supreme Soviet election. Brezhnev accused China and America of causing Soviet intervention and said that 'the need for Soviet forces would no longer exist' when outside interference ended. Early peace proposals put forth by the United States, France and the European Community in the summer of 1981 were rejected because they failed to include the Afghan government in early discussions. These proposal included the direct representation by rebel forces, and they spoke of 'neutralization', which the Soviets viewed as an unacceptable alteration of Afghanistan's nonaligned status.[72] These proposals would have required the end of the Karmal regime, and from the Soviet perspective they violated Brezhnev's public pledge at the Twenty-sixth Party Congress in 1981 that the gains of revolution were permanent. 'We do not object to the questions connected with Afghanistan being discussed together with the questions of Persian Gulf security. Naturally, this applies only to the international aspects of the Afghan problem, and not to internal Afghan affairs. Afghanistan's sovereignty, like its nonaligned status, must be fully protected.'[73] The United Nations, in accordance with a General Assembly resolution of November 1980, began negotiations with Pakistan and Afghanistan. These negotiations, known as 'proximity talks', were held through UN mediators. The two sides would not correspond directly, thus relieving the Pakistanis of the need to recognize officially the Karmal regime or admitting to the Soviet charge of outside interference. The Pakistani position was clear. It wanted a complete withdrawal of Soviet forces, a restoration of Afghanistan's nonaligned and independent status, freedom from outside interference and the safe return of the Afghan refugees.[74] The refugee problem was of special concern for

Pakistan, which had been forced to provide for over three million Afghans since 1982.[75]

When Brezhnev died in November 1982, there was hope that Andropov, who was rumoured to have been against the invasion, would move to end the war. President Zia of Pakistan noted that there was 'a hint of flexibility' in the Soviet attitude toward Afghanistan.[76] The chief editor of *Pravda*, Victor Afanasyev, a Central Committee member, told a Japanese newspaper that a political settlement was desired that did not require an Afghan government to 'be a Soviet-type socialist government'.[77] The Soviet press soon denied Afanasyev's statements and retorted that the USSR's position remained unchanged. Andropov personally laid to rest any rumours of change in the Soviet view:

> Our plans for a political settlement of the Afghan problem are no secret ... We consider that as soon as outside interference in the affairs of Afghanistan has been terminated and non-resumption of such interference guaranteed, we shall withdraw our troops. Our troops are staying in that country and are there at the request of the lawful Afghan government ... headed by Babrak Karmal ... It is, however, far from being a matter of indifference to us what is happening directly on our southern border.[78]

Overall, the Soviet military strategy remained relatively unchanged from 1979 to 1986. According to General Muhammad Nawroz, a veteran of the Army of Afghanistan allied with the Red Army, Soviet strategy for the military occupation centred around six main objectives:

(1) stabilizing the country by garrisoning the main routes, major cities, air bases and logistic sites;

(2) relieving the Afghan Government forces of garrison duties and pushing them into the countryside to battle the resistance;

(3) providing logistic, air, artillery and intelligence support to the Afghan forces;

(4) providing minimum interface between the Soviet occupation forces and the local populace;

(5) accepting minimal Soviet casualties;

(6) strengthening the Afghan forces, so once the resistance was defeated, the Soviet Army could be withdrawn.[79]

On a number of these points we see similarities between the US and Soviet approaches. Perhaps learning from the American experience in Vietnam, the Soviets never intended to bear the brunt of the fighting, expecting their

Afghan allies to carry the fight to the resistance in the countryside. However, as many before them have learned, in war the best intentions and plans often come to naught. Like the Americans in Vietnam, the Soviets were forced to bear the major burden of combat, primarily because of the huge proportion of Afghan government troops that joined the resistance rather than fighting alongside foreigners against their fellow Afghans. However, in stark contrast to the United States, the Soviet Union did not escalate the level of their involvement to the degree witnessed in Vietnam. Essentially, under Brezhnev and Andropov the Soviets were satisfied with keeping the war limited. Under Konstantin Chernenko, who served as general secretary very briefly for less than a year in 1984 and 1985, a marginally greater effort was made to win the war. In this period the Soviet forces in Afghanistan adopted much more aggressive tactics, launching the noted 'Panjshir 7' offensive into the Panjshir Valley, which included 15,000 Soviet and 5,000 Afghan troops, as well as heavy bombing from Tu-16 aircraft based in the Soviet Union. According to Mark Galeotti, the author of one of the most well-received analyses of the Afghan War published in the 1990s,

> Soviet casualties increased during this period, but it is important to stress how limited the war remained. There was no major increase in the size of the OKSV [Limited Contingent of Forces in Afghanistan], nor was there much recourse to such measures as cross-border bombing, as practiced by US forces in Vietnam. Nevertheless, Chernenko's iron fist did not lead to a convincing military success, just temporary victories which, in turn, sparked a more assertive response from the USA and other backers of the rebels.[80]

The Gorbachev years

After the selection of Mikhail Gorbachev as the General Secretary of the CPSU in March 1985, real changes began to occur in the Soviet position toward Afghanistan. The shift in the Soviet position can be directly linked to Gorbachev's domestic policies, which were attempting a 'restructuring' of the Soviet economy and society. Gorbachev's plan, known as *perestroika*, called for major changes in the Soviet economy as well as increased political freedoms. According to Kremlin documents, the secret decision to withdraw from Afghanistan was made on 13 November 1986. Gorbachev initiated a debate that would alter the course of world history in stating, 'We have been fighting in Afghanistan for six years now. If we don't change approaches we will be fighting there for another 20 or 30 years … We must finish this process in the swiftest possible time.'[81] However, it would be a year before the Soviets were ready to implement the changes. In a speech at the 70th anniversary celebration of the Bolshevik Revolution in November 1987 Gorbachev severely compromised the ideological rationale for the Brezhnev Doctrine in admitting that there was 'no model of socialism to be emulated by everyone'.[82] In his book *Perestroika*, Gorbachev provides a clear statement of the foreign policy metamorphosis:

> Every nation is entitled to choose its own way of development, to dispose of its fate, its territory and its human and natural resources. International relations cannot be normalized if this is not understood in all countries. For ideological and social differences and differences in political systems are the result of the choice made by the people. A national choice should not be used in international relations in such a way as to cause trends and events that can trigger conflicts and military confrontation … it is high time to recognize that the Third World nations have the right to be their own bosses.[83]

Taken at face value, this statement indicates that as early as 1987, when *Perestroika* was first published, if a nation were to decide a new form of government, even if it meant changing from a socialist government to some other form, the Soviets under Gorbachev were prepared to accept the change. This idea clearly contradicts the core precept of the Brezhnev Doctrine and can be interpreted as a rejection of the principle that once a country becomes socialist, it must always remain socialist. Therefore Gorbachev, still a committed communist in 1987, was building the ideological basis for changing the Soviet Union's foreign policy with the goal of reducing the huge economic burden of military spending that foreign commitments which the 'socialist commonwealth' required.

The decision to withdraw from Afghanistan was a fundamental turning point in Moscow's foreign policy. For the first time since Soviet forces were reluctantly removed from Iran at the end of the Second World War and the signing of the Austrian peace treaty in 1955, the Soviet Union retreated from an occupied territory. This overt divergence from past behaviour signalled the first stage of a comprehensive policy reorientation that was later clearly affirmed by the encouragement that Moscow provided for the democratic revolution in Eastern Europe. Lenin's zero-sum world-view of *kto kovo* had been replaced by Gorbachev's positive-sum world-view of global inter-dependence and common interests.

Gorbachev's ideological gerrymandering had begun to affect the Soviet relationship with Afghanistan soon after he assumed leadership of the Soviet Union. Three days after returning from a trip to Moscow in May 1986, Babrak Karmal was peacefully replaced by Dr Muhammad Najibullah, the head of the Afghan secret police (KhAD). Karmal's replacement coincided with a new round of indirect US-sponsored peace talks in Geneva between Afghan and Pakistani negotiators. Karmal's removal brought about demonstrations in Kabul on his behalf, which caused the Soviets to surround key government buildings and army barracks with tanks. Karmal did retain his membership in the Afghan Politburo and the ceremonial post as president, but his tenure as Afghanistan's political leader was over.[84]

Like President Nixon in Vietnam, despite making the political decision to leave Afghanistan, Gorbachev would not do so without punishing the Soviet Union's enemies on the battlefield. He appointed General Mikhail Zaitsev, a younger and more energetic commander formerly in charge of Soviet forces in East Germany, to try to break the military stalemate. Zaitsev successfully used special forces (Spetsnaz) and helicopter gunships to inflict significant damage on rebel operations. Analyses of Soviet tactics (which began appearing in print mostly after the downfall of the Soviet empire) have found that like the United States in Vietnam, a great deal of learning did take place on the battlefield. Soviet ground forces developed the innovative (and risky) *bronegruppa* concept, which used the firepower of BMP, BMD and BTR armoured personnel carriers in the capacity of an independent reserve once the motorized rifle soldiers had dismounted. Likewise Soviet air assault tactics and the use of helicopter gunships steadily improved throughout the war. However, according to one study, 'Ten large, conventional offensives involving heliborne and mechanized forces swept the Pandshir Valley with no lasting result.'[85]

The improved battlefield performance was countered in part by the US decision in April 1986 to supply the Mujahideen with sophisticated Stinger anti-aircraft missiles. One well-respected analyst downplayed their importance. The Stingers, he said, 'did not change the face of the war, but they were a powerful symbol of the continuing will of the West and the Arab world to support the rebels'.[86] However, most analysts of the Afghan War believe that the Stingers were a major factor in significantly altering the battlefield dynamic. According to Richard Litwak, 'The arrival of these new American weapons marked a turning point in the war. With air losses estimated at one aircraft per day, the Soviet military command was forced to change tactics. They were no longer able to use helicopter gunships and tactical aircraft in close ground support roles ... Zaitsev's activist strategy based on mobility ground to a halt as Soviet military operations reverted back to their prior form.'[87] Litwak's analysis is similar to that of Lester Grau of the US Foreign Military Studies Office: 'Without the helicopter gunship the Soviets may have withdrawn years earlier ... The guerrillas adapted. They fought at night when the helicopter was least effective ... The masterful employment of the Stinger by the Afghan freedom fighters heavily tilted the balance in favor of the Mujahideen. Even the extensive use of Soviet airpower that was stationed across the northern border could not change the situation.'[88]

In July 1986 the Soviets announced their intention to remove six regiments of troops by December of that year. Although these troops consisted mainly of anti-aircraft personnel and were useless in fighting the Mujahideen, the removal, when completed, was the first instance of a Soviet reduction in forces. In late summer 1986 the Soviets began to suffer substantial losses in aircraft because of the growing supply of Stinger missiles reaching the rebels. The Soviet dominance of the air was reduced considerably, and rebel forces were able to consolidate their hold on many areas that had previously been subjected to Soviet aerial bombardment.[89] Political reforms under Karmal and Najibullah did little to increase the regime's popularity with the Afghan people. Factionalism within the PDPA remained a problem, and there was little hope for change in the battlefield stalemate. Like Johnson in 1968, Gorbachev was faced with three basic options. First, he could escalate the conflict by increasing Soviet troop levels and possibly striking at rebel base camps in Pakistan. Second, he could continue to suffer what he described as the 'bleeding wound' by extending existing policies indefinitely. Or third, he could make the difficult decision to withdraw Soviet troops.

The first option carried the greatest risk. It was not clear that military escalation would fundamentally change the battlefield situation – as the Soviets may have learned from the US experience in Vietnam. Short of Soviet incursions into Iran, Pakistan and China, the rebel's base camps would remain relatively secure even if more Soviet troops were in-country. Like the United States in Vietnam, the Soviet Union could widen the bombing campaign to these countries, but doing so would undoubtedly elicit a greater response from an already hostile Reagan administration in the United States and an equally hostile China. Furthermore, escalation in Afghanistan might result in a greater degree of Sino-American detente. In the strategic picture on the global scale, even though the situation in Afghanistan might improve, any cooperation between the Kremlin's two major rivals would be detrimental to fundamental Soviet national security interests. Nor would more troops increase the political viability of the Kabul regime, again a lesson perhaps learned from the American experience in Vietnam. Moreover, escalation would carry increased economic and political costs at a time in which Soviet resources had been already overextended by external commitments. Any further acts of Soviet aggression in Afghanistan might inspire the Reagan administration to respond with even greater increases in defence spending, which historically the Soviets had routinely tried to match.

The second option, continuing with the status quo, also held little appeal for Gorbachev. Unlike President Johnson, who was in large part responsible for the escalation in US commitments to Vietnam, Gorbachev had not been part of the senior politburo members who had sent Soviet forces into Afghanistan. Because of his predecessors' decisions, the war had caused a deterioration in Soviet prestige around the world, and it had proved to be especially damaging to relations with countries in the Middle East. Likewise, Gorbachev's *glasnost* (openness) policies had uncovered a widespread dissatisfaction among the Soviet population with the war. The growing numbers of casualties and disillusioned veterans had brought home the negative aspects of the war. By the end of 1987 unprecedented statements by Soviet veterans were appearing in the Soviet press attacking both the Soviet leadership and war itself:[90]

> There is talk that the war in Afghanistan would have ended long ago if the sons of leaders were sent as well.
>
> (*Pravda*, 25 November 1987)

> The main question about Afghanistan is not the truth about the horrors and the death, but why are we there?
>
> (*Ogonyok*, November 1987)

Although unusual in terms of status-quo Soviet politics, these criticisms were part of Gorbachev's grand strategy for changing the Soviet Union under the umbrella of *glasnost* and *perestroika*. In order that his own version of the Great Society policies might have a chance of success, Gorbachev required a peaceful international environment. Both the United States and China had made a Soviet withdrawal from Afghanistan a prerequisite for improved relations. Therefore the third option, reversing Brezhnev's decision to intervene, appeared to be the optimal solution for Gorbachev in 1987.

In December 1987, one week before the US–Soviet summit in Washington, Afghan president Najibullah announced the Afghan version of 'new thinking', which he called 'National Reconciliation'. This programme offered amnesty to all rebels and called for a coalition government made up of all elements of Afghan society. For the first time since the communist coup, the various Mujahideen organizations were recognized as legitimate political groups in Afghanistan.[91] One week later, at the summit meeting with President Reagan, Gorbachev announced in regard to the Soviet withdrawal from Afghanistan: 'The political decision has been taken. We've named the time limit – 12 months, maybe less.'[92] After Gorbachev's announcement, high-level talks between Soviet Foreign Minister Shevardnadze and President Najibullah resulted in an agreement for the withdrawal of Soviet troops. Shevardnadze explained that the Soviet decision to withdraw its forces was based on the Afghan National Reconciliation. The Soviet press reported on the Afghan–Soviet talks of 7 January 1988:

> Weapons in hand, Afghan patriots have been wholeheartedly defending the gains of the April Revolution. Soviet internationalist fighting men have been at their side ... But the new political thinking has persistently sought ways and means that rule out a military solution to the problem. This is how the draft political settlement around Afghanistan and the policy of national reconciliation came into being ... *When the outside*

interference has ended, we will leave Afghanistan with a clear conscience and with the awareness that our duty has been fulfilled.[93]

Although the Soviet position regarding the cessation of outside interference as a precondition for withdrawal appeared unchanged from that consistently argued since the beginning of the invasion, the doctrine behind it had changed entirely. The Afghan policy of 'National Reconciliation' transformed the official characterization of the Mujahideen from imperialist-sponsored 'bandits' into 'internal opposition forces'. Therefore, the official justification for Soviet containment policies in Afghanistan – outside interference – was erased with a clever bit of 'new thinking'. By recognizing the conflict as a civil war rather than an international war, the Soviet Union could now see the struggle as an internal Afghan affair, which, since Gorbachev's repudiation of the Brezhnev Doctrine, was no longer a matter of concern to the Soviet Union and could be dealt with by the Afghan government. Thus the need for Soviet troops no longer existed. Clearly, this reinterpretation was an attempt to give the Soviets a way to withdraw 'honourably'. In doing so, it confirms that the original Soviet goal – containment of imperialist aggression – was a falsehood. Like the Americans in Vietnam, containment of outside aggression was a pretence used to detain a population under the control of an illegitimate government, a government that the Soviet Union would end up abandoning to its own fate, just as the Americans had done in Vietnam in 1973.

On 8 February 1988 Gorbachev announced that the Soviets would begin removing their forces from Afghanistan on 15 May, if an agreement was signed in Geneva by 15 March. He proposed that all Soviet troops would be withdrawn within ten months after an agreement was signed.[94] Gorbachev was apparently so eager to begin the process of withdrawal that he agreed to a US proposal that military supplies to both the Kabul regime and the rebels be symmetrically reduced. Thus, if the United States stopped arming the Mujahideen, the Soviets would apparently abandon their clients in the PDPA. After a Soviet announcement on 17 March that they would withdraw troops even if no official agreements were reached,[95] the Geneva peace talks, which had been stalled by demands from both sides, soon ironed out the numerous technical difficulties that were delaying an agreement. On 6 April Gorbachev and Najibullah met in the Soviet Central Asian city of Tashkent. In a joint statement issued the next day, the two sides announced 'that the last obstacles to concluding the agreements have now been removed thanks to the constructive cooperation of all who are involved in the settlement, and favor their immediate signing'.[96] On 14 April Pakistan, Afghanistan, the Soviet Union and the United States signed agreements providing for the withdrawal of Soviet forces from Afghanistan and the restoration of a nonaligned Afghan state.[97]

The United States in Afghanistan, 1979–88

In a news conference on 28 December 1979, President Jimmy Carter described the Soviet military intervention in Afghanistan as a blatant violation of international norms and a 'grave threat to peace'. On the same day the National Security Council began a series of meetings to formulate the US reaction to the Soviet move. In his memoirs Carter recalls,

> The worst disappointment to me personally was the immediate and automatic loss of any chance for the early ratification of the SALT II treaty. Furthermore, the situation created a threat to both Iran and Pakistan which had not existed previously. If the Soviets could consolidate their hold on Afghanistan, the balance of power in the entire region would be drastically modified in their favor, and they might be tempted toward further aggression. We were resolved to do everything feasible to prevent such a turn of events.'[98]

In various speeches during 1980 the president and his cabinet members revealed that the administration saw the Afghan invasion both as an extension of the Brezhnev Doctrine, and as a qualitatively new event. Secretary of State Cyrus Vance characterized the invasion as 'the first time since World War Two' that the Soviet Union had 'used its own armed forces beyond the Warsaw Pact sphere to impose its authority directly over a Third World country'.[99]

The US response further hardened in the president's annual State of the Union address on 23 January 1980. This speech was noted for the enunciation of the so-called 'Carter Doctrine'. Carter declared that in defence of the region's oil supply, 'An attempt by any outside force to gain control of the Persian Gulf region will be regarded as an assault on the vital interests of the United States of America, and such an assault will be repelled by any means necessary, including military force.'[100] The president went on to declare that the invasion 'could pose the most serious threat to peace since the Second World War', and announced a series of punitive measures:

(1) blocking the export of 17 million metric tons of grain;

(2) stopping the sale of computers and high-technology equipment;

(3) reducing the allowable catch of the Soviet fishing in US waters from 350,000 tons to 75,000 tons;

(4) delaying the opening of the new Soviet consulate in New York;

(5) postponing a renegotiation of the cultural agreement that was under consideration;

(6) boycotting the Moscow Olympics: an action later joined by fifty-five other countries, including Germany, Japan and China.[101]

It was only the beginning of US support for the Afghan resistance. During Carter's last year in office and continuing throughout the Reagan presidency, the United States put unrelenting diplomatic pressure on the Soviets to withdraw from Afghanistan. The most important US contribution to the war in Afghanistan, however, was its material support for the Afghan Mujahideen. By the end of 1984 Washington had provided the rebellion with over $400 million in aid, and another $250 million came through in 1985. Washington's planned support was increased that year when the president signed National Security Directive 166, which promised $470 million in 1986 and $630 million in 1987. Simultaneously the US Agency for International Development provided approximately $40 million by 1988 for aiding refugees displaced by the fighting.[102] In all, during the 1980s the United States funnelled well more than $2 billion in weapons and money to the rebels. It was the largest covert action programme since the Second World War. Supply levels rose from 10,000 tons in 1983 to 65,000 tons in 1987. CIA officers helped to plan rebel attacks using Pakistani intelligence officers as intermediaries. As mentioned earlier, the Stinger missiles helped to turn the tide in the war by forcing upon Gorbachev the choice between further escalation, maintenance of the status quo, and withdrawal.[103] In the United States there was wide support for the Afghan programme, both among the population and among the often divided houses of Congress. US Representative Charles Wilson summed up the prevailing sentiment in Congress stating, 'there were 58,000 dead in Vietnam, and we owe the Russians one'.[104]

On the diplomatic front, the United States was less active than might have been expected. Like the Soviet involvement in Vietnam during the American war, the national interests of the United States were not necessarily best served by a rapid conclusion to the conflict. When it became apparent during the 1980s that the Soviet Union did not appear likely to expand further into the Persian Gulf, the Soviet 'bleeding wound' was a relatively low-cost, high-benefit situation for the United States. The Americans were willing to allow Pakistani negotiators the main task of settling the details of the dispute with the Soviet Union and only became involved in the diplomatic negotiations during the final phases in Geneva in the late 1980s.[105] During the zero-sum game of the Cold War, Soviet difficulties in Afghanistan were perceived as benefiting the United States. For instance, during the Reagan administration, US–Iraqi relations steadily improved, and by the late 1980s the United States had essentially weaned Iraq away from the Soviet Union.[106] Although US policy toward Iraq proved in 1991 ultimately to have been a major policy-making failure, at the time events in Afghanistan helped to improve US relations with it and other countries, including communist China. Likewise, by helping the Islamist rebels in Afghanistan, the United States was perceived more positively in the Arab world. By taking actions on behalf of both Iraq and Afghanistan, the United States clearly signalled to Iran that it would actively protect its interests in the region and would not sit idly by in the wake of Iran's successful anti-Shah, anti-US revolution.

In retrospect, the enunciation of the 'Carter Doctrine' also provided a clear rhetorical demarcation of the limits of US toleration of Soviet activity in the Middle East and South Asian regions. Although appearing to be a new strategy, Carter simply reaffirmed in a more publicly bellicose fashion US policy toward Afghanistan since the Truman administration: the United States would not directly challenge the Soviet Union's regional sphere of influence as long as it did not move beyond Afghanistan's borders. However, the threat of direct US military confrontation if Soviet troops moved into Iran or Pakistan was consistent with US containment policies over the previous three decades. Even though the United States may have 'lost Iran' as a close anti-Soviet ally when the Shah was overthrown, Washington was not willing to allow Iran to fall directly under Soviet control.

FROM ESCALATION TO WITHDRAWAL: A COMPARISON OF FAILED DETAINMENT

After intervening unilaterally in the pursuit of self-determined national interests, both superpowers ended their military occupations under the diplomatic cover provided by agreements negotiated in Paris and Geneva. After the US withdrawal from Vietnam in 1973, President Nixon attempted to use a secret $4.75 billion war reparations package as leverage to keep the North from invading the South. However, the evolving Watergate scandal increased Nixon's vulnerability and Congress displayed no intention of approving any further appropriations, either to pay the promised funds to the communist North, or to assist the Southern regime. Nixon continued the bombing campaign in Cambodia, but his efforts were curtailed by Congress through fiscal legislation. In November 1973 Congress overrode the president's veto of the War Powers Act in a direct challenge to presidential war-making capabilities.[107]

In August 1974 Richard Nixon resigned the office of the presidency. To a significant degree, the Vietnam War played an important role in this political disgrace, unprecedented in US history. During his tenure in office, Nixon had become the nation's most emboldened 'imperial president', believing himself and his acts to be above the rule of law. Nixon's 'tough decisions' in Vietnam, Cambodia and Laos had not damaged him in the 1972 election, which he won with a huge majority; however, his decision to send American troops and bombers into these countries had a definitive impact on his eventual downfall. In July 1973 Congress had begun investigations over the possible criminality of Nixon's actions in Cambodia. When the first press accounts of US bombing began to appear in the American press, the president and his advisers had responded with a wide assortment of illegal wiretaps of White House aides and reporters. Each act of lawbreaking, ranging in scope from the burglary of the offices of Daniel Ellsberg's psychiatrist (Ellsberg was responsible for the *Pentagon Papers* leak) to the eventual break-in at the Democratic Party headquarters located in the Watergate Hotel, fed the next. Eventually the president and his aides decided that their lawbreaking could be managed only by further illegal acts, which resulted in the now infamous cover-up conspiracy. Nixon's attempt to deceive Congress and the American people was judged to be his greatest crime, and the cover-up conspiracy constituted the core arguments in the Congressional bill of impeachment that was drawn up in 1974. Also in 1973, Nixon's open defiance of a clear Congressional desire to withdraw from Vietnam spurred the Watergate investigation and contributed to a Congressional override of Nixon's veto of the War Powers Act, which placed some limits on the president's near-unilateral power to deploy US forces. Of equal significance at the time was the passage of the yearly Military Procurement Authorization bill, which included an amendment banning the funding of any direct US military actions in Indochina.[108] Congress was acting rapidly to end US involvement in the Vietnam War, and in his attempts to obstruct the process, Richard Nixon was driven from office. As a result, the war in Vietnam had claimed the career of a second American president.

By the end of 1974 the United States had reduced its aid to South Vietnam to $700 million. The vast reduction of US support had devastating effects on the South Vietnamese government, economy and military apparatus, all of which had been created by and were totally dependent on American means. In early 1975 Northern troops stationed in Southern Vietnam launched a small offensive that avalanched into a final attack on the South. When the United States failed to respond, the North pushed toward Saigon. After heated debate, Congress approved only $300 million to help evacuate Americans, but no military assistance was offered. Congress rejected President Ford's appeals that the United States was bound by Nixon's promises to Thieu. Less than two months after the initiation of the Northern assault, Vietnam was unified. On 1 May 1975 the thirty-year war for Vietnamese independence was over; detainment had failed.[109]

In Afghanistan the Mujahideen's war against the regime of Najibullah was less conclusive from the perspective of national unity, which remains an elusive goal nearly a decade after the Soviet troops were withdrawn. In Vietnam, the artificial division between North and South had pitted a unified nationalist movement of North Vietnamese and NLF forces against the Americans and a much less unified polity in the South. Whereas in Vietnam national liberation and national unity were merged, in Afghanistan the forces opposing the Soviet invaders and Afghan communists were more diverse and factionalized along traditional ethnic and religious lines. The downfall of the

Najibullah regime evolved over a three-year period. Soon after the departure of the last Soviet troops on 15 February 1989, the Afghan president began successfully exploiting divisions among the ranks of the Mujahideen. These divisions, which had existed throughout the rebellion, had deepened during the Soviet withdrawal as the struggle for post-Soviet Afghanistan began. According to analyst Barnett Rubin, 'The fragmentation of the political and military structures of the resistance prevented the mujahidin from turning local victories into a national one. For many of the fighters and the commanders, the personal obligation (*farz-i'ain*) of jihad ended with the Soviet withdrawal. As in normal times – but with more weapons – they engaged in struggles for local power.'[110] The government projected itself as the only force in the country capable of maintaining order, a claim partially substantiated by infighting among the resistance. However, Najibullah's success in maintaining power until 1992 was also directly tied to events in the Soviet Union. Despite the Soviet withdrawal, the Soviet Union continued to provide $300 million in monthly military and economic aid to the Kabul regime, support which lasted until November 1991. The Kabul government survived by adhering to a conservative military strategy that concentrated on defending urban areas, strategic lines of communication and logistics, the model left to them by their Soviet patrons.[111]

On 25 April 1992 the Afghan civil war symbolically ended. Exactly fourteen years after the leaders of the PDPA seized power in their coup against Daoud, Kabul was finally overrun by Mujahideen forces under the military command of Ahmed Shah Massoud, an ethnic Tajik whose power base is located in northeast Afghanistan. As with the final attack on Saigon, the guerrillas moved into the capital mostly unopposed by the remaining government troops.[112] However, the Afghan civil war has continued intermittently up until the present. As things stand (in the spring of 1998), a group known as the Taliban occupies Kabul and controls approximately three-quarters of Afghan territory. The Taliban, a group promoting a radical vision of Islam so conservative and traditional that even the Iranians have denounced them, draws its strength primarily from ethnic Pathans (the tribal group that has traditionally ruled Afghanistan). It has solid support from the government of Pakistan, which remains the primary foreign actor in Afghan domestic politics. However, it would be a mistake to view the Taliban as simply a new expression of traditional tribal politics. Their unifying message of radical Islam is being embraced (or at least tolerated) by many non-Pathans as well. Nonetheless, they have not yet been able to consolidate power, and they face significant opposition from Uzbeks and Tajiks living north of the Hindu Kush.[113] Whatever the outcome of the Afghan civil war, the dramatic failure of Soviet detainment in Afghanistan has shown that the political future of the country will be decided primarily by Afghans, not by outside powers.

In Vietnam more than 58,000 Americans lost their lives: in Afghanistan over 15,000 Soviet soldiers were killed. In both wars more than a million Vietnamese and Afghans died.[114] The failure of detainment was damaging for the Americans, ruinous to the Soviets and catastrophic for the people of Vietnam and Afghanistan. The United States survived its ordeal in Vietnam, the Soviet Union dissolved shortly after its Afghan débâcle, but the major victims in both struggles were the millions of Vietnamese and Afghans who became pawns in the global struggle for hegemony between the superpowers.

In the aftermath of Vietnam and Afghanistan, impassioned arguments were put forward by a multitude of critical voices within the United States and the Soviet Union proclaiming that 'the war could have been won if only we had ...'. For instance, in 1977 General Bruce Palmer Jr, the former commander in Vietnam and Vice-Chief of Staff, claimed that the army should have taken the offensive across the Laotian and Thai borders in order to isolate the battlefield from communist incursions along the Ho Chi Minh trail. Palmer claimed that his plans would have succeeded without having to increase the number of US forces in Vietnam. According to Palmer, 'the bulk of these [US] forces would have fought on ground of their choosing which the enemy would be forced to attack if he wanted to invade South Vietnam'. He went on to claim, 'cut off from substantial out-of-country support, the Viet Cong was bound to wither on the vine and gradually become easier for the South Vietnamese to defeat'.[115] In part, this rationale was confirmed during the war. Palmer's reasoning was correct in purely military terms. In order to win the war without changing its strategy, the United States would have had to supply more troops to General Westmoreland, or the troops already in Vietnam would have had to have been deployed as a part of a different strategic plan that would fulfil the classical principles of war as suggested by Palmer.

Similar lines of analysis have been offered by analysts of Soviet strategy in Afghanistan. In responding to the claim that Afghanistan was a military defeat, Mark Galeotti declares: 'This is incorrect: had the USSR ever deployed the sort of forces the US had used in Vietnam ... the war could have been won.'[116] However, Galeotti then undermines his own conclusion in stating, 'Since the Kremlin was never prepared to accept commensurate losses or the political risks of cross-border incursion into Pakistan, it is more fair to say, as Mark Urban has in his *War in Afghanistan*, that this was a war the Soviets never really tried to win.'[117] This is the key point. In order to understand superpower war loss in Vietnam and Afghanistan, the focus should not be primarily on an analysis of the battlefield, but rather on the analysis of the politics that ruled the battlefield. As von Clausewitz reminds us: war is an extension of politics by other means. It is correct to observe that neither of the superpowers actually 'lost' on the battlefield. In every single major engagement, in both wars, US and Soviet troops dominated their opponents. However, domination of the battlefield in a strict military sense did not produce political victory for the superpowers. Likewise, battlefield defeat was not equivalent to political failure for those resisting the superpowers in Vietnam and Afghanistan. We must remember that devoid of its ultimate political significance, war has no worthy moral, intellectual, or social meaning. Without politics, war is simply murder on an aggregate scale. Therefore, arguing over how these wars were won militarily on the battlefield but lost by the politicians at the diplomatic table is a misguided adventure in armchair strategic sophistry. War can never and should never be separated from the political context that gives it meaning.

In the superpower interventions in Vietnam and Afghanistan the global politics and history of the Cold War set the intellectual milieux in Washington and Moscow. In Vietnam, the political history of the Korean War and the possibility of military intervention by the Chinese did not necessarily amount to false perceptions by US policy-makers. In order to achieve what General Palmer described as being necessary to win the war, without an official declaration from Congress the US president would have had to break international and domestic law twice again by violating the territorial sovereignty of Thailand and Laos – the latter having been officially declared 'neutral' in treaties signed during the Kennedy administration. Military incursions into Laos and Thailand might have indeed been the best solution to the problem. However, widening the war in such fashion was judged to be politically impossible by President Johnson, who perceived a growing erosion in his own ability to pursue the war as Congress and the American media began asking serious questions about his veracity in explaining the war – and Johnson's inability to come to terms with the repercussions of his earlier subterfuge on Vietnam was one of many factors that eventually drove him from office. In ordering US bombers into Cambodia and Laos President Nixon had embarked on a strategy somewhat akin to General Palmer's post-war analysis; however, he did so as part of a negotiating strategy for bringing about an 'honourable' peaceful withdrawal of US forces from the Vietnam quagmire. It was not part of an attempt to win the war itself, and it was in violation of US domestic law in the process.

Even if the war in Vietnam had been conducted along more strategically correct lines, short of total annihilation using nuclear weapons, the Vietnamese seemed willing to continue their nationalist struggle indefinitely, making it difficult for leaders in the United States to perceive anything more than a military stalemate. The same holds true for the Soviets in Afghanistan. The only way to eliminate the Afghan rebels was to invade both Iran and Pakistan, with the almost certain probability that such an action would cause a direct confrontation with the United States. Therefore, both superpowers were constrained politically, and they eventually perceived that they could only achieve victory or acceptable compromise through political means. General Westmoreland's three-year pattern of troop requests eventually raised the question of how much would be enough in the end. There was no certain answer. In this regard, one clear difference between the two wars is the fact that the Soviets never abandoned their enclave strategy in an attempt to control the rural areas of Afghanistan, and after the Stingers had neutralized the effectiveness of helicopter assaults, Soviet ground operations, which had seen significant changes in the early Gorbachev period, were again curtailed.

What must be remembered also is the importance of how the superpowers finally came to realize that the Vietnamese and the Afghans, in keeping with their traditional patterns of undiminished hostility to foreign invaders, were refusing to compromise. As long as their patrons continued to provide war materiel, the Vietnamese north of the 17th parallel and the Afghans both inside and outside of the country were willing to bear the blood sacrifice. Their dogged commitment to the armed struggle – to ensure national liberation and unity in Vietnam, and to fight Allah's *jihad* in Afghanistan, guaranteed that indefinite stalemate was inevitable. In reflection, Dean Rusk summarizes this reality concisely: 'As Secretary of State I made two serious mistakes with respect to Vietnam. First, I overestimated the patience of the American people, and second, I underestimated the tenacity of the North Vietnamese.'[118] According to General Nawroz of the Army of Afghanistan,

> Whatever else these lessons may show, the most fundamental of them is that no army, however sophisticated, well trained, materially rich, numerically overwhelming and ruthless, can succeed on the battlefield if it is not psychologically fit and motivated for the fight. The force, however destitute in material advantages and numbers, which can rely on the moral qualities of strong faith, stubborn determination, individualism and unending patience will always be the winner.'[119]

An important battlefield fallacy clearly demonstrated in both wars was the superpowers' seduction by their own technical military superiority. Modern machines can provide battlefield superiority and inflict massive destruction and suffering, but alone they cannot bring political victory. The Vietnamese and the Afghans were not stupid. They realized that they could not confront the military forces of the superpowers in conventional head-to-head, force-on-force fashion and that attempting to do so would be suicide. As one analyst put it,

> The Afghan freedom fighter came from a traditional warrior society and proved highly resourceful in fighting the Soviets. They saw no point in remaining under aerial and artillery barrages or in facing overwhelming odds and firepower. They were adept at temporarily withdrawing from Soviet strike areas and then returning in hours, days or weeks to strike the enemy where he was exposed.[120]

This description aptly portrays the guerrilla war fought by the NFL and North Vietnamese troops while the United States was occupying South Vietnam.

However, unlike the Afghans, on two separate occasions the anti-US forces in Vietnam attempted to challenge the US superiority in firepower directly, first during the Tet offensive in 1968 and later during the 'Eastertide' offensive in 1972. In both cases overwhelming American firepower decimated the communists' concentrated formations of troops and heavy weapons.

The fallacy of technology-as-power reasoning is further illustrated by a look at the industrial capacities of the combatants. Unlike the heavy impact of strategic bombing on the war-fighting capabilities of Germany and Japan in the Second World War, bombing in North Vietnam and Afghanistan was relatively ineffective because of the industrial underdevelopment of those countries. Both the Vietnamese and the Mujahideen relied heavily on outside suppliers for their war-fighting capabilities, and with the two exceptions listed above, neither attempted to pursue the wars as the superpowers might have wished. However, the psychological impact on the bombed populations was similar to that of Germany and Japan in the Second World War, working in the favour of the bombed regime. Aerial bombing increased support for the government in North Vietnam, just as it helped to swell the ranks of the Mujahideen – in both cases helping to unify the nationalist sentiments of the superpowers' opponents. Any advantage that was provided by technological superiority in helicopters and bombers eroded over time because of increasingly effective countermeasures. Like the Stingers in Afghanistan, Soviet supplied anti-aircraft missiles and gun systems took a heavy toll on US planes in Vietnam. During the notorious 'Christmas Bombing' in 1972, thirty-four B-52 strategic bombers were lost, raising concerns among the Joint Chiefs of Staff that the American air deterrent might be indefinitely crippled if such losses continued.[121] Both wars thus confirmed one of the maxims of military conduct – wars are won on the ground. Bombing of any type is only effective when the bombed territory is occupied and defended by soldiers. Neither the United States nor the Soviet Union was willing to supply enough troops to achieve a victory in the ground wars, and neither was supporting a client government that had the necessary domestic support among the people to build an effective fighting force that could achieve internal security. Over half of the Afghan army deserted after the Soviet invasion, and the million-man ARVN almost evaporated during the first major Northern attack that was not subject to American bombing.

Hence, to compare the two, the Soviets were not willing to escalate the war to a level that might have enabled them to establish a significant degree of sovereignty over Afghan territory, whereas the United States had in fact made such an attempt in Vietnam – although clearly an insufficient one. The Soviet Union spent only 1–2 per cent of its total defence budget on the war, whereas US expenditures in Indochina reached 23 per cent of its defence budget in the peak year 1969. In crude terms, US forces in Vietnam attained a force-to-space ratio of more than seven troops per square mile when nearly a half million troops were in-theatre; the Soviets never reached a troops-to-terrain ratio of more than 0.7 troops per square mile, with a numerical peak of less than 110,000.[122] The Soviet's five divisions, four separate brigades and four separate regiments, and smaller support units of the 40th Army were hard pressed to provide security for the twenty-one provincial centres, let alone to extend this security comprehensively to the thousands of small villages, roads and strategic terrain features that spanned Afghanistan, whose territory is five times the size of Vietnam's.[123] Thus it is clear that the United States made a more concerted military effort to 'win' the war in Vietnam than the Soviet Union did in Afghanistan.

At the root of the failures is the fact that each of the superpowers committed itself to an indigenous political leadership that had already lost the 'hearts and minds' of the people. It is undeniable that in 1965 that the North Vietnamese became integral to the NLF's campaign to undermine the Southern regime, and it is true that the United States, Pakistan, China and others were involved in an effort to overthrow Afghan communists. However, the presence of the armed forces of the superpowers was the *only* thing that allowed their allied 'governments' to exist at all. The indigenous rebellion in Southern Vietnam existed during the French period, and it remained active without large-scale Northern support for many years. The Afghan rebels also were a creation of grassroots anti-government indigenous forces. The claim of containing outside aggression is highly misleading in both cases. Outside aggression did exist, but only as a function of pre-existing and overwhelming internal dissent that had been driven across international borders by the military actions of the superpowers. South Vietnam would never have survived for more than a short period without the direct military power of the United States, and neither would the Afghan communist regime have survived without the backing of the Soviet Red Army.

In each instance the superpower strategy of containment failed, in part because detainment of a rebellious population, rather than containment of outside aggression was the primary problem that military force attempted to redress. The root cause for defeat had already been firmly established at the onset of US and Soviet intervention – in the view of most of their own subjects the governments in Saigon and Kabul were illegitimate creations of hated foreign interlopers. Both the Americans and the Soviets attempted to change this fundamental problem by using military force. In this aspect, the United States and the Soviet Union were clearly invoking von Clausewitz's principle that war is an extension of politics by other means. It was believed that military might could ensure security for a period of time during which an effective indigenous governing apparatus could be created. With the clarity of hindsight we now know that this was a mistaken belief. However, it is difficult to conclude authoritatively that this belief was patently wrong at the time simply because of an erroneous or capricious reading of history by reckless policy-makers. During the course of the previous two and a half decades the armed forces of the United States had helped to defeat impressively armed enemies and to create new and friendly governments in Germany, Italy, Japan and South Korea – countries that had never been closely allied with Washington and that most recently had been at war with the United States. Likewise, throughout the countries of Eastern Europe and in North Korea the armed forces of the Soviet Union had helped to defeat enemies and create new governments in countries that had never been allied with Moscow and often had been hostile and at war with Russia and the Soviet Union. Hence the assertion that the United States should have learned the lessons of the French in Vietnam is perhaps a valid one with the infallible accuracy of hindsight, but it is an overly simplified conclusion that fails to grasp the complexity of power and circumstance in the given historical context. If leaders in Washington and Moscow had taken all of their cues from France's and Britain's historic experiences in deciding their foreign policies, Fascism might still reign throughout Europe.

Nonetheless, despite many historic examples of the successful use of military power, the superpowers' use of force clearly failed in Vietnam and Afghanistan. What makes them different? Again we must turn to a discussion of the politics of legitimacy. As noted in the previous chapter, Michael Walzer's concept of self-help and legitimacy is a useful one. According to Walzer, in the case of new regimes, there is supposedly a length of time, 'a period of grace', to build support for any new government. During that period, it is arguably both morally and legally legitimate for outside powers such as the United States and Soviet Union to lend a hand. Nonetheless, even during the transition period, political legitimacy cannot simply be conferred upon a regime from the outside powers. Legitimacy of all governments is ultimately rooted in the domestic polity, embedded in the relational nexus between the rulers and the ruled. Walzer provides no set parameters for his time limit or grace period when the new regime must inculcate popular support. Clearly, when relying on outside assistance, that period is very much dependent on the political will of the supporting regime. I concur with Walzer's view that coercive control by a state over its citizens is simply not sufficient:

> … a government that receives economic and technical aid, military supply, strategic and tactical advice, and is still unable to reduce its subjects to obedience, is clearly an illegitimate government. Whether legitimacy is defined sociologically or morally, such a government fails to meet the most minimal standards. One must wonder how it survives at all. It must be the case that it survives because of the outside help it receives and for no other, no local reasons. The Saigon regime was so much an American creature that the US government's claim to be committed to it and obligated to ensure its survival is hard to understand.

It is as if our right hand were committed to our left. There is no independent moral or political agent on the other side of the bond and hence no genuine bond at all ... When the US did intervene militarily in Vietnam, then, it acted not to fulfil commitments to another state, but to pursue polices of its own contrivance.[124]

This is the 'lesson' that Americans did not learn from the Korean War – or, if not a lesson, it is certainly the key factor that makes Vietnam different from Korea. In Korea the southern regime of Syngman Rhee achieved self-help *vis-à-vis* the United States, but more important, it was also supported by a majority of the citizens under its control. In South Korea no indigenous rebellion equivalent to the Viet Minh, NLF, or Viet Cong ever developed. Containment of outside aggression accurately describes events in Korea; detainment of a rebellious population is more the case in Vietnam. In Vietnam the communist leadership in the North had been able to seize the Mandate of Heaven in 1945 at the end of the Second World War, briefly proclaiming an independent and unified Vietnamese state. When France was allowed to regain its colonial rule in Vietnam as part of Washington's strategic vision of postwar Europe, the communists again became the leading nationalist force for independence and liberation in Vietnam. For nearly a decade the Viet Minh fought against French control, successfully waging a nationalist struggle that finally broke France's will to fight in 1954 at Dienbienphu. The partition of Vietnam into North and South was only meant to be a temporary arrangement pending elections that would unify the country and allow the French to withdraw with some semblance of their pride intact. The transition regime in the South led by President Diem was created with the intent of offering the Vietnamese people a noncommunist nationalist alternative. However, nationalism is, by definition, something that cannot take root when heavily tainted by foreign support and the presence of foreign troops. In the end, the civil dispute had to be settled by the Vietnamese themselves, something once recognized by President Kennedy, who observed, 'In the final analysis it is their war. They are the ones who have to win it or lose it. We can help them, we can give them equipment, we can send our men out there as advisers, but they have to win it – the people of Vietnam against the Communists ...'.[125] What Kennedy and his successors seemed to forget was that the communists too were people of Vietnam, and they were able to lay claim and hold on to the Mandate of Heaven despite the best efforts of the French, the Americans and other challengers among the Vietnamese themselves.

In the case of Afghanistan we see a very similar situation. The Afghan communists and their allies in the armed forces successfully seized power from the previous regime in a classic palace coup. The new regime most likely could have survived, but only if it assimilated to and governed within traditional Afghan political structures and codes of behaviour. The regime of Prince Daoud had done so, even though he had changed the government to a republic with himself as president rather than king. President Daoud had instilled incremental changes in Afghanistan, and he had used coercive force when resistance mounted. This was acceptable behaviour for an Afghan sovereign. However, Daoud did not fundamentally attack the basic social elements that bonded Afghanistan's loosely knit polity: respect for Islam, respect for traditional culture, and maintenance of a relatively decentralized governing apparatus that ceded local authority clan and tribal elders. On all three of these fundamental elements, the Afghan communists fell short. They promoted secularism over religion. They challenged the fundamental elements of Afghan tradition by pursuing the alien ideology of communism, which, in addition to being a serious affront to Islam, directly challenged basic social customs ranging from gender roles and family relations to education and health care. Unlike their Bolshevik predecessors, who seventy years earlier had managed to alter Russia radically during the tumultuous creation of what became the Soviet Union, the Afghan communists failed to engender both a significant measure of popular support and to marshal enough military assets to protect their new regime.

We can now understand that superpower intervention in Vietnam and Afghanistan created an irreconcilable contradiction: without direct military support, the regimes in Saigon and Kabul could not survive; yet with superpower intervention the regimes undermined their chances of convincing their populations that they were legitimate national governments. During the period of transition, the superpowers attempted to create an environment in which their allies could generate enough popular support that a significant component of the citizenry would believe that the government was worth fighting for. In both Vietnam and Afghanistan, Walzer's open 'grace period' lasted for slightly less than a decade before the superpowers themselves gave way to internal pressures to withdraw their forces. It is not clear how much time (if any) would have been enough for these regimes to create or coerce a more supportive domestic polity; however, it is clear that during that period, their opponents were able to do so.

NOTES

1. George Herring, *America's Longest War: The United States and Vietnam, 1950–1975* (New York: John Wiley, 1979) pp. 137–40.
2. Cited in Larry Berman, 'The US in Vietnam', in Ariel Levite, Bruce W. Jentleson and Larry Berman (eds), *Foreign Military Intervention: The Dynamics of Protracted Conflict* (New York: Columbia University Press, 1992) p. 42.
3. Ibid., pp. 42–3.
4. Ibid.

5. Raphael Littauer and Norman Uphoff (eds), *The Air War in Indochina* (Boston: Beacon Press, 1972) pp. 39–40.
6. Herring, *America's Longest War*, pp. 149–11.
7. Guenter Lewy, *America in Vietnam* (New York: Oxford University Press, 1978) pp. 389–90.
8. Ibid. See also Herring, *America's Longest War*, p. 154.
9. For two important works on the strategic failures of the Vietnam war, see Harry G. Summers, *On Strategy: A Critical Analysis of the Vietnam War* (New York: Dell, 1982) and Norman Hannah, *The Key to Failure: Laos and the Vietnam War* (New York: Madison Books, 1987).
10. *The Pentagon Papers*, Gravel Edition (Boston, MA: Beacon Press, 1971) (*PP*), Vol. IV, pp. 427–8.
11. Marlin B. Young, *The Vietnam Wars, 1945–1990* (New York: Harper Perennial, 1991) pp. 167–70.
12. Herring, *America's Longest War*, pp. 158–9.
13. Stanley Karnow, *Vietnam: A History* (New York: Viking, 1983) p. 451.
14. Ibid., pp. 451–2. See also Herring, *America's Longest War*, pp. 160–61.
15. Berman, 'The US in Vietnam', p. 44.
16. Young, *The Vietnam Wars*, pp. 192–205.
17. Cited ibid., p. 205.
18. See the JASON study in *PP*, Vol. IV, pp. 222–5.
19. Cited in Leslie Gelb and Richard Betts, *The Irony of Vietnam: The System Worked* (Washington, DC: Brookings Institution, 1979) pp. 169–70.
20. Ibid., p. 170.
21. An excellent overview of the Tet offensive is provided by Don Oberdorf, *TET!* (New York: Doubleday, 1991).
22. Cited in Young, *The Vietnam Wars*, p. 218.
23. Herring, *America's Longest War*, pp. 187–8.
24. Berman, 'The US in Vietnam', p. 46.
25. Herring, *America's Longest War*, p. 199.
26. Berman, 'The US in Vietnam', p. 48.
27. Herring, *America's Longest War*, pp. 201–3.
28. Cited ibid., p. 205.
29. Lewy, *America in Vietnam*, p. 166.
30. Henry A. Kissinger, 'The Vietnam Negotiations', *Foreign Affairs* 47 (Jan. 1969) p. 219.
31. Richard Nixon, *RN: The Memoirs of Richard Nixon*, Vol. 1 (New York: Warner Books, 1978) p. 349.
32. Cited in Berman, 'The US in Vietnam', p. 53.
33. Young, *The Vietnam Wars*, p. 238.
34. Herring, *America's Longest War*, p. 232.
35. Ibid., pp. 235–6.
36. Ibid., pp. 236–7.
37. Reported in the *New York Times*, 30 June 1974.
38. Cited in Herring, *America's Longest War*, p. 241. See also Berman, 'The US in Vietnam', pp. 54–5.
39. Ibid., pp. 242–3. By the end of the offensive, it was estimated that the North had suffered 100,000 casualties, and the South 25,000. In June alone American planes dropped 112,000 tons of bombs on North Vietnam.
40. Ibid., p. 242.

41. Berman, 'The US in Vietnam', p. 56.
42. Cited ibid., p. 56.
43. Herring, *America's Longest War*, pp. 249–50.
44. *Rand Vietnam Interviews*, Series DT, No. 135, pp. 5, 138–9, cited in unpublished paper by Mark Moyer, 'Villager Attitudes During the Final Decade of the Vietnam War'.
45. Ibid., Series AG, No. 372, p. 28.
46. James Trullinger, *Village at War: An Account of Conflict in Vietnam* (Stanford: Stanford University Press, 1994) p. 110.
47. Tay Ninh Province Report, February 1968, p. 1, cited in Moyer, 'Villager Attitudes During the Final Decade of the Vietnam War'.
48. Douglas Pike, *Vietnam and the Soviet Union: Anatomy of an Alliance* (Boulder, CO: Westview Press, 1987) p. 139.
49. Ibid., p. 83–4.
50. Ibid., pp. 83–4. See also Herring, *America's Longest War*, pp. 149–50.
51. Cited ibid., pp. 87–8.
52. Ibid., pp. 91–3.
53. Ghulam Muradov, 'The Democratic Republic of Afghanistan: Second Stage of the April Revolution', in *Afghanistan Past and Present* (Moscow: USSR Academy of Science, 1981) pp. 187–8.
54. Thomas Hammond, *Red Flag over Afghanistan: The Communist Coup, the Soviet Invasion, and the Consequences* (Boulder, CO: Westview Press, 1984) p. 149.
55. Henry S. Bradsher, *Afghanistan and the Soviet Union* (Durham, NC: Duke University Press, 1983) pp. 187–8.
56. Ibid., p. 151.
57. Anthony Arnold, *Afghanistan's Two-Party Communism: Parcham and Khalq* (Stanford: Hoover Institution Press, 1983) p. 112.
58. *New York Times*, 7 Sept. 1983, pp. 1–4.
59. 'Facts and Figures', *Kabul New Times*, 25 April 1984, cited in Arnold, *Afghanistan's Two-Party Communism*, p. 105.
60. Anthony Arnold, *Afghanistan: The Soviet Invasion in Perspective* (Stanford: Hoover Institution Press, 1985) p. 98.
61. Bradsher, *Afghanistan and the Soviet Union*, p. 206.
62. Joseph J. Collins, *The Soviet Invasion of Afghanistan: A Study in the Use of Force in Soviet Foreign Policy* (Lexington, MA: Lexington Books, 1986) p. 144.
63. Ibid., p. 145.
64. Ibid., p. 147.
65. US Department of State, *Chemical Warfare in South Asia and Afghanistan* (Washington, DC: US Government Printing Office, 1982) p. 23, cited in ibid.
66. Arnold, *Afghanistan*, p. 100.
67. Ibid., pp. 109–10.
68. Collins, *The Soviet Invasion of Afghanistan*, p. 141.
69. Ibid., p. 146.
70. Arnold, *Afghanistan*, p. 110.
71. Collins, *The Soviet Invasion of Afghanistan*, p. 147.
72. *Pravda*, 5 Aug. 1981, p. 4, cited in *CDSP*, 31 (Sept. 1981) pp. 5–6.
73. *Pravda*, 24 Feb. 1981, pp. 2–9, cited in *CDSP*, 8 (March 1981) p. 13.
74. Collins, *The Soviet Invasion of Afghanistan*, p. 157.
75. *New York Times*, 22 Nov. 1982, p. A5.
76. *New York Times*, 10 Dec. 1982, p. 8.

77. Collins, *The Soviet Invasion of Afghanistan*, p. 157.
78. *Tass*, 24 April 1983, cited in Collins, *The Soviet Invasion of Afghanistan*, p. 158.
79. Mohammad Yahya Nawroz and Lester W. Grau, 'The Soviet War in Afghanistan: History and Harbinger of Future War?', US Army, Foreign Military Studies Institute (Fort Leavenworth, KN, 1996), http://leav-www.army.mil/fmso. Boris Gromov, *Ogranichennyy Kontingent* [Limited Contingent] (Moscow: Progress Publishers, 1994) p. 172; Scott R. McMichael, *Stumbling Bear: Soviet Military Performance in Afghanistan* (London: Brassey's, 1991) p. 10.
80. Mark Galeotti, *Afghanistan: The Soviet Union's Last War* (London: Frank Cass, 1995) pp. 17–18.
81. Michael Dobbs, 'Dramatic Politburo Meeting Led to End of War,' *Washington Post*, 16 Nov. 1992, p. A1.
82. *New York Times*, 5 Nov. 1987, p. 1.
83. Mikhail Gorbachev, *Perestroika: New Thinking for Our Country and the World* (New York: Harper & Row, 1987) pp. 177–8.
84. 'Afghanistan: Bad to Worse?' *Newsweek*, 19 May 1986, p. 50.
85. Nawroz and Grau, 'The Soviet War in Afghanistan'.
86. Galeotti, *Afghanistan*, p. 18.
87. Robert S. Litwak, 'The Soviet Union in Afghanistan', in *Foreign Military Intervention*, p. 84.
88. Nawroz and Grau, 'The Soviet War in Afghanistan'.
89. Litwak, 'The Soviet Union in Afghanistan', p. 84.
89. Ibid.
90. Cited in Riaz M. Khan, *Untying the Afghan Knot: Negotiating the Soviet Withdrawal* (Durham, NC: Duke University Press, 1991) p. 367, note 100.
91. 'Show 'em a Way to Go Home', *Time*, 14 Dec. 1987, p. 52.
92. *US News and World Report*, 21 Dec. 1987, p. 25.
93. *Pravda*, 7 Jan. 1988, p. 14, cited in *CDSP*, 1 (Feb. 1988) p. 13, italics added.
94. *New York Times*, 9 Feb. 1988, pp. 1, 7.
95. *New York Times*, 18 March 1988, p. 7.
96. *New York Times*, 8 April 1988, pp. 1, 4.
97. *New York Times,* 15 April 1988, p. 1.
98. Jimmy Carter, *Keeping Faith: Memoirs of a President* (New York: Bantam Books, 1982) p. 473.
99. Cyrus Vance, *Hard Choices: Critical Years in America's Foreign Policy* (New York: Simon & Schuster, 1983) p. 391.
100. Cited in Raymond Garthoff, *Détente and Confrontation: American–Soviet Relations from Nixon to Reagan* (Washington, DC: Brookings Institution, 1985) p. 954.
101. See Collins, *The Soviet Invasion of Afghanistan*, p. 87.
102. Galeotti, *Afghanistan*, pp. 17–18.
103. For an authoritative review of American policies in Afghanistan in this period, see Steve Coll's two-day series in the *Washington Post*, 19–20 July 1992.
104. *Daily Telegraph* (14 Jan. 1985). Cited in Galeotti, *Afghanistan*, p. 18.
105. The best two studies to date of the diplomatic negotiations on the Afghan war are provided in Khan's *Untying the Afghan Knot* and Diego Cordovez and Selig S. Harrison, *Out of Afghanistan: The Inside Story of the Soviet Withdrawal* (New York: Oxford University Press, 1995).
106. Bruce Jentleson, *With Friends Like These: Reagan, Bush, and Saddam, 1982–1990* (New York: W.W. Norton, 1996).

107. Herring, *America's Longest War*, pp. 254–6.

108. Young, *The Vietnam Wars*, pp. 284–5.

109. Herring, *America's Longest War*, pp. 256–62.

110. Barnett R. Rubin, *The Fragmentation of Afghanistan: State Formation and Collapse in the International System* (New Haven, CT: Yale University Press, 1995) p. 247.

111. Rasul Bakhsh Rais, 'Afghanistan after the Soviet Withdrawal', *Current History*, 91, 563 (March 1992) p. 123.

112. *Washington Post,* 26 April 1992, p. A1.

113. M.M. Ali, 'Afghanistan's Taliban Draw World Attention Again', *Washington Report on Middle East Affairs*, 16, 2 (Aug./Sept. 1997) p. 48.

114. *Washington Post,* 2 April 1992.

115. General Bruce Palmer Jr (US Army, Retired), 'Remarks to USAWC Elective Course, The Vietnam War', 31 May 1977, cited in Summers, *On Strategy*, pp. 171–2.

116. Galeotti, *Afghanistan*, p. 153.

117. Ibid.

118. Dean Rusk, *As I Saw It* (New York: W.W. Norton, 1990) p. 497.

119. Nawroz and Grau, 'The Soviet War in Afghanistan'.

120. Ibid.

121. Herring, *America's Longest War*, p. 248.

122. Galeotti, *Afghanistan,* p. 153, italics added.

123. Lester W. Grau, *The Bear Went Over the Mountain: Soviet Combat Tactics in Afghanistan* (Washington, DC: US Government Printing Office, 1997) p. xii. Grau's book is a translation of a 1991 book entitled *Combat Actions of Soviet Forces in the Republic of Afghanistan*, compiled at the Frunze Academy in Moscow, the Soviet Army's elite officer-training institution.

124. Michael Walzer, *Just and Unjust Wars: A Moral Argument with Historical Illustrations* (New York: Basic Books, 1977) pp. 98–9.

125. Cited in G.M. Kahin and John W. Lewis, *The United States in Vietnam* (New York: Dial Press, 1967) p. 146.

5

Superpowers Defeated:
The Impact of War Loss at Home

Was Afghanistan the Soviet Vietnam? Was Vietnam the American Afghanistan? Our comparison now has a solid foundation from which to proceed to the final object of enquiry: the process of disengagement and the political impact of war loss at home. At the outset, both invasions were judged to be vital to the national interests of the superpowers that launched them. Likewise, nearly a decade later the decisions to withdraw were seen to be in the vital national interests of both countries. In both cases what constituted the national interest had changed over time. Although it is clear that a mixture of international and domestic factors were involved at the time of these interventions, there is little doubt that the international considerations manifested in the Cold War ideological struggle for global power were primarily responsible for influencing President Johnson and General Secretary Brezhnev. However, while the decisions to disengage from these conflicts were also driven by an amalgam of domestic and international factors, the emphasis had switched, with domestic considerations playing the dominant role in the minds of President Nixon and General Secretary Gorbachev. In this chapter I will attempt draw together the underlying conceptual lines of enquiry that have sustained the analysis to this point: political legitimacy in the domestic polities of the United States and the Soviet Union, and credibility in the international sphere.

THE IMPACT OF VIETNAM ON THE UNITED STATES

In American history no other event, with the exception of the Civil War, has had as great an impact on the domestic tranquillity of the United States as the Vietnam War. The United States survived its Vietnam experience as it had the Civil War – battered, changed, bloodied, but intact. The withdrawal of US forces in 1973 and the unification of Vietnam under a communist government in 1975 did not produce the dire consequences predicted by those who argued for intervention. The Asian communist dominoes did fall in Cambodia and Laos; however, the original American belief in a monolithic international communist movement shed its last vestiges of credibility when

Vietnam invaded its communist neighbour Cambodia in 1978 to oust the genocidal regime of Pol Pot – an act that in turn caused China to invade Vietnam briefly in 1979 to reassert Chinese regional hegemony. But the dominoes stopped falling in parts of Indochina, and communism did not spread as predicted to Japan, which lay at the root of the original US justification for containment in Vietnam. Thus one of the most significant impacts of the Vietnam War was the stark clarity with which the original domino theory was rebutted as the other Asian 'dominos' – Thailand, the Philippines, Malaysia, Indonesia and Japan – all remained 'standing'. George Herring provides a poignant critique of containment and the domino theory:

> By wrongly attributing the Vietnamese conflict to external sources, the United States drastically misjudged its internal dynamics. By intervening in what was essentially a local struggle, it placed itself at the mercy of local forces, a weak client and a determined adversary. It elevated into a major international conflict what might have remained a localized struggle. By raising the stakes into a test of its own credibility, it perilously narrowed its options. A policy so flawed in its premises cannot help but fail, and in this case the results were disastrous.[1]

Much of the disaster was felt at home. Before its end, US involvement in Vietnam had inspired some of the most violent protests in the nation's history, and the final US withdrawal and swift unification of Vietnam under the communists also had a profound impact on the United States. In April 1975 Americans watched in stunned disbelief as the last helicopter lifted off from the roof of the US embassy in the final hours before Saigon's fall. The first televised war ended with scenes of chaos as thousands of Vietnamese tried to flee the invading communist forces. Many Americans believed that they had abandoned Kennedy's 'child' to the communists, and that the United States had failed to uphold its commitments. For the families of over 58,000 dead American service personnel there was no satisfactory answer to the question of what they had died for. To some US citizens the American military had failed the country, either for acts that violated morality, human rights and justice, or for the simple dereliction of duty in failing to strongly protest political decisions which were strategically culpable. For many, images of the My Lai massacre, in which American soldiers had slaughtered over 500 unarmed Vietnamese civilians, drove home the vision that the true enemy was us. Others adopted a 'stab in the back' analysis that blamed the government for not allowing the army to win the war, and 'tying the military's hands' – a common response on the part of the losing side of wars throughout history. Others blamed the protesters – 'the hippie–freak/pinko/commie/fags' – for undermining the system and for being 'un-American'. The simplistic slogan 'America – love it or leave it' was hurled like an epitaph on those who protested against the war. Others blamed the press for distorting the images of the war, arguing that the horror of Vietnam was no different from that any other war, and that the atrocities committed by America's enemies had been lost in the sensationalism of live coverage showing only the death and destruction caused by US forces. Still, many others reacted with a combination of denial, confusion and amnesia. Immediately after the war there was little debate outside the halls of academia as to who 'lost' Vietnam. In the political realm, the latest Cold War rendition of 'losing China' to communism could not easily be used again for political purposes, as both major US political parties had been deeply involved in the war's beginning and its outcome. Even the leading members of American media were reluctant to raise the issue, having become sensitized to the accusation of undercutting public support.[2] Only one year after America's 'child' was lost in Asia, Vietnam was scarcely mentioned in the 1976 presidential campaign.[3]

The economic impact of the war, although less spectacular than the emotional trauma, was possibly equally damaging to American society. A study by Anthony Campagna estimates that the direct total cost of the Vietnam War to the US economy was $515 billion. If indirect costs (such as war-consequent recessions and long-term inflation, the deterioration of trade conditions, etc.) are included, the cost of the Vietnam War exceeds $900 billion. In his analysis of the costs Campagna notes:

> It takes little imagination to wonder what sums like these could have accomplished if used for other purposes. The Great Society was sacrificed, urban problems were allowed to fester and grow, mass transportation was discarded, schools were ignored, and so on. There is little point in belabouring the issue or listing the social ills – the butter that was sacrificed for the guns. Whether or not these problems would have been addressed in the absence of the war is problematic anyway, and little is gained in speculation. It is sufficient to point to the enormous waste of resources in the pursuit of unspecified goals and thereby hope to avoid its repetition.

He then reaffirms the critique with an assessment of the war's positive value:

> The enormity of the folly is evident when one looks at the benefits of the war. That no one, except perhaps for defense contractors, seems to have benefited appears distressing in view of the costs involved ... costs may be easier to measure than benefits, but more gains should be readily identifiable. Only the military sector appears to show temporary gains, either for contractors or in promotions for officers who reported for battle. The rest of society was badly divided with little in economic gains to smooth over the dissension.

Campagna concludes, 'Considering the total costs minus the total benefits leaves only one conclusion – it was not a worthwhile endeavour. Looking at costs and benefits are one way to pass judgment, but whether considered from an economic, legal, moral, or military view, the same conclusion emerges – the war cannot be justified.'[4]

The American economy was also damaged by Vietnam on the international level. During the Johnson administration, worldwide confidence in the dollar began to erode because of growing deficits both in balance-of-trade figures and in federal budget outlays. In his 1984 analysis of the evolution of America's role in the global debt crisis, economist John Makin states:

> The decade that had forged ahead on hope for the future had reached its extravagant goal, to put a man on the moon, with no great amount of thought given to just why it was being done and how it was going to pay for itself. All of this along with Vietnam began to take its toll. Inflation reached 6.1% in 1969 – its highest level since the Second World War. Americans were beginning to feel the weight of Vietnam on their spirits and their pocketbook ... wage increases were starting to fall behind inflation. The federal government's $3.2 billion surplus that year was the last Americans have seen to date. By the mid 1970s Vietnam, social programs, and the politicians' imperative to postpone as much of their cost as possible to an inevitably more prosperous future brought in the first $50 billion deficit since World War II.[5]

The federal budget deficit was tied to Johnson's guns-and-butter policies, with the war directly blamed for the outflow of dollars. The global economy of that time, still tied to the gold standard, became volatile and unstable. The United States was increasingly unable to exchange gold for dollars to investors; thus the price of gold rose, and the value of the dollar fell. The United States, still committed to the Bretton Woods monetary regime, was also committed to sustaining the dollar's parity against other international currencies. Investors responded by selling dollars *en masse* to foreign central banks, so creating a run on the dollar. Because of massive intervention by the US Federal Reserve Bank in 1968, the dollar's slide was temporarily halted. However, the decline in the postwar US economic hegemony had begun. It accelerated during the Nixon 'shocks' of 1971 – a trend that continued throughout the 1980s when the United States moved from being the world's largest creditor nation to being its largest debtor. It cannot be said that the Vietnam War itself was more than a small part of this overall trend, and a detailed analysis of the impact of Vietnam on global US economic hegemony is beyond the scope of my analysis. However, according to political economist David Calleo, 'the Vietnam War undoubtedly cost the country's economy a great deal. Enormous defense budgets throughout the postwar era may well have distorted and weakened American economic growth. Steady overseas investment may well have slowed the modernization of domestic industry.'[6] While America was 'investing' in the Vietnam War, Japan, Germany and others were investing in their domestic economic infrastructure.

One positive result of American defence spending in Vietnam was on other US allies, especially those in East Asia. In the late 1950s and 1960s, industrialists based in Japan, South Korea and Taiwan were given privileged access to the US market as part of economic development strategies to undermine communism's appeal. Major contracts for war materials and spending by soldiers on leave helped to stimulate the local economies in the region. The meteoric economic rise of the East Asian 'Tigers', widely hailed in the late 1980s and early 1990s, was part of a wider matrix of US policies in Asia during the Cold War, of which Vietnam was the most visible location. The United States tolerated tightly protected markets in Japan, South Korea and Taiwan while pressuring other countries to pursue open or 'free' trade – a practice that began to unravel only in the late 1980s as the Cold War wound down. In Vietnam the anticommunist crusade was fought with dollars, guns and soldiers; in the rest of Asia dollars were the primary instrument of US influence, much to the benefit of East Asian economies.[7]

The economics of war loss are often of secondary importance to the more significant shocks to a society's political culture. As with the impact of the Second World War on Japan's culture, Vietnam has had a lasting impact on American society. In the case of Japan, a polity once distinguished by its glorification of the individual warrior and the *samurai* code is now fundamentally pacifist, with a deep-seated suspicion of the military and its role in Japanese society. In the case of the United States, a polity historically distinguished by the glorification of the ideals of democratic governance is now fundamentally suspicious of and cynical about both governing institutions and politicians. In the years since Vietnam, general public distrust in government has grown, even as Americans are increasingly more willing to discuss the war. Academic texts as well as anecdotal accounts by American veterans are continually added to a growing body of literature. The trauma and drama of Vietnam are replayed (and often history is rewritten) in television shows, documentaries and major movie productions.[8] Vietnam veterans, who were initially perceived as drug-crazed, gun-toting, hair-trigger maniacs, have been in great part socially rehabilitated in movies and television shows, with much of the rest of American society feeling a collective sense of guilt and shame for having treated veterans so poorly on their return.

The war also continues to have a tangible impact on the lives of its combatants. In the 1980s evidence emerged that many veterans (both United States and its allies) were dying from various cancers that are linked to 'Agent Orange', the chemical defoliant that had been used indiscriminately to destroy the jungle vegetation that had served so effectively as a cover for the

Vietnamese combatants. In the 1990s the long-festering issues of prisoners of war and soldiers missing in action again became prominent. During the 1992 US presidential campaign new and as yet unsubstantiated evidence and allegations emerged that Americans had been left behind in Vietnam and Laos. The candidacy of Governor Bill Clinton was questioned on the grounds of 'character', with some seeking political advantage by questioning Clinton's patriotism on account of his opposition to the war as a college student. Other contentious issues continue to resurface, including the plight of Vietnamese 'boat people', refugees and unpaid war reparations. Even the US army has begun to come to terms with Vietnam. In March 1998 two American soldiers, Lawrence Colburn and Hugh Thompson, received medals for heroism under enemy fire in a moving ceremony at the Vietnam Veterans Memorial in Washington, DC: a site that continues to affect profoundly virtually everyone who visits it. The bestowing of medals on these soldiers was a monumental act, as it acknowledged their heroism for risking their own lives to protect Vietnamese civilians from rampaging American troops during the My Lai massacre in March 1968.[9]

In the realm of foreign affairs, the impact of Vietnam remains the most clearly tangible component of American politics. After the Vietnam War, the doctrine of communist containment remained the centrepiece of US foreign policy; however, the use of military force came under great scrutiny, with comparisons to Vietnam being raised thereafter whenever military intervention has been contemplated. In relations with its allies the US's global position was perhaps shaken, but it was not structurally altered in the immediate wake of the Vietnam War. The Western European alliance structure remained intact, and new organs of international cooperation (most notably the Conference on Security and Cooperation in Europe or CSCE) were born. On a strategic level both the Soviet Union and China were eager to maintain the status quo or to proceed with arms control negotiations and confidence-building measures. In the age of nuclear interdependence, it was clear to all sides that the vital national interests of the members of the nuclear club could not be directly assailed. The American defeat in Vietnam was actually followed by improved relations with China and the Soviet Union – and the fall of Vietnam did not inspire an entirely new wave of communist aggression or communist-inspired rebellion. In the late 1970s socialist forces did gain ground in some countries. However, in countries where communists gained power (Angola, Ethiopia, Afghanistan) US national interests were not threatened, and eventually the support of these new allies became major economic burdens for their Soviet patrons, adding to the eventual communist collapse.

In a more direct challenge to US national interests, in Latin America and the Caribbean various communist insurgencies also made tangible gains. However, the Vietnam War had clearly shattered the anticommunist consensus that had existed under US containment doctrine since the late 1940s. Even before the fall of Saigon, public opinion polls had indicated that only one-third of Americans felt that the United States should intervene militarily to protect any of its allies, with only the defense of Canada being endorsed by a majority.[10] During the second half of the Carter administration American anger was rekindled in the humiliation of the Iranian seizure of the US embassy; however, Carter refused to use military force in an attempt to challenge the outcome of the Iranian Islamic revolution. His ill-fated hostage rescue mission, which ended with the death of a number of US troops, cannot be considered as significant use of military force comparable to an operation with strategic ramifications.

American nationalism and a renewed emphasis on military force re-emerged to a greater degree with the election of Ronald Reagan in 1980. Like many cold warriors of the 1950s, Reagan embraced a relatively simplistic view of world affairs – the source of all evil was communism, primarily communism centred in Moscow and spread by the Soviets and their proxies. During his tenure in office, Reagan ordered US troops to intervene globally on a number of occasions, the most successful operation taking place on the small Caribbean island of Grenada in October 1983. Reagan ordered 6,000 US troops (supported by 300 troops from the Organization of Eastern Caribbean States) to liberate the island from a pro-Cuban communist faction that had seized control. The US troops quickly overwhelmed the Marxist forces and restored a representative government to the island. The Reagan administration bragged that it had reversed the 'Vietnam syndrome' by showing that Washington would use military force when necessary to block communist expansionism in the Western hemisphere. However, the US act was viewed by many countries as an illegal act of aggression, and even Reagan's closest ally, British prime minister Margaret Thatcher, joined in the condemnation.[11]

Grenada clearly marked the re-emergence of military intervention as a tool of US foreign policy after approximately a decade of post-Vietnam inhibition. However, Grenada was an operation of limited scope, with a mission against a tiny number of lightly armed forces located in a small, isolated and easily controlled geographic space – a qualitatively different matter from an operation the size and scope of Vietnam. A more comparably valid scenario presented itself in Nicaragua, a country that had witnessed the overthrow by leftist forces of the pro-US Somoza regime in Nicaragua in 1979. For the next decade the shadow of Vietnam openly influenced the domestic political debate on what US response was appropriate in Nicaragua, a country located in a region the United States had long considered as its exclusive sphere of influence. Turning back Marxism in Nicaragua became a personal obsession for Reagan; however, the strong fear that US policy might be headed toward a Vietnam-style military intervention was prevalent among members of the US Congress, who sharply curtailed the president's ability to act in Nicaragua. Congressional limits were imposed on spending by the CIA for the support of the Nicaraguan 'Contras', a group consisting mainly of ex-National Guard troops from the Somoza dictatorship. When in 1982 members of Congress raised questions about the scope and purpose of US covert operations, CIA director William Casey falsely assured them that neither the Reagan administration nor the Contras sought to overthrow the government of Nicaragua. With the memories of the Gulf of Tonkin deception echoing in the background, Congress revealed its lack of trust in the executive branch by passing a series of laws that steadily undercut funding for the Contras. In April 1984, when it was revealed that the CIA had illegally mined Nicaraguan ports and harbours, Congress acted to bar the CIA or any other US intelligence agencies from aiding the Contras.[12]

Reagan, like his Republican predecessor Richard Nixon in Vietnam, would not be deterred by legal constraints. Members of his national security staff, including the NSC director Robert McFarland and his deputy and successor Admiral John Poindexter, supervised an effort organized by Lieutenant Colonel Oliver North to bypass the Congressional restrictions. In part of a highly controversial and illegal strategy, North's plan called for covertly selling arms to Iran in an attempt to free US hostages in Lebanon who had been seized by pro-Iranian militants. The profits from the illegal arms sales would then be channelled to the Contras. After a US transport plane was downed in Nicaragua in October 1986 the Iran–Contra scandal erupted, nearly bringing the Reagan presidency to an end. Reagan's Secretary of State, George Shultz, warned the president that his order to circumvent Congress by soliciting foreign funds for the Contras might constitute an impeachable offence, to which Reagan responded that if the story ever got out 'we'll all be hanging by our thumbs in front of the White House'.[13] Reagan would publicly deny his knowledge of the transfer of funds from the Iranian operation to the Contras, a denial contested by Colonel North, who claimed that the president had full knowledge of his activities. During the Iran–Contra Congressional hearings it was revealed that North had conducted extensive planning for a US military invasion of Nicaragua, which appears to be modelled on US policies in Vietnam under the Eisenhower administration. North's plans included the creation of a new Nicaraguan government made up of pro-US leaders who would declare their sovereign independence from the leftist Sandinista regime. The United States could then recognize the new government as legitimate, thereby justifying the invasion of US forces to protect an allied state. As a veteran of the Vietnam era, North knew that an explosion of anti-government protest in the United States would erupt after any invasion. Thus his contingency plans included a declaration of martial law in order to prevent any repeat of the domestic upheavals that had plagued the country in the late 1960s.[14]

Although President Reagan avoided impeachment in the Iran–Contra scandal, and his various aides' direct criminal activities were mostly absolved on the basis of legal technicalities and grants of Congressional immunity, for many observers the entire Nicaraguan scenario in the 1980s was a replay of the US approach to Vietnam. Rather than focusing on the political history of Nicaragua and the local conditions that led to the overthrow of the Somoza regime by a populist uprising that included both communists and noncommunist forces, Reagan blamed Latin America's problems on the evil influence of the Kremlin. As in Vietnam, in Nicaragua the Reagan administration seemed unable to comprehend that the nationalism could be championed by those who also professed a pro-socialist political ideology, and that the majority of Nicaraguans viewed the Sandinista regime as their legitimate government. As in Vietnam, it was falsely believed that a military solution could be found to what fundamentally was a question of political legitimacy, with the US-created Contras being viewed as illegitimate in the domestic polity of Nicaragua. As in Vietnam, in order to achieve the administration's policy goals in Nicaragua, both Congress and the American people were lied to repeatedly, and illegal acts were pursued by the White House. However, unlike in Vietnam, Congressional oversight and influence of US foreign policy were much greater, primarily through the aggressive control of funding measures. It is also clear that Colonel North's views on Nicaragua did not represent those of the majority of the US military establishment, which, like Congress, was hesitant to become embroiled in what was clearly a domestic political upheaval with numerous parallels to Vietnam. The military did not want to be blamed again for losing a war, and with the perspective gained from Vietnam, it seemed unlikely that a US war in Nicaragua could be won without great cost. It was clear that an invasion of Nicaragua would require the US military to re-engineer fundamentally the politics of a revolutionary state that was strongly unified by the drama and sacrifice of a recently won popular struggle against a highly unpopular dictatorship. The potential quagmire in Nicaragua in the early 1980s was analogous to that in Vietnam in the mid 1950s, and the majority of the US military understood this, despite the simplistic illusions of their commander-in-chief.

Most Americans supported President Bush's decision to send troops to Panama in December 1989, though criticism abroad was widespread. Bush's intervention had deep roots in the tangled history of US–Panamanian relations. In May 1989 Panama's presidential elections were annulled by Manuel Noriega, the head of the armed forces who had been indicted in the United States on drug-trafficking charges the year before. Despite the irony that Noriega had long been on the CIA's payroll, the Bush administration, embarrassed by this affront to democracy in a long-time US vassal state, urged Panamanians to overthrow Noriega. In mid December 1989 the Noriega-controlled National Assembly declared war on the United States and sanctioned the continued harassment of US service personnel and their dependants, who were stationed in Panama as part of long-standing agreements. Bush responded with what can only be described as overwhelming force, including over 25,000 troops and the most advanced weapon systems in the US arsenal. Within days organized resistance was destroyed, and Noriega soon surrendered to US troops. Bush's objectives were achieved: to protect the lives of US citizens and the security of the Panama Canal, to take Noriega into custody, and to re-establish the elected government of Panama. The forces used in the operation were withdrawn less than two months after the operation.[15] Most important, however, is that many Panamanians also strongly supported the US action. Before the invasion Noriega had attempted to foment support for his regime by accusing the United States of 'Yankee imperialism'. Although the mass of citizens were not willing to confront the Panamanian military forces, as urged by Bush, nor were they willing to support Noriega's desire for an anti-American nationalist uprising. The dreaded Vietnam-like quagmire did not develop, showing clearly that local conditions in Panama were unlike those in Indochina.

The problematic issues of post-Vietnam US military intervention were again raised during the Persian Gulf War of 1991. The Bush administration's public relations campaign to gain both Congressional and public support was largely built around the strategy of explaining why Iraq's invasion of Kuwait and the proposed American response comprised a set of circumstances entirely different from those that led to defeat in Vietnam. Bush's major task was to overcome opponents who argued that 'Iraq was Arabic for Vietnam', envisioning another unpopular, unwinnable war, this time in the desert. During these debates the average American was exposed to a series of useful and informative comparisons. Vietnam was largely a civil disorder between domestic Vietnamese factions struggling to control the national government. Kuwait was the victim of a conventional invasion by an outside aggressive force bent on territorial expansion. In Vietnam, America had attempted to create a legitimate government; in Kuwait, it would restore a legitimate government. In Vietnam, the military had been constrained by political considerations that limited its ability to win the war. In Kuwait, the military would not be constrained, with maximum force being employed as rapidly as possible. According to Bush, the war in the Persian Gulf would 'not be another Vietnam', and he and his military advisers, many of whom had fought in Vietnam, would pursue the war and achieve victory on the basis of the lessons of the Vietnam defeat. In retrospect, it would appear that they kept their word. On the eve of certain victory, Bush refused to widen the war and destroy the Iraqi regime outright, instead acting within the existing framework of the international agreements that provided a legal mandate only for the liberation of Kuwait. In a euphoric victory statement, President

Bush claimed, 'By God, we've kicked the Vietnam syndrome once and for all!'[16]

The president was only partially correct. The Gulf War had shown citizens of the United States that their military was capable of victory, and it had convinced decision-makers that the government could rally popular support for the use of force abroad. However, the Gulf War's success also clarified the vast differences between the types of struggles involved in Vietnam and the Gulf. Vietnam was not forgotten; the victory in the Gulf War reminded Americans of just how different the war in Vietnam was, a fact confirmed by the president's own behaviour. Bush's refusal to try to solve the 'Saddam problem' was not only contingent upon the international agreements that authorized the transition from Operation Desert Shield (to protect Saudi Arabia) to Operation Desert Storm, which liberated Kuwait by force. Rather, Bush's decision to limit the operation was also a recognition of the political and military quagmire that might have ensued if the United States had continued the invasion of Iraq with the intent of installing a new government. Who would that government consist of? How would it remain in power? Would the Iraqi people rebel against foreign occupation? Would US troops be forced to prop up the new government indefinitely? What would happen to US credibility in the Middle East and elsewhere? Would the American people support an extended operation that had no clear resolution, massive costs and continual casualties? These and other questions clearly echoed Vietnam's lasting influence on policy-making in the Bush White House.

In the years since the Gulf War, the United States has been willing to send forces into various operations, each of which has been closely scrutinized through the Vietnam lens. In the post Cold War era, the argument over ideology has largely disappeared; however, the arguments over the utility and limits of military force remain highly salient. Perhaps the two best examples are the operations in Somalia and Bosnia. Bush was supported by the American public in his decision to send US forces to Somalia in 1992, with the goal of averting a humanitarian disaster. Domestic turmoil by warring Somali factions had paralysed the food distribution system and threatened hundreds of thousands of Somalians with starvation. The initial mission to feed the population was remarkably successful. However, by the autumn of 1993 the US mission had incrementally changed, with US troops becoming embroiled in the domestic dispute. When eighteen US soldiers were killed the shade of Vietnam immediately re-emerged in the domestic debate. Critics from both liberal and conservative poles of the political spectrum cited the lesson of Vietnam that the United States could not be the world's 'policeman' in the 'new world order' envisioned by President Bush. President Clinton agreed, ordering the withdrawal of American forces and making it clear that the 'Vietnam syndrome' remained alive and well in the hearts and minds of both citizens and policy-makers.[17]

However, Clinton too has been willing to send US forces to intervene abroad. Troops were sent to Haiti in 1994 to ensure the safe return of the democratically elected President Jean-Bertrand Aristide, and to the Republic of Bosnia in 1995 to help enforce the Dayton peace accords that had been negotiated between various warring factions. Both operations were limited in scope and took place within multilateral frameworks in close conjunction with UN and NATO allies. After providing the initial bulk of soldiers, materiel and logistics, US military forces were withdrawn from Haiti by the end of 1997, and have been steadily scaled back in Bosnia. Although the Bosnia mission has been a clear-cut success story in peace enforcement into the early months of 1998, many Americans both inside and out of government remain fearful that deep-seated historical animosities in the Balkans make long-term peace in the region highly unlikely. Thus far Clinton has been able to maintain support for the operation; however, the Somalian operation suggests that the administration's commitment is highly contingent on both public opinion and Congressional support. If US and NATO forces become the target of attacks that result in even small numbers of casualties, it is highly unlikely that US troops will remain in the Balkans for long.

The lessons of Vietnam have been applied to each subsequent use of force in American foreign policy. However, Vietnam was a unique historical experience that may have only limited utility in determining the proper course of action in any subsequent scenario. Furthermore, there is little agreement on just what the lessons of Vietnam are. The Gulf War's success has rekindled the notion that massive uses of force can be the means to achieve moral, legal and practical interests that serve both the United States and the international community. However, because the nature of the conflict in the Vietnam War was so fundamentally different from that of the Gulf War, the liberation of Kuwait has confirmed the notion that old-style forms of cross-border aggression between sovereign states are much easier to deal with using counterforce methods than are domestic civil disputes.

Thus Panama, Somalia, Haiti and Bosnia all provide a different amalgam of lessons as a result of their own comparisons with Vietnam. Americans will support intervention in a domestic civil dispute when they perceive US national interests to be at stake. However, the determination of national interest, always a problematic endeavour among the nation's foreign policy elite, will remain a matter of rancorous public discourse in the post-Vietnam era. In the cases of Grenada and Panama, Presidents Reagan and Bush did not seek public support; they acted unilaterally, correctly gambling that if rapid victory could be achieved with minimal costs, the American people would deferentially accept *fait-accompli* justifications of US national security interests. With the war won and their sons and daughters coming home, most Americans were willing to overlook the complex moral, legal and ethical issues that both of these interventions raised in the international community.

However, the American public and Congress will not deferentially accept justifications for the use of force when given the opportunity to express themselves. Any proposed or ongoing intervention must pass the 'Vietnam test' before approval is given, and such approval is always highly qualified. Clearly Americans are willing to support intervention when they perceive a significant moral rationale, either to avert a massive humanitarian crisis or to prevent the gross violation of human rights. However, as Somalia shows, such support can rapidly be withdrawn when American casualties are incurred and there is no clear and compelling national interest at stake that justifies further sacrifice of American lives. As shown in Panama, Haiti and Kuwait, Americans are willing to support intervention when they perceive that a legitimate government has been wrongly overthrown by either internal or external forces. However, Somalia clearly lacked such a government, and in the Balkans the new governments are understood to be the frangible creations of a peace imposed by the outside world – a peace that could rapidly unravel into a new quagmire of ethnic violence, from which American troops would most likely be rapidly withdrawn. In their deep-seated anxiety about Bosnia, Americans remember the most fundamental the lesson of Vietnam: no matter how much military force is brought to bear, governing legitimacy cannot be created for people by outside powers; they must create it themselves.

THE IMPACT OF AFGHANISTAN ON THE SOVIET UNION

The end of the Afghan War coincided with the end of the Soviet Union itself. However, it was not a coincidence, even though it certainly was a surprise. In the late 1960s and early 1970s, the Soviet Union was perceived by many statesmen and scholars to have increased its relative power and influence *vis-à-vis* the United States. Even though Eisenhower's apocalyptic 'domino effect' did not materialize in Asia in the wake of the communist victory in Vietnam, the Soviet Union was able to achieve nuclear parity, and it maintained a modest numerical advantage in conventional weapons. In addition, the states conquered in Eastern Europe at the end of the Second World War remained chastened, and military and political ties with leftist or 'socialist-oriented' states were strengthened in Africa, Asia and Central America. However, it is clear now that by the mid 1980s, severe economic problems were developing in the Soviet Union – problems that coincided with a renewed challenge from Washington – and that cracks in the system were widening. The United States under President Reagan had renewed the arms race for techno-military superiority. Protected by a well-armed NATO, a vibrant and wealthy European Community stood in stark contrast to the comparative poverty of the Eastern bloc, and many Third World revolutionary regimes began to buckle under the heavy burdens of internal corruption, civil war and Western political pressure. In the late 1980s these cracks had become full-blown fissures which in 1989 destroyed the Warsaw Pact, and then in 1991 shattered the very existence of the Soviet Union as a unified state.

What role did Afghanistan play in the downfall of the Soviet Union? As with the debate over the impact of Vietnam on the United States, this is a question that is not easily or simply answered. Most scholars agree that the war in Afghanistan certainly played some role in the Soviet collapse; however, the degree of its importance remains a topic hotly debated. A well-received recent book by Mark Galeotti concludes with the following emphatic assertion:

> [T]o suggest that the defeat in Afghanistan doomed the Soviet Union is patently unfounded, even if we accept the popular perception that the Soviet Union was defeated rather than the more clinical verdict that it failed to win much of a success. The events of 1991 were rooted, after all, in economic decay and the associated loss of legitimacy for a state which had long since abandoned ideology in favour of legitimation by managerial success. From a personal point of view, having spent years studying it, it would be satisfying to be able to identify the war as a pivotal event in late Soviet history: the cause of perestroika, the last gasp of Sovietised Russian imperialism, the final nail in the USSR's coffin. Yet of course it was none of these things. It was part and parcel of the catastrophes, blunders, tensions and crises which brought the Soviet system down, from Chernobyl to food queues, the Tbilisi massacre to the collapse of the Eastern Bloc. Perhaps at most it added a particularly sanguine red hue and some dramatic imagery to the collage.[18]

Galeotti's conclusion is representative of many mainstream Soviet and Russian area studies specialists: Afghanistan played a part in the collapse of communism, but only a minor one. Despite some empathy with his conclusion, I believe Galeotti goes too far in undervaluing the importance of Afghanistan. While I do not believe that Afghanistan was the only important factor in the myriad of elements that combined to bring down the communist regime, I do think that its role in influencing events cannot be degraded to the level of insignificance that he expresses. In making my case for the importance of the Afghan experience, I will turn once again to the discussion of political legitimacy and the important role that Afghanistan had in undermining the Soviet state's own of legitimacy within the context of Gorbachev's reform policies. As first proposed in the introduction of this book, I believe that the departure from Afghan soil by the last Soviet combat soldier on 15 February 1989 represented a significant and crucial event in the rapid ideological, foreign and domestic policy reforms undertaken by

President Gorbachev. Furthermore, concurrent with the repudiation of the Brezhnev Doctrine, the withdrawal from Afghanistan marks the first significant example of Gorbachev's reforms in Soviet foreign policy. The Soviet withdrawal was important internationally because it bolstered the existing forces for reform in the Soviet bloc. In essence, I will argue that Afghanistan was the first 'domino' in the systematic collapse of the pro-Soviet regimes in Eastern Europe, and in the fall of the supreme domino itself – the Soviet Union.

Afghanistan: communism's first domino

Like the American withdrawal from Vietnam, the Soviet retreat from Afghanistan was firmly rooted in domestic factors. However, unlike the Vietnam War, the primary pressure for a change in policy did not emanate from the domestic population. Rather, the decision to leave Afghanistan was made at the highest level of Soviet politics – within the leadership cadre of General Secretary Mikhail Gorbachev. Gorbachev's change in policy on Afghanistan was embodied by his sweeping ideological programs of *perestroika* (restructuring) and *glasnost* (openness). The revolution from above began with the intent to strengthen the Soviet Union through what was perceived as imperative internal reform measures. However, the Cold War presented Gorbachev with a difficult predicament. His plans for domestic revitalization were seen as being indefensible to conservative criticism from within the Communist Party while the Soviet Union was confronted by powerful enemies in a hostile international environment. Therefore Gorbachev launched his reform agenda first in the realm of foreign policy with the belief that when international peace and cooperation were obtained, the regime could turn to rebuilding socialism at home. From Gorbachev's perspective, withdrawing from Afghanistan was the logical first step toward revitalizing detente with the Soviet Union's global competitors, America and China, which had become significantly more confrontational after the 1979 invasion of Afghanistan. Thus the withdrawal from Afghanistan was perceived as part of a larger strategic plan to achieve domestic political and economic goals.

Although the direct economic impact of Afghanistan is difficult to judge, the war was clearly one of the most significant components of the multiple foreign policy expenditures draining Soviet coffers. Beginning with Khrushchev, one of the major tools of Soviet foreign policy had been to provide economic incentives to reinforce friendly regimes and, it was hoped, to buy nonaligned ones. Like American containment policies, Soviet foreign policy under the guise of Brezhnevian 'internationalism' required massive outlays, usually in the form of exceedingly cheap weapons systems, overcompensation for exports from 'fraternal' countries, low-interest or no-interest loans and outright charity. However, the indirect costs were significant as well, as noted shortly after the intervention in a first critical report by Oleg Bogomolov, the director the Institute for Economics of the World Socialist System, a leading government think-tank: 'Our policy has evidently gone beyond the brink of confrontation tolerance in the "Third World" as a result of the move to send forces into Afghanistan. The benefits of the action proved insignificant compared to the damage caused to our interests ... Detente has been block-aded ... Economic and technological pressure against the Soviet Union has sharply grown ... The Soviet Union has now got to shoulder a new burden of economic aid to Afghanistan.'[19] Although Bogomolov and others (includ-ing Evgennii Primakov, who would be Russia's foreign minister under Yeltsin) were ignored at the time, their influence emerged when Gorbachev came to power. In his critique of the Brezhnev Doctrine Gorbachev fully acknowledged the fact that Soviet national interests had been damaged. He stated 'the foreign policy that served the utopian aim of spreading communist ideas around the world, had led us into the dead end of the Cold War, inflicting on the people an intolerable burden of military expenditure and dragged us into adventures like the one in Afghanistan'.[20] The war itself cost the Soviet Union approximately five billion roubles a year, with a total direct cost of approximately sixty billion roubles. During the glasnost era, one of the major public criticisms of Gorbachev's foreign policy was in regard to continued Soviet economic support for Afghanistan after withdrawal of the last troops in 1989. Many wondered why the state was spending money abroad when the average Soviet citizen was living so poorly at home. Like Americans, the Soviet masses clearly overestimated the burden of foreign aid as a percentage of overall government expenditure.[21] Nonetheless, in terms of political importance, absolute truth is often irrelevant. If Americans or Russians believe that their government is spending too much on foreign aid, the government must either act to change that perception, or pay the price in terms of the erosion of popular support.

In contemplating the withdrawal from Afghanistan, General Secretary Gorbachev and Foreign Minister Eduard Shevardnadze were faced with credibility quandaries analogous to those that had plagued Nixon and Kissinger in Vietnam. In both wars each country's guiding ideology had provided the rationale and justification for intervention, but that same ideology became a great liability during the withdrawal process. Just as the US containment doctrine had morally and philosophically committed America to any conflict in which communists were involved, Soviet foreign policy as driven by the Brezhnev Doctrine had raised the stakes in the Soviet response during any crisis in the socialist camp. Having drawn the Cold War battle lines around its clients, the Soviet Union required these states to conduct their domestic and foreign policies within the confined space of Soviet consent. If any state failed to correct what Moscow deemed unaccept-able behaviour, military intervention became a probable solution. Although some ideological variation was tolerated in the Eastern bloc, once military intervention was threatened, Soviet prestige and international credibility demanded that military action be taken if Moscow's policies were openly defied. From the Kremlin's perspective, any loss of prestige risked the spread of dissent in the Eastern bloc. If one state were to defy Moscow, they all might follow suit. Just as the United States feared the fall of dominoes in Asia if a noncommunist South Vietnam was not preserved, the Kremlin feared the fall of dominoes in Eastern Europe if any regimes under Moscow's control were allowed to act as independent sovereign nations.

In the early 1980s Poland's communist leaders were confronted with a serious dilemma. Soviet intolerance of the increasing popularity of the independent Polish labour union Solidarity clearly showed the limits of their own power and independence. If the Polish authorities did not take action to repress Solidarity, the Soviets would most likely react as they had in Hungary in 1956 and Czechoslovakia in 1968. In 1981 the threat of a Soviet invasion was very real. Before the declaration of martial law in Poland, Soviet theorist Oleg Bykov plainly restated the Brezhnev Doctrine in warning Poland that 'no one should have any doubts about the common determination of the fraternal countries to protect the socialist gains of the Polish people from infringement by counter-revolution, internal or external'.[22] His warning was substantiated by a significant build-up and mobilization of Soviet forces on the border. As a result, the Polish military authorities heeded this omen and imposed martial law.

However, by the late 1980s the demands for ideological and political loyalty had changed dramatically. Gorbachev had determined that the Soviet economy was collapsing under the dual pressures of overextended foreign commitments and inefficient internal organization. New policies on Afghanistan would begin the process of changing the nature of Soviet foreign commitments, and these changes would affect Poland. Shortly before the revolt against communism in the winter of 1989, the state-controlled Eastern European press agencies had provided routine coverage of the negotiations that led to the Geneva Accords on Afghanistan, and the press had reported on the Soviet troop withdrawal from that country. According to a brief survey of the Czechoslovakian, Romanian, Polish, Bulgarian and East German press conducted by Australian political analyst Robert Miller, Poland's news agencies provided the most complete and detailed coverage of events.

Trybuna Luda, for example, carried an only slightly abridged version of Aleksandr Prokhanov's article in *Literaturnaia gazeta* featuring the argument that the Afghan adventure had been a grievous mistake, which would have 'painful after-effects' on the USSR, its culture, internal politics, social conditions and the life of a significant part of a whole generation of Soviet citizens. In reporting the meeting between

Gorbachev and Najibullah in Tashkent on 7 April, *Trybuna Luda*, like other Eastern European papers, noted ... 'the problems of Afghanistan and their solutions are Afghanistan's own business and no one else's', to be solved by that country as an 'independent, non-aligned, neutral state'.[23]

Perhaps the most significant coverage occurred in the Polish weekly *Polityka*, which acknowledged the 'electrifying effect' of the news of the Soviet withdrawal, citing the 'many open questions' on the past, present and future of Afghanistan.[24] Clearly, the authors of these articles were raising in the minds of Polish citizens suggestive questions which, with little imagination, could be extended to Poland's own relationship with the Soviet Union and the role that military force had played in coercing Polish fealty toward Moscow since the Second World War. As Miller notes, 'the implications of this formulation for the autonomous forces in Eastern Europe were obvious, but no one seemed inclined to mention them'.[25] However, even after making this perceptive statement on the possible implications of the Soviet withdrawal, Miller concludes that 'it was clear that different rules applied to Soviet allies in the second world, namely, the members of the Warsaw Treaty Organization'.[26] Clearly, with the benefit of hindsight his initial analysis of the potential impact of these news stories was correct; yet, like the majority of Western scholars at that time, Miller's cautious conclusion on Gorbachev's willingness to extend the Afghan model to Eastern Europe was in error.

Despite variations in the degree of coverage and in accuracy in the Eastern press, it is clear that the knowledge of the withdrawal of Soviet troops from an occupied country was not withheld from the masses of Eastern Europe. It is true that the impact of these press reports is hard to ascertain, and it cannot be said with certainty that the Soviet withdrawal from Afghanistan had a direct causal impact in spurring on the Eastern European revolutions. Yet it is impossible to ignore the fact that the revolutionary wave that exploded throughout Eastern Europe emerged only after reports that Soviet troops had actually pulled out of Afghanistan.

Further empirical evidence exists that more substantially connects these two events. Writing from prison, Adam Michnik, one of Poland's leading political dissident writers, declared in 1982: 'They have no program; they have no principles; they have no respect; they have only guns and tanks.'[27] However, Michnik was also one of the first to recognize the potential changes that Gorbachev's reform policies had initiated. In 1987 and 1988 Michnik and others in the Polish opposition began increasingly to assert that there was a growing disparity between the pace of reform in the Soviet Union and that in Poland.[28] Once Gorbachev's reform policies began to be accepted as genuine, the Polish military government became the first in Eastern Europe to test seriously the limits of perestroika and glasnost as they applied to Soviet foreign policy and the Brezhnev Doctrine. During the last month of the Soviet retreat from Afghanistan, Solidarity was declared a legal trade union by General Wojciech Jaruzelski's government, and six months later, in June 1989, Solidarity candidates stunned the Eastern bloc by capturing ninety-nine out of a hundred open seats in Poland's first partially free parliamentary elections.[29] When the results of the election were allowed to stand both by the Polish military and, more important, by the Soviet Union, the rules of power politics had explicitly changed in Eastern Europe. In Afghanistan, the Soviets had first abandoned one of their allied communist regimes. By not forcing the Polish military to crack down on internal dissent as it had on all previous occasions since the Second World War, the Soviets had clearly revoked the Brezhnev Doctrine in Eastern Europe.

The more direct connection between the Soviet withdrawal from Afghanistan and the Eastern European revolution is made by Czech President Vaclav Havel in the preface of a book in which he states: 'Many journalists and scholars will look for the correlation of that chain of spectacular transformations that changed, as if at one blow, the fates of tens of millions of individuals and hitherto firm bipolar picture of the modern world. I believe this book will be one of the first important impulses in that direction.'[30] One of the contributing authors to the book clearly states that Havel's 'one blow' was first struck in Afghanistan. Andrei Piontkowsky, an active participant in the 'Democratic Russia' movement and adviser to the liberal Inter-Regional Group in the Congress of Peoples' Deputies, wrote:

> The experience in Afghanistan was crucial in stimulating this re-thinking. Afghanistan showed the limitations of military power very clearly and convincingly. Even the most hard-line generals and political and military analysts in the Kremlin understood this message. So it would be fair, if a little surprising to Europeans, to say that it was not so much thinkers in the corridors of the Kremlin as the Mujahadin in the hills of Afghanistan who were the real liberators of Eastern Europe.[31]

Perestroika and glasnost, the new Soviet ideology that made these changes possible, would have been made morally bankrupt if any military action had been taken in Eastern Europe. In December 1988, during the final months of the Afghan withdrawal, Gorbachev announced in a speech at the United Nations that the Soviet Union would unilaterally withdraw some of its military forces from Eastern Europe, without insisting on a quid pro quo from Washington and NATO. It was a particularly candid expression of Moscow's sincere intentions to retreat from the globalist/imperialist posture that had characterized its foreign policy in Eastern Europe since the Second World War. In a speech in Italy in September 1989, Soviet Foreign Ministry spokesman Gennediy Gerisomov said that the Soviet Union has 'replaced the Brezhnev Doctrine, which exists no longer and perhaps never existed, with the Frank Sinatra Doctrine from the title of one of his famous songs, "I did it my way".[32] Thus Gorbachev's new policies, which had been received with much scepticism in the West in 1987, had become institutionalized in Soviet foreign policy by 1989. The Brezhnev Doctrine, which had justified the deaths of thousands in Eastern Europe and Afghanistan, was officially laid to rest with a light-hearted quip from Gerisomov. Lenin's Machiavellian *kto kovo* ('who will do in whom') ethic, which had guided Communist Party politics internally and externally since the creation of the Soviet state, was becoming null and void in the Gorbachev era.

There is no question that the multiple political, social and economic forces that fuelled the democratic movements in Eastern Europe had been slowly multiplying since the beginning of the Cold War. Nor is there a debate that parts of Eastern Europe had been sovereign between the two world wars, and the dissident movements that led the 1989 revolution had continued to operate underground even in the most oppressive periods of Soviet-backed totalitarian rule. Gorbachev's abandonment of the Brezhnev Doctrine contained a critically important political message: the Soviet Union would no longer defend its allied regimes against populist uprisings from their own peoples. As noted in the case of Poland, it was a message not lost either on government officials or their domestic opponents, and throughout the rest of Eastern Europe, domestic grassroots opposition to the Stalinist-modelled one-party-statist regimes coalesced quickly among the general population. In Hungary and Poland the less rigid communist regimes reached out to the rapidly germinating democratic elements and within a year were peacefully replaced in power by the democratic forces. In Czechoslovakia, East Germany, Bulgaria and Romania the communist regimes resisted change more forcefully, with the Romanian democratic revolution being marked by significant bloodshed. However, the result was the same – the communist governments were all overthrown, in large part because of their inability to dissociate themselves from their past connection with the Soviet Union. In the case of Afghanistan the regime of Najibullah had little choice but to fight on. The somewhat surprising three-year survival of Najibullah's government was assisted by the historical fissures in Afghan politics, which quickly invoked infighting among the tribe-based groups after Soviet forces were withdrawn in 1989. However, as different as they may appear to be at first glance, the countries of Eastern Europe and Afghanistan shared the common fate of having been invaded and occupied by Soviet troops when their internal political situations threatened perceived Soviet national interests. Because of this shared trauma, the Soviet withdrawal from Afghanistan was a signifier of hope. Actions in Afghanistan were the first concrete sign to the rest of the 'socialist commonwealth' that Moscow was willing to match the rhetoric of perestroika with action. Even though Eastern Europe's predisposition for revolution existed long before the late 1980s, the actual expression of any people's revolution occurred only after Gorbachev's removal of troops from Afghanistan, and his subsequent affirmations that the Red Army would not again be used to support the communist regimes in Eastern Europe. Afghanistan was the first place where this revolution in foreign policy took place. The withdrawal from Afghanistan was a harbinger of the fall of the communist 'dominoes' in Eastern Europe. In 1992 this sequential reality was confirmed by perestroika's foremost patron in foreign policy. Former Soviet Foreign Minister Eduard Shevardnadze makes the final connection by declaring, '*The decision to leave Afghanistan was the first and most difficult step ... Everything else flowed from that.*'[33]

END OF FORCE – END OF UNION

From the founding of the Soviet state in 1917, the declared enemies of socialism were either imprisoned, forced into exile, or shot. State violence was used extensively in order to maintain complete political control within Soviet society. When the Soviet Union expanded its sphere of influence after the Second World War, military and secret police forces were the primary tool used to maintain Soviet dominance in the outer empire. The need to use force, fear and terror to Sovietize most of Eastern Europe demonstrated the primary weakness of the Soviet system, and once force had been used to keep its titular 'allies' in line, the Soviet Union became largely dependent on force to remain in control. At its core, military force was the key ingredient in holding both the outer empire and the internal union together. Ironically, Gorbachev's breaking this dependence on force led to the destruction of the entire system. The last communist 'domino' to fall in the wave of democratic political reform that swept the Eastern Bloc in the dramatic period of 1989–91 was the Soviet Union itself.

By 1988 the Soviet public had become much more attuned to the problems of Afghanistan. On the domestic level, Gorbachev was faced with growing public dissatisfaction with the war as the human costs became increasingly tangible over the years. Like the United States in Vietnam, the Soviet military's inability to win the Afghan War decisively brought home the negative aspects of the war: battlefield deaths, POWs and MIAs (Missing in Action), wounded veterans, mentally and physically ill veterans, and veterans with drug addiction. Veterans of the Afghan War, all conscripts, rotated back home at periodic intervals, which permitted the travails, frustrations, self-doubts and horror stories of the common soldier to be shared by the entire population. The problems exposed in the wartime army soon became a microcosm for the internal weakness of the society as a whole. According to one study:

The messages of doubt were military, political, ethnic and social. In the end they were corrosive and destructive. One needs only review the recently released casualty figures to underscore the persuasiveness of the problem. Soviet dead and missing in Afghanistan amounted to almost 15,000 troops, a modest per cent of the 642,000 Soviets who served during the ten-year war. Far more telling were the 469,685 other casualties, fully 73% of the overall force, who were wounded or incapacitated by serious illness. Some 415,932 troops fell victim to disease, of which 115,308 suffered from infectious hepatitis and 31,080 from typhoid fever. Beyond the sheer magnitude of these numbers is what the figures say about Soviet military hygiene and the conditions surrounding troop life. These numbers are unheard of in modern armies and modern medicine and their social impact among the returnees and the Soviet population was staggering.[34]

Because of Gorbachev's policy of glasnost, press reports on the Afghan War were also being printed that did not simply promote a glossy official line, thus increasing public awareness and dissatisfaction with the war. During the Brezhnev years, there had been no war at all, Soviet soldiers were simply helping the Afghans, who welcomed them with open arms. Under Andropov and Chernenko some fighting was reported; however, most reports simply glorified the prowess of the Soviet fighting machine. Under Gorbachev the extent of coverage widened rapidly, with stories of veterans' experiences being used to enhance the reform process, undermine conservative critics inside the Communist Party, and outflank the ossified bureaucracy. At the 27th Party Congress in February 1988 Gorbachev had called the war a 'bleeding wound', a statement that inspired members of the Soviet press to steadily test the limits of glasnost. Politically Gorbachev wanted the war to be linked to the failed foreign and domestic policies of the Brezhnev era. Any opposition to the Afghan withdrawal was therefore linked to support of the previous regime. Gorbachev perceived that the battle to restructure Soviet society at home could only be helped by ending the war in Afghanistan and by unmasking its dark side by freeing censorship in television, movies, music, art and literature. On all levels, in various forms and degrees, reports on the horrors and heroism of Afghanistan extensively penetrated the cultural space of Soviet society.[35] The political sphere was penetrated directly as well. After a remarkable series of heated debates between dissident Andrei Sakharov and various conservative members of the Supreme Soviet it was declared in December 1989 that the Afghan War had been an immoral act in violation of international human rights standards and illegal under international law. No similar declaration of guilt has ever been adopted by the US government regarding Vietnam. In 1990 the Soviets continued to confess old sins, apologizing for the invasion of Czechoslovakia and going so far as to declare the

Molotov–Ribbentrop Pact illegal, thus opening a Pandora's box of territorial legal questions and igniting the long-smouldering embers of Baltic independence into open flame.

In an interview on the granting of independence to the Baltic states, Alexander Karpienko, a Soviet veteran wounded in Afghanistan, cites the importance of Afghanistan in the destruction of the Soviet empire. 'Afghanistan was a crucial link in the chain. Our failure in Afghanistan and Gorbachev's decision to introduce glasnost raised questions about the proper role of the Soviet army. Russian mothers began insisting that their sons be brought home.'[36] Once Gorbachev broke the ideological constructs of the 'socialist commonwealth' and denounced the use of force to maintain Soviet influence, there was little else to hold the empire together. Internally, the empire crumbled because violent force was no longer seen as a legitimate and effective tool of state power. Military force was used to keep the Baltic states in line from 1988 to 1991. However, when Soviet soldiers refused in late August 1991 to obey the coup leadership's orders to crack down in Moscow, the independence movement was destined to succeed. By removing Soviet troops from Afghanistan, Gorbachev had set into motion a tide of social forces that eventually destroyed the Soviet Union as a unified state.

In April 1992 the last Soviet-installed leader of Afghanistan, President Najibullah, surrendered power. Oddly, Afghanistan, where the end of Soviet hegemony was initiated, was the last Soviet-backed regime to fall, surviving longer than its patron. In commenting on Najibullah's departure, Robert B. Oakley, US ambassador to Pakistan (1988–91), summarized Afghanistan's importance: 'The unraveling of the Cold War began there. When the Soviet people asked why their leaders were wasting lives and treasure in a remote, backward country in a time they were facing massive domestic problems, it was the beginning of the end for the whole Soviet experiment.'[37] Oakley's view was echoed by Afghanistan's first postcommunist president, Sibghatullah Mujaddidi. During the ceremony that officially transferred power from Najibullah's regime to the Islamic rebels, Mujaddidi claimed credit on behalf of the Afghans for the Soviet Union's demise: 'No one believed that our resort to arms would destroy a superpower and destroy communism. But we believe God is the only superpower.'[38] Mujaddidi's words are revealing, if somewhat exaggerated. The Afghans' resort to arms was one of many factors that led to the destruction of a superpower. However, Soviet communism was finally destroyed after its leaders renounced the use of force by arms to maintain power and, once fear of arrest or execution had dissipated, the citizenry rebelled.

In addition to the linkage between the breaking of the Brezhnev Doctrine in Afghanistan and the revolution in Eastern Europe, the Soviet/Afghan experience has more direct generative linkage to the final days of the Soviet state. As widely narrated in newspaper and television reports from the makeshift blockades in the streets of Moscow, the vast majority of anti-coup forces were young men between the ages of twenty and forty, most of whom had military experience under the Soviet system of universal conscription. Veterans of the Afghan War were present in large numbers and were largely responsible for guarding the Russian Republic parliamentary building during the critical hours of the aborted coup in Moscow. Artyom Borovik, a Soviet journalist and author of *The Hidden War: A Russian Journalist's Account of the Soviet War in Afghanistan*, helped to man the barricades while reporting for the American television network CBS's highly acclaimed '60 Minutes' programme. After numerous interviews, he reported that Afghan War veterans were committed to the internal reforms started by Gorbachev and would die before allowing a return of the old leadership that had sent them to Afghanistan.[39] Clearly, many Afghan War veterans in Moscow were willing to lie down in front of tanks to protect the reform process symbolized by Boris Yeltsin and the Russian parliament building. After having personally experienced the failure of Brezhnev's socialist internationalism in Afghanistan, opposing the coup was of paramount importance to these veterans. Two of the three men killed on the night of 20 August 1991, Dmitri Komar and Iliya Krichevsky, were Afghan War veterans.[40]

On the other side of the barricades the legacy of Afghanistan was also at work. Soviet generals who had served in Afghanistan were involved in carrying out the coup, and many of their soldiers were veterans of the Afghan War. However, in the final test of loyalties, three of the last commanders in Afghanistan, Aleksandar Rutskoi, Pavel Grachev and Boris Gromov, joined with Yeltsin's forces. Both Grachev and Gromov had been involved in coup plans to storm the Russian parliament building, but during the second day of the coup Grachev and Gromov refused to give orders for the attack when it became apparent that a massive loss of life would result. Gromov took a series of steps that effectively sabotaged the coup by informing his fellow Afghan War veterans inside the building that an attack was being planned. Grachev was responsible for urging the Russian leadership to summon as many supporters as possible because 'the attacking forces will not dare open fire on the people'.[41] Rutskoi, who had been once been shot down by a Stinger missile on one of his 428 combat missions in Afghanistan, had become on his return from service a leading champion of parliamentary democracy and a major figure during the August coup.

Elite Soviet KGB troops of the celebrated Alpha group also refused to participate. Many Alpha members were Afghan War veterans and had been responsible for the death of Amin during the storming of the presidential palace in Kabul in December 1979. Anatoly Savelev, one such member, stated, 'Everyone is free to act as his conscience determines. But I personally will not take part in a storming of the White House.' His words were echoed by General Grachev, who informed Yeltsin, 'I am a Russian and will never allow the army to spill the blood of my own people.' Yeltsin was informed also that Grachev was so committed to stopping the coup that he had arranged plans to bomb the Kremlin if coup leaders attempted to storm the building. Yeltsin rewarded Grachev's loyalty by appointing him minister of defence in his new government; Rutskoi became Yeltsin's vice-president; and Gromov, the 'Lion of Afghanistan' remained a deputy commander of ground forces after the coup, even though he had run for president against Yeltsin in 1991 and at one time was seen as one of Yeltsin's many rivals.[42]

The return of history: war loss and reform

From the vantage point of history the monumental changes brought about in Soviet foreign and domestic policy during the war loss and withdrawal from Afghanistan are part of a distinct and continuous pattern. Throughout Russian history, foreign wars have influenced the character, size and politics of the Russian empire. In victory, the central regime became stronger, the empire larger and the political system more rigid. In defeat, the regime became unstable, the empire was diminished, and political restructuring occurred. I have elaborated this argument in detail elsewhere and here offer the following summary.[43]

From the beginning of the Moscow-centred state in the fifteenth century to the downfall of the Soviet empire at the end of the twentieth century, fundamental political changes in Russian politics have only occurred when war loss was a concurrent factor. The pattern of war loss and reform began with the creation of modern Russia under the leadership of Ivan III, who was responsible for defeating the Mongols and concentrating state power in Moscow. The pattern repeated itself under Boris Gudunov, who took power in the late sixteenth century, after the disastrous results of Russia's Livonian Wars against Sweden and Poland had further magnified Ivan IV's self-induced domestic crisis. Gudunov is largely responsible for the early institutionalization of Russian feudalism, which would serve as the social basis of imperial control until the nineteenth century. Peter the Great's reign again witnessed the pattern of war loss and political reform, beginning with his immediate predecessor's military defeats at the hands of the Crimean Tartars in 1687 and the Tartars and Chinese in 1689 – defeats that catalysed Peter's seizure of the throne in a *coup d'état* in 1689. Peter's own armies were routinely over-matched by Swedish forces from 1700 to 1709; however, Peter was able to reorganize and modernize his forces while Charles XII attempted to solidify Swedish control over Poland. The major 'lesson' learned in the early reversals of the 'Great Northern War' was a need for fundamental domestic change, in both economic and political structures. Under Peter the Russian nobility was reorganized and became completely dependent on and subservient to the Tsar, and industrialization for modern war production was introduced.

The pattern of war loss and reform again occurred after Russia's disastrous defeat in the Crimean War in 1856. The Russian defeat had exposed the military strength of the modernizing West, whose war machines were years ahead of Russia's. After the Crimean War, economic and social reformers pushed for and eventually achieved radical internal changes. In order to retain Russia's place among the world powers, the post-Crimean War Tsars began the difficult task of creating an industrialized society. In order to create an industrial labour pool, serfdom had to be abolished, which radically restructured the Russian socioeconomic system. Eventually the Communist Party headed by Lenin, which was first created in the social upheaval produced by this economic reform process after the Crimean War, would rule Russia. The post-Crimean period is one of the best examples of a pattern of internal changes that occur in the Russian system after a disastrous foreign war.

This pattern of defeat and reform recurred after Russia's even more embarrassing defeat in the Russo-Japanese War of 1905. For two years after Russian forces had been soundly trounced by the Japanese, a tide of popular rebellion brought the Tsarist regime to near collapse. Nicholas II, aided by the ineffectiveness of a poorly organized and weak opposition, was able to bring the country under control only after a series of ruthless military campaigns against the peasantry, combining coercive means with promises to implement political and social restructuring. The reforms designed by Nicholas II's chief adviser, Peter Stolypin, launched the process of restructuring; much like Gorbachev's perestroika, however, these plans were hindered by resistance from conservative opposition. The Russian monarchy and nobility (much like the Communist Party hardliners) never honestly embraced political reform, choosing rather to cling to their monopoly on state power even to the point of self-destruction.[44] However, significant structural changes at the local and regional governing levels helped to sustain and nurture the liberal and radical anti-monarchical political movements that remained abundant in Russian society after the 1905 revolt, and successfully resurfaced during the trauma of the First World War.

The radical transformation of state and society after the First World War is the most notable example of the pattern of defeat and reform in Russian history. The Soviet state that finally crumbled in December 1991 was created in the massive social upheaval fomented during the bloody civil war (1918–21) that followed Russia's withdrawal from the First World War. The anti-war Bolsheviks seized power in a society torn between forces supporting and opposing Russia's involvement in the war. The magnitude of the Imperial Army's defeat caused widespread desertion and mutiny among the armed forces. This military disintegration, combined with the country's paralysed economy and widespread famine, resulted in the final victory by the Bolsheviks in 1921.

Likewise, during periods of military gain, recent war victory, or peace, all attempts at fundamental political reform in Russia's governing structures have failed. Without war loss as a contributing factor, structural political change has never occurred. Three examples of this 'pattern in absence'[45] are notable. The first occurred in 1730 during the transition of power to Tsarina Anne, when an attempt to usurp power by the nobility and create a less absolutist state was checked by the Tsarist imperial guards. The second phase of the pattern in absence occurred after the Napoleonic Wars when Alexander I's highly touted reforms were suppressed by conservative reaction, with political liberalization being killed outright in 1825 at the bloody end of the Decembrist revolt. The third example of the pattern in absence occurred during and after the Second World War, when Stalin's basic governing structures remained intact domestically and the Stalinist order was exported to the newly conquered states of Eastern Europe. Although Stalin's death brought about a great reduction in the use of terror by the state, the basic form of the system that he created endured until the arrival of Mikhail Gorbachev in 1985.

The Soviet defeat in Afghanistan is the latest cycle of war loss and political reform. Like every previous upheaval in Russian history, war loss has directly influenced the dynamics and structures of Russian politics. By his own admission, Gorbachev's decision in 1986 to end the war was embedded in a wider logic that linked multiple global and local considerations, all of which contributed to the eventual demise of the Soviet Union. The crucial decisions regarding Afghanistan were both cause and effect: when implemented, they imprinted a logic for expanded political reforms throughout the Soviet sphere, soon producing a momentum that Gorbachev would be unable to control. According to Afghan scholar Anthony Arnold, who describes the Afghan War as 'the fateful pebble' that began the avalanche of social upheavals, 'The Soviet system collapsed thanks in large part to the weaknesses in its supporting pillars that the war in Afghanistan revealed. By exposing those weaknesses and helping trigger the collapse of the system, the Afghans opened the way to fundamental reform …'.[46] Again, losses in war themselves have not been the sole cause of fundamental political reform. Rather, war loss has always been a necessary accompanying event when fundamental political change has taken place in Russian history. The argument that the Soviet experience in Afghanistan was purely coincidental in the downfall of the Soviet Union simply does not withstand the scrutiny of the historical pattern.

The pattern I have outlined applies nicely to the broad processes of political change in Russian history. However, the pattern now may be at an end, because the narrow base of political legitimacy and claims of infallibility that previously characterized Russian politics are rapidly receding. Since the adoption of the new constitution in 1993, a greater degree of rational legal authority has become systematically embedded in Russian politics. Though it is not clear as of early 1998 whether democracy has become so ingrained in Russian society that it cannot be jettisoned if the government faces some new legitimacy crisis, with each election cycle the democratic process and new institutions should become stronger. As discussed further below, democracies often show a greater flexibility in dealing with war loss than do non-democracies. Thus the Russian Federation, because it is a political state qualitatively different from all of its predecessors, may in fact break the cycle of defeat and reform that is a hallmark of Russian political history.

In terms of military intervention abroad, the post-Soviet foreign policy of Russia has yet to find a guiding ideological doctrine similar to that articulated by Brezhnev after the invasion of Czechoslovakia. Like the United States after Vietnam, Russia has been very hesitant to promote the use of force in the greater international sphere. Furthermore, the readiness and capabilities of the Russian military to project power have declined dramatically as post-Soviet economic decay and massive budget cuts have combined to disembowel the armed forces. With the demise of the Soviet Union and the succession of the fourteen non-Russian republics, the Russian Federation emerged as the emaciated heir to Soviet and Tsarist imperial glory. For Russia, having lost approximately one-quarter of the territory and 40 per cent of the population of the Soviet Union, most foreign policy issues pertaining to the use of force are now focused on relations with states that now comprise the Commonwealth of Independent States (CIS), otherwise known as 'the near abroad' in Russian policy-making circles. However, despite a radical change in context, Russian foreign policy during the 1990s can be usefully compared to that of the United States after Vietnam. Both countries initially retreated from globalism, with acts of force projection re-emerging first in countries of close geopolitical proximity. The United States was restricted by strong domestic opposition to foreign adventures, a restraint that collapsed first in Grenada and Panama, two countries within the US's traditional sphere of influence. Russia's force-projection capabilities, although in rapid decline, have been limited to the CIS. In the mid 1990s forces under Moscow's control were stationed in every CIS state. In many countries, such as Moldova, Georgia, Belarus and Tajikistan, the Russian forces have played a significant role in influencing domestic politics. Russia has a variety of motives for the placement of these troops, including: the wish to protect significant Russian ethnic populations in these countries; the fear of losing strategically important border states; suppression of internal conflicts that may have negative spillover effects in Russia; and the traditional imperial desire for control over resources and territory. For some of these operations, Russia has received the endorsement of the UN, although Russian 'peacekeeping' troops have been denied the status of UN peacekeepers. Russian forces have also been deployed on sensitive border regions of the old Soviet Union, in Belarus on the Polish border and in Tajikistan on the Afghan border.

Despite the slowly maturing democratic component of Russia's political culture, the use of military force to ensure the ruling authority of the state also remains a significant component. The historical continuity of state violence is perhaps best expressed in Moscow's dealing with the Republic of Chechnya (which had declared independence in 1991).[47] Yeltsin ordered Russian armed forces into the Republic of Chechnya to restore Moscow's sovereignty in the region. At the outset, Yeltsin's decision to crush the Chechens was seen as a public-relations disaster by some observers. In early December 1994, Russian troops began their assault on the rebels and ran into fierce opposition, failing to take the capital city of Grozny in the short period promised by Yeltsin's military advisers (most notably Defence Minister Pavel Grachev, who predicted that the war would be over in a few hours). In keeping with the Russian great-power tradition, Yeltsin responded by taking a more hard-line position, and he began surrounding himself with more hawkish advisers. He replaced hesitant military ground commanders, fired doves in the defence ministry, denounced his critics in the press, and ordered the use of massive force, including heavy artillery and aerial bombardment, which produced a level of indiscriminate carnage that many observers found reminiscent of the Afghan War. After weeks of intense attacks, which resulted in thousands of military casualties and massive butchery among civilians and rebels alike, the Russian Army took control of the Chechen capital and began a string of difficult but steady victories over the separatist forces throughout Chechnya. However, the Chechens proceeded to launch raids into Russia proper, attacked economic targets, seized hostages, occupied villages.[48] As a result of the extreme violence and the large numbers of civilian casualties and refugees, many of Yeltsin's long-time supporters in the Parliament, namely, the liberal 'Democratic Russia' and 'Russia's Choice' factions, denounced the attack and stated that they would not support Yeltsin in the 1996 presidential election.[49] In turn, Yeltsin's decision to use military force was supported by many of his harshest critics among the Russian nationalist forces that held the balance of power in the Parliament after the 1993 elections. Among the general public the war was very unpopular, and the military intervention had the exact opposite of the planned effect on Yeltsin's popularity – which plummeted to single digits in public opinion polls.[50]

Yeltsin's future as a two-term president seemed highly unlikely in the early months of 1996. As shown by Lech Walesa's defeat by the communist Aleksander Kwasniewski in Poland's 1995 election, even the most prominent and popular figures in the democratic upheavals of 1989–91 could be replaced in the system they helped to create; such are the risks of democracy. However, Yeltsin once again highlighted his stature as Russia's ultimate political phoenix by staging a dramatic comeback to win the presidency in the second round of voting on 3 July 1996.[51] During the campaign, Yeltsin had signed a widely publicized cease-fire with the Chechen leadership, whose ground forces had been decimated by heavy military assaults and who were politically fractured after the death of their charismatic leader, Dzhokhar Dudaev, at the hands of a well-aimed Russian artillery barrage.

CONCLUSIONS

This book has been an attempt not only to provide a greater degree of substance to the suggestion that Vietnam and Afghanistan are analogous events but also to explore the important differences between two of the most important events that shaped the dynamics of the Cold War and helped to bring about its end. I have sought to answer two fundamental questions. First, why were the United States and the Soviet Union and their respective allies in Vietnam and Afghanistan unable to create and maintain political legitimacy, while their opponents were successful? Second, why was the American political system (in both the international and domestic spheres) able to survive the stresses of war loss in the Vietnam War, while the Soviet Union and the 'socialist commonwealth' in Eastern Europe collapsed so soon after the end of the Afghan War?

In Chapter 1 I concluded that before large-scale military intervention, the superpowers historically had pursued significantly dissimilar policies toward Vietnam and Afghanistan. The United States had little if any interests or relations in Vietnam before the Second World War, and Washington's focus on the country during that war was wholly derived from Japan's occupation of French Indochina. In contrast, the Soviet Union had a much greater degree of involvement, and a good deal of historical continuity in its relations, with Afghanistan – relations that had been shaped primarily by the dynamics of the Russo-British balance-of-power geopolitics of the previous century. Despite their revolutionary fervour in domestic policy and in other foreign affairs, the Bolsheviks sought in their relations with Afghanistan to maintain the status quo in South Asia. Unfortunately for the superpowers and for the peoples of Vietnam and Afghanistan, the lessons of history should have convinced both the United States and the Soviet Union that intervention in these two countries was ill-advised – these lessons were not unknown. For instance, in 1965 President Johnson was reminded of the French experience by Undersecretary of State George Ball, who advised him with prophetic accuracy that

> ... we may not be able to fight the war successfully enough – even with 500,000 Americans in South Vietnam we must have more evidence than we now have that our troops will not bog down in the jungles and rice paddies – while we slowly blow the country to pieces ... the French fought a war in Vietnam, and were finally defeated – after seven years of bloody struggle and when they still had 250,000 combat hardened

veterans in the field supported by an army of 205,000 South Vietnamese. To be sure the French were fighting a colonial war while we are fighting to stop aggression. But when we have put enough Americans on the ground in South Vietnam to give the appearance of a white man's war, the distinction as to our ultimate purpose will have less and less practical effect.[52]

Johnson rejected Ball's analysis, not believing that the United States would fail as the French had done; however, he certainly was not unaware of the risks involved. By the time Johnson decided to escalate the war, the leadership mantle of Vietnamese nationalism had been in the possession of Ho Chi Minh and his communist followers for twenty years. When these new forces were deployed to villages in provinces throughout the country, the communists were able to portray themselves as the protectors of Vietnamese tradition in the fight against yet another foreign invader. Americans saw themselves as being different from the French; however, the average Vietnamese simply saw more heavily armed white men who spoke an even more obscure foreign language. The blue, white and red of one flag was replaced by the red, white and blue of another. The leadership cadre of the South Vietnamese had very poor credentials for laying claim to the Mandate of Heaven. The pre-eminent leaders of the North, Ho Chi Minh and Vo Nguyen Giap (the military mastermind of the communist forces) had successfully fought against both the Japanese and the French. Ngo Dinh Diem, the first US choice to lead the South, had a very limited personal history of anti-French nationalism, and his successors Nguyen Cao Ky and Nguyen Van Thieu both had served in the French armed forces, which further enhanced the credibility of the communist claims to legitimacy. Although the programmatic ideals of communism did not fit well with Vietnamese tradition, the NLF and communist forces simply did a better of job of drawing support. The average villager was a 'rational peasant'[53] who made decisions based on self-interest. South Vietnamese government officials were largely seen as cosmopolitan snobs who were estranged from the people by simple and basic criteria: their dress, demeanour and social background. This image contrasts with that of the average NLF cadre, who seemed much closer to the peasants socially. Moreover, the communists often did a better job of focusing on social issues linked to village politics than did the government.

A similar misreading of the ability of military force to challenge the power of domestic nationalism was made by the Brezhnev politburo. The Soviet Union's involvement in Afghan affairs during the 1980s indicates a clear rejection of the lessons learned by the British in the three Anglo-Afghan Wars of the nineteenth century. Although there are many differences between British and Russian involvement in Afghan affairs, the similarities are remarkable. The First Anglo-Afghan War was started when the Afghan leader

Dost Muhammad incurred the wrath of the British by partaking of a small degree of independent behaviour. The British overreacted, sent in the troops, and installed their own puppet – Shah Shuja. Although they possessed complete dominance in military firepower, and had all the resources of the British Empire to back them, the British were unable to defeat the resolute Afghans. Eventually they were forced to withdraw after suffering terrible losses. By the middle of the nineteenth century the Afghans had provided ample forewarning of their fighting tenacity and intolerance of foreign invaders – no matter what the odds. The British suffered similar defeats in the Second and Third Anglo-Afghan Wars after unwisely choosing again to intervene in Afghan internal affairs.

Soviet intervention in Afghanistan from 1979 to 1989 was a modern version of the same story. Before the invasion the Soviets were the dominant economic, political and military force having influence over Afghan affairs. However, they remained dominant only when they exerted influence from within their own borders. The Soviets' ability to dictate events within Afghanistan ceased as soon as the Red Army became directly involved in Afghan internal affairs. Historically the Afghans have always stopped fighting among themselves when a common enemy enters the scene. As soon as the Soviets departed the country, the Afghan civil war (which began as a fight among Afghans in 1978) resumed its historical patterns and continues to this day. Thus both the Vietnamese and the Afghans reacted in a historically predictable fashion. The leadership of both superpowers were aware of this history. They were advised by dissenting voices in their governments not to intervene, but they decided to follow the advice of other advisers who promoted military intervention. As discussed in Chapter 3, containment of outside aggression was used as a justification for intervention, but this was a falsehood in both cases, because the regimes that the superpowers sought to support were largely bereft of domestic legitimacy. Thus, I argued, detainment of a rebellious population, not containment of outside aggression, better describes both interventions. In this regard, Afghanistan was the Soviet Vietnam, and Vietnam was the American Afghanistan.

In Chapters 2 and 3 I showed that while the processes and time-frames of military intervention were markedly different in the two cases, the basic driving motivations and perceptions behind superpower military intervention were very similar. Because the ideological struggle between American liberalism and Soviet socialism had taken on global proportions, many key members of the elite leadership of both superpowers believed that their national security was directly linked to the outcomes of the Vietnamese and Afghan civil wars. The superpower decisions to go to war in Vietnam and Afghanistan were thus entangled in the existing logic and history of the Cold War. Here a second lesson of history can be derived from the superpowers' interventions: beware misplaced analogies from one's own historical experience. In Vietnam the United States essentially believed that it was fighting a different version of Korea. In Afghanistan the Soviet Union believed that the success of its most recent invasion, that of Czechoslovakia a decade earlier, could be repeated. In both cases previous interventions produced overconfidence in the utility of military solutions. Because of the hubris of self-perceived power, history is full of losers whose decision to venture down the road to war seems, in hindsight at least, to be the ultimate act of folly. Could not the Japanese see that they had no chance of defeating the United States? Could not the Germans see that attacking both the United States and Soviet Union would doom them to failure? Of course none of the initiators of war throughout history entered into combat expecting to lose. And in cases such as Vietnam and Afghanistan the perceived power imbalances led the politicians to believe themselves incapable of losing. The unknown perils hidden in the fog of war can claim even the mightiest of warriors.

In Chapter 4 we saw that the manner in which the superpowers conducted themselves in war had many similarities but also many differences. Because of their experiences in Korea and Europe, both superpowers believed that overwhelming military force could be used to alter the political landscapes in Vietnam and Afghanistan to a point where their client regimes could survive internal challenges by their own devices and join their patron's international Cold War alliance system. After nearly a decade of fighting, the superpowers in both cases had to admit that this belief was false. Detainment could achieve a military stalemate, but it could not produce internal political reforms and legitimacy. The regimes with which the superpowers were allied were so weak that they could not even provide for their own internal security, let alone protect themselves from outside forces. The many governments of South Vietnam and communist-led Afghanistan during those years were seen as the creation of foreigners and thus forever stigmatized in the highly nationalistic anti-outsider traditions that imbued the Vietnamese and Afghan cultures. Also in both cases, the political restraints imposed by Cold War geopolitics made it very difficult to achieve battlefield victory. In order to isolate their clients from attack by opposing forces, both the United States and the Soviet Union could either drastically increase the number of troops in-theatre, or widen the war to neighbouring countries. In Vietnam, the United States made such an attempt at the first option between 1965 and 1969; however, domestic political constraints limited the number of troops that could be called up, with President Johnson drawing the line at the mobilization of the reserves. In Afghanistan, the Soviet Union never made such an attempted escalation. Although the reasons for this remain unclear, it is logical to conclude that the Kremlin leadership simply was unwilling to make a larger troop commitment when the numbers that might be necessary for victory were unclear in the first place, and the political and economic costs of such escalation would be too high. As a result, in both cases the superpowers decided to conduct these wars with heavy reliance on air power and bombing – a strategy which certainly kept their enemies from achieving quick victory but which in itself could not destroy the Vietnamese communists or the Afghan Mujahideen. As long as the Vietnamese and the Afghans were willing to suffer the punishment required to maintain their struggles for national independence, and neighbouring states allowed their movements to and from the battlefield, stalemate was the inevitable outcome in both cases.

War loss and the lessons of legitimacy at home

Perhaps the most important lesson that can be derived from this comparison has to do with our understanding of political legitimacy in the domestic polities of the United States and the Soviet Union. Both superpowers ended their interventions because of domestic pressures, although in the United States it was pressure from the masses, and in the Soviet Union it was pressure from within the government. In the American case President Johnson was driven from politics because of his inability both to win the war and to fulfil his vision of a 'Great Society' for all Americans. Although the Tet offensive in 1968 was a military disaster for communist forces located south of the 17th parallel – a defeat from which they never fully recovered – it marked the turning point in the war's legitimacy crisis in the United States: the ruling political elite were willing to continue the war, but ordinary people increasingly were not. Americans had been given numerous promises and assurances that their sons and daughters would be home soon, that the war was being won, that South Vietnam was a bastion of democracy, and that the United States had always pursued the war in accordance with the laws and ideals of American society. Thus, the very fact that the communist's Tet offensive could happen at all came as a great shock to Americans. The trauma of Tet began to peel away the multiple layers of naïve trust that Americans held in their government – or, perhaps more accurately, Tet ultimately revealed the façade of Cold War illusions that the government had fabricated around an overly trusting public.

Ironically, Tet also undermined the legitimacy of the communist forces in the South, which were rendered militarily destitute by their near destruction by the United States and GVN forces. After Tet, the war fought in the South was much less that of the detainment of a population which was willing to take up arms against the government. From 1956 to 1968 the war was fought in the South by members of the local population supported by those in the North. However, from 1969 to 1975, the war in South Vietnam was fought primarily by soldiers from the North who infiltrated South Vietnam via the Ho Chi Minh Trail. As for the American commitment to fight on behalf of Vietnam, the war was essentially over after Tet, in no small part because of its influence on the 1968 election in the United States and President Johnson's decision to end his otherwise brilliant political career. Nixon was elected in large part because of his promise to end the war in Vietnam while keeping intact America's international credibility and honour.

Although Nixon fulfilled this promise, he too was driven from office. Why? To answer this question it is useful to revisit Max Weber's three-part typology of legitimacy. Nixon may have fulfilled his promise, but in terms of Weber's sources of legitimacy he violated both traditional authority (that consisting of values, norms and accepted behavioural codes) and rational–legal authority (that consisting of positive law and constitutional mandates). In the politics of the United States, the ends do not always justify the means – especially if the means violate the sources of legitimacy in American politics. Due process, the separation of powers, and constitutional legality are the fundamental sources of political legitimacy in the American political system. Nixon eventually ended the war in Vietnam, but in doing so he violated the lawful boundaries of the office of the American presidency.

Both Nixon and Johnson were ruined in part because they violated the accepted norms of American politics – in Weber's framework, the traditional sources of legitimacy. Both presidents were caught in half-truths, deception and outright lies regarding various aspects of the war. This behaviour was unacceptable, especially in the context of a war that would cost 58,000 American lives, over a million Vietnamese lives, and uncounted billions of dollars in national treasure. Furthermore, once the process began, Americans wanted to know what other forms of duplicity had been perpetuated upon them. Deception regarding the war, including its origins in Vietnamese history; the US's original support for Ho Chi Minh during the Second World War; Eisenhower's abrogation of the democratic elections promised in the Geneva Accords of 1954; and Kennedy's involvement in the *coup d'état* that killed President Diem, were some of the major dishonourable acts dredged up for US citizens to consider. They did not (and do not) enjoy the flavour of this slice of American history.

Nevertheless, despite being shaken to its core, the American constitutional system remained intact and mostly legitimate in the view of the American people. American democracy, like all modern democratic regimes, has a number of self-correcting mechanisms, primarily in the form of elections, but also in the form of laws for the removal of figures from high office. Hence when the rational–legal authority of the modern state is violated, the state itself – the 'system' – has the ability to survive by addressing its shortcomings through legislation. The system may in fact have flaws, but individuals are usually seen as the cause for failures of the system. Individuals are replaced during elections, and the system is tinkered with, but the basic constitutional structure remains the same. It is possible to argue that the greatest damage inflicted by Vietnam was that it destroyed the trusting and confident attitude of Americans toward their government, themselves and their place in the world. However, this, in many ways, was no bad thing since in the wake of Vietnam Americans once again became willing to question their leaders. Only after Vietnam had destroyed the self-righteous illusions and myths that the United States had constructed around itself after the Second World War did Americans remember that blind trust in their leaders was a recipe for disaster. Vietnam was a searing experience for the nation, but at some level perhaps the United States emerged improved by the experience. For a time, the hubris of superpower was humbled, and I suspect that until the last generation of Americans who lived through the Vietnam War passes into history, the United States will not again be involved in a war in which its citizens fail to keep close tabs on what their government is doing, both in rhetoric and in reality.

There were no Tets in Afghanistan; there was no similar battlefield crisis to foment a legitimacy crisis in Soviet society comparable with the Tet offensive's impact on the United States. The Mujahideen, unlike the NLF in Vietnam, never attempted to overthrow the Soviet forces in a single, co-ordinated, country-wide military assault and popular uprising. In all likelihood, such a unified effort was impossible in Afghanistan, simply because it would have required the cooperation and coordination of too great a number of disparate political groups which, although unified in the struggle to oust the Soviet army, were not unified under a single umbrella of Afghan nationalism to the extent seen in Vietnam. In political terms, however, the Soviet Union perhaps did experience something of its own Tet offensive in the form of the crisis of legitimacy caused by Mikhail Gorbachev and his policies of perestroika and glasnost, which were first rendered into tangible policy acts in Afghanistan. Like Nixon, Gorbachev pulled out of Afghanistan to achieve objectives that he perceived as crucial to the national interests of the Soviet Union. Like the Tet offensive, the message to the Soviet people was delivered primarily through decreasing controls on the press, which became the vehicle for promoting change. Still, the fate of the Soviet Union stands in sharp contrast to the final fall-out of Vietnam on American society. In making his reforms, Gorbachev employed a public relations strategy which, instead of strengthening the Union, ultimately destroyed it entirely. Why?

Once again, Weber's typology of the sources of governing legitimacy provides some useful guidance for our comparison and analysis. During the Soviet era, the authority of the state was *officially* portrayed in rational–legal terms, and the regime had all the accoutrements of rational–legal authority that characterize modern states: a written constitution, an elective legislative body, an executive bureaucracy and regular elections. Viewed collectively, the various drafts of the Soviet constitution all *officially* guaranteed the Soviet citizens an extensive complement of civil, political and economic rights, often exceeding that of Western democracies. Likewise, elections and voting took place on the national, regional and local levels. However, in reality, all aspects of Soviet politics – from the construction of the organs of the state, to relations among the fifteen republics, to the rights and obligations of the average citizen – were contingent on the monopoly on power held by the Communist Party of the Soviet Union. Although political parties are often considered to be a characteristic of modern, rational–legal politics, in the Soviet case power and legitimacy in the Communist Party was characterized by a peculiar amalgam of all three of Weber's categories: charisma, traditional and rational–legal sources of authority. For example, charismatic elements were seen in the 'cult of personality' that sprung up around each successive Soviet leader. The longer any individual leader served in the office of General Secretary of the Communist Party, the more that person began to accrue the absolute power of the Tsar, as the office and the person merged. Continuity in traditional sources of legitimacy were best expressed by the use of military force and police terror to maintain the state. Rational–legal elements of legitimacy existed in form, but lacked true substance in comparison to the other sources. Despite Gorbachev's reforms, the rule of law never was able to free itself from the rule of the Party during the Soviet era.

In a broader historical context, then, we can perhaps best understand the Soviet Union as a transition regime between what political sociologists describe as premodern and modern states. As noted in Chapter 2, in the Tsarist order, power, authority and legitimacy were deeply embedded in traditional and charismatic elements, and these remained vibrant in the Soviet era. In essence both Tsars and commissars justified their monopoly of absolute power on a very narrow set of criteria. At the foundation of the Tsarist order lay tradition, orthodox mysticism, the divine right of aristocratic rule and coercive military power as the final arbiter of rule. At the foundation of the Soviet regime lay a superior ideology, the principal role of the Party to propagate and to guarantee the survival of that ideology, and coercive military power as the final arbiter of rule. As such, both regimes based their ruling legitimacy on claims of superiority, the guardianship of truth, basic infallibility and fear. When challenged by internal dissent, both Tsarist and Soviet regimes remained in power through the extensive use of military force, state violence and terror. As discussed above, during both the Tsarist and the Soviet era, war loss challenged the basic legitimacy of the state and resulted in structural reforms. The claim of superiority and infallibility could only be maintained in time of military success. In defeat, the state was seen as unreliable and possibly inferior to its worldly opponents. Only in times of war loss, when a regime had fallen into a condition of proven fallibility, did political change ever take place in Russia.

The crucial importance of repressive means of control for the survival of these regimes is perhaps best illustrated in its absence. The end of the Soviet empire would not have occurred in the period of 1989–91 without Gorbachev's rejection of the use of force as enshrined in his glasnost and perestroika policies. In an ideal sense, these policies were an attempt to reform the Soviet Union by abandoning traditional authority asserted from within the Communist Party by institutionalizing a more genuine form of rational–legal authority and the rule of law. In true rational–legal authority, democracy can be authentic only if people can choose their political leaders. Elections can be genuine only if they are free from manipulation by the state. Due process can be certain only if the rules apply to everyone equally. However, despite Gorbachev's desire to reform the Communist Party, the ruling regime could not be separated from the instruments of power upon which it relied. Once Gorbachev had renounced the use of force to maintain Communist Party dictatorship, there was very little left to make the government legitimate in the minds of the population. End of force resulted in end of empire and end of union.[54] Although he clearly did not intend the Soviet Union to collapse, in a transcendent sense Gorbachev succeeded in creating a more modern rational–legal democracy in Russia. In the wake of Vietnam, Americans learned again to beware of unsupervised power. In the wake of Afghanistan, Russians and others living in the territorial space of the old Soviet empire have been provided with a similar opportunity as part of the ongoing evolution of politics in the newly democratized states.

Throughout history war has always been the ultimate test of a state's ruling legitimacy, and the superpowers' experiences in Vietnam and Afghanistan reaffirm this age-old truth. Vietnam is the only war that the United States ever completely lost, and Afghanistan is the only war that the Soviet Union ever completely lost. From a comparative perspective, it is clear that Afghanistan's impact on the ultimate fate of the Soviet Union was much greater than Vietnam's impact on the United States. The United States survived Vietnam, and the Soviet Union did not survive Afghanistan. Therefore, despite multiple layers of analogy, in comprehensive terms Afghanistan was not the Soviet Vietnam; and mercifully, Vietnam was not the American Afghanistan.

NOTES

1. George Herring, *America's Longest War: The United States and Vietnam, 1950–1975* (New York: John Wiley, 1976) p. 270.
2. See Guenter Lewy, *America in Vietnam* (New York: Oxford University Press, 1978) pp. 433–4.
3. Herring, *America's Longest War*, p. 265.
4. Anthony S. Campagna, *The Economic Consequences of the Vietnam War* (New York: Praeger, 1991) p. 109.
5. John H. Makin, *The Global Debt Crisis: America's Growing Involvement* (New York:

Basic Books, 1984) pp. 98–9.
6. David P. Calleo, *The Imperious Economy* (Cambridge: Harvard University Press, 1982) p. 88.
7. See Mark T. Berger and Douglas A. Borer (eds), *The Rise of East Asia: Critical Visions of the Pacific Century* (London: Routledge, 1997) p. 7.
8. For an excellent overview of movies, see James S. Olson and Randy Roberts, *Where the Domino Fell: America and Vietnam, 1945–1990* (New York: St Martin's Press, 1991) pp. 264–80.
9. *Washington Post*, 7 March 1998, p. A1.
10. *Washington Post*, 22 March 1975. Cited in George C. Herring, *America's Longest War: The United States and Vietnam, 1950–1975*, 3rd edn (New York: McGraw-Hill, 1996) p. 308.
11. Ronald E. Powaski, *The Cold War: The United States and Soviet Union, 1917–1991* (New York: Oxford, 1998) pp. 234–5.
12. Ibid.
13. Michael Schaller, *Reckoning with Reagan: America and its President in the 1980s* (London: Oxford University Press, 1992). Cited ibid., p. 236.
14. *Cover-up behind the Iran Contra Affair* (Empowerment Project: MPI Home Video, 1988). See also, Lawrence E. Walsh, *Firewall: The Iran–Contra Conspiracy and Cover-up* (New York: Norton, 1997). Walsh was the special prosecutor assigned to the case.
15. Richard N. Haass, *Intervention: The Use of American Military Force in the Post-Cold War World* (New York: Carnegie Endowment, 1994) pp. 30–31.
16. See George Herring, 'Refighting the Last War: The Persian Gulf and the "Vietnam Syndrome"', *New Zealand International Review*, 16 (Sept./Oct. 1991) pp. 15–19.
17. Herring, *America's Longest War*, 3rd edn, pp. 311–13.
18. Mark Galeotti, *Afghanistan: The Soviet Union's Last War* (London: Frank Cass, 1995) pp. 232–3.
19. Cited ibid., p. 165.
20. Mikhail Gorbachev, *The August Coup* (New York: HarperCollins, 1991) p. 119.
21. Ibid., pp. 161–2.
22. Quoted by Margot Light, *Soviet Theory of International Relations* (New York: St Martin's Press, 1988) p. 200.
23. Robert F. Miller, 'Afghanistan and Soviet Alliances', in Amin Saikal and William Maley (eds), *The Soviet Withdrawal from Afghanistan* (Cambridge: Cambridge University Press, 1989) p. 113.
24. Ibid.
25. Ibid.
26. Ibid., p. 116.
27. Adam Michnik, *Letters from Prison and Other Essays* (Berkeley: University of California Press, 1985) p. 42. Cited in Andre W. Gerrits, *The Failure of Authoritarian Change: Reform, Opposition, and Geo-Politics in Poland in the 1980s* (Brookfield: Dartmouth Publishing, 1990) p. 31.
28. Adam Michnik, 'Gorbatschow und die Polen', *Der Spiegel*, 41 (Oct. 1987) pp. 154–5. Cited ibid., p. 163.
29. Charles Gati, *The Bloc that Failed* (Bloomington: Indiana University Press, 1990) p. 167.
30. Vaclav Havel, preface in Gwyn Prins (ed.), *Spring in Winter: The 1989 Revolutions* (Manchester: Manchester University Press, 1990) p. vi.
31. Andrei A. Piontkowsky, 'The Russian Sphinx: Hope and Despair', ibid., pp. 168–9.

32. Cited in W. Raymond Duncan and Carolyn McGiffert Ekedahl, *Moscow and the Third World Under Gorbachev* (Boulder: Westview Press, 1990) p. 69.
33. Michael Dobbs, 'Dramatic Politburo Meeting Led to End of War', *Washington Post*, 16 Nov. 1992, p. A16; italics added.
34. Mohammad Yahya Nawroz and Lester W. Grau, 'The Soviet War in Afghanistan: History and Harbinger of Future War?' US Army, Foreign Military Studies Institute (Fort Leavenworth, KN, 1996).
35. For an excellent overview, see Galeotti, *Afghanistan*, pp. 141–50.
36. *New York Times*, 7 Sept. 1991, p. A14.
37. *The Washington Post*, 17 April 1992, p. A27.
38. *The Washington Post*, 29 April 1992, p. A25.
39. CBS News weekly television programme, '60 Minutes', 25 Aug. 1991.
40. *USA Today*, 26 Aug. 1991, p. 2A.
41. Michael Dobbs, 'Coup Lifted War Heroes to Top of Russian Military', *Washington Post*, 27 Sept. 1992, p. A37. See also Galeotti, *Afghanistan*, pp. 125–38.
42. *The Washington Post*, 27 Sept. 1992, p. A44.
43. Douglas A. Borer, 'War Loss and Political Reform: A Pattern in Russian History', *Studies in Conflict and Terrorism*, 20: 4 (Oct.–Dec. 1997) pp. 345–70.
44. Theodore H. VonLaue, *Why Lenin? Why Stalin?: A Reappraisal of the Russian Revolution, 1900–1930*, 2nd edn (New York: J.B. Lippincott, 1971) pp. 52–69.
45. See Borer, 'War Loss and Political Reform', pp. 345–70.
46. Anthony Arnold, *The Fateful Pebble: Afghanistan's Role in the Fall of the Soviet Empire* (Novato, CA: Presidio Press, 1993) p. 207.
47. 'Yeltsin's Iron Fist', *Newsweek International*, 9 Jan. 1995, pp. 46–7.
48. *OMRI Daily Digest*, 1, pp. 1–76 (Jan.–April, 1995). Russian military spokesmen admitted that approximately 2,000 Russian troops had died after four months of conflict. See *OMRI Daily Digest*, 1, p. 72 (11 April 1995). See also The Jamestown Foundation, *MONITOR: A Daily Briefing On the Post-Soviet States*, 1, p. 165 (26 Dec. 1995).
49. John Thornhill, 'Liberal Faction Abandons Yeltsin', *The Australian*, 14 March 1995, p. 11.
50. McFaul, 'Eurasia Letter', *Foreign Policy* (Summer 1995) pp. 153–5.
51. *OMRI Russian Presidential Election Survey*, 13 (4 July 1996).
52. Cited in Larry Berman, 'The US in Vietnam', in *Foreign Military Intervention: The Dynamics of Protracted Conflict*, ed. Ariel Levite, Bruce W. Jentleson and Larry Berman (Princeton: Princeton University Press, 1992) p. 34.
53. Samuel L. Popkin, *The Rational Peasant: The Political Economy of Rural Society in Vietnam* (Berkeley: University of California Press, 1979) pp. 260–61.
54. Borer, 'The Afghan War: Communism's First Domino', *War and Society*, 12, 2 (Oct. 1994) pp. 130–42.

Bibliography

AFGHANISTAN SOURCES

Adamec, Ludwig W., *Afghanistan, 1900–1923: A Diplomatic History*. Berkeley: University of California Press, 1967.

Adamec, Ludwig W., *Afghanistan's Foreign Affairs to the Mid-Twentieth Century*. Tucson: University of Arizona Press, 1969.

'Afghanistan: Bad to Worse?' *Newsweek*, 19 May 1970, p. 50.

Anwar, Raja, *The Tragedy of Afghanistan: A First-Hand Account*, trans. Khalid Hasan. London: Verso Press, 1988.

Arnold, Anthony, *Afghanistan's Two-Party Communism: Parcham and Khalq*. Stanford, CA: Hoover Institution Press, 1983.

Arnold, Anthony, *Afghanistan: The Soviet Invasion in Perspective*, 2nd edn. Stanford, CA: Hoover Institution Press, 1985.

Arnold, Anthony, *The Fateful Pebble: Afghanistan's Role in the Fall of the Soviet Empire*. Novato, CA: Presidio Press, 1993.

Beloff, Max, *The Foreign Policy of Soviet Russia 1929–1941*. London: Oxford University Press, 1949.

Bhargave, G.S., *South Asian Security After Afghanistan*. Lexington, MA: Lexington Books, 1983.

Bonosky, Philip, *Washington's Secret War Against Afghanistan*. New York: International Publishers, 1985.

Borer, Douglas A., 'The Genesis of a Forgotten War: Containment in Afghanistan 1947–1956'. *Comparative Strategy*, 11 (July–Sept. 1992) pp. 343–56.

Borer, Douglas A., 'The Afghan War: Communism's First Domino', *War and Society*, 12, 2 (Oct. 1994) pp. 130–42.

Borovik, Artyom, *The Hidden War: A Russian Journalist's Account of the Soviet War in Afghanistan*. New York: The Atlantic Monthly Press, 1990.

Bradsher, Henry S., *Afghanistan and the Soviet Union*. Durham, NC: Duke Press Policy Studies, 1983.

Chaffetz, David, 'Afghanistan in Turmoil'. *International Affairs* (Jan. 1980).

Collins, Joseph J., *The Soviet Invasion of Afghanistan: A Study in the Use of Force in Soviet Foreign Policy*. Lexington, MA: Lexington Books, 1986.

Cordovez, Diego and Harrison, Selig S., *Out of Afghanistan: The Inside Story of the Soviet Withdrawal*. New York: Oxford University Press, 1995.

Cristostomo, Rosemarie, 'Muslims of the Soviet Union'. *Current History*, 81 (Oct. 1982) p. 327.

Current Digest of the Post Soviet Press, 1993–98.

Current Digest of the Soviet Press, 1954–92.

Degras, Jane (ed.), *Soviet Documents of Foreign Policy, 1917–1924*. London: Oxford University Press, 1951.

Degras, Jane (ed.), *Soviet Documents of Foreign Policy, 1925–1932*. London: Oxford University Press, 1951.

Duncan, Raymond W. and Ekedahl, Carolyn McGiffert, *Moscow and the Third World Under Gorbachev*. Boulder, CO: Westview Press, 1990.

Dupree, Louis, *Afghanistan*. Princeton: Princeton University Press, 1973.

Farr, Grant M. and Merriam, John G. (eds), *Afghan Resistance: The Politics of Survival*. Boulder, CO: Westview, 1987.

Fletcher, Arnold, *Afghanistan: Highway of Conquest*. Ithaca, NY: Cornell University Press, 1965.

Franck, Peter, *Afghanistan: Between East and West*. Washington: National Planning Association, 1960.

Fraser-Tytler, W.K., *Afghanistan: A Study of Political Developments in Central and South Asia*, 2nd edn. London: Oxford University Press, 1953.

Freedman, Robert O., *Moscow and the Middle East: Soviet Policy Since the Invasion of Afghanistan*. Cambridge: Cambridge University Press, 1991.

Galeotti, Mark, *Afghanistan: The Soviet Union's Last War*. London: Frank Cass, 1995.

Gankovsky, Yu V., *et al.*, *A History of Afghanistan*, trans. Vitaly Bashakov. Moscow: Progress Publishers, 1982.

Gati, Charles, *The Bloc that Failed*. Bloomington: Indiana University Press, 1990.

Gerrits, Andre W., *The Failure of Authoritarian Change: Reform, Opposition and Geo-Politics in Poland in the 1980s*. Brookfield: Dartmouth Publishing, 1990.

Gibbs, David, 'Does the USSR Have a "Grand Strategy"?: Reinterpreting the Invasion of Afghanistan', *Journal of Peace Research*, 24: 4 (1987) pp. 365–79.

Gorbachev, M.S., *Perestroika: New Thinking for Our Country and the World*. New York: Harper & Row Publishers, 1987.

Gorbachev, M.S., *The August Coup*. New York: HarperCollins, 1991.

Government of the Republic of Afghanistan: First Seven-Year Economic and Social Development Plan 1355–1361, Vols. I and II (text). Kabul: Ministry of Planning, 1355.

Gregorian, Vartan, *The Emergence of Modern Afghanistan: Politics of Reform and Modernization 1880–1946*. Stanford: Stanford University Press, 1969.

Griffiths, John, *Afghanistan: Key to a Continent*. Boulder, CO: Westview Press, 1981.

Gromov, Boris, *Ogranichennyy Kontingent* [Limited Contingent]. Moscow: Progress Publishers, 1994.

Habberton, William, 'Anglo-Russian Relations Concerning Afghanistan (1837–1907)'. *University of Illinois Studies in the Social Sciences*, 21 (1937) pp. 30–47.

Halliday, Fred, 'Revolution in Afghanistan'. *New Left Review*, 112 (Nov./Dec. 1978).

Halliday, Fred, 'War in Afghanistan'. *New Left Review*, 3 (Jan./Feb. 1980).

Hammond, Thomas, *Red Flag over Afghanistan: The Communist Coup, the Soviet Invasion, and the Consequences*. Boulder, CO: Westview Press, 1984.

Hauner, Milan and Canfield, Robert L. (eds), *Afghanistan and the Soviet Union: Collision and Transformation*. Boulder, CO: Westview Press, 1989.

Havel, Vaclev, 'Four Essays: Cards on the Table' in William M. Brinton and Alan

Rinzler (eds), *Without Force or Lies: Voices from the Revolution of Central Europe in 1989–90*. San Francisco: Mercury House, 1990.

Heathcote, T.A., *The Afghan Wars 1939–1919*. London: Osprey Publishing, 1980.

Hunt, R.N. Carew, *The Theory and Practice of Communism: An Introduction*. New York: Macmillan, 1957.

Hussain, Syed S., *Afghanistan Under Soviet Occupation*. Islamabad: World Affairs Publications, 1980.

Hyman, Anthony, *Afghanistan Under Soviet Domination 1964–1981*. New York: St Martin's Press, 1982.

Jain, Rajaendra K. (ed.), *US–South Asian Relations 1947–1982*, Vol. 2. Atlantic Highlands: Humanities Press, 1983.

Kanet, Roger E. (ed.), *The Soviet Union and the Developing Nations*. Baltimore, MD: Johns Hopkins University Press, 1974.

Katsikas, Suzanne J., *The Arc of Socialist Revolutions: Angola to Afghanistan*. Cambridge, MA: Schenkman Publishing Co., 1982.

Katz, Mark, *Gorbachev's Military Policy in the Third World*. New York: Praeger, 1989.

Khan, Riaz M., *Untying the Afghan Knot: Negotiating the Soviet Withdrawal*. Durham, NC: Duke University Press, 1991.

Khrushchev, Nikita, 'The Disintegration of the Imperialistic Colonial System', *Report of the Central Committee of the CPSU to the Twentieth Party Congress*. Moscow: Foreign Languages Publishing House, 1956, in Alvin Rubinstein, *The Foreign Policy of the Soviet Union*. New York: Random House, 1966, pp. 404–6.

Khrushchev, Nikita, 'Some Fundamental Questions of Present-Day International Development – Report of the Central Committee of the CPSU to the Twentieth Party Congress', in Robert Goldwin (ed.), *Readings in Russian Foreign Policy*. New York: Oxford University Press, 1959, p. 439.

Khrushchev, Nikita, *Khrushchev Remembers: The Last Testament*, trans. and ed. Strobe Talbott. Boston: Little, Brown & Co., 1974.

Klass, Rosanne (ed.), *Afghanistan: The Great Game Revisited*. New York: Freedom House, 1987.

Laber, Jeri and Rubin, Barnett R., *'A Nation is Dying': Afghanistan Under the Soviets*. Evanston, IL: Northwestern University Press, 1988.

Lenin, V.I., 'Imperialism: The Highest Stage of Capitalism', *Sochinenia*, 2nd edn. Moscow: State Publishing House, 1929. Vol. 19, pp. 120–75, in Alvin Rubinstein, *The Foreign Policy of the Soviet Union*. New York: Random House, 1966, pp. 17–21.

Lenin, V.I., *V.I. Lenin Selected Works*, 12 vols, New York: International Publishers, 1943.

Levengood, Richard L., 'The Soviet Doctrine of National Self-Determination in Theory and Practice', MA dissertation, Montana State University, 1964.

Light, Margot, *Soviet Theory of International Relations*. New York: St Martin's Press, 1988.

Litwak, Robert S., 'The Soviet Union in Afghanistan', in Ariel E. Levite, Bruce W. Jentleson and Larry Berman (eds), *Foreign Military Intervention: The Dynamics of Protracted Conflict*. New York: Columbia University Press, 1992.

Maprayil, Cyriac, *Britain and Afghanistan in Historical Perspective*. London: Cosmic Press, 1983.

Maprayil, Cyriac, *The Soviets and Afghanistan*. New Delhi: Reliance Publishing House, 1986.

Marx, Karl and Engels, Friedrich, *The Communist Manifesto*. New York: Penguin Books, 1967.

McMichael, Scott R., *Stumbling Bear: Soviet Military Performance in Afghanistan*. London: Brassey's, 1991.

Menon, Rajan, *Soviet Power and the Third World*. New Haven, CT: Yale University Press, 1986.

Michnick, Adam, *Letters from Prison and Other Essays*. Berkeley: University of California Press, 1985.

Miller, Robert F., 'Afghanistan and Soviet Alliances', in Amin Saikal and William Maley (eds), *The Soviet Withdrawal From Afghanistan*. Cambridge: Cambridge University Press, 1989.

Monks, Alfred L., *The Soviet Intervention in Afghanistan*. Washington, DC: American Enterprise Institute for Public Policy Research, 1981.

Muradov, Ghulam, 'The Democratic Republic of Afghanistan: Second Stage of the April Revolution', in *Afghanistan: Past and Present*. Moscow: USSR Academy of Sciences, 1981.

Nawroz, Mohammad Yahya and Grau, Lester W., 'The Soviet War in Afghanistan: History and Harbinger of Future War?' US Army, Foreign Military Studies Institute. Fort Leavenworth, KN, 1996. http://leav-www.army.mil/fmso

Newell, Richard, *The Politics of Afghanistan*. Ithaca, NY: Cornell University Press, 1972.

Newell, Richard, 'Foreign Relations', in Louis Dupree and Linette Albert (eds), *Afghanistan in the 1970s*. New York: Praeger Publishers, 1974.

Piontkowsky, Andrei A., 'The Russian Sphinx: Hope and Despair', in Gwyn Prins (ed.), *Spring in Winter: The 1989 Revolutions*. Manchester: Manchester University Press, 1990.

Poullada, Leon B., *Reform and Rebellion in Afghanistan, 1919–1929*. Ithaca, NY: Cornell University Press, 1973.

Poullada, Leon B., 'Afghanistan and the United States: The Crucial Years', *The Middle East Journal*, 35 (1981).

Poullada, Leon B., 'The Road to Crisis 1919–1980: American Failures, Afghan Errors and Soviet Successes', in Rosanne Klass (ed.), *Afghanistan: The Great Game Revisited*. New York: Freedom House, 1987.

Radek, Karl, 'The Bases of Soviet Foreign Policy', *Foreign Affairs* 12 (Jan. 1934): 193–206.

Radio Liberty Report on the USSR (1979–1991).

Rais, Rasul Bakhsh, 'Afghanistan After the Soviet Withdrawal', *Current History*, 91: 563 (March 1992): 122–8.

Rubinstein, Alvin, *The Foreign Policy of the Soviet Union*. New York: Random House, 1966.

Saikal, Amin and Maley, William (eds), *The Soviet Withdrawal from Afghanistan*. Cambridge: Cambridge University Press, 1989.

Scott, Harriet F. and Scott, William F., *Soviet Military Doctrine: Continuity, Formulation, and Dissemination*. Boulder, CO: Westview, 1988.

Shevardnadze, E.A., 'The 19th All-Union CPSU Conference: Foreign Policy and Diplomacy', *International Affairs* (Moscow), Oct. 1988.

'Show 'em a Way To Go Home', *Time*, 14 Dec. 1987, p. 52.

Sokolovskii, V.D. (ed.), *Soviet Military Strategy*, trans. Herbert S. Dinerstein, Leon Goure and Thomas W. Wolfe. Englewoods Cliffs, NJ: Prentice-Hall, 1963. Originally published by the Military Publishing House of the Ministry of Defence of the USSR.

Teplinksy, Leonid, 'Soviet–Afghan Cooperation: Lenin's Behest Implemented', in *Afghanistan: Past and Present*, Moscow: USSR Academy of Sciences, 1981.

The Bear Went Over the Mountain: Soviet Combat Tactics in Afghanistan, trans. Lester W. Grau. Washington, DC: US Government Printing Office, 1997.

The Spokesman-Review, 15 April 1988: 1.

The Truth About Afghanistan: Documents, Facts, Eyewitness Reports. Moscow: Novosti Agency Publishing House, 1980.

Toynbee, Arnold, 'Afghanistan as a Meeting Place in History', *Afghanistan*, 25 (April–June, 1960).

Triska, Jan F. and Finley, David D., *Soviet Foreign Policy*. New York: Macmillan, 1968.

Trotsky, Leon, 'Manifesto of the Communist International', in *The Communist International, 1919–1943*, ed. Jane Degras. London: Oxford University Press, 1951.

Ulam, Adam B., *Expansion and Coexistence: The History of Soviet Foreign Policy 1917–67*. New York: Praeger, 1968.

Urban, Mark, *War in Afghanistan,*, 2nd edn. New York: Macmillan, 1990.

Valkner, Elizabeth Kridl, 'Soviet Economic Relations with the Developing Nations', in *The Soviet Union and Developing Nations*, ed. Roger Kanet. Baltimore, MD: Johns Hopkins University Press, 1974.

VonLaue, Theodore H., *Why Lenin? Why Stalin?: A Reappraisal of the Russian Revolution, 1900–1930*, 2nd edn. New York: J.B. Lippincott Co., 1971.

Vorobiev, Colonel K., 'The Incarnation of Leninist Ideas on the Armed Defense of Socialism', *Kommunist Voorushennykh Sil*, 1 (Jan. 1980) p. 22. In Alfred L. Monks, *The Soviet Intervention in Afghanistan*. Washington: American Enterprise Institute for Public Policy Research, 1981.

Vorobiev, Colonel V., *Krasnaya Zvezda*, 6 Sept. 1979. In Alfred L. Monks, *The Soviet Intervention in Afghanistan*. Washington: American Enterprise Institute for Public Policy Research, 1981.

Wilber, Donald N., *Afghanistan*. New Haven, CT: Hraf Press, 1962.

Wriggins, Howard W., 'US Interests in South Asia and the Indian Ocean', in Lawrence Ziring (ed.), *The Subcontinent in World Politics: India, its Neighbors, and the Great Powers*. New York: Praeger, 1982.

Zhukov, E., 'The Colonial Question After the Second World War', *Pravda*, 7 Aug. 1947. In Alvin Z. Rubinstein, *The Foreign Policy of the Soviet Union*. New York: Random House, 1966, pp. 398–9.

VIETNAM SOURCES

Anderson, David L., *Trapped by Success: The Eisenhower Administration and Vietnam 1953–1961*. New York: Columbia University Press, 1991.

Bain, Chester A., *Vietnam: The Roots of Conflict*. Englewood Cliffs, NJ: Prentice-Hall, 1967.

Barnet, Richard, *Roots of War: The Men and Institutions Behind US Foreign Policy*. New York: Atheneum, 1972.

Berke, John P. and Greenstein, Fred I., *How Presidents Test Reality: Decisions on Vietnam 1954 and 1965*. New York: Russell Sage Foundation, 1989.

Berman, Larry, 'The US in Vietnam', in Ariel E. Levite, Bruce W. Jentleson and Larry Berman (eds), *Foreign Military Intervention: The Dynamics of Protracted Conflict*. New York: Columbia University Press, 1992.

Buttinger, Joseph, *The Smaller Dragon: A Political History of Vietnam*. New York: Praeger, 1958.

Buttinger, Joseph, *Vietnam: A Dragon Embattled*, 2 vols. New York: Praeger, 1967.

Buttinger, Joseph, *A Dragon Defiant: A Short History of Vietnam*. New York: Praeger, 1972.

Buttinger, Joseph, *Vietnam: The Unforgettable Tragedy*. New York: Praeger, 1977.

Cady, John, *The Roots of French Imperialism in Asia*. Ithaca: Cornell University Press, 1954.

Calleo, David P., *The Imperious Economy*. Cambridge, MA: Harvard University Press, 1982.

Cameron, Allan W., 'The Soviet Union and Vietnam: The Origins of Involvement', in W. Raymond Duncan (ed.), *Soviet Policy in Developing Countries*. Waltham: Ginn–Blaisdell, 1970.

Campagna, Anthony S., *The Economic Consequences of the Vietnam War*. New York: Praeger, 1991.

Chomsky, Noam, *At War With Asia*. New York: Pantheon, 1970.

Chomsky, Noam, *For Reasons of State*. New York: Vintage Books, 1973.

Duiker, William, *The Rise of Nationalism in Vietnam, 1900–1941*. Ithaca, NY: Cornell University Press, 1976.

Dunn, Peter M., *The First Vietnam War*. New York: St Martin's Press, 1985.

Falk, Richard A. (ed.), *The Vietnam War and International Law*, 4 vols. Princeton: Princeton University Press, 1967–76.

Fall, Bernard, *The Two Viet-Nams: A Political and Military Analysis*, 2nd edn. New York: Praeger, 1964.

Fishel, Wesley R. (ed.), *Vietnam: Anatomy of a Conflict*. Itasca, IL: F.E. Peacock, 1968.

FitzGerald, Francis, *Fire in the Lake: The Vietnamese and the Americans in Vietnam*. Boston: Little, Brown & Co., 1972.

Fulbright, William J., *Old Myths and New Realities*. New York: Random House, 1964.

Fulbright, William J., *The Arrogance of Power*. New York: Random House, 1966.

Fulbright, William J., *The Crippled Giant: American Foreign Policy and its Domestic Consequences*. New York: Random House, 1972.

Gallucci, Robert L., *Neither Peace nor Honor: The Politics of American Military Policy in Vietnam*. Baltimore, MD: Johns Hopkins University Press, 1975.

Gardner, Loyd C., *Approaching Vietnam: From World War II Through Dienbienphu*. New York: W.W. Norton, 1988.

Gelb, Leslie H. and Betts, Richard K., *The Irony of Vietnam: The System Worked*. Washington, DC: The Brookings Institution, 1979.

Gibbons, William Conrad, *The US Government and the Vietnam War: Executive and Legislative Roles and Relationships*, Parts I, II and III. Originally prepared for the Committee on Foreign Relations of the United States Senate. Princeton: Princeton University Press, 1986, 1989.

Halberstam, David, *The Best and the Brightest*. New York: Random House, 1972.

Hall, D.G.E., *A History of Southeast Asia*, 4th edn. New York: St Martin's Press, 1981.

Hannah, Norman B., *The Key to Failure: Laos and the Vietnam War*. New York: Madison Books, 1987.

Herring, George C., *America's Longest War: The United States and Vietnam 1950–1975*. New York: John Wiley, 1979.

Herring, George C., *America's Longest War: The United States and Vietnam 1950–1975*, 3rd edn. New York: McGraw-Hill, 1996.

Hilsman, Roger, *To Move a Nation: The Politics of Foreign Policy in the Administration of John F. Kennedy*. New York: Doubleday, 1967.

Isaacs, Harold, *No Peace for Asia*. Cambridge, MA: MIT Press, 1947.

Johnson, Lyndon B., *The Vantage Point: Perspectives on the Presidency 1963–1969*. New York: Holt, Rinehart & Winston, 1971.

Karnow, Stanley, *Vietnam: A History*. New York: Viking Press, 1983.

Kissinger, Henry A., 'The Vietnam Negotiations', *Foreign Affairs* 47 (Jan. 1969).

Kolko, Gabriel, *The Roots of American Foreign Policy*. Boston: Beacon Press, 1969.

Lewy, Guenter, *America in Vietnam*. New York: Oxford University Press, 1978.

Littauer, Raphael and Uphoff, Norman (eds), *The Air war in Indochina*. Boston: Beacon Press, 1972.

Lomperis, Timothy J., *The War Everyone Lost – and Won: America's Intervention in Viet Nam's Twin Struggles*, rev. edn. Washington, DC: CQ Press, 1993.

Lomperis, Timothy J., *From People's War to People's Rule: Insurgency, Intervention and the Lessons of Vietnam*. Chapel Hill: University of North Carolina Press, 1996.

Marr, David G., *Vietnamese Traditionalism on Trial 1920–1945*. Berkeley: University of California Press, 1981.

Miller, Robert H., *The United States and Vietnam, 1787–1941*. Washington, DC: National Defense University Press, 1990.

Miller, Robert H., 'Vietnam: Folly, Quagmire, or Inevitability?' *Studies in Conflict and Terrorism* 5 (April–June 1992) pp. 99–123.

Morgenthau, Hans J., *Vietnam and the United States*. Washington, DC: Public Affairs Press, 1965.

Nixon, Richard M., *RN: The Memoirs of Richard Nixon*, 2 vols. New York: Warner Books, 1978.

Oberdorf, Don. *TET!* New York: Doubleday, 1991.

Pentagon Papers (*PP*), Gravel Edition, Vols 1–5. Boston: Beacon Press, 1971.

Pike, Douglas, *Vietnam and the Soviet Union: Anatomy of an Alliance*. Boulder, CO: Westview Press, 1987.

Podhoretz, Norman, *Why We Were in Vietnam*. New York: Simon & Schuster, 1982.

Poole, Peter A., *The United States and Indochina from FDR to Nixon*. Huntingdon, NY: Robert E. Kreiger, 1976.

Popkin, Samuel L., *The Rational Peasant: The Political Economy of Rural Society in Vietnam*. Berkeley: University of California Press, 1979.

Porter, Gareth (ed.), *Vietnam: A History in Documents*. New York: Meridian Books, 1981.

Rand Vietnam Interviews.

Rusk, Dean, *As I Saw It*. New York: W.W. Norton, 1990.

Schlesinger, Arthur M., *A Thousand Days*. Boston: Houghton Mifflin, 1965.

Schlesinger, Arthur M., *The Bitter Heritage: Vietnam and American Democracy, 1941–1966*. New York: Houghton Mifflin, 1967.

Sharov, V.A. and Tyrurin, V.A., *Southeast Asia: History, Economy, Policy*. Moscow: Progress Publishers, 1972.

Summers Jr, Harry G., *On Strategy: A Critical Analysis of the Vietnam War*. New York: Dell, 1982.

Taylor, Keith W., *The Birth of Vietnam*. Berkeley: University of California Press, 1983.

Taylor, Maxwell D., *Responsibility and Response*. New York: Harper–Row, 1967.

Taylor, Maxwell D., *Swords into Plowshares*. New York: W.W. Norton, 1972.

Trager, Frank, *Why Vietnam?* New York: F.A. Praeger, 1966.

Trullinger, James, *Village at War: An Account of Conflict in Vietnam*. Stanford, CA: Stanford University Press, 1994.

US Overseas Loans and Grants and Assistance from International Organizations: Special Report Prepared for the House Foreign Affairs Committee. Washington, DC: US Agency for International Development, 29 March 1968.

Vance, Cyrus, *Hard Choices: Critical Years in American Foreign Policy*. New York: Simon & Schuster, 1983.

Young, Marilyn B., *The Vietnam Wars 1945–1990*. New York: HarperPerennial, 1991.

Zinn, Howard, *Vietnam: The Logic of Withdrawal*. Boston: Beacon Press, 1967.

GENERAL SOURCES

Carter, Jimmy, *Keeping Faith: Memoirs of a President*. New York: Bantam Books, 1982.

Clemens, Jr, Walter C., *Can Russia Change?: The USSR Confronts Global Interdependence*. Boston: Unwin Hyman, 1990.

Combs, Jerald A., *American Diplomatic History: Two Centuries of Changing Interpretations*. Berkeley: University of California Press, 1983.

Commager, Henry S. (ed.), *Documents of American History*, Vol. 2. New York: Appleton-Century-Crofts, 1968.

Cumings, Bruce, 'The Wicked Witch of the West is Dead. Long Live the Wicked Witch of the East', in Michael J. Hogan (ed.), *The End of the Cold War: Its Meaning and Implication*. Cambridge: Cambridge University Press, 1992.

Current Digest of the Post Soviet Press.

Current Digest of the Soviet Press.

Daily Telegraph.

Fitzsimons, David M., 'Tom Paine's New World Order: Idealistic Internationalism in the Ideology of Early American Foreign Relations', *Diplomatic History*, 19: 4 (1995) pp. 569–82.

Foreign Broadcast Information Service, Daily Reports.

Gaddis, John Lewis, *Strategies of Containment: A Critical Appraisal of Postwar American National Security Policy*. New York: Oxford University Press, 1982.

Gaddis, John Lewis, *The Long Peace: Inquiries into the History of the Cold War*. New York: Oxford University Press, 1987.

Gartoff, Raymond, *Détente and Confrontation: American–Soviet Relations from Nixon to Reagan*. Washington, DC: The Brookings Institution, 1985.

Guardian Weekly.

Kennan, George F., 'X', *Foreign Affairs* 54 (July 1947) pp. 566–82.

Kennan, George F., *The Decision to Interview*. Princeton: Princeton University Press, 1961.

Kennan, George F., *The Nuclear Delusion*. New York: Pantheon Books, 1982.

Levite, Ariel E., Jentleson, Bruce W. and Berman, Larry (eds), *Foreign Military Intervention: The Dynamics of Protracted Conflict*. New York: Columbia University Press, 1992.

Luttwak, Edward, *The Grand Strategy of the Soviet Union*. New York: St Martin's Press, 1985.

Makin, John H., *The Global Debt Crisis: America's Growing Involvement*. New York: Basic Books, 1984.

Markovits, Andrei S. and Silverstein, Mark, 'Introduction: Power and Process in Liberal Democracies', in Andrei S. Markovits and Mark Silverstein (eds), *The Politics of Scandal: Power and Process in Liberal Democracies*. New York: Holmes & Meier, 1988.

Mayers, David, *George Kennan and the Dilemmas of US Foreign Policy*. New York: Oxford University Press, 1988.

Merquior, J.G., *Rousseau and Weber: Two Studies in the Theory of Legitimacy*. London: Routledge & Kegan Paul, 1980.

Miller-Unterberger, Betty, *The United States, Revolutionary Russia, and the Rise of Czechoslovakia*. Chapel Hill: University of North Carolina Press, 1989.

New York Times.

OMRI Daily Digest of the Post-Soviet Press. Open Media Research Institute (OMRI).

Pipes, Richard, *Survival is Not Enough*. New York: Simon & Schuster, 1984.

Rubin, Barry, *Paved with Good Intentions: The American Experience and Iran*. New York: Oxford University Press, 1980.

Spokesman-Review.

Starr, Richard F., *USSR Foreign Policies after Détente*. Stanford, CA: Hoover Institution Press, 1985.

Stoessinger, John G., *Nations in Darkness: China, Russia, and America*, 4th edn. New York: Random House, 1986.

The Australian.

Tucker, Robert W. and Hendrickson, David C., *Empire of Liberty: The Statecraft of Thomas Jefferson*. New York: Oxford University Press, 1990.

Tyroler, Charles (ed.), *Alerting America: The Papers of the Committee on the Present Danger*. New York: Pergamon–Brassey's International Defense Publishers, 1984.

US Department of State, *Foreign Relations of the United States*. Washington, DC: United States Government Printing Office.

US News and World Report.

Wall Street Journal.

Walsh, Lawrence E., *Firewall: the Iran–Contra Conspiracy and Cover-up*. New York: Norton, 1997.

Walzer, Michael, *Just and Unjust Wars: A Moral Argument with Historical Illustrations*. New York: Basic Books, 1977.

Washington Post.

Wiarda, Howard J., *Ethnocentrism in Foreign Policy: Can We Understand the Third World?* Washington, DC: American Enterprise Institute, 1985.

Index